DRAGON AGE

THE WORLD OF THEDAS

VOLUME 2

DARK HORSE BOOKS

BIOWARE

Project Leads
Ben Gelinas (writing) and Nick Thornborrow (art)

Writing
Brianne Battye, Joanna Berry, Sheryl Chee, Sylvia Feketekuty, David Gaider, Ben Gelinas, Mary Kirby, Lukas Kristjanson, Ann Lemay, Karin Weekes, and Patrick Weekes

Editing
Cameron Harris and Cori May

Cover Art
Casper Konefal and Nick Thornborrow

Artwork
Matthew Goldman, Steve Klit, Casper Konefal, Tom Rhodes, Matt Rhodes, Ramil Sunga, Nick Thornborrow with Fran Gaulin, Ben Huen, Jae Keum, Ville Kinnunen

Recipes
Joan Berry, Leanne Brown, Sheryl Chee, Melanie Fleming, Ben Gelinas, Matthew Goldman, Sarah Hayward, Mary Kirby, Lukas Kristjanson, Jannose Le Bray, Tulay McNally, Vivi and Jessica Merizan, Elizabeth Neustaeter, Evelyn Ostoforoff, Chantel Rogers, Kim Wall and Janine Rogers

Dragon Age Leadership
Mark Darrah, Executive Producer
Mike Laidlaw, Creative Director
Matthew Goldman, Art Director
Chris Bain, Business Development Director

Special Thanks
Jason Baxter, Dan Fessenden, Arone Le Bray, Liane Merciel, Rion Swanson, and the many team members who donated recipes to be considered for this lore book. Sorry we couldn't use them all. Also, *Dragon Age* leadership for trusting us to make this monster, which somehow got done alongside *Inquisition*. And lastly, the readers of our books and players of our games. We hope you love volume 2 as much as we loved making it. Ben and Nick sleep now.

DARK HORSE

Publisher
Mike Richardson

Designer
Amy Arendts

Digital Production
Chris Horn

Assistant Editor
Roxy Polk

Editor
Dave Marshall

DRAGON AGE: THE WORLD OF THEDAS VOLUME 2

Published by Dark Horse Books
A division of Dark Horse Comics, Inc.
10956 SE Main Street
Milwaukie, OR 97222

DarkHorse.com
DragonAge.com

First edition: April 2015
ISBN 978-1-61655-501-6

10 9 8 7 6 5 4 3 2
Printed in China

CONTENTS

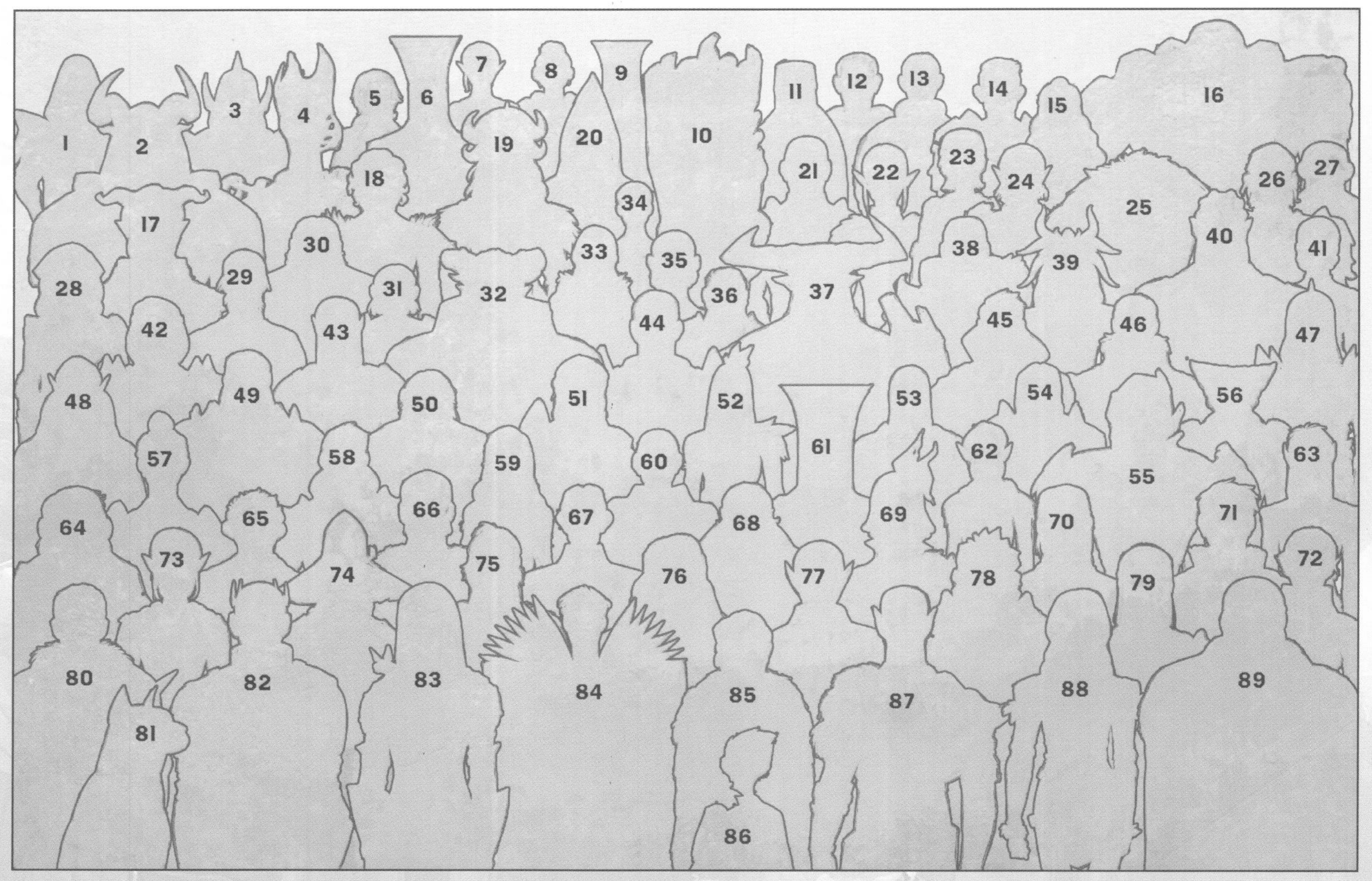

1 Abelas
2 The Arishok
3 Alexius
4 The Architect
5 Bianca
6 Justinia V
7 Briala
8 Harding
9 Giselle
10 Xenon the Antiquarian
11 Roderick
12 Erimond
13 Clarel
14 Krem
15 Florianne
16 Shale
17 Rasaan
18 Maevaris
19 Flemeth
20 Aurelian Titus
21 Barris
22 Marethari
23 Dagna
24 Fenris
25 Swiftrunner
26 Samson
27 Harrowmont
28 Isabela
29 Wynne
30 Endrin
31 Sigrun
32 Ketojan
33 Sebastian
34 Kieran
35 Calpernia
36 Bhelen
37 The Iron Bull
38 Gaspard
39 Yavana
40 Sten
41 Anora
42 Aveline
43 Zevran
44 Stroud
45 Dorian
46 Alistair
47 Meredith
48 Orsino
49 Cailan
50 Bartrand
51 Blackwall
52 Morrigan
53 The Withered
54 Loghain
55 Corypheus
56 Vivienne
57 Josephine
58 Cassandra
59 Lady of the Forest
60 Genitivi
61 Beatrix III
62 Merrill
63 Sera
64 Bodahn
65 Sandal
66 Duncan
67 Rendon Howe
68 Varric
69 Prosper
70 Teagan
71 Carver
72 Velanna
73 Tallis
74 Cole
75 Anders and Justice
76 Maric
77 Zathrian
78 Oghren
79 Nathaniel Howe
80 Cullen
81 Dog
82 Marlowe Dumar
83 Leliana
84 Celene
85 Isolde
86 Connor
87 Solas
88 Bethany
89 Eamon

AN EXPANDING UNIVERSE

It's been more than twenty years since BioWare officially became a game-development studio. *Dragon Age* has played a pivotal role in that time. Why?

For me, it comes down to what the book you have in your hands represents: Lore. Stories. A rich universe full of characters, conflict, and consequences.

It's always been remarkable to me how so much can come from the simplest of ideas and the humblest of beginnings. When I was a developer on *Dragon Age: Origins*, the richness of the world explored in these books seemed an eternity away. Yet here we are, thanks to the passion and effort of the people creating and enlarging the *Dragon Age* universe. A world as expansive as Thedas is only possible after an entire team have put their hearts and souls into making something from nothing. I learn new things every time I go through these books, so I get to count myself as much a fan as a team member when I sit back and appreciate what has been created.

I'd like to extend a personal thanks to Mark Darrah for his supreme commitment to Thedas through the games he helps lead. These are monumental efforts that take an entire team yet still need someone to try to hold the whole thing together. Even after working with him for fifteen years, I'm still amazed and humbled by his commitment to exceeding the expectations of the best fans anyone could hope for.

When I think of the miles upon miles of Thedas we've explored, and all the stories we've told, I feel genuinely privileged to have played a small part in making *Dragon Age*. Enjoy the book.

—*Aaryn Flynn, General Manager, BioWare Edmonton/Montréal*

STORIES ABOUT CHARACTERS

When we make a game, we'll often introduce a core crisis, something like the Breach or a Blight, to give momentum to the story and pull the action in a particular direction. But while ultimately the game may come to a head with the resolution of this crisis, the most memorable story moments often spring from the many characters along for the ride.

First and foremost, our stories are about characters and their reactions to events, to each other, and, of course, to the player. We want our characters to feel like real people. They need compelling reasons for their actions. While the characters in a *Dragon Age* story may do bad things, some do them for good reasons—or at least convince themselves of this. They may even think themselves the hero of their own story, even if they end up the villain of ours.

For believable characters to exist, they need a believable world. This goes beyond the ground they stand on. The culture and lore of *Dragon Age* permeate the cobblestones of the farthest-flung town and nearly every word uttered there. The way the world works influences the way its people think, forging unique and complex characters. Even the smallest detail matters, from a nation's architecture to its fashion and even its cuisine.

By exploring and expanding upon the stories of many memorable characters, this book will take you even deeper into the world of Thedas. A special thanks to Nick Thornborrow and Ben Gelinas for bringing together such an excellent reference. After three games, numerous novels and comics, and countless other platforms, we still have a lot more stories to tell.

—*Mark Darrah, Executive Producer,* Dragon Age

chapter one

LEGENDS OF THEDAS

WELCOME BACK TO THEDAS, A DOMAIN OF GREAT diversity, guided by the politics of magic and belief in still-greater powers. Held together, albeit loosely, by disparate peoples, each with their own aspirations and views of the world, Thedas is nothing without the humans, dwarves, elves, and Qunari who call it home. A proud and powerful few are remembered in the histories you hold in your hands. These are the legends of Thedas: nation builders and prophets, the heroes and villains of five Blights and countless wars.

CHANTRY LEADERS

The Chantry was founded upon belief in the Maker as defined by the teachings of the prophet Andraste. Through the edicts of its leader, the Divine, the religious authority has taken root across most of Thedas, influencing kings and emperors from Orlais to the Anderfels. The predominant orders of justice and conflict act in the Chantry's name, and for all but outliers in Thedosian society, its word is law.

ANDRASTE & MAFERATH

The Chantry starts and ends with Andraste: its mother, the Bride of our Maker. But while any learned child can recount her rise and fall, and indeed recite her words on command, there is much historians do not know about her life.

The Family & Lineage of Our Lady

Maferath's father was Heggar II. His mother was Thelois. Both were prominent Alamarri, their union creating a powerful tribe that controlled much of what would become eastern Ferelden. They died of sicknesses common to the day but ensured the future of their people by training their son well in matters of tactics and arms. Their legacy is all but forgotten, except as parents to the Betrayer. But let us return to him later.

Of Our Lady, we begin with mortal truths.

Andraste's father was Elderath, chief of the northernmost tribes of the Alamarri. He held vast stretches of territory, though the Alamarri cared little for the specifics of their borders. Tevinter struggled in an environment the barbarians had mastered. Elderath also benefited from relations with a number of small but wealthy tribes in what would come to be known as the Fertile Crescent, and married Brona of the Ciriane to secure this arrangement.

The birthplace of Andraste is believed to be what would become Denerim. Elderath sired another daughter, Halliserre, but her mother was not Brona. Rather, she was the product of a union with an unnamed advisor on matters of alchemy. This was frowned upon but not unheard of, and Halliserre was welcome in the family line, if not the family home. The fate of her mother is uncertain. She was likely exiled, if not killed by Brona. Halliserre would die young in events not properly recorded.

"Andraste, still a youth, awakened, unquiet, to a storm," the Orlesian emperor Kordillus Drakon wrote of the Prophet. "She glimpsed her sibling following lights into a wood. Our Lady pursued, and an event of some violence occurred, followed by fires throughout the forest. Andraste was found pale and uncertain of what she had seen. The remains of Halliserre were lying in a burned clearing, her body having suffered wounds beyond weapons. The Ciriane blamed animist spirits or a blighted beast. The Alamarri suspected rival tribes."

Andraste was scarred in many ways by this event. The storm's cold left her with a sickness in the lungs

Depictions of Andraste range from more traditional iconography to regional variations, like this distinctly Fereldan woodcarving.

that persisted for years, and despite her eventual strength, it would be a decade before she recovered enough to bear children. As a young woman, she would become still for long moments, unable to be moved or roused. After, she would report voices, as though from a lost memory, and talk of strange auras or the sounds of bells. It was some years later when she began to recall the events of Halliserre's death as a matter of heresy, suggesting the alchemist consort whispered of the Old Gods. Our Lady would frame her early experiences with her rising sense of destiny, becoming her own first historian. As with all such interpretations, we must guard against misunderstanding.

Andraste was married to Maferath to create a unified Alamarri border that stretched from the Planasene, through the Fertile Crescent, to the Bannorn. It was, at that point, the largest such alliance the barbarians of the South had attempted. The result was not certain, as many small tribes were slow to acknowledge the unions, having not personally felt the sting of Tevinter. That would change in due course, as Tevinter reeled from its own failings, inspiring a new faith as its own withered.

Death of Elderath

The empire was slow to recover from its First Blight, due to growing civil unrest over the silence of the Old Gods. Outposts ran short of supplies as the strength of the empire drew back. Andraste's father, Elderath, was killed when soldiers and mages seized an Alamarri settlement, kidnapping the young Andraste into slavery and razing the settlement to the ground. This was an act more brutal than mere colonization. Tevinter generally appeased or bribed common citizens of its conquered territory. Martyrs lead to revenge at any cost, which is not a recipe for holding barbarian tempers in check.

Elderath's death passed command to Maferath, now in control of all northern Alamarri territory, the largest potential force outside the Imperium. In truth, since the population was largely composed of those loyal to Elderath, most held allegiance to his daughter, Andraste. They would follow Maferath, but only after he successfully negotiated Andraste's freedom from the Tevinter slavers who held her.

Faith

What begins now is the too-detailed and opinionated account of the rise of Our Lady, augmented as it is by her own tellings and the weight of future history. To be responsible, we must act as apologists for the sometimes-harsh truth that makes the historian unwelcome in halls of worship.

"Andraste had always held the traditions of her people close to her heart, and in the years following the death of Halliserre, that became her source of strength," wrote Drakon. "Physically weak in her early life, she spent a great deal of time searching for meaning in what she had seen, and this slowly became a search for the Maker Himself. She sought and found His influence in everything."

By separate account, visions and periods of immobility troubled her. In an age when the beliefs of Tevinter had recently been tested and failed, Andraste found many who were willing to listen to her dreams of the Maker and His sadness at what had been done by His children. Had there not been a catalyzing incident, Andraste might have passed as a gentle current through Alamarri beliefs. But in the wake of the Blight and the death of Elderath, Andraste became a focus for the rage of an entire people.

Rebellion and Intervention

As her people rallied, Andraste's visions became more vivid and personal, her understanding of the will of the Maker less abstract and more driven. She began to see herself as a conduit to the truth of the Maker and what He required for the salvation of her people.

No doubt it helped that Tevinter was in its own throes of change. The borders of the Imperium were not fortified like they were at the height of empire, and the people there were mostly indigenous barbarians. In these settlements, few objected to returning to the leadership of their own kin.

As the Alamarri pressed against the true borders of the empire, several events convinced the faithful that theirs was a divine mission. Some were a result of the Blight, so even if there was doubt about the Maker's role, it could still be seen as Tevinter paying for its own mistakes.

"The Maker, seeing the will of Our Lady, struck down mighty Tevinter with drought, wildfires, and the weakening of the very earth beneath them," wrote Sister Damson in her *Secrets of the Most Holy*.

The miracles of the day are now assumed to have been assisted by natural consequence. When the hordes of darkspawn carved their way to light during the Blight, they didn't dig with a careful eye. They bludgeoned the earth, and in the years

Andraste may be represented as warm and maternal.

SHARTAN'S LEGACY

There, see the Winter Palace at Halamshiral. Gaze upon its white walls and golden spires, built on the broken dreams of a people. Our people.

The human prophet Andraste was a slave in the Tevinter Imperium, as our ancestors were. When she rose up against them, we rose up with her. Together, we fought for freedom. In gratitude and kinship, Andraste promised the elves a new land: the Dales. And although she died, her sons kept her promise.

Our people came from farthest Tevinter to claim this new land. Here, our journey ended. This was our Halamshiral. As we laid the first stone for the city, our people vowed that no human would ever set foot on our lands. The greatest of our warriors swore to uphold this vow. One by one they came, invoking the names of Elgar'nan and Mythal, Andruil and Ghilan'nain. Before all our gods, they dedicated themselves to Halamshiral, becoming our protectors, our Emerald Knights. They would ensure that the Dales remained free.

It *was* free. For over three centuries. But the humans and their new Andrastian Chantry would not let us be. They pushed against our borders. They sent missionaries to spread the word of their prophet. They sought ways to subjugate the People once more. When we refused, we angered them.

They destroyed us. Even the Emerald Knights could not stand against the might of their army, armored in faith. In the name of their Andraste, they burned Halamshiral, scattering us to the winds. They forgot that once, long ago, Andraste's followers and the elves marched together. They forgot that Andraste called Shartan "brother."

—"A Promise Lost," as told by Keeper Gisharel to the young hunters of the Ralaferin clan on the outskirts of Halamshiral

following, the effects continued even though their scrabbling claws were gone. It is suspected that many rivers were diverted as natural caverns fractured and water found a new path. Thaigs reported underground reservoirs drying up, which corresponded to surface fields in some locations becoming parched and spare.

"The lands of the Imperium were forsaken and cruel, as was their deserving," Damson wrote. "Famine taxed the empire, and fire brought them low. The red glow of the sky was the wrath of our Maker, readying the enemy for her arrival. And when Our Lady did come, they were found weary."

There were isolated areas where the problem was not where the water had left, but where it had arrived. These changes could take years and be gentle, like a settling of hills into valleys, but on at least one occasion it was violent and sudden. The advancing Alamarri found the earth had shifted beneath a legendary fortified pass, making it useless as a barrier. While not carved like a bolt from the heavens, the destruction was described as more violent in each retelling. So convincing was this, that when they later crossed another area where the land had recently shifted, it was also hailed as a divine act, even though it made no difference in the defenses of nearby Tevinter holdings.

The Battle of Valarian Fields

Lest it seem like the Alamarri were unopposed, there were real military victories in addition to the turns of fate. Maferath was a masterful tactician, and he capitalized on the inspiration his wife provided. They made short work of outposts equipped to fight banditry, pushed reluctant troops back to fortify the heart of the empire, and proselytized among a population reeling from the silence of their leaders and gods. But their true test came as they approached the real borders of the enemy. We can now draw on the records of the Imperium itself and know that Tevinter was suffering civil unrest over the Blight and the silence of the Old Gods. The barbarian menace was a real threat, but while some magisters were committed, the full resources of the empire were not. Domestic unrest was still seen as the greater menace.

While the forces available to face those of Our Lady were

Often, Andraste is depicted as a noble warrior.

considerable, they were not the full might of the empire. But as the first truly difficult resistance, the Battle of Valarian Fields is recounted by the Alamarri as Tevinter's best showing. The Battle of Valarian Fields was bloody and turned from siege to open fighting and back again several times. Maferath was masterful, and the inspiration of Andraste was a focusing element that drove her people on. But, and this is said with full knowledge of the controversy, it is perhaps unfortunate that Andraste won.

Andraste Unbound

In the end, the Alamarri were victorious. But it wasn't the rout that the faithful remember. There were losses, including most of the Alamarri leadership. The last reins on Andraste were lost, and they were no longer a people fighting for freedom; they were an arrow launched by the Maker. Scholars of war know that the best an arrow can hope for is a quick kill, because if the enemy is not slain, there is no returning to the bow.

Examining the resources of the day, the Alamarri knew they didn't have the ability to fortify the outposts they took, and Tevinter reversed a number of Our Lady's early victories by reoccupying abandoned conquests. This had the effect of slowly flanking the Alamarri. In addition, the farther into the Imperium Andraste pressed, the more resistance she encountered. Her army was running out of governed territories eager to accept liberation. The closer they came to the heart of the empire, the more they faced the enemy on its home ground. There were a number of outright losses that history all but ignores. Andraste was now fully enraptured by her role as a messenger for the Maker.

"These fringe defeats were instructions," wrote Drakon. "Our Lady was not to aim the wrath of the Maker's children at peripheral holdings. She was meant to guide this sacred force directly into the heart of the heretical monster. She was not meant to diminish Tevinter as a neighbor; she was meant to destroy it, and guide the Chant of Light from every living mouth."

Maferath and Doubt

Maferath was a tactician, not a philosopher. As his anger after the death of Elderath waned, it appears he did not find it replaced with divine purpose. There are few records of his intent, but modern generals insist that he would have been skeptical of early victories. Had the Alamarri secured their progress, they might have rivaled Tevinter in perpetuity, ensuring stability for generations. The unending press of the faithful was not concerned with that. But Maferath certainly was.

The Tevinters were a people with understandable and predictable reactions. We know what the leaders of today would do in their place: needing a distraction from civil unrest, they would target the Alamarri as a convenient threat. If Tevinter found its full strength and its people were rallied against this heretic, Andraste, the Alamarri would be faced with the reversal of their success. And the magisters of Tevinter had vast power to draw upon.

Maferath must have known that they would lose all they had gained and possibly more. Because they had not fortified, because they had not considered failure, they faced the threat of not just a major defeat, but a total rout.

Artists take some license with their depictions of Maferath, the Betrayer.

Here begin the tales of Maferath's jealousy of the Maker and his conniving betrayal. And betrayal it was but for whose benefit? Perhaps he betrayed the faithful, but looking at his actions that followed, did he truly betray their spirit?

Maferath's Betrayal and Andraste's Death

The facts are plain. Maferath conspired with Archon Hessarian and allowed disguised Tevinter forces to enter Andraste's stronghold in the city of Nevarra. Our Lady was captured and taken to Tevinter, where she was burned at the stake, the most painful and cruel punishment that Tevinter could impose. It was meant to set an example, but there was no celebration in her death.

"Until that moment, Andraste was a barbarian who threatened all of Tevinter," Damson wrote. "It was the truth, in a way, but in person she must not have seemed such a creature. The gathered crowd were not citizens of the borders who had felt the sting of the Alamarri, so they held no burning hatred for Our Lady. Before them was merely a woman. All who witnessed the brutality of the moment were shamed."

Hessarian must have realized that the effect was not what he had hoped. He killed Our Lady to end the spectacle and would be remembered as the Sword of Mercy. But the Alamarri now had a martyr, and the Tevinter people had doubt in their leaders. By his actions, we can only assume Maferath predicted what would come. This is the often-overlooked element of self-sacrifice to the story: we must grant the Betrayer humanity and forethought. His actions are fact, both that he was instrumental in her death and that he acted to preserve her legacy.

Key figures in Andraste's story like Maferath, Hessarian, and Havard (*left to right*) are depicted in a variety of aspects and mediums.

THE CHILDREN OF ANDRASTE

Andraste and Maferath had five children, but the eldest three were born of Maferath and the concubine Gilivhan. The pairing was allowed because, as noted, Andraste in her youth was too weak to bear children.

Evrion and the Free Marches

The middle son, Evrion, led a nomadic group in what would be the Free Marches. During the decade of peace before the reveal of the betrayal, he was the son least concerned with holding power, preferring only to spread the word of his mother and her sacrifice. When the truth of the event came out, Evrion and his children abandoned their lineage and dispersed their holdings to the various tribes. As a result, that area did not gel into a cohesive nation, and many of its cities would change hands repeatedly.

Two of Evrion's children would lay claim to the legacy of Andraste but wouldn't survive the backlash. The rest have fallen to obscurity.

Verald and Nevarra

Nevarra was ruled by Verald, the youngest of Maferath's sons. By all accounts, he tried to leverage his connection to Maferath and gain sympathy because of his mother's legacy. It worked in the short term, but when the actions of his father came to light, he was instantly vilified, along with Maferath. Verald's court was killed to a man, and the young king fled to the neighboring lands that would become Orlais, where his brother Isorath was still in power. The two engaged in a lengthy power struggle, until Verald conspired with Isorath's wife, Jeshavis. Verald murdered his brother and married Jeshavis to bring legitimacy to his claim to the throne. Verald was later killed by Jeshavis, who became the first Ciriane leader of Orlais.

Isorath and Orlais

Isorath, the eldest, was charged with the greatest challenge: uniting the Ciriane into a people who could stand as one. He was just and wise and worked diligently to fortify the idea of Orlais and instill an identity among the disparate tribes. His grand unification is both celebrated and reviled, but he began a course that would result in centuries of stability for one of the greatest empires Thedas has known.

When Maferath's betrayal came to light, Isorath initially kept his rule. He had separated himself enough from that legacy that he was seen as a victim. It was a temporary reprieve, however. Isorath was eventually killed by the machinations of his own wife, angered not by the death of Andraste, but by the upheaval caused by unifying Orlais. The actions of Jeshavis spurred the radically different direction that Orlesian culture would follow. Isorath and all his direct children were killed.

The True Daughters

Our Lady had proved stronger than predicted and was able to bear two daughters, Ebris and Vivial. They were never presented as heirs, in deference to the elder sons, and were not permitted to marry. But the daughters were neither shunned nor cloistered—they were welcome in the home and were permitted to have relationships.

Ebris partnered and had children young but was physically weak as her mother had been. She died of plague in her late twenties. Her daughter, Alli Vemar, married young, but died in an accident during a voyage to Denerim. She had no children, but her husband would remarry and have a girl and a boy.

Vivial dared to proclaim affection for a Tevinter mage, Regulan. They went into exile before the betrayal and sought no connection to any of the resulting chaos. Vivial had several children, all daughters. The record is vague as to their names, for their mother actively sought to destroy any record, sometimes appealing to sects of Our Lady's believers to aid her.

HAVARD'S STEPS

Find the gnarled pine near the old Haven chantry, climb a foot or two up into the branches, and look east. You'll see them far away in that porcelain line of the snowy Frostback Mountains, if the day's clear: three or four notches that stand out in the peak. Havard's Steps, they call them. They're named after the disciple of Andraste who carried the ashes of Our Lady up into the mountains from Tevinter, seeking a final resting place for her.

"Carried her ashes . . ." It's only a moment to write those words, but Maker's breath, I've been in those mountains in winter. Even with good gear and supplies and dwarven merchants keeping the passes open, it's miles of frozen nothingness, under a sky like the arch of the world. Imagine being a band of refugees staggering from Tevinter through that snow, starved, hunted, with the murder of the Prophet still vivid in your mind.

Then imagine you're the man who has to lead them forward to . . . where? You don't even know, and you still have the scars from your last journey.

For that's the tale. Havard had been the strong right arm of Maferath since childhood—they were inseparable. When Maferath betrayed Andraste to their Tevinter enemies, Havard tried to stand between Our Lady and harm and was cut down for his loyalty. But Havard survived and made his way to Minrathous, bleeding, praying he could stop Andraste from being burned at the stake.

Miles and miles, with mortal wounds, all the way to the gates of Minrathous, where they were already laughing about the death of the upstart barbarian. Havard's suffering led him to a pile of cold ashes in the rain. But the touch of the ashes healed him and gave him courage, and so Havard gathered Our Lady's remains to keep them from being defiled. He came back to the lands of the Alamarri, seeking a safe refuge for her ashes, followed by what was left of Andraste's faithful.

The revered mother here once gave a sermon on Havard's journey as an allegory, or metaphor, or one of those. It was about how we put our faith in mortal things, only to be disappointed, and then have to suffer step by step to find grace again in the Maker. It was fine enough, but I don't think it's right to reduce Havard to some smiling example in a stained-glass window. This is the man who staggered to Minrathous soaked in his own blood and then forged through thigh-deep snow, urging his followers on with the urn containing Andraste's ashes lashed to his back, watching for pursuers behind. That's the Havard that inspires me. Not the holy disciple ascending those steps to the sky, but the man who simply refused to lie where he fell.

—Annotations in a prayer book belonging to Maella Tarren, Inquisition scout

In the decade after Our Lady's death, Maferath took the throne as king in future Ferelden but did not rule as the jealous tyrant portrayed by scripture. Instead, he divided power among his children. By all accounts, this was because Maferath intended these four nations to stand as a barrier if the Tevinter Empire returned to its colonial ways. He distanced himself from the rule of his sons when he could have held power alone over all the spoils of his betrayal. And so generous were these spoils, he must have known they could not last.

When his betrayal was revealed, Maferath and his court were slain. His death is not talked about in the acknowledged verses of the Chant of Light. There is no known burial site.

DIVINE JUSTINIA I

The appointment of Justinia I as Divine by Emperor Kordillus Drakon saw the beginning of the Divine Age and, with it, the creation of a new Chantry calendar and era in history. According to Chantry writings, Justinia I was, before her coronation, the only female general in Emperor Drakon's armies and a devout missionary of Andraste. For her devotion to both the arts of war and her faith, she was named "the Warrior-Priest" by many who knew her. When Drakon was tasked with selecting the leader for the Chantry, he chose this woman who most embodied Andraste: both a maiden of war and a spiritual leader. The name "Justinia" was chosen by the newly crowned Divine in honor of one of the first disciples of Andraste.

Divine Justinia I is most well known for compiling the Orlesian Chantry's interpretation of the Chant of Light. Her version of the Chant has survived with few changes to this day and is still recognized as part of the canon.

DIVINE JOYOUS II

The tension in the Chantry both within and outside Tevinter reached its peak shortly after Joyous II was elected to the Sunburst Throne. The issue of contention was the Maker's second commandment: "Magic must serve man, not rule over him." Beyond the Imperium borders, the commandment was interpreted literally, stating that mages should have no part in governing, or ruling, the people. But as the cornerstone of Tevinter culture, magic was revered in the Imperium, and for mages to occupy the most powerful positions in the government was common and encouraged.

After her ascension, Joyous II attempted to bring Tevinter in line with Orlais, demanding that mages and priests in Tevinter adhere to the Orlesian Chantry's interpretation of the commandment. When Tevinter refused, Joyous II declared all members of the Tevinter clergy heretics. This proclamation

OTHER MAJOR DIVINES

There have been dozens of Divines. Some served the Chantry with nary a whisper; others, with a heavy hand. Not every Divine is noteworthy, but the ones who use their power to its fullest have a way of making history.

Ambrosia II

The second Ambrosia famously tried to order an Exalted March against her own cathedral after protesting mages barricaded themselves inside.

Galatea

Galatea was a commoner said to be chosen by the Maker to assume the role of Divine when elections came to a standstill. In 2:83 Glory, she granted the Right of Annulment to all grand clerics of the Chantry to purge Circles of Magi ruled irredeemable.

Innocente

In 2:99, Innocente consecrated the newly completed Grand Cathedral in Val Royeaux and decreed that the Chant would be sung round the clock in its halls so that the faithful would always be able to hear Andraste's message. She also named the Towers Age in honor of the two towers of the Grand Cathedral.

Beatrix I

Beatrix I declared the Black Age and called for retribution against the Imperium when the Imperial Chantry celebrated the death of Joyous II by declaring a holiday. The Exalted March didn't actually occur till 4:40 Black, since most nations were still recovering from the Third Blight. The Chantry spent the next several decades fearmongering and warning nations of Tevinter's intent to expand and invade.

Amara III

Elected in 5:71 Exalted under what are considered dubious conditions, Amara III was the sister of the newly elected Emperor Alphonse and never obtained the rank of revered mother. During her reign, Amara III was said to enjoy bonfires fueled by burning maleficarum, and she ruled the Chantry with an iron fist until her death under suspicious circumstances in 5:85. A hunt for conspirators in her death was championed by Emperor Alphonse, and though it led to the imprisonment of many revered mothers and three executions, no one was actually convicted of killing Amara III. To this day the truth behind her death is a mystery.

Theodosia II

Theodosia II is said to have given birth while ascending the steps of the Grand Cathedral, in front of a crowd of faithful Andrastians. She was removed from the seat of the Divine shortly after.

Divine Justinia V

Justinia V will be remembered as one of the most progressive Divines in the history of the Chantry. Before her untimely death at the Temple of Sacred Ashes, she made strides to break down barriers for both mages and elves, as well as encouraging free thought among the Maker's many children. For her views, she won as many enemies as she did supporters.

led to the schism in 3:87 Towers, during which the Tevinter clergy broke completely from the Orlesian Chantry and named their own Divine.

DIVINE ROSAMUND

Divine Rosamund, the only one of her name, was born Lilette Montbelliard to the wealthy and noble Montbelliard family and was one of the numerous granddaughters of Queen Asha Subira Bahadur Campana. She was groomed from birth for the post of Divine by her predecessor, Hortensia II, achieving the rank of revered mother at the age of nineteen. Shortly thereafter, Hortensia II passed, and Rosamund ascended to the throne. Crowned before twenty, she remains the youngest Divine ever to be appointed.

Rosamund reigned for fifty-five years and is remembered as one of the most compassionate and gentle Divines in Chantry history. Despite all these distinctions, she is best known for the reams of erotic art and literature, circulated among Orlesian nobles, in which she featured. The Knights-Divine took steps to eradicate this material and, when they failed, tried instead to protect Rosamund from it. This latter endeavor met with greater success; Divine Rosamund seems to have lived out her life unaware that she appeared in the fantasies of Orlesian nobles.

PROMINENT GREY WARDENS

The Grey Wardens are an ancient order dedicated to protecting Thedas from once and future Blights. Since the Order's founding by the legendary Warden known as Carinus, each Blight has ended with the eradication of an Archdemon—and with its death, the birth of a Warden martyr. Before the rise of the Hero of Ferelden during the Fifth Blight, no Warden was more famous than Garahel, hero of the Battle of Ayesleigh.

GARAHEL

The name "Garahel" stands for much of what the Grey Warden Order values most and would prefer to be known for: Pride. Honor. Selflessness. Warden Garahel was a notable elven hero whom even humans must revere for his bravery and sacrifice as slayer of the Archdemon Andoral.

The Warden's legendary charm, intelligence, and keen political sense drew countless allies to battle against the darkspawn hordes of the Fourth Blight, a fight that lasted well over a decade. In addition to recruiting Wardens from the Anderfels and Orlais, Garahel negotiated the support of Free Marcher

Garahel slew the Archdemon Andoral.

royalty, creating a united army that finally broke the infamous siege of Hossberg, setting into motion the end of the Blight. War and circumstance shaped the young elf into a canny commander. He was very aware that Blights are not defeated by a single hero. He once noted to his sister Isseya that "heroism is just another word for horror."

Less well documented is the person behind the legend: the golden-haired elf, whose green eyes twinkled as he shared a story, told a joke, or flirted shamelessly. It is written that people from all walks were drawn to Garahel, as his manner and wit drove life's unpleasantness from their minds and allowed them to think of a better tomorrow.

As a Warden recruit in the Fourth Blight's early years, Garahel made his first griffon flight in 5:12 Exalted on a beast he'd only just met and would dub Crookytail. The odd griffon was not solid gray like most of his brethren. Crookytail's feathers were tinted with dusky brown; white patches decorated his chest and belly. One of his ears flopped forward, and he had a distinctive, bushy tail with a prominent kink in it—giving him his name. Nevertheless, Crookytail's strength, speed, and exceptional ability to find advantageous cracks in darkspawn formations made the beast and his rider one of the Grey Wardens' best battle teams.

From their first flight, made to rescue the nobles of Antiva City from the pressing darkspawn hordes, to their final battle at Ayesleigh in 5:24 Exalted, where they sacrificed all to slay Andoral, Garahel and Crookytail were said to be inseparable.

ISSEYA

Even during the Fourth Blight, few knew the name of Garahel's younger sister, Isseya. While her brother was outgoing, charming, and prone to heroism, Isseya was more modest and enjoyed studying and building her formidable magical skills. Her focus and determined nature, however, made her arguably as important to ending the Blight as her brother. He landed the killing blow upon the Archdemon; she helped ensure the survival of those most affected by the horrors of the age after Andoral's defeat.

VALYA'S GIFT

It was bad enough that Valya got to spend so much time with Caronel in the Warden library when we first arrived. Now with these griffons, there's no chance of him ever looking at me again.

Yes, it was pretty terrible after the mages rebelled and tore up our Circle, and I'd certainly be happy to never have to walk that far and then straight up a cliff again. But the Wardens were kind enough to take us in—and my gorgeous Caronel can take me anywhere he wants.

He is everything that a Grey Warden should be: smart, daring, and *so* handsome. I know things are getting bad with the mages trying to fight off the templars, but we need something good to focus on, right? Focusing on Caronel really calms me down.

So why he ended up spending so much time with plain old Vanya, I have no idea. She grew up in an *alienage,* for Andraste's sake. And she's always got her nose in some musty old book. Maybe it's because they're both elves. I guess I can see how he'd like that. She probably understands some of their old language. Better than me, anyway.

But she actually used one of their old books to find some griffon eggs. Griffon eggs! Can you imagine?! And they hatched! I have to admit they are quite cute, in a sort of prickly baby goose way. They must get fluffier when they grow up a bit. As babies, they have so many colors; I expected they'd just be gray, like the Wardens. I bet people will start coming from all around to see them. Could be a few handsome young men I can show around the castle and let peek at the griffons. Maybe Vanya and her old books aren't so bad, actually.

Berrith

—From the journal of a young mage who fled to Weisshaupt after mages in her Hossberg Circle rebelled, dated 9:41 Dragon

Garahel and his sister Isseya were instrumental in ending the Fourth Blight.

One of Isseya's most important achievements was enchanting makeshift aravels: wagons, boats, any conveyance large enough to fit a number of people. These were fastened together, held above the ground by her skillful magic, and pulled by teams of griffons. Isseya conceived of and executed the first of many journeys using the aravels to move citizens of Wycome out of the Blight's path and safely to Starkhaven.

Isseya's other major impact on Thedas reached beyond the boundaries of the Blight and was both a blessing and a curse. As the desperate times called for equally serious measures, she turned to her fellow mage Calien to learn the basics of blood magic to fight the darkspawn. In trying to save a griffon that had been tainted by a darkspawn bite, she used a process similar to a Grey Warden Joining and inadvertently started a chain of events that led to the extinction of all griffons in Thedas.

However, it is rumored that, shortly before she left on her own Calling, Isseya found a way to preserve a clutch of griffon eggs, protected with a complex weave of magical guards. It is written that she hoped a like-minded mage could recover the eggs and perhaps find a way for the mighty griffons to again soar through the skies of Thedas.

CORIN & NERIAH

The Second Blight was a bad one. This is not to say any Blight is good. Just that this one was particularly bad. It lasted ninety years—spanning nearly the entirety of the Divine Age—and stretched to all corners of the continent.

Though he made significant ground, Emperor Drakon of Orlais succumbed to old age in the middle of the Blight, and his son did little to strengthen anyone's position in the face of the darkspawn hordes that surfaced. By the time of the Second Blight's last battle, countless lives had been lost and entire villages wiped off the map.

The Wardens met the Archdemon Zazikel at Starkhaven, coaxing it into what was supposed to be a trap. Somehow, Zazikel expected the assault. Darkspawn surrounded the city. The Warden mage Neriah and her lover, a Warden named Corin, met the blighted dragon head-on while fighting off a legion of darkspawn. It is said that Neriah died protecting young Corin, that she flung herself in front of a striking emissary. She was killed, and Corin went on to deliver the fatal blow to Zazikel, turning the tide on the Blight and finally forcing the darkspawn back underground.

SOPHIA DRYDEN

Sophia Dryden lived during the Storm Age. She was the cousin of Arland Theirin of Ferelden and a rival for his crown when the previous king died without naming a successor. She refused to let go of her claim to the throne, even after Arland was crowned, and was accused of treason. As punishment, Dryden was forced to join the Grey Wardens.

A charismatic leader, Dryden eventually became Commander of the Grey and used her influence and power to start a rebellion against King Arland, a violation of the Wardens' vow to remain politically neutral. In response, King Arland's forces laid siege to Soldier's Peak, where Dryden's Wardens were stationed. The attack ended her life and the rebellion she'd founded.

During the Fifth Blight, sightings of Warden-Commander Dryden were reported, along with her mage counterpart, Avernus, ages after they should have died. The Wardens remain resolutely silent on the matter.

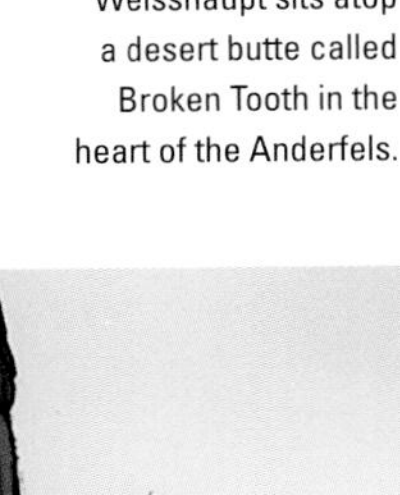

The Warden fortress Weisshaupt sits atop a desert butte called Broken Tooth in the heart of the Anderfels.

NOTES ON THE SEARCH FOR BREGAN

Details surrounding the last days of the Warden-Commander known as Bregan have been kept largely classified by Order leadership at Weisshaupt. What we do know is that Bregan descended into the Deep Roads for his Calling in 9:10 Dragon. His sister, Genevieve, replaced him as commander but did not last long in the post. For a reason the Wardens refuse to provide, an unprecedented expedition was organized to retrieve Bregan from the Deep Roads.

Some have speculated that the sentient darkspawn known as the Architect may have been involved, though it is nearly impossible to prove this. The expedition included a number of prominent Wardens, many of whom never returned to the surface. Of the documented members of the party, only the Wardens Duncan and Fiona survived, and neither has publicly spoken on the subject. Rumors persist that Maric Theirin also accompanied the Wardens on the journey, though his duties as king of Ferelden make it hard to believe even this notoriously brash royal would take such a risk.

What follows is a summary of what is known of the Wardens involved in the expedition:

Bregan: Those who knew Bregan well said the Orlesian was a reluctant Warden; he joined for the sake of his sister, Genevieve, who dreamed of being a member, when the Order refused to take her without him. Eventually, Bregan's respect for his fellow Wardens and his belief that he was no more deserving than them of advancement made him an excellent, if paradoxical, candidate for leadership, and he was made Commander of the Grey. The day he left the Warden ranks to see through his Calling was a day of mourning among Wardens across southern Thedas.

Genevieve: The former Warden-Commander was a cold and competent leader of considerable strength. She was loyal to her brother during his time in command and was likely the one to give the order to seek out her brother in 9:10. When she took his post, many cried nepotism, and she did not occupy the role of commander long enough to prove anyone wrong.

Fiona: The grand enchanter of the troubled Circle of Magi during the explosion at the Temple of Sacred Ashes is the only Warden on record who was actually able to reverse the effects of her Joining—an apparent product of the expedition. The fiery elven mage was present at the White Spire conflict and, before the violence, preached for mage independence, even going so far as to controversially proclaim, "Fuck the Divine."

Duncan: Much of Duncan's legacy is tied to the part he played in defending Ferelden from the Fifth Blight. But earlier in his career, he was young and reckless—forced onto the expedition by Genevieve as punishment for the murder of her fiancé. Though she likely did not expect him to survive, Duncan was one of only two Wardens to return from the Deep Roads.

Kell ap Morgan: An Avvar who trained as an Ash Warrior, Kell ap Morgan died on the expedition after years of service to the Wardens. He rose to the rank of lieutenant in the Order with his mabari at his side. The hound was named Hafter after the Fereldan figure of legend, and with Hafter's help, Kell developed a reputation among his peers for the ability to track any prey.

Julien: A senior Warden of considerable skill, Warden Julien is remembered for his calm, terse demeanor and deep belief in the Maker. He insisted on saying prayers before major battles.

Nicolas: Warden Nicolas's boisterous personality starkly contrasted with that of his partner, Julien. But by all accounts, the two Wardens were inseparable. They died together in the Deep Roads.

Utha: The dwarven Silent Sister used signs to communicate with other members of the Order. Like most Silent Sisters, she used her fists to fight, though she also carried two lengths of steel connected by a short chain. There are reports that Utha actually survived the search for Bregan. More than twenty years later, a dwarf matching Utha's general description was reported working with the Architect when his disciples surfaced. These reports cannot be verified.

ORLESIAN EMPERORS & EMPRESSES

The grand nation of Orlais occupies a full quarter of the Thedosian continent and extends its influence far beyond its shifting borders. In ages past, Orlais flexed its military muscle, threatening territory belonging to Nevarra and Tevinter and outright invading Ferelden. One could argue that the Emperor or Empress of Orlais, regardless of competency, is the second most powerful person in Thedas—the first, of course, being the Divine.

KORDILLUS DRAKON

When Lord Vanderin Drakon married his youngest son, Septimus, to Castana, the daughter of a prominent Ciriane chieftain, no one in Tevinter thought anything of it. A declining family simply wished to rid itself of an unwanted, non-mage child. For almost two ages, the nation of Orlais had been ruled by a gothi, or queen, chosen by the clans of Ciriane and Alamarri. Each time a new gothi was selected, the old hatreds between the myriad clans grew stronger and the process grew bloodier. Septimus Drakon may have lacked magical ability, charisma, and military prowess, but he had survived the cutthroat Tevinter nobility. He shared his expertise with his bride, Castana, who rose to be named gothi in -36 Ancient.

Their son, Kordillus Drakon, was born soon after. He was raised knowing that his mother's throne would only be his if he had the strength to claim it. At the time, the "nation" his mother ruled over was not even half the size of modern-day Orlais, and unified only in their love of Andraste and shared hatred of everyone else. Prince Drakon believed it could be much more. For he had a vision. He believed Andraste had appeared to him in a dream when he was a child and charged him with redeeming the world in the eyes of the Maker.

He began his holy quest at the ripe old age of sixteen by taking to the battlefield. At the time, each clan had its own variety of the cult of Andraste, its own rituals, traditions, and versions of Andraste's words. Young Drakon unified them by the sword.

When Drakon reached the age of majority, the prince courted and married Area Montlaures, one of the daughters of a Val Chevin lord. This sealed an alliance between their clans. Far more importantly, Area was both an unequaled archer and a shrewd tactician—the perfect person to stand at Drakon's side.

Even in Drakon's time, the eccentricities of contemporary Orlesian style were already emerging.

Together, the two transformed Orlais from a few squabbling clans controlling their own city-states into an empire. Hand in hand, they conquered well into modern-day Ferelden and Nevarra, stamping out any worship of the Old Gods as well as lingering Alamarri and Ciriane deities.

Their campaign of expansion stalled as they met heavier resistance in the North. Drakon, fearing that his cause was failing because the Maker questioned his devotion, refocused his attention on glorifying his god. He began by demolishing the ancient Ciriane fortress that was once home to Jeshavis herself and using its foundations to build, he said, "a chantry where the one true song of Andraste shall forever after be heard."

The search for a suitable leader for Drakon's new Chantry took four years. When Justinia I was finally chosen as Divine, the coronation festivities lasted a full year. Many hoped the first age, named for the Divine, would be the dawning of a peaceful and prosperous era, a time for Orlais and far beyond to bask in the protective light of the Maker.

That hope was short-lived. The Second Blight struck just four years later in the Anderfels. Emperor Drakon rallied every able-bodied warrior to march north against the Archdemon Zazikel, but he knew this would not be enough. In a controversial move, Drakon called every mage in his empire to join him.

The emperor's zeal in driving back the darkspawn did far more to spread the Chant than his earlier campaigns of conversion or expansion. His timely intervention in the Anderfels prompted both the recently independent Anders and the Grey Wardens to convert to Drakon's faith. The grateful Anders went even further and declared themselves part of the Orlesian Empire. As the battles against the darkspawn moved south and east across the continent, Drakon won much of the Free Marches and parts of modern-day Nevarra both spiritually and politically.

At the time of his death in 1:45 Divine, Drakon had created the most powerful nation in Thedas, united much of the continent under the grace of his god, and laid the groundwork to stop a Blight. He had fulfilled the destiny Andraste revealed to him.

THE GANDER

The reign of Empress Michele de la Tour de Fermin saw the brief adoption of the gander as a standard unit of measurement, being as far in one direction as Her Majesty might gaze before losing interest. Borders fluctuated daily, with negotiations regularly disrupted by the deliberate placement of small, distracting dogs. The tactic is widely credited for the popularization of the domestic pets that plague many royal estates to this day.

—*From* The Emperors of Orlais *by Brother Harlon Ascari*

REVILLE, THE MAD EMPEROR

"In a ring of silver, who shall stay? One little child gets away."

Children chant this rhyme as they stand in a circle. One child taps his or her fellows' backs as the words are sung. When they reach the word "away," whichever child is tapped must run until they are caught by the others. It is a simple game, often accompanied by much laughter. While the children are no doubt ignorant of the rhyme's meaning, scholars give it a dark origin. The poem is said to represent the "Mad Emperor," Reville. The "ring of silver" is the ring of daggers Reville placed around his bed to ward against threats. In 8:47 Blessed, Reville infamously ordered the assassination of his twin brother, the grand duke, and saw to the death of the duke's wife, their three grown children, and their eight grandchildren. It was rumored that eleven-year-old Verene escaped—the little child who "gets away."

Under Reville's rule, Orlais began a successful invasion of Ferelden beginning in 8:24 Blessed. The Orlesian occupation would ultimately last until 9:00 Dragon, significantly shaping the history of the two nations and influencing relations to this day. Unfortunately for Reville, he's remembered more for his behavior than for his contributions to history.

Reville was possessed of an increasing paranoia throughout his reign, the extent of which is difficult to determine. Even at the time, stories from the palace were exaggerated for dramatic effect. Reville was said to douse himself in self-made tonics, the rumored ingredients ranging from the mundane to the outlandish. Fearing betrayal, the emperor famously wore armor everywhere but the bedchamber. While some accounts state only that, others claim Reville oversaw the armor's crafting, then murdered the armorer, fearing the man had put a weakness in the metal that could be passed to Reville's enemies. In Ferelden, one might hear stories of chevaliers sent in search of Calenhad's legendary silver armor, said to render its wearer invulnerable. Knights who returned without it were killed on the spot—inspiring more than one to bring back a counterfeit set.

OTHER ORLESIAN ROYALS

Kordillus II: The son of the first emperor of Orlais famously floundered. A mere twenty years after his father's death, the Anderfels declared its independence from the empire. However, he clung to power well into old age. One of his last acts was aiding Divine Renata in the Exalted March on the Dales.

Jeaneve I: Following the lengthy reign of Kordillus II, the first empress of Orlais ushered in an era of "cultural betterment." Her rule spurred the creation of a great many customs still alive in Orlesian society today, including the popularization of masks and the founding of the Empress Arm, her guard and precursor to the chevaliers.

Etienne I: This emperor went twenty-eight years without fathering an heir. When his third bride finally gave birth to twin boys in 7:99, the Chantry named the eighth age "Blessed."

Florian: The overseer of the invasion of Ferelden famously eschewed all cosmetics and powders due to an intense dislike of being, as he saw it, dirty.

Etienne I strengthened trade with Orzammar.

Florian rarely appeared at court.

Etienne II was assassinated by dissatisfied nobles.

Judicael I rebuilt the Winter Palace.

Judicael II lost all heirs to illness.

DWARVEN PARAGONS

The dwarves venerate ancestors who have contributed in some substantial way to the betterment of dwarven society. A Paragon may be named for an invention, like Hirol, or acts of bravery, like Gherlen. However, the title may be bestowed upon a dwarf for all manner of contributions and discoveries. Varen is a favorite Paragon among surface historians; he was the first dwarf to eat a nug.

CARIDIN

The Paragon Caridin was born in the Ancient Age, while the First Blight ravaged the surface world. Caridin was the product of a love affair between a noblewoman from House Ortan and a Smith Caste worker. As a male child, he took on his father's caste instead of his mother's. She fought to keep him close to her in Ortan Thaig and devised a plan in which both father and son would serve House Ortan exclusively as smiths.

Caridin was a talented smith from the start and often employed creative techniques in his work. By the time he was a young man, he had taken over many of his father's commissions for the noble house and was entrusted with the task of outfitting their best and proudest warriors, many of whom were his close friends.

As more and more of the Deep Roads were lost to the darkspawn, the dwarves knew they were watching the fall of their once-great empire and were desperate to drive the intruders away from their cities. A seed of an idea had formed in Caridin's mind years before, and as battle raged through the Deep Roads, he sequestered himself in his workshop, where he spent years refining his plans for a contraption that would turn the tide in favor of the dwarves. When he finally emerged, he displayed his infamous Anvil of the Void to the Assembly. A device that melded the disciplines of blacksmithing and lyrium enchantment,

A striking tribute to Astyth the Grey. Statues of Paragons will vary in style and scope depending on the artist.

THEDOSIAN ARTISTS: AMBROSE DUMONT

A newly discovered talent, Ambrose Dumont has quickly become a darling of the Orlesian court. Older and of more humble origins than the usual newcomer thus favored by the peerage, he has nonetheless settled into his newfound popularity quite well. Dumont's patronage now includes many nobles and richer merchants. Indeed, it is rumored that the empress herself has commissioned a unique set of precious woodcuts and prints. Dumont's work ethic is irreproachable, the volume of his pieces since his ascent to preeminence having fulfilled even the most ambitious of commissions.

Dumont's determination to craft every single one of his woodcuts, rather than allow an apprentice to handle his work, has drawn the glowing approval of his patrons and a very high price for original woodcuts of his own carving. Though some would argue that the work of Dumont is without equal, it is perhaps hasty to offer him such accolades with other promising artists rising to fame, most notable among them the young Griselda Reiniger. It is, however, absolutely correct to attribute to Dumont the most sought-after trifecta of Orlesian skills: impeccable composition, discerning use of rare materials, and a newly discovered yet dazzling social acumen. One could point to his modest and somewhat drab attire as a possible flaw, but rumors of his consultations with the distinguished clothier Selvages should lay this issue to rest.

Dumont's gift of an exquisite series of woodcuts to the University of Orlais is now being used as the primary reference for any naturalist wishing to study the physiology of livestock and other such manner of creatures. A smaller and equally detailed series on the anatomy of nugs can be found in the Great Library of the University of Orlais.

It was briefly rumored that Dumont made use of blood magic to transfer his work to the woodcut with indelible artistic fidelity. These accusations were first levied by the once-notable art critic DeCassoulet during the beginnings of Dumont's fame. However, no proof was ever brought to light, and DeCassoulet has since fallen from grace after consorting with art forgers.

—*From* A Still Life of Modest Artistic Discernments: Thedosian Artists Through the Ages *by Plume*

the Anvil allowed the dwarves to forge golems: huge, powerful creatures of stone or steel. The golems were tougher than any warrior, could not be weakened by the blight, and knew no fear—perfect guardians for the thaigs that had not yet fallen to the darkspawn scourge. It was for this Anvil that Caridin was named Paragon.

There was a catch, however. The spark of life was essential to the building of a golem. Each golem created required the sacrifice of a warrior, for it would be that warrior's soul that powered the creature. Made bold by the hope that their lands could be reclaimed from the darkspawn, countless dwarven warriors volunteered to lie down upon the Anvil and be transformed into unyielding, immortal constructs.

The golems Caridin forged won many victories against the darkspawn, driving them off from thaigs long considered lost. As time passed, King Valtor demanded greater numbers of golems and forced casteless, criminals, and even his political enemies to go under the hammer.

But Caridin's conscience would not allow him to subject the unwilling to the agonizing process of being turned into a golem.

For that defiance, King Valtor commanded Caridin's apprentices to turn the Paragon himself into a golem. Caridin was strapped to his own Anvil and forged into a stone giant. When he rose, his apprentices were unable to control him; Caridin, unlike the golems before him, retained his memory. Now keenly aware of the horror of the procedure, Caridin vowed that no more souls would be sacrificed to the hammer. He took the Anvil of the Void and disappeared into the Deep Roads, taking the secret of his craft with him.

ENDRIN STONEHAMMER

Endrin Stonehammer, often known as the First Paragon, was king of the ancient dwarven kingdom that ran the length and breadth of Thedas, connected by the sprawling Deep Roads. Stonehammer, supported by his predecessor, King Orseck Garal, was responsible for establishing trade alliances with Archon Darinius of Tevinter, and the relationship between the Imperium and the dwarves survives to the modern age.

In the wake of Archon Darinius's death, the Imperium was thrown into chaos—a situation that some believe prompted the move of the dwarven capital from Kal Sharok to the smaller thaig of Orzammar, many hundreds of miles distant from the Imperium. Some credit Stonehammer for the move, while others dispute this, arguing that the idea was originally put forth to the Assembly by King Orseck. As in most things, the truth likely lies somewhere in between, with King Orseck making the decree and his ally Stonehammer enforcing it. When King Orseck died, Stonehammer was named his heir.

For his contributions to dwarven civilization, Endrin Stonehammer was named Paragon on his deathbed. His last act as king and his only act as Paragon was to name his late friend and ally, Orseck Garal, Paragon as well.

AEDUCAN

Paragon Aeducan was the progenitor of House Aeducan, the foremost noble house of Orzammar, which produced generations of Orzammar's rulers. Born to the Warrior Caste, Aeducan was responsible for taking command of the armies of Orzammar and defending the city from the First Blight when the Assembly and the Warrior Caste were paralyzed by interhouse feuds.

Aeducan's quick thinking saved Orzammar from the darkspawn and later earned him the title of Paragon. Aeducan is the only Paragon in dwarven history whom the Assembly unanimously voted to raise up, with no debate necessary and only a single abstention.

ASTYTH THE GREY

Astyth the Grey was the first female warrior Paragon and the woman for whom the order of the Silent Sisters was founded. Ages ago, dwarven culture forbade women from becoming soldiers. Astyth, who was born into the Warrior Caste, opposed this tradition. However, her arguments were ignored by the elders of her caste. To protest their silence, Astyth cut out her own tongue. Freed from the distraction of speech, she was able to dedicate her life to training. Years of intense preparation turned her into a warrior without equal. After she triumphed at the Grand Provings with nothing but her bare fists, demonstrating to all dwarves that a woman could be a worthy warrior, she won the right for female dwarves to become soldiers. Astyth herself was called upon by her king to serve him personally as his second and bodyguard,

The long-abandoned Deep Roads hide many secrets.

which she did proudly until she died while saving him from an assassin's dagger. For her sacrifice and her commitment to her caste and womankind, she was named Paragon.

To honor Astyth's memory, the Silent Sisters—an order of female warriors—was later founded. All Silent Sisters cut out their tongues out of reverence for Astyth.

FAMOUS FERELDANS

The dog lords of Ferelden. A kingdom of provincial agrarian fur wearers. It is easy to dismiss Fereldans for their rough-around-the-edges customs and culture, but the nation has given birth to some of the most important figures in Thedosian history, including the Bride of the Maker herself.

FLEMETH

Called the Witch of the Wilds by the people of southern Ferelden, Asha'Bellanar or the Woman of Many Years by Dalish elves, and the Mother of Vengeance by Chasind tribesmen, Flemeth is a shapeshifting mage who—if the legends are to be believed—has lived in the Korcari Wilds for centuries, sometimes involving herself in the lives of prominent heroes of Fereldan myth, sometimes luring men to sire one of her many daughters, all of whom are said to be witches like her.

The tales of Flemeth originate from the Alamarri in the Towers Age. According to a tale told among their tribes, an Alamarri lord by the name of Bann Conobar Elstan took a wife with a secret talent for magic: Flemeth of Highever. The marriage lasted until a young poet named Osen captured Flemeth's

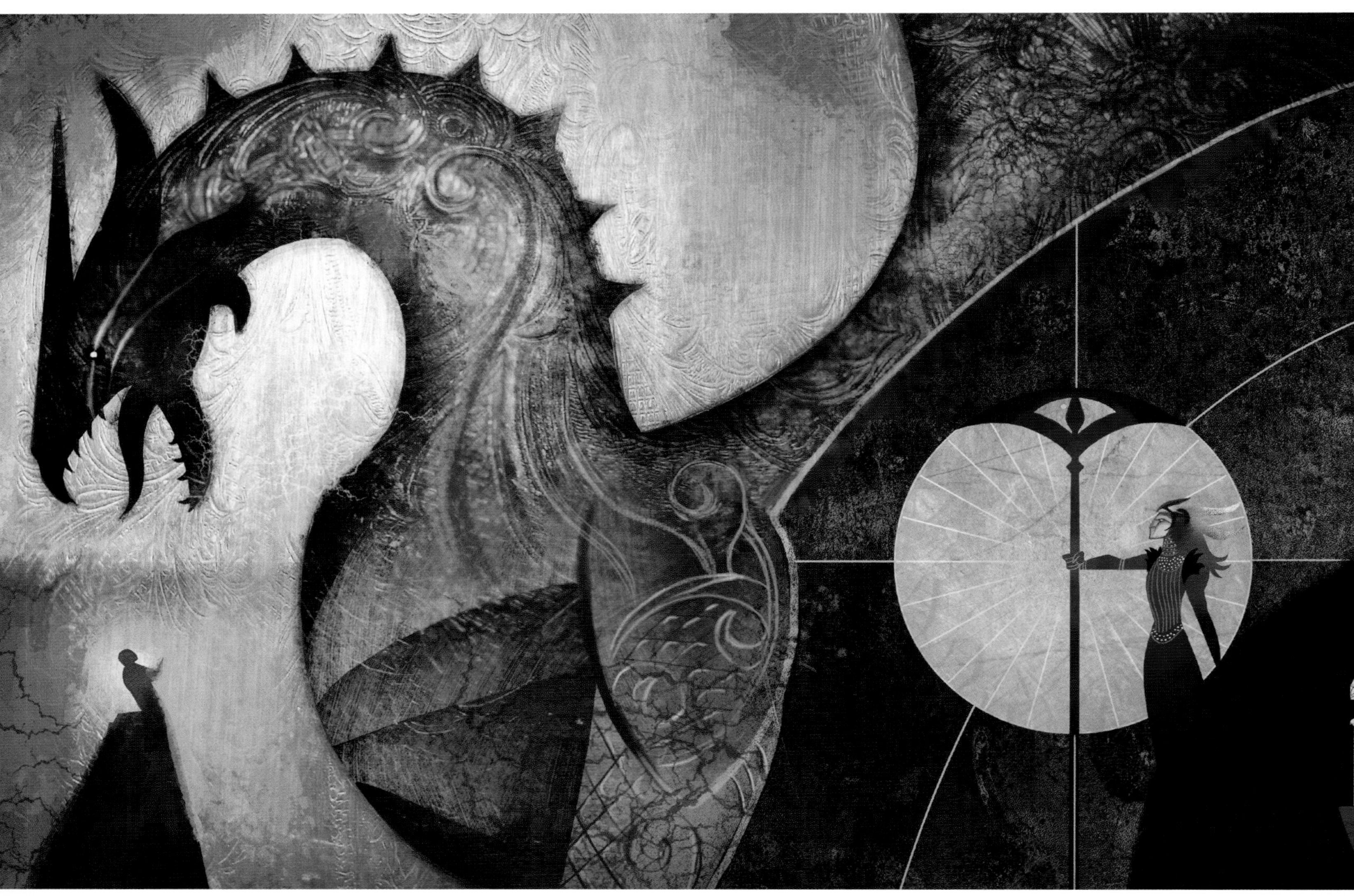

Flemeth, the Witch of the Wilds, has been known to take many forms.

heart, and the two fled into the Korcari Wilds, hiding from Conobar's wrath among the Chasind wildlings. When the couple received word that Conobar was dying and his wish was to see his former wife one final time, they returned to him, only to discover a trap. Osen was slain and Flemeth imprisoned.

In her dark prison, trembling with grief and rage, Flemeth is said to have summoned a powerful spirit to wreak vengeance upon Conobar. The spirit possessed her, turning her into a twisted abomination that slaughtered Conobar and all his people before fleeing back into the Korcari Wilds. From there, Flemeth plotted revenge on the Alamarri people, stealing Chasind men to produce many daughters.

These daughters led the Chasind in a massive invasion of the Alamarri lowlands, only to be defeated by the hero Cormac.

"It's difficult to say how much of Flemeth's legend is true and how much is false," Brother Ferdinand Genitivi has said of the stories. "Alamarri records before the creation of Ferelden as a nation are sparse, leaving us only with oral histories that changed over time. There is no actual evidence of a 'Bann Conobar' having ever existed, nor a 'Flemeth of Highever.' Some speculate that the legend actually refers to Teyrn Talemal, son of Caedmon, who tried to unite Ferelden and was eventually slain by his own wife—a woman he had imprisoned for her unfaithfulness, yet who had been released by sympathetic servants. It is also interesting how Flemeth's legend intersects with later history regarding the Chasind invasion that actually occurred almost a hundred years later. Alamarri stories of Chasind witches within their army abound and perhaps were tied to this earlier legend, even if the two had absolutely nothing in common."

Regardless of what became of the original Flemeth, stories of the mysterious Witch of the Wilds have persisted ever since. Flemeth, or a version of her, appears often in Fereldan tales. In one legend, an old witch is said to have approached Calenhad the Great to offer him the power to unite the Alamarri tribes and form a kingdom. She appears in many versions of *Dane and the Werewolf* and was even said to have aided King Maric the Savior in retaking the Fereldan throne.

There is, of course, a darker side to Flemeth's tale. Her daughters, for instance, are always represented as being far more sinister than their mother. They are the wicked seducers, slaying men who cross them. They are the shapeshifters, turning into vile beasts and killing anyone who trespasses in their forest domain.

So, too, does Flemeth herself take on darker aspects. The Dalish say Asha'Bellanar is a vengeful and sometimes-capricious being whom clan members seek out for aid—but only when desperate, as she is just as likely to kill a supplicant as help them. The Chasind, meanwhile, often paint Flemeth as a dragon or a serpent that dwells in caves. Desperate Chasind will seek out this monster when they desire revenge upon another. In such tales, those who are granted vengeance never get it in the way they expect. Flemeth always makes them regret their decision; in the end they lose more than they bargained for.

Ultimately, it seems unlikely for there to have been a single being alive for over seven hundred years in the Korcari Wilds. Perhaps there was once a Flemeth, and she had daughters who assumed her name and title. Today, the idea of the "Witch of the Wilds" is simply a handy cloak for apostates to wear, hiding them behind a veil of superstition. These are stories, after all, which have spread far beyond Ferelden. There is a Witch of the Wilds in Antiva, in the Nahashin Marshes, in the Planasene Forest of Nevarra. They surely cannot all be the product of one immortal woman and her daughters.

"If we actually had such a being living among us, one who has evaded Chantry detection for centuries, it seems difficult to imagine what dark and sinister goals she would have," concluded Genitivi in his research on the subject. "Either it is all smoke and mirrors, or we should be far more afraid than we realize."

CALENHAD

Calenhad's rise to power began when he met Arl Myrddin on the field of battle. At the time, Ferelden was little more than a collection of independent arlings vying for power. In a bid for kingship, Myrddin had moved against Arl Tenedor. During the ensuing battle, Tenedor was killed, and Myrddin found himself facing a young squire named Calenhad in one-on-one combat. Calenhad, of course, proved victorious. In front of his allies, Myrddin knelt before the squire. As outlined in Brother Herren's *The Legend of Calenhad,* Myrddin declared that while he now knew he would never be king, he'd realized who should be.

Myrddin stood by his conviction, and his allegiance brought more allies to the would-be king's side. Calenhad eventually married Myrddin's daughter, Mairyn. While some resisted the notion of following a commoner, the years to come would see many victories fall to Calenhad. His reputation for honor spread, as did the knowledge that he was a firm believer in the Chantry—qualities that garnered further support from the people of Ferelden. The final battle for Ferelden came in 5:42 Exalted, with Calenhad facing the forces of Simeon, teyrn of Denerim. Though Calenhad's friend Simeon nearly felled him, the peerless warrior Lady Shayna took the blow, and the teyrn was slain. That same year, Calenhad was crowned king with Mairyn his queen. The two were well loved by the people, and for a time, the fledgling nation of Ferelden knew peace and prosperity. It would not last.

Shayna had proven a steadfast comrade throughout Ferelden's unification. However, her love for the king far exceeded the bonds of friendship.

Calenhad is the founding father of modern-day Ferelden. His silver armor was said to be enchanted.

Compelled by honor, Shayna kept her love secret for years. But when offered a love potion from a witch, she gave in to temptation. When Mairyn discovered her husband with Shayna that night, the heartbroken queen fled to her father. Furious, Arl Myrddin threatened to pull his support from Calenhad.

Guilt-ridden, Shayna admitted her use of forbidden magic to the court, but Calenhad refused to have her killed. This did little to assuage Myrddin's outrage, and he roused the arls against Calenhad. When Shayna went to see Mairyn, hoping to make a plea for peace, she was discovered by Myrddin and killed. Calenhad challenged Myrddin to an honor duel and killed him. Calenhad's triumph over Myrddin was both bitter and brief. The other arls refused to back down, and Ferelden stood on the brink of civil war. To preserve the country he had forged, Calenhad chose to leave it.

It's said that Calenhad went to see Mairyn one last time, though what passed between them remains unknown. He left behind a proclamation abdicating the throne to Mairyn's unborn child. Thus began the Theirin dynasty, which would hold the Fereldan throne for ages to come.

As for Calenhad, he vanished without a trace, his fate unknown.

NOTES ON THE ORLESIAN INVASION

The Orlesian invasion of Ferelden was a long and violent period of recent history that few speak of openly now that the two nations enjoy peace. This outcome may not have occurred without the actions of key figures on both sides of the conflict.

Rowan Guerrin
Rowan Guerrin was a famed and decorated battlemaster of the rebel army. Betrothed to Maric, she became queen of Ferelden following its liberation. With Orlais expelled, Rowan's brother Eamon inherited their father's post as arl of Redcliffe, while her brother Teagan became bann of a province in Redcliffe's jurisdiction.

Meghren
An Orlesian usurper to the Fereldan throne, Meghren fostered a strong dislike and distrust of the Fereldan people. He refused to marry a Fereldan woman, despite Mother Bronach's counsel that it would give his reign legitimacy. He saw Fereldans as dogs who should fear him and his post as little more than a means to restore favor with the Orlesian aristocracy.

Severan
Severan was a Rivaini mage and Meghren's right hand. He acted as Meghren's military advisor, but the inattentive, selfish ruling style of Meghren meant Severan was essentially the commander of Orlesian forces in Ferelden during the occupation.

Bronach
Revered Mother Bronach was grand cleric of the Fereldan Chantry during an era of Orlesian occupation. A native Fereldan, she defected to sit at the side of the Orlesian usurper, Meghren, advising him on cultural and political matters. Bronach ineffectually advised Meghren to embrace Fereldan culture to earn trust from the populace and to marry a Fereldan woman to give legitimacy to his rule. He often ignored her advice.

When the tide turned against Meghren, Bronach declared Maric the rightful ruler of Ferelden.

Katriel
Katriel was an elven bard Severan dispatched to get close to Maric during his successful attempt to overthrow the occupying Orlesians in Ferelden. Katriel lured Maric's rebel army into an ambush at West Hill.

Nalthur
Nalthur was a prominent member of the Legion of the Dead. He led Maric and key leaders of the rebel army through the Deep Roads to Gwaren, then fought alongside them in some of the most important battles of the rebellion in Orlesian-occupied Ferelden.

Nalthur was killed in the historic Battle of River Dane. For his sacrifice, Maric agreed to tell the Assembly at Orzammar of his honorable actions.

MOIRA THEIRIN, THE REBEL QUEEN

The Orlesian occupation of Ferelden took a great many lives, but none greater than Moira's. The legendary Rebel Queen rose in the face of overwhelming odds to take on the occupying forces and no small number of Fereldan traitors.

When Orlais invaded and drove out King Brandel, it was Meghren, a disgraced Orlesian noble and cousin to the emperor, Florian, who was sent to usurp the throne. Moira took up her father's rightful claim to the Fereldan throne. With her son, Maric, at her side, she traveled between rebel camps, raising an army to take on Meghren and building a reputation for bravery.

Bann Ceorlic led a group of Fereldans who had allied with Meghren to betray and murder Moira. Maric was with his mother when she died but escaped the same fate. It is said that Meghren had Moira's head placed on a pike at Denerim as a symbol to any who would try to unseat his stolen authority.

MARIC THEIRIN

Kings are not rare in Thedas. Neither are heroes. But to be a hero-king is considerably less common.

Maric Theirin was forced to carry Ferelden's crown under dire straits when his mother was slain. He escaped the clutches of her Fereldan killers and landed in the care of Loghain Mac Tir, then a young poacher hiding in the hills with his family. The two young men were slow to trust each other, in no small part because of Maric's reluctance to admit his birthright. But circumstance made them friends: Maric, the reluctant king, and Loghain, his knight.

The Orlesian sympathizers who'd killed Moira tracked Maric to Loghain's camp. When Maric was revealed to be the rightful heir to Ferelden's throne, Loghain's father Gareth stood strong, sacrificing himself to fend off Ceorlic's troops while the young king and Loghain escaped into the Korcari Wilds.

In the possessed woods, they are said to have encountered Flemeth, who led them to safety. Free of the forest, Maric and Loghain met up with Rowan Guerrin, Maric's betrothed and a commanding officer in the rebel army. She led them to the army proper, under the command of Arl Rendorn, her father.

Celebration of Maric's survival was tempered by the approach of Orlesian forces. It was at this crucial moment, when everything was at risk, that Loghain hatched a now-legendary plan to split the defending fronts, salvaging a seemingly impossible fight. It would be the first of many daring calls Loghain made over the course of the war, earning him a reputation for keen military strategy. Maric fought on the front lines in the battle, despite Rendorn's misgivings.

Following the battle, the rebel army under Maric spent years traveling the fringes of Ferelden, gathering support and bolstering their numbers.

Taking Gwaren

Three years after the Rebel Queen's death, the rebel army took the remote settlement of Gwaren at the edge of the Brecilian Forest, their first major victory under Maric. During the battle for the town, Maric saved an elven woman named Katriel from an apparent assault. She told him that she was a messenger, carrying scrolls from his defeated ally Arl Byron that warned of approaching forces. Though Katriel earned Maric's trust with this act, she was later revealed to be an Orlesian bard—hired by Severan, Meghren's right hand, to infiltrate the rebels.

Loghain had the rebel army pose as Gwaren townsfolk to make it look like they had fled to the sea. When Meghren's chevaliers arrived, they found Gwaren empty and were surprised by an attack. Though the rebels won the battle and pushed the Orlesians back, Maric was seriously wounded in the fight, stabbed deeply by a chevalier.

Once Maric recovered, he and much of the army, acting on fraudulent information from Katriel, launched an attack at West Hill. It proved to be a trap. The rebels were decimated, and Arl Rendorn was killed.

Maric, Rowan, Loghain, and Katriel were left on their own following the Battle of West Hill. But they were not the last of the rebel army. Others survived, retreating to Gwaren with the usurper's forces giving chase. The party ventured into the Deep Roads to reach Gwaren before the Orlesians, a daring move, considering the darkspawn present on the roads.

Underground, they encountered a band of dwarven warriors, members of the Legion of the Dead led by Nalthur, who helped them to the surface under Gwaren.

Maric Becomes King

With the reemergence of Maric, Gwaren was able to fight back Meghren's forces. Word of Maric's rise, apparently from the dead, spread. Riots broke out in Redcliffe, with unrest spreading through the Hinterlands. Meghren ordered public executions for any Fereldan suspected of having rebel sympathies and told Mother Bronach, Ferelden's grand cleric, to spread word that Maric was actually dead and possessed by a demon.

It is not known how Maric finally learned of the bard Katriel's betrayal at West Hill, but most historians believe he could not have known until after they surfaced at Gwaren. He likely would not have let her live so long

Maric delivered Ferelden from its Orlesian occupiers and served as king for nearly twenty-five years.

had he known. Katriel was killed sometime after that second battle at Gwaren, presumably by Maric—though this has never been proven.

As the whole country erupted in rebellion, Bann Ceorlic and the other men who betrayed the Rebel Queen were brought to Maric in a Bannorn village, where he executed them.

The rebels pressed on. Loghain and Rowan led a battle against chevaliers at the River Dane, joined by the Legion of the Dead, Nalthur included. As Denerim burned, the grand cleric declared Maric the rightful ruler of Ferelden.

At the Battle of River Dane, Loghain emerged a hero, leading the army to victory, though many men were lost, including Nalthur. Orlais committed no more troops to the invasion, and over a bloody three years, they were expelled from Ferelden.

Meghren made his last stand at Fort Drakon. Maric challenged him to a duel and won, finally killing the usurper. Meghren's head was placed on a pike in Denerim square, an act of revenge for his treatment of Moira.

With Meghren's death, Maric assumed the throne of Ferelden and won a fragile peace with Orlais that exists today. Rowan became Maric's queen, and they had a son, Cailan, before Rowan died of an illness untreatable by magic.

Maric would lead Ferelden through much of the early Dragon Age and was rumored to bear another child, a bastard named Alistair. By all accounts, Maric was a far from attentive father to either child. Indeed, following Rowan's death, the king was notoriously reckless, said to be more interested in wild excursions abroad than in tending to his duties at Denerim.

King Maric was presumed lost at sea in 9:25 Dragon, leaving Cailan to assume the throne as hints of a Fifth Blight began to surface. Rumors of his survival persist to this day.

King or peasant, death's blade finds us all.

DANE

Dane was a great hunter from Fereldan legend and the father of the hero Hafter. According to the story *Dane and the Werewolf*, Dane was stalking a rare white hart through a forest. When he finally caught and killed it, a werewolf appeared to claim tribute for the hart, which had been killed in woods belonging to his pack. Surrounded by the werewolf's pack, Dane had no choice but to strike a bargain: he would exchange lives and bodies with the werewolf, one becoming the other. For more than a year, Dane roamed the forest—part man, part wolf—running with the pack, while the werewolf lived the life Dane left behind.

The truth of this tale has never been proven. While Dane almost certainly existed, the claim that he spent a year and a day as a werewolf is often challenged by Fereldan scholars. Regardless of academic skepticism, some Fereldan nobles believe they are descended from the lines of Dane and Hafter, and the most superstitious among them even claim to be part wolf themselves.

HAFTER

Hafter was a legendary warrior said to be the son of Dane. During the Second Blight, he united the disparate Alamarri tribes to defeat darkspawn hordes attacking what would become the nation of Ferelden. The long, grueling campaign to free Alamarri lands from the Blight devastated the Alamarri's numbers, and both Chasind and Avvar, hoping to take advantage of this weakness, came together to destroy Hafter and his people. Under Hafter's leadership, the Alamarri prevailed against the other clans, forcing them to flee to the wilds and the highlands.

For his heroism, Hafter earned the esteem of all the Alamarri tribes, who came together in a rare show of cooperation and named him teyrn—the first teyrn of Ferelden. Hafter's victories against the Chasind and the Avvar established the Alamarri as the dominant clan in the Fereldan Valley.

It is said that Hafter never died, but sailed away on a ship to lands unknown, where he may dwell still.

THE BARONESS OF THE BLACKMARSH

When you travel through the Blackmarsh, keep your mind on the Maker, a leaf of the Prophet's laurel under your tongue, and a vial of lyrium in your pocket. Sing the Chant so you cannot hear the whispers on the foul wind. Keep your eyes on the path so you do not see the faces of the dead in dark water. And keep your hands clasped as in prayer so they may not be caught in the clawing branches of the trees.

Do all this because the Blackmarsh is a terrible place, steeped in blood, where spirits of desolation roam, cursed to eternal wandering by a cruel baroness.

—An old Fereldan superstition

There are many who speak ill of our baroness, and it pains me to hear their words. It is as though they have forgotten that it was she who banished the dragon. Now all they can think of is that Orlais rules here when it should be Moira. What has the Rebel Queen done for us? She hides in the forests, afraid to show herself.

The baroness is here. She sees to this land and its people. She is stern, yes, but a firm hand is required for governance. I would not ask less from any ruler.

They say she is a witch. They say she calls for the most beautiful maidens of Ferelden to come to this very place and, deep within her cellars, drinks their blood to keep herself young. But I have seen no maidens, no blood, and no magic.

What I have seen is the baroness in her chambers, in the light of a single candle, reading a book of old poetry. She looks forlorn and alone. She often has a mirror beside her and observes herself within its glass. When I bring her wine, she takes it with both hands and thanks me kindly.

I asked her once why there was no baron. She replied that there had been one, but he turned away from her when her hands began to crease, her hair lost its luster, and her lips were no longer as red. I told her that she was still beautiful. She thanked me and told me to turn in, for she no longer needed me that night.

Those who speak poison about her do not know. They do not see who she really is.

—From a tattered journal signed "Fenella" and found in the Blackmarsh

LUTHIAS DWARFSON

Luthias, given the name of Dwarfson later in his life, was a legendary warrior of the Alamarri tribes. As a young man, he was sent to Orzammar, capital of dwarven civilization, to propose an alliance between his tribe and the dwarves. The alliance was refused, but while in Orzammar, Luthias fell in love with the dwarven king's daughter, Scaea. The two fled to the surface and returned to Luthias's tribe, where she taught him the way of the dwarven berserkers in battle. This new skill earned Luthias the reputation of invincibility.

The beautiful and terrible Avvar chieftain Morrighan'nan killed Luthias Dwarfson at the Battle of Red Falls. Morrighan'nan had declared war upon Luthias and his tribe for the murder of their son, who was conceived during a tryst. According to the legend, Luthias's body was retrieved by dwarven warriors, who carried it back to Orzammar to be interred.

The Ash Warriors of Ferelden believe they follow in the footsteps of Luthias and continue to practice the art of battle wrath.

TEVINTER ARCHONS

It is rare for someone outside the Tevinter Imperium to celebrate even its greatest Archons. So deep runs the disdain that the rest of Thedas holds for this nation of magic and backward Andrastianism that few faithful could even name its current leader, Archon Radonis. Yet it is difficult to deny the impact the Imperium has had on the greater continent. At the height of its power, the Imperium held land in all corners of Thedas, linked by the magnificent Imperial Highway still in use today. It's been said, "If it weren't for Tevinter, we wouldn't have alienages, blood magic, and the Blight."

DARINIUS

Before Darinius united the Tevinter Imperium, the lands of northern Thedas were occupied by three smaller kingdoms: Tevinter, Neromenian, and Qarinus.

The story of Darinius began in the kingdom of Tevinter. Livia, high queen of the kingdom and high priestess of Razikale, was pregnant with her first child when her brother, Tarsian, made a bid to usurp her throne. Because Tarsian had no magic, he could not make a legitimate claim to the throne, and he doubted his chances in a fair fight against his sister. So it was only as the queen went into labor that Tarsian made his move, slaughtering the priests and all the soldiers who would not swear allegiance to him.

When Tarsian broke into the queen's bedroom, he found it empty save for the royal signet of Tevinter cleaved in two. Half was missing. Frantic, Tarsian tracked his sister to the Temple of Razikale, where she waited, exhausted but fully armed and armored. Their battle claimed her life, and Tarsian lost his right eye and right arm—the price of betraying a Dreamer queen. No sign of the child was found.

A day later, Calpurnia, a priestess of Dumat serving in the temple at Vyrantium, found a baby boy in a basket on the seashore. The infant had nothing but a blanket and half of a broken ring. She took the child and raised him as her own son, naming him Darinius.

Darinius was raised in the Temple of Dumat and from an early age showed remarkable magical talent. By the age of ten, he could bend the Fade to his whim with the same ease and skill as somniari (another word for Dreamers) who had trained for twenty years. He is said to have been able to charm animals and was often found surrounded by birds or cats, whom he employed as agents and spies. They were such effective spies that many in Vyrantium believed the child was able to foretell the future. Statues of Darinius often depict him with a crow or a raven perched on his shoulder and a cat at his feet, holding a ferryman's pole.

Darinius united the Tevinter Imperium.

When Darinius was only nineteen, the high priest of Dumat lay dying. He sent for all the senior acolytes as well as Darinius, who was only a novice. The high priest said that Dumat had spoken and that his successor must prove their worth by bringing him that which has no legs yet must dance, has no lungs but must breathe, and has no life yet lives and dies. The acolytes grumbled among themselves that the high priest had lost his wits while Darinius cast a spell, lighting a brazier, and carried it to the high priest's bedside—the thing described was *fire*. The high priest named Darinius his heir and died. Darinius became high priest the following day.

When the high king of Neromenian died without an heir, a successor had to be chosen from the ranks of the Dreamers. The high priests of Dumat, Toth, and Lusacan, the three patron gods of the kingdom, were summoned to the palace at Neromenian and called upon to complete a test to see which was most blessed by the gods. The high priests were told they had until sunrise

the following day to tie an egg in a knot and place this knot on a pedestal set before the throne. The pedestal was enchanted so that when a correct solution was set there, only then would the crown of the high king be released from the palace vaults. If none of the high priests could solve this puzzle in the time allotted, they would all be put to death, and their successors would come and be tested. While the high priests of Toth and Lusacan put themselves into trances to roam the Fade for a solution, Darinius smashed his egg, tore a strip of cloth from his clothing, soaked the cloth in the egg, and tied it in a knot. He placed it on the pedestal, and all of the city of Neromenian heard the sound of a great bell ringing as the magic sealing the royal vault unlocked.

On the evening of Darinius's coronation, Calpurnia gave her son the broken ring and revealed to him how he had been found on the seashore. His war chief recognized the ring as the royal seal of Tevinter, which put the new high king in a very difficult position. If Darinius was the true heir to the throne of Minrathous, then he was obligated to avenge his mother's murder. If he failed to do this, it was generally believed the gods would put a curse upon his lineage. But the usurper Tarsian was well fortified in Minrathous, the city was known to be impregnable, and all diplomatic contact between the royal court of Minrathous and the other kingdoms had been cut off for more than twenty years. The rulers of Qarinus and Neromenian refused to recognize a Soporati, or non-mage, as the high king.

That night, Darinius had a dream. In it, he crossed a mighty river in a small ferry piloted by a man whose face was always in shadow. When he reached the other side, Darinius looked back and saw that he himself was the ferryman. When the young king awoke, he took this as a message from Dumat.

The next day, Darinius sent messengers with gifts to Tarsian, bearing the message that the new high king of Neromenian wanted to parley with Tevinter and mend the deplorable rift that had opened between the kingdoms. Tarsian was flattered enough that he invited Darinius to the palace at Minrathous.

Darinius took only an honor guard of seven soldiers with him on his supposed state visit to the usurper, and Tarsian welcomed him into the palace with open arms. Once inside the great hall, Darinius ensorcelled the palace, preventing any guard from entering, and challenged his uncle to a duel. When the spell was lifted, Tarsian was dead, and Darinius had reforged the broken seal of Tevinter, proving his claim to the throne. The kingdoms of Tevinter and Neromenian were united under a single high king.

Darinius now turned his attention to the dwarves. He realized that a military campaign in the Deep Roads was never going to succeed, so he sent his scouts to locate an entrance to their domain and traveled there himself. When his escort was met by dwarven warriors, Darinius offered himself as a hostage and asked to be taken to see their king in order to negotiate a treaty between their peoples.

In Minrathous, buildings that might otherwise crumble are kept standing through magical means.

The Imperium spent generations constructing the Imperial Highway that still stretches across Thedas.

Darinius traveled for weeks in darkness until they emerged in the city of Kal Sharok. He was not permitted to see the king, however, until he had been sent to the Provings to show that the ancestors and the Stone would favor this meeting. Darinius fought alone, and after many rounds of battle against the champions of the Warrior and Noble Castes, stood against a lone dwarf in magnificent armor wielding a war hammer forged from pure lyrium. This champion was far more cunning than the others Darinius had faced in the Provings, and the lyrium hammer shattered spells like spun glass. Still, Darinius fought bravely, and after hours on the sand battling the warrior, his opponent suddenly called a halt to the combat. He was, of course, King Endrin Stonehammer himself, and Darinius was declared—to the astonishment of the exhausted spectators—to have *valos atredum*, the voice of the Ancestors.

Endrin Stonehammer and the high king forged a trade agreement between their two nations, and Darinius returned from the Deep Roads bearing numerous gifts. Within a few years of healthy trade with the dwarves, Darinius's army wore dwarven steel, and his priests had lyrium fonts to fuel their spells. It was clear that Darinius had no equal.

Rather than risk a war that could not possibly be won, Rathana, the high queen of Qarinus, proposed marriage to Darinius. With their union, the Three Kingdoms were finally united, and Darinius took the title of Archon. He established the first Magisterium from the priesthood of the seven dragon gods and built the first embassy for the dwarves. The age of the Tevinter Imperium had begun.

THALSIAN, THE FIRST DREAMER

Little is known of the life of the man credited with bringing worship of the Old Gods to Tevinter. Although he lived well before the Imperium was founded and never held the throne of Minrathous, Thalsian of Neromenian is historically considered the first Dreamer and was awarded the honorary title of Archon by the Magisterium some four hundred years after his death. He claimed to have communicated with the Old God

ELENI ZINOVIA

Archon Darinius once said, "The wise are wary of prophecy: to seek knowledge of the future is to grip a sword by the blade." While this is quite true, few take the idea to heart. Immense magical power tends to go hand in hand with ego, and the idea of exploiting one's fate, or somehow avoiding it, reliably comes up sooner or later.

Although few aside from somniari can see the future with any degree of success, how much lyrium has been widdled away over the years by ambitious mages trying to prove otherwise?

A colleague once believed that, being timeless, Fade spirits could know the future. Indeed they do—from their point of view. They warned him of an assassination attempt from five years ago.

Even when the future can be known, it's those who are born with the gift, like Darinius himself, who are most likely to bleed for it. Consider Eleni Zinovia, mistress and advisor to Archon Valerius and mother of Andraste's judge and executioner, Archon Hessarian. Zinovia's prescient dreams helped Valerius's rise to power, but when she claimed to foresee his downfall, Valerius was so outraged that he bound her spirit to a statue and set it outside the entrance to his fortress. There, she could speak her prophecies and be mocked for them.

It is curious. The young Hessarian must have passed that statue many times, hearing the voice of his mother from unmoving stone lips—even after Zinovia's predictions proved correct and Valerius's fortress burned to the ground. Years later, Hessarian would stand before another prophet, one he had sentenced to burn at the stake, and show her mercy.

I have sometimes wondered what Hessarian was thinking the moment he made that fateful decision to put Andraste out of her misery. Perhaps he indeed heard the voice of the Maker, as he would later claim. One could imagine, however, that he was remembering his mother's fate: that such mercy had been denied to her, leaving her trapped for years in a form not her own. Perhaps Zinovia had even foreseen this moment and whispered of it to her son, in some small way shaping the world to come.

This, I think, is the best possible argument to not meddle with the future: whenever one tries, the Maker sees to it that the outcome is as ironic as possible.

—From Mapping Ephemera *by Cetaphina of Perivantium*

Dumat, who taught him the secrets of blood magic; Thalsian used this art to make himself king of Neromenian.

For the glory of his god, he established the first temples worshiping Dumat, and the dragons became a symbol equated with divine power. Thalsian is also credited with creating a mage ruling class; his own pupils founded many of the noble houses that have ruled over Tevinter for millennia. Mages of the Imperial Chantry today believe that blood magic was likely learned from the elves of Arlathan rather than from the Old Gods, but there is not enough direct evidence to support this.

THALASIAN THE DESTROYER

As Tevinter began to expand its borders eastward, the Imperium first encountered the elves. Elven scouts were sometimes spotted at the edge of the forest of Arlathan by the settlers who had previously believed the forest uninhabited. The Imperium initially dismissed the settlers' stories as superstition—the forest had a reputation for being haunted—but revised their stance when their legionnaires began to report skirmishes with strange creatures with pointed ears who used magic. When the Tevinters realized the forest was held by a nonhuman race, they were cautious. They sent emissaries into the forest of Arlathan to make contact with the elves, but none returned alive. The Imperium built a fortress near the border and stationed soldiers on permanent watch over the forest.

Over the next few decades, contact with the elves became more frequent and more violent. In the summer of -998 Ancient,

THE BODY CANTO

Tonight, in the desert, with emptiness all around,
The sky, endless, the earth, desolate,
Before my eyes the contradiction opened like a night-blooming flower.

Emptiness is illusion. Beneath my feet,
Grains of sand beyond counting.
Above my head, a sea of stars.
Alone, they are small,
A faint and flickering light in the darkness,
A lost and fallen fragment of earth.

Alone, they make the emptiness real.
Together, they are the bones of the world.

Solitude is illusion. Alone in the darkness,
I was surrounded on all sides.
The starlight dripped from the petals
Of cactus flowers,
A chorus of insects sang across the dunes.

How much abundance the world carries
If every fistful of sand
Is an eternity of mountains.

—Koslun, Qunari prophet who introduced his people to the Qun

several Tevinter settlements in Arlathan vanished into the forest, never to be seen again. The frightened Tevinter people cried out for war.

In -981 Ancient, the Magisterium and the reigning Archon, Thalasian, agreed to a reprisal. The legions of the Imperium marched into Arlathan, found the city hidden in the heart of the forest, and laid siege to it.

The siege lasted for six long years, consuming much of the Imperium's resources. With the legions' attention on Arlathan, the Inghirsh took the opportunity to rise up and strike the southern settlements. Under increasing pressure to bring a swift end to the war with the elves, the magisters and Thalasian combined their efforts to work a blood-magic spell against the city of Arlathan. The spell sank the elven capital into the ground, destroying it utterly. The legions captured the fleeing elves, and a vast new population of elven slaves was brought into the Imperium almost overnight.

The dwarves were among the first allies of the ancient Tevinter Imperium.

ALMADRIUS & TIDARION

With the conquest of Arlathan, the Imperium acquired a growing population of magically gifted citizens. But magic in Tevinter culture had always been a mark of the favor of the gods, not an accident of birth. The magisters and the temples refused to acknowledge this mage underclass of elves and other newly "liberated" foreigners.

During Archon Almadrius's reign, the problem was exacerbated: he took a lowborn mage of Planasene blood named Tidarion as one of his apprentices. The outraged Magisterium refused to consider the boy a possible heir to the throne. Almadrius's rivals within the Magisterium plotted against the boy as well as his master. Almadrius survived several attempts on his life, but his Altus apprentices did not. When the magisters finally assassinated Almadrius, only Tidarion remained as his heir. The magisters refused to recognize him, so he took the throne by force, marching the legions into the Magisterium and slaughtering all those who would not swear fealty.

The Seven Temples declared Tidarion a usurper, and the legion was divided. Some generals supported the temples, and some the Archon. The mages of the Laetan class overwhelmingly supported Tidarion, and so mages fought mages for the first time since the fall of Arlathan. The Imperium plunged into a civil war.

Archon Tidarion died in the midst of the war without naming an heir, and the magisters fought among themselves over the vacant throne for twenty years. When Parthenius, the former high priest of Dumat, took his place as Archon, he ended the war by admitting the Laetans to the temples for the first time and giving them three seats in the Magisterium.

HESSARIAN THE REDEEMED

Most Andrastians can recite the story of Hessarian and Andraste, at least in the barest of terms.

As most Chantry sisters would recite it, Andraste's mortal husband, Maferath, approached Archon Hessarian, ruler of the Tevinter Imperium. Jealous of his wife's influence, Maferath offered to arrange for Andraste's capture. Believing her death would end her cult and strengthen the Imperium, Hessarian eagerly agreed. He arranged a public execution so that her followers could see their prophet fall. However,

Though Hessarian murdered Andraste, some would argue that he showed mercy.

as Andraste burned, he was plagued with sudden remorse. Too late to stop her death, but able to end her suffering, Hessarian took mercy on Andraste as outlined in multiple versions of Apotheosis 2:11:

Before any among his advisors could draw breath
Hessarian took blade to hand and himself
Dared the fire that consumed the Prophet,
With one swift strike, pierced her heart.

Though Hessarian had originally intended to end Andraste's following, her cult did not fall, and he refused to take action against them following the Prophet's death. Ten years later, Hessarian declared that he heard the voice of the Maker when his blade touched Andraste. He named himself a disciple of Andraste and revealed that Maferath had betrayed her. What came next shook the Imperium to its core. Hessarian declared the Maker the one true god and made Andrastianism the religion of the Imperium. His forceful conversion of the empire effectively outlawed Tevinter's long-held worship of the Old Gods.

Today, Hessarian is widely revered in Tevinter but remains a complicated figure for the true Chantry. His hands are stained with the blood of Andraste, yet the Chantry teaches that his conversion was sincere. He heard the voice of the Maker, yet some scholars question why he took ten years to confess it. Hessarian wrote the Canticles of Erudition and Penance, both of which are sung in the Chantry today. However, his Canticle of Silence is considered by some to be Tevinter propaganda. He created an alternate version of Transfigurations, only taught by the Imperial Chantry, which removes references to prohibitions against magic. It is unsurprising that much of Hessarian's impact is reduced in Chantry teachings for simplicity's sake.

The uncertainty surrounding what Hessarian represents—or *should* represent—is clearly reflected through works of art commissioned by the Chantry over the centuries. At times Hessarian is depicted as a terrifying figure, fire rising around him and stained with Andraste's blood. Other times, Hessarian weeps as his blade pierces Our Lady, the two figures bathed in light as he hears the voice of the Maker. How Hessarian is portrayed often reveals less about the disciple himself and more about the philosophical and political leanings of the Divine or revered mother who commissioned the piece. Regardless of how he's portrayed, Hessarian's contributions to the Chantry are felt, if not always acknowledged. He is held up as an example of the penitent man, and his Sword of Mercy is proudly displayed on the uniforms of templars throughout Thedas.

The glory of Andraste knows no bounds.

NEVARRA, ANTIVA & BEYOND

Kirkwall's notorious Orlesian viscount Perrin Threnhold. The Antivan queen Madrigal, whose brutal death by four Crow blades ushered in the Steel Age. Cathaire, an often-overlooked disciple of Andraste who commanded the Prophet's armies when she marched on Tevinter. There are libraries dedicated to the myriad figures of minor nations and their equally colorful histories. While this text cannot possibly do justice to the thousands of years and thousands of lives that came before it, it can highlight some of Thedas's most important and influential figures beyond the greater empires of Orlais, Tevinter, and Ferelden.

TYLUS VAN MARKHAM

King Tylus Van Markham of Nevarra was the founder of the short-lived but influential Van Markham dynasty. Originally a general in the Nevarran army, he claimed to have descended from the Orlesian emperor Kordillus Drakon. He rose to prominence in the midst of the Fourth Blight, while defending Nevarra from the ravages of the darkspawn. After the defeat of the Archdemon Andoral, the general was greeted by his fellow countrymen as a hero. Tylus took this opportunity to stir the populace against the corrupt Pentaghast dynasty and eventually led a coup to overthrow then-king Nestor Pentaghast.

A popular king, Tylus was able to rally his people against the Orlesians, winning several decisive military battles and establishing Nevarra as a power not to be taken lightly. He started its expansion from city-state to nation, but that continued after his death. Over the course of three generations, his descendants transformed Nevarra from yet another dot on a Free Marcher map into a proud nation and a world power in its own right.

AURELIAN PENTAGHAST

Aurelian Pentaghast was notoriously a false member of the Pentaghast family whose failed attempt to assume the Nevarran throne in the Blessed Age exposed him as a fraud. Disgraced, he joined the Legion of the Dead, the only human ever recorded to do so.

Aurelian's father, Gustav LaFleur, was a minor Orlesian noble who married Sotiria Pentaghast following her divorce from the Orlesian emperor Etienne I. Gustav came to the marriage with a son, Aurelian. Aurelian was raised as a Pentaghast and very much looked on Sotiria as a mother.

SEASONS IN NEVARRA

To My Lady Gennel,

I would, of course, be honored to host you at the embassy whenever you care to arrive. As to your question of what diversions there are for visitors to Nevarra City, that requires something of a more detailed answer. The Nevarrans love their arts and entertainments, but each season brings its own particular flavor.

For example, in high summer, as it is now, I can glance out my study window and see the colored flags from street markets strung along the Minanter River—and on more than a few boats as well. One can buy any manner of leather goods, candied fruit, or rare wines, while the lower classes risk the danger of the trade boats to swim and cool off in the waters.

For someone of your rank, my lady, the attraction of this season would be the so-called "Duchess's Games" at the Anaxas estate here in the city. Scholars from Cumberland are invited to travel up the Imperial Highway to test their minds and mettle against the best of the Free Marches, in contests of philosophy and rhetoric usually taking place over tea with the Duchess Ravria Anaxas. I can confess only to you, my lady, that some of my better witticisms have been stolen from such gatherings.

When the leaves start to turn, the street markets drift away, and the best entertainments can be found in the evenings. This is the season of ancestral pageants. Lanterns are lit in the streets, illuminating the statues—there must be hundreds of them across the city, my lady, of powerful generals, dragon hunters, and heroes. The Nevarran people adore their heroes almost as much as they venerate their dead, and these pageants combine the best of both traditions. Great families drape statues of their respected ancestors in their colors and hire troupes of actors to stand about them at night, dressed in elaborate costumes, acting out the ancestors' most famous exploits for any passersby. Traditionally, one pays the actors in copper coins, though I imagine the largesse of the nobility is somewhat more practical, since the actors return every year.

The very best pageants take place along the boulevard stretching up to the Castrum Draconis. Here, statues of kings and queens of Nevarra stand amid columns of polished black marble. I tell you, my lady, the reflections of hundreds of lanterns in the stone is a beautifully eerie sight. The Pentaghasts and Van Markhams compete to put on the better show, and these pageants are your best chance to see the famed ebony dragon armor of the kings, donned to act out the greatest battles in Nevarran history.

There are rumors that the Mortalitasi, mage-keepers of the Grand Necropolis, where the dead are mummified and laid to rest, perform rites of their own during these autumn nights. But I shall say no more, even in a personal letter. The Mortalitasi are powerful at court, and one never wishes to offend.

Winter comes hard to Nevarra, and the city is soon swept with frost. Stretches of the Minanter River freeze, and one can see daring skaters enjoying the ice, while vendors on the banks sell roasted chestnuts or hot spiced tea. The winds here are bitter, so the best entertainments are found indoors, where—if you'll permit me—a little of Nevarran history makes itself felt.

When high dragons menaced Thedas in ages past, dragon hunters traditionally tracked them in winter, when the beasts were sluggish. The Nevarran dragon hunters pursued them almost to extinction in the Steel Age, and before our own Dragon Age saw the return of the creatures, the winter excitement of dragon hunts was lost to Nevarra City's culture. However, the hunt balls continued to be held, and are still held in winter today. Few have the traditional dragon's head or heart as the centerpiece, a fact for which this humble ambassador is grateful. No amount of incense can mask the smell.

Instead, the dances changed to incorporate the thrill of the hunt itself. Couples dress in armor or flowing red costumes, according to their preference, and the early dance is often a lively galliard, where steel flashes and red cloth flutters. It is as close to a dragon hunt as I am likely to see, my lady, with the virtue of being able to enjoy a glass of good Antivan wine while watching.

By the time spring arrives, everyone is glad to be out of doors. With the river unfrozen, the trade ships return, and the marketplaces overflow. The Wintersend tournaments are particularly grand in Nevarra, since the nobility have vast treasuries and deep-seated rivalries to spend them on. There are fewer jousts, however, and more tests of arms in archery or sword fighting, something better suited to the Nevarran character, I feel. They are generals and hunters, queens and kings, for whom death is a noble friend long anticipated. It gives them a love of life rarely equaled elsewhere.

—Letter from Galen Vedas, Starkhaven ambassador to Nevarra, to Lady Gennel of Starkhaven, 9:10 Dragon

When the time came to crown the next king of Nevarra, Aurelian made a bid for the throne. He was a pious man, his firm beliefs in the Maker a product of his Orlesian father. He believed the Maker demanded that he return his adopted homeland to Chantry rule. When it was exposed in 8:60 Blessed that he was actually not directly linked to the Pentaghast bloodline, he retreated, disgraced, into dwarven lands.

With little recourse but to live out his days as a dishonored exile, he joined the Legion of the Dead and went into the Deep Roads to find honor as an unlikely dwarven hero. He was never seen again, but pieces of his enchanted armor turned up on the surface in the ensuing decades. Some say the armor was scavenged off his body; others, that he sold the pieces after secretly returning to the surface. The truth, as always, is known only to the Legion, whose motto has always been "Our secrets die with us."

THE CRYPT OF CASPAR PENTAGHAST

Uncle insisted I accompany him to the Grand Necropolis today. I heard him saying, "I want my niece dressed in something befitting her station for once," to the maids. They descended like wolves, lacing this and buttoning that. He was surprised when I asked what was happening, as if he mentions anything to me. He neglected to tell me today we would see Caspar Pentaghast.

Uncle would not stop talking all the way to the Necropolis about the "noble legacy" of King Caspar the Magnificent. The stories in the family books say he was a most ferocious knight who threw the former king out of Nevarra. I asked if that made him a traitor, and Uncle grew cross and told me King Caspar was a great hero, saying, "If the king that Caspar deposed had had his way, we would be *Orlesian*." I do not care, but did not say so. I asked instead if King Caspar hunted dragons.

Uncle says King Caspar killed many dragons, because in the Glory Age there were so many in Nevarra, they ate whole villages and roads were not safe. King Caspar organized great hunts with hundreds of knights from other noble families to drive the dragons back. Uncle says the armor in the grand foyer in our house is made from the bones and scales of a high dragon Caspar killed by himself, alone. It is so large I did not think anyone could actually fit inside it. I asked what Caspar used to kill the dragon. Uncle actually smiled, and said that I would see.

We arrived in the Grand Necropolis and went into a part of the family crypts I had never been in before. Uncle walked past all the staring dead until we came to a set of doors as tall as the ceiling. They swung open, and a dozen Mortalitasi were waiting inside the largest place I have ever seen. At the top of a set of stairs was a throne, and on the throne was a body wearing a gold crown.

The Mortalitasi went through their chants. It did not stir. I bowed and did not look where its eyes should be. Everything on the throne was gold or marble and very fine, except the sword on King Caspar's lap, dull silver, but very sharp. I thought what a waste that a good weapon should lie buried, and stepped forward to look at it, and then I heard a soft noise and saw the corpse looking at me.

On the way home, Uncle said that was a singular honor and praised me for remaining calm when older children sometimes flee the dead. I was not afraid of what I saw. I do not understand why it matters if a spirit finds me interesting or not. I only think for a moment, when it was looking at me, King Caspar's face looked very sad.

—A page taken from the journal of Cassandra Pentaghast, written when she was a young child

FYRUSS

King Fyruss was the notoriously ambitious ruler of Starkhaven during the Glory Age. Since Starkhaven was the largest and most prosperous city-state in the Marches at the time, Fyruss concluded that the rest of the Free Marches should follow its lead. Thus he carried out a long and ultimately fruitless campaign to unite all of the Free Marches under his banner.

Fatally, Fyruss's expansionist aspirations were not limited to the Marches; he also invaded some of Antiva's southernmost cities. His recklessness turned diplomatic agreements with Starkhaven from an asset into a liability—prompting his betrayal by his Tevinter allies, who staged a coup against the king and annexed Starkhaven.

Fyruss was exiled from Starkhaven and forbidden to return. According to some stories, he drowned himself in the Minanter River, throwing himself off an escarpment on the riverbank across from Starkhaven, so that his last sight would be of his beloved city. Starkhaven would not be reclaimed from Tevinter till much later in the Glory Age.

ASHA SUBIRA BAHADUR CAMPANA, QUEEN MOTHER OF THEDAS

Most people believe that Antiva maintains its independence on the backs of the Crows, but most people are wrong about nearly everything.

In the Black Age, the matriarchs of Rivain arranged a marriage between the crown prince of Antiva, Alonzo Campana, and the young gana of Ayesleigh, Asha Bahadur. Most at the time thought that all the advantage of the match fell to the young lady. Gana Asha was the daughter of wealthy merchants who had been elevated to nobility; for her to wed the future king of Antiva was a stroke of extraordinary luck. Once again, those people would be idiots. The advantage of the match was entirely on the prince's side.

Princess Asha understood that her new kingdom was in danger. It was becoming too prosperous to avoid attracting the attention of envious powers with better armies. It was only a matter of time before Tevinter, the Marcher states, Nevarra, and Orlais began trying to claim a share of Antiva's wealth, and when they did, she knew her kingdom would be no match for them on the battlefield. So Asha planned to outmaneuver her enemies before it could ever come to war.

By the time Alonzo Campana took the throne, his queen had already arranged marriages in rival countries for three of their children. Over the next several decades, Queen Asha's plan was revealed. She married her children and grandchildren into strategically selected families in every nation on the continent. Each marriage sealed an alliance.

Within thirty years, no country in Thedas could risk hostilities against Antiva without bringing half of Thedas into war. Today, the blood of Queen Asha flows in the veins of Empress Celene and the prince of Starkhaven, the king of Nevarra, most of the dukes of the Anderfels, and even prominent magisters of the Imperium. More than any document or agreement, her bonds of blood force most of Thedas to remain at peace with Antiva or risk terrible consequences at family gatherings.

Many Thedosians live isolated, simple lives, unaware of any history outside of what is present in the Chant of Light.

THE SEARCH FOR MARIC

There are stories that say King Maric did not in fact die at sea in 9:25 Dragon—that he survived, and lived years longer. These stories, which stretch in setting from Antiva to Seheron and are said to involve dragon eggs and Qunari women and Tevinter magisters, are at best not credible and at worst preposterous, given that they also involve Alistair Theirin, his rumored bastard son. That Varric Tethras may be involved only further discredits the stories. Still, there is some evidence that supports the rumors, and there is value in learning what one can about the others involved.

MAEVARIS TILANI

In the Tevinter Imperium, mages have all the power—but they are not all equal. A mage who does not hold a seat in the Magisterium or who does not adhere to exacting standards of behavior—at least in public—is a pariah at best and an outcast at worst. As with any such society, however, there are exceptions.

One such exception is Maevaris Tilani. Called male at birth, Maevaris lived as female beginning at the age of fifteen, permitted to do so by a kind and understanding father despite the scandal it caused. Magister Athanir Tilani was considered too inoffensive, and had too many allies, to be driven out of the Imperial Senate for such an offense—and he was unwilling to lose his only heir, despite the hardships this would cause them both.

Maevaris watched as her father was used constantly for his gentle nature, passed around in the ranks of the Magisterium like currency and discarded whenever convenient. When the Imperial templars arrested her father and executed him for treason in 9:32 Dragon, she was certain it was the result of his becoming involved in a scheme he didn't even believe in, and then being abandoned by his allies when it went awry. She took revenge, quietly. It was enough, however, for others to take notice and realize she would not truly be her father's daughter. This made her enemies, enough so that her inheritance of her father's seat in the Magisterium was called into question.

It was a challenge that could not be allowed to stand. Fortunately, while the Tilani family had never been known for its political clout, it was well known for its wealth through long-standing ties to the dwarven Ambassadoria. Having forged an alliance with Thorold Tethras, the dwarven merchant and representative of Orzammar, Maevaris successfully outmaneuvered opponents and secured her inheritance, as evidenced by the following letter between two magisters from 9:35 Dragon:

"It's unimaginable. This woman flies in the face of every tradition we hold dear, and rather than being turned out of the Magisterium as she deserves, she is now welcomed! To top it off, I understand she's now promised her hand in marriage to a status-grubbing dwarf, of all things. Yes, together it appears they have enough coin to buy off every vulgatis and honoratus in the eastern empire, but why should that make a difference to us? I am disappointed you've refused to sponsor my bill, and even more disappointed that you attended the Tilani gala. Yes, everyone says they are magnificent, but we must stand on our principles, or we have nothing!"

Maevaris never officially married Thorold, but their union was universally recognized in social circles as being a sincere and affectionate one. Thorold died in 9:37 Dragon—the victim of an accidental fall while visiting Minrathous, though some claimed it was the doing of Maevaris's embittered enemies. She inherited all of Thorold's fortune, retaining his contacts in the Ambassadoria even though some tried to cast suspicions on her for his death, and during the following year of mourning, she was rumored to spend much of that coin and clout exacting quiet vengeance. As a result, Maevaris has become a magister of unique reputation: she walks the balance of fear and respect, with few who oppose her willing to do so openly. In recent years, it is said that she has become part of a league of magisters seeking massive reform within the Tevinter Imperium, and it remains to be seen whether this will propel her further into the limelight or spell her ultimate doom.

AURELIAN TITUS

Common wisdom holds that worship of the Old Gods was stamped out in the Tevinter Imperium during the period of its history known as the Transfiguration, which followed Archon Hessarian's conversion to the Andrastian religion. This is, of course, not entirely the case. Dragon cults persist in the Imperium and, in more recent ages, have sometimes acquired a great deal of political power—usually in secret, with no one aware of their existence until far too late.

Such was the case of Aurelian Titus, a Tevinter mage who surprised many by suddenly gaining an Imperial Senate seat in 9:28 Dragon with no history, no family name, and no lands to speak of. He had been granted the seat by Archon Davan, who'd presented Titus at a Minrathous social event not a month earlier. The presence of a new player with the Archon's ear sent the Magisterium into a frenzy. Everyone wanted to know who this man was or be his friend. Within the span of a year, Titus had accumulated a web of magister allies without having anything more concrete to offer in return than the vague promise of currying favor with the Archon on their behalf—a promise that Davan did nothing to dispute, particularly since it deflected attention from the various other scandals of his reign.

Of those who did their best to discover who Titus was and how he came by his position, they found very little.

The man's name is much like the man himself: conjured from nothing. The only Titus family on record was eradicated during the Black Age, and even if he belonged to such a lineage, it would give him no benefit to claim it. The rumors that he appeared suddenly are, of course, untrue. Our sources say that he has been aiding Archon Davan from the shadows for several years and has a veritable army of fanatics—all of whom he has put at the Archon's disposal. It worries me, however, that the man has "fanatics," and yet nobody seems to know what they are fanatical about.

—An anonymous magister investigating Titus

Archon Davan was assassinated in 9:29 Dragon. Though the list of those with cause to kill him, up to and including his successor, Archon Radonis, was long, there are many who say Davan's death came after a falling-out between him and Titus. Even with the Archon's death, Titus's star continued to rise, to the point where even quiet revelations about his worship of dragons caused little stir. Whispers claimed that he would inherit the legacy of Thalsian, the First Priest of Dumat, and lead the Imperium to the old ways once more. A struggle with the Imperial Chantry and the Black Divine ensued, made all the more impressive because Titus actually appeared to be winning. This lasted until 9:40 Dragon, when Titus disappeared. Some say he perished during a Qunari assault on his coastal fortress of Ath Velanis in Seheron, but considering the power of his cult was simultaneously broken, it seems likely that larger forces were at play.

CLAUDIO VALISTI

The Antivan Crows are an order of assassins so entrenched in the nation of Antiva that they have become a political force unto themselves. More than once they have all but dictated who would ascend to the throne of Antiva, regardless of who originally stood in the line of succession, and members of the royal family and the merchant princes routinely join their ranks.

Claudio Valisti was born in 9:08 Dragon to the Valisti dynasty, a family of merchant princes operating out of the city of Treviso. They had been enmeshed in the business of the Antivan Crows since the dynasty's founder, Princess Liviana (an actual princess, as opposed to a merchant), joined the assassins and eventually became First Talon—before her marriage into the then-floundering Avastana merchant house.

Family fortunes have risen in recent years after Claudio Valisti took over as head of the family in 9:34 Dragon, following his father's death. Seeing as the Valistis had fallen to the rank of Eighth Talon due to mismanagement and were threatening to fall into the ranks of the minor cuchillos, his ascension was viewed positively by the rest of the Crows. In short order, Claudio had restored the house to Sixth Talon and was on his way to even greater heights.

By the time of his death in 9:40 Dragon, Valisti had risen to Third Talon and was strong enough to pose a threat to the current guild leadership. It is rumored that this quick rise was due to an alliance with a dragon cult of the Tevinter Imperium, providing him and his assassins with access to dark magic. Whether this led directly to his death is unknown, but Valisti was found brutally murdered in the Tellari swamps of southern Antiva.

While control over the Valisti house will undoubtedly pass to Claudio's sister, Orlanda, a woman with a fearsome reputation of her own, it will likely also spawn another battle for leadership among the Crows.

RASAAN

The order of female priests known as tamassrans, roughly translated as "those who speak" in Qunlat, play a large and complicated role in Qunari society. These women are the first Qunari an outsider is bound to meet when they are captured. Tamassrans interview captives to determine their possible role among the Qunari, if any. Among the Qunari, they are the ones who raise the children and provide each Qunari with their name and role in society.

Such a position, particularly in a society where one's role means everything, conveys a great deal of authority. Thus it would be easy to mistake tamassrans as being in command of their fellow Qunari. Many times, outsiders have witnessed the priests giving orders to Qunari soldiers and even their commanders. It is important to note, however, that this authority only applies to things covered by their domain. A tamassran will determine what is done with captives and will interpret the Qun with regards to how it applies to those outside it. They do not determine military strategy and have no place when it comes to fighting battles.

The Qunari known as Rasaan is a prominent member of the tamassrans. She is said to serve directly under the Ariqun—the member of the Qunari ruling triumvirate responsible for spiritual welfare—and was long ago chosen as the Ariqun's eventual successor by the rest of the priesthood. As such, she is required to accompany the Arishok—the military leader of the triumvirate—on expeditions, acting as the Ariqun's representative and advising the Arishok as to the will of the Qun. Rasaan's name means "emissary," though in Qunlat it also equates to "chosen heir."

In 9:31 Dragon, the Arishok was shipwrecked and stranded in the city of Kirkwall. Unwilling to call for aid from Par Vollen, he remained in the Marcher city until the Champion drove the Qunari out in 9:34 Dragon. During this period, Rasaan remained in the Qunari city of Qunandar, unable to perform her duties. A successor to the Arishok was chosen in 9:34, a sten who had traveled much in non-Qunari lands, and since then Rasaan has been at his side almost constantly. She was most recently seen at the fortress of Akhaaz in Seheron. There are many rumors that the new Arishok is amassing a force of dreadnoughts—perhaps for an eventual invasion. If this is true, it seems likely that the humans of Thedas will soon see a great deal more of Rasaan than they care to.

The names of many ancient elven heroes have been lost to ages of cultural oppression. Dalish Keepers do their best to pass on what little is remembered.

YAVANA

Of the many daughters said to belong to the Witch of the Wilds known as Flemeth, few have cast such fear into the hearts of men as Yavana of the Tellari swamps. The length of time she has inhabited these swamps of southern Antiva is unknown, but there are many tales among locals that feature the involvement of a mysterious witch, most famously in the legend of Queen Madrigal, the namesake of the Steel Age who was found dead in a forest with four steel blades stabbed into her chest. According to the legend, Madrigal had been informed of her impending death by a black-haired witch of the swamps and had bargained for the life of her young son, Prince Eladio, who was supposed to die with her. When the young prince grew deathly ill, it is said that Madrigal rode into the forest to find the witch and challenge her—and this is when she died.

Is there any truth to the tale? That is unknown. Most historians attribute Madrigal's death to the Antivan Crows. Some credit the secret society known as the Executors. Still, Prince Eladio recovered from his illness and succeeded his mother, only to vanish a year before his adulthood and coronation.

During the more than three hundred years that have passed since Madrigal's death, stories of the Antivan Witch of the Wilds have persisted. They say she was present at the Qunari siege of Seleny in 6:90 Steel, calling down a dragon upon the attackers and forcing them into wild retreat. They say she appeared on a cliff side in the Weyrs in 8:95 Blessed, shouting a prophecy that dragons were about to return to the world after ages of absence.

Antivans tell stories of Yavana to this day. Travelers in the swamps have spoken of a dark-haired witch who claims the many dragons of the area are under her care. They say those who mean no harm may have a chance to bargain. Those who do not will almost certainly die. More recent rumors persist that Yavana herself may have been slain by one such visitor in 9:40 Dragon, though whether a witch of such power and longevity can actually be killed is difficult to say.

OF CONCERNS NUMISMATIC

We are familiar with the standards demanded when trading with the various merchant guilds. Be it a sovereign (Ferelden), a royal (Orlais), a king's gulder (Nevarra), a double griffon (Anderfels), or any of a dozen others, one gold coin is worth one hundred silver coins or ten thousand copper coins. Let us instead concern ourselves with the art of the minter, how coins stand apart, and the more unusual currencies now falling by the wayside.

Antivan Andris: Value Equivalent to One Royal

Andris are of note because of the practice of striking them with images of the leaders of major guilds, rather than current or storied rulers. Also, an amount of five thousand andris has, for some reason, come to be known as "one bastard," which is occasionally used as a veiled insult in negotiations.

Andraste's Tear: Value Equivalent to One Hundred Gold or Five Royals

The Andraste's tear was an experiment in striking nonmetallic coinage. One tear was a drop of glass pressed flat, as a signet is used to mark wax. Influenced by the methods of the Serault Glassworks, the design of the glass was laced with elements to show the lot of the mintage. Surprisingly, breakage was not a concern. A coin worth one hundred gold was made in limited quantities, said to include a bubble that contained "the still of the air as they watched Our Lady breathe her last." This was a beautiful but dubious claim, and one collector remarked—after purposefully smashing one—that given the smell, Andraste and the local glass blowers may have shared a favorite brewer.

Orlesian Caprice: Value Varies

Caprices are adorned with family heraldry or details specific to a personal event, and serve as social amusements at high-profile Orlesian gatherings. Their weight in gold is usually small, as the coins are intended to be disposable. Nobles exchange caprices over the course of an evening, rewarding dashing remarks and impeccable grace. At the end of the event, all collected coins are thrown into a fountain—or, in the rare rural setting, a fireplace. Despite the low inherent value of these coins, the craftsmen who make them are in great demand. There is an art to creating a pleasing relief that also commands the light as the coin arcs to its watery destination. One legendary example was an entire set that, when thrown in unison, not only tumbled in a beautiful pattern but also rang the exposition of the patron's anthem. Reusing a caprice is thought to be bad luck and a great embarrassment.

Imperial Tesserae: Valued at Various Denominations or by Barter

Tesserae are tokens or tiles struck to allow entry to specific events, including magisterial appointments, celebratory gatherings, and wagering or sporting contests. There is a great deal of competition to produce accurate portraiture or other spectacular details. Collectors often focus on those coins created for combat or racing events, of which a favorite athlete or animal is the subject. Great sums are commanded for tokens from the subject's early career, especially if they went on to either greatness or absolute obscurity.

The rarest tesserae are created for intimate events, such as private performances by celebrated minstrels. They do not command much value after the fact, however, as there is little demand for souvenirs of a rival's vanity.

The Travelers' Bend: Value Varies by Source Currency

The travelers' bend was a practice common along what would become the Imperial Highway. As a means of thwarting bandits, gold coins were beaten into a curved shape so they could be hidden beneath the tongue or upon the palate, away from prying eyes or searching fingers. Though the intent was to protect small amounts for emergencies or perhaps bribery, misuse could be risky. It was not unknown for a hoarder to choke on his cache. The bend was also linked to a condition highwaymen called "miser's madness"—caused by hiding lesser Hunter Fell currency struck from lead.

Chant of Light

Foreword to the Abridged Reader's Edition

The first printing of the Reader's Edition of the Chant in 7:45 Storm was the work of decades of historical research and translation of the Chantry archives by myriad sisters and brothers. It represented, in its time, the greatest work of Chantry scholarship ever completed. It is my joy and honor to continue the tradition of my predecessors in keeping this important work available to readers of all faiths.

This edition is designed to bring forward, as much as possible, the beauty of the original dialects and languages of the canticles into the modern tongue—and make the history and culture of the Chant accessible to both casual readers and scholars alike.

The Chant is the song of our own histories—sometimes conflicting, sometimes imagined—changing with each voice that takes up the tale, in many diverse lands, for many reasons. It is political, spiritual, personal, visionary, manipulative, exultant, and tragic all at once. It is a work with many purposes and interpretations, and it is my hope that this edition will help future readers discover their own within its verses.

Divine Justinia V

Val Royeaux, 12 Harvestmere 9:38 Dragon

CONTENTS

The New Cumberland Chant of Light

WITH DISSONANT VERSES

Canticle of Threnodies: Cosmogenesis & First Sin

The earliest recorded version of this canticle was written between -31 and -11 Ancient by Justinia I, and for many ages Threnodies, along with the rest of the Chant, has been attributed to her. However, modern study reveals a variety of inconsistent styles, as well as repetitions and contradictions in the narrative of the saga, which indicates multiple authors at work. It is now believed that the first Divine's work was primarily a translation and transcription of a much older oral tradition. Tevinter legal documents dating from as far back as -182 Ancient make reference to "The Slave Dirge" being sung during uprisings. The Canticles of Threnodies, Andraste, Transfigurations, and Trials are collectively known as "the Portents" and are believed to compose the original Chant of Light as sung by the disciples of Andraste at the time of her death.

Justinia's original text was written in Ciriane, then the language of Orlais, and was likely translated from a song in Tevene, the language Imperium slaves would have spoken. Scholars can discern distinct literary traditions within the canticle. The *Spiritual* specifically names the first children of the Maker "spirits." The *Dynastic* refers to the first children as "firstborn." The *Demonic* calls them "demons."

Threnodies repeatedly tells the story of the creation of the world and the fall of man. Chantry scholars generally believe that the multiple tales arose from local interpretations of Andraste's vision by the individual cultures to which the Chant spread during and after her lifetime. It is in many respects the most successful part of the Chant, as the portion that has been claimed and sung most often by the largest number of cultures across Thedas, and for that reason, the regional differences in the tale have been preserved in Chantry canon.

Threnodies sets the history of the world in the center of an ongoing mystical battle over existence itself. The early stanzas describe the creation of the Fade and the world and set up a conflict between the Maker and His children that leads into the First Sin and eventually the origin of the Blight. The events of its narrative are mirrored in the dissonant canticles of Erudition and Silence.

Threnodies 5

The Maker creates the Fade and the spirits

(1) There was no word
For heaven or for earth, for sea or sky.
All that existed was silence.
Then the Voice of the Maker rang out,
The first Word,
And His Word became all that might be:
Dream and idea, hope and fear,
Endless possibilities.
And from it He made His firstborn.
And He said to them:
"In My image I forge you,
To you I give dominion
Over all that exists.
By your will
May all things be done."

The Golden City

(2) Then in the center of heaven
He called forth
A city with towers of gold,
Streets with music for cobblestones,
And banners which flew without wind.
There, He dwelled, waiting
To see the wonders
His children would create.

The Maker becomes disillusioned with the spirits

(3) The children of the Maker gathered
Before His golden throne
And sang hymns of praise unending.
But their songs
Were the songs of the cobblestones.
They shone with the golden light
Reflected from the Maker's throne.
They held forth the banners
That flew on their own.
And the Voice of the Maker shook the Fade,
Saying: "In My image I have wrought
My firstborn. You have been given dominion
Over all that exists. By your will
All things are done.
Yet you do nothing.
The realm I have given you
Is formless, ever changing."

The Fade is separated from the World

(4) And He knew He had wrought amiss.
So the Maker turned from His firstborn
And took from the Fade
A measure of its living flesh
And placed it apart from the Spirits,
and spoke to it, saying:
"Here, I decree
Opposition in all things:
For earth, sky.
For winter, summer.
For darkness, Light.
By My Will alone is Balance sundered
And the world given new life."

Man is created

(5) And no longer was it formless, ever changing,
But held fast, immutable,
With Words for heaven and for earth, sea, and sky.
At last did the Maker
From the living world
Make men. Immutable, as the substance of the earth,
With souls made of dream and idea, hope and fear,
Endless possibilities.
Then the Maker said:
"To you, My second born, I grant this gift:
In your heart shall burn
An unquenchable flame,
All consuming, and never satisfied.
From the Fade I crafted you,
And to the Fade you shall return
Each night in dreams,
That you may always remember Me."

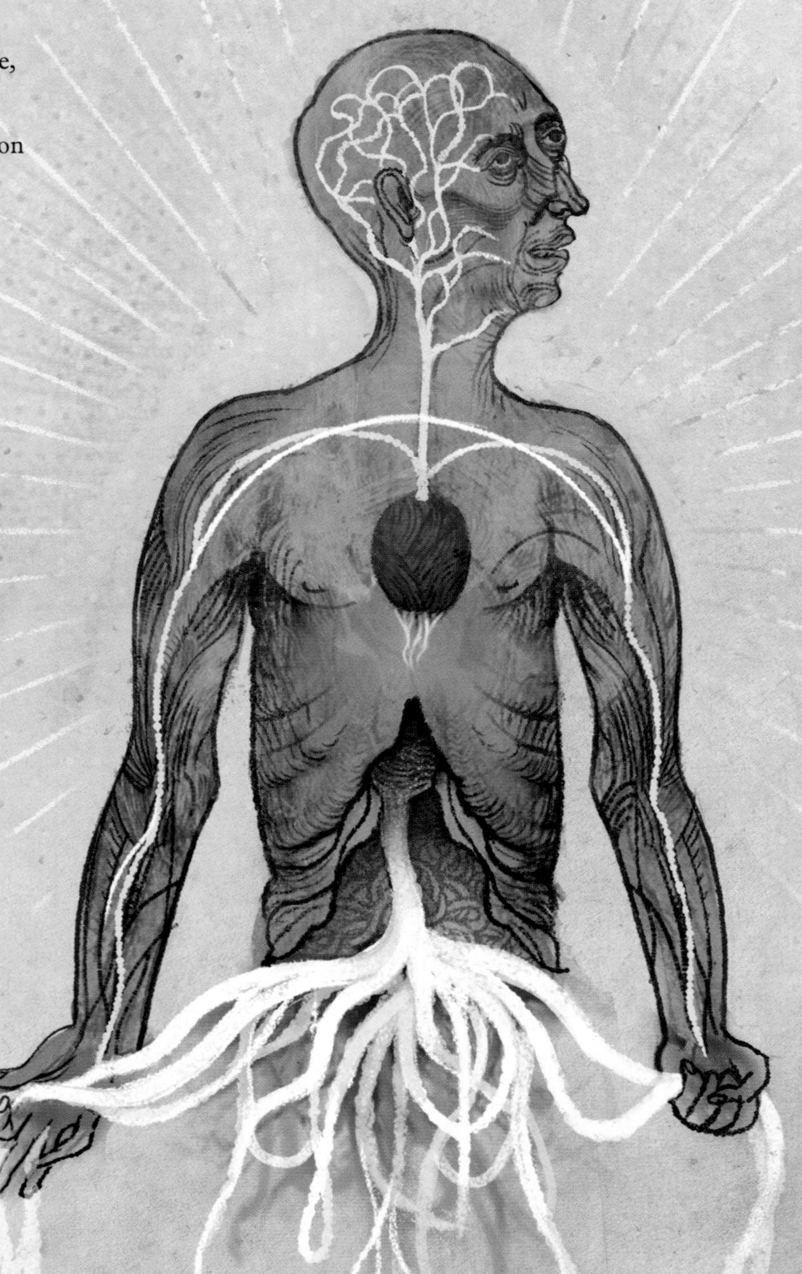

Man is created

The Maker seals himself in the Golden City

(6) And then the Maker sealed the gates
Of the Golden City
And there, He dwelled, waiting
To see the wonders
His children would create.

The rise of the Old Gods

(7) Now, with their Father's eye elsewhere, the firstborn
At last created something new:
Envy. They looked upon the living world and the favored
Sons and daughters there, covetous of all they were.
Within their hearts grew
An intolerable hunger.
Until, at last, some of the firstborn said:
"Our Father has abandoned us for these lesser things.
We have power over heaven.
Let us rule over earth as well
And become greater gods than our Father."

(8) The demons appeared to the children of earth in dreams
And named themselves gods, demanding fealty.
And a mighty voice cried out,
Shaking the very foundations of heaven:
"Ungrateful children! I gave you power
To shape heaven itself,
And you have made only poison.
As you crave the earth, the earth shall be
Your domain! Into the darkness
I cast you! In tombs of immutable rock
Shall you dwell for all time."
Those who had been cast down,
The demons who would be gods,
Began to whisper to men from their tombs within the earth.
And the men of Tevinter heard and raised altars
To the pretender gods once more,
And in return were given, in hushed whispers,
The secrets of darkest magic.

Threnodies 6

War between Neromenian and Inghirsh

(1) On the shores of the Nocen, in the lands of Neromenian[1]
King Antoridus girded his people for war. A thousand strong
Carried spear and bow to the East. To be forged anew
And rise on burning wings,[2] heroes of Neromenian.
Mighty were the Inghirsh,[3] who returned numbers beyond counting
To the lands of their fathers, carried on the shields of their kin.

(2) Antoridus demanded victory, and so his many Oracles
Consulted the stars and drank the blood of unclean beasts,[4]
Seeking counsel from the Maker that they might deliver
To their king the lands of the Inghirsh people.
And the Maker gave them signs and portents
That no victory was theirs to claim.

The first Dreamer

(3) But among the king's Oracles was one, Thalsian, who sought counsel
Not from the Maker of the World, but from a demon of the Fade.
And he returned to his king with its tidings.

Antoridus turns away from the Maker

(4) If Antoridus would make burned offerings of oxen and horses
And swear that he would follow the Maker no more,
The demon would grant him the lands of all the Inghirsh people.
So Antoridus sought the best oxen and horses
And made burned offerings to the demon. And he turned his back
Upon the Maker of the World.

Conquest of the Inghirsh

(5) So did the demon gift to Antoridus victory
Over the mighty Inghirsh, and they who had held forth
Against ten thousand spears were laid low.
And their people were made chattel, and their lands claimed
In the name of Neromenian.

---

[1] One of the original three kingdoms of Tevinter, believed to cover the region from the modern city of Neromenian south and east to the Hundred Pillars.

[2] Refers to the Tevinter belief that the souls of their honored dead were reborn as dragons.

[3] Perhaps refers to ancient people in southern Tevinter. Historians have found signs of cities and settlements across the Silent Plains whose destruction predates the Blight.

[4] Most likely wyverns.

War with the Planasene

(6) The power of Neromenian grew sevenfold.

And with it, Antoridus's heart grew hard.
And he looked

Upon the lands of the Planasene[5] to the south, and said:

"There upon the plains I see a land of plenty.

The branches bear fruit until they bow to the ground,

And sheaves of wheat go to rot, forgotten, in the fields."

[5] Ancient name for the people of Nevarra.

(7) So once again, in the lands of King Antoridus

The people of Neromenian girded for war. Seven thousand strong

Carried spear and bow to the South. To forge anew

The land of plenty in the name of the king.

(8) In the lands of the South, on the banks

Of the River Pnemoix,[6] the people heard the croaking of ravens

And were afraid. They cried out to their king, Damertes,

To save them from the coming storm.

Damertes consults his Oracles

(9) The king of the Planasene, sorely troubled,

From amongst the wisest of his people gathered

A council to prepare for the arrival of the enemy.

And the sages went forth and looked to the stars,

Drew water from the sacred River Pnemoix,

With hope that the fate of Inghirsh might not be shared.

[6] Ancient name for the Minanter River

The Magisters are tempted by the Old Gods

(10) And the Great Blade of Heaven revealed

An attack would come in secret, from the East.

And the Swift carried with it news that the men of the North

Would set the fields of Planasene alight before them.

(11) And lo, the sages returned to their King Damertes

And girded the warriors of Planasene with talismans

Carved from serpentstone and anointed their brows

With the waters of the sacred Pnemoix,

And sent them forth to battle with Neromenian.

(12) Damertes decreed that all the men and women of the kingdom

To the fields of the East journey with vessels drawn

From the Sacred Pnemoix. And for three days and three nights

They anointed the fields that the river's blessing

Might keep the fires of the dragons' children at bay.

The armies clash

(13) On the eve of battle, the armies of Antoridus raised their voices

In praise to their demon gods for the victory to come,

While the armies of Damertes called out in supplication to the Maker.

No darkness could hide the fears of Planasene,

No star could outshine the sureness of Neromenian.

(14) As the sun rose, the armies girded themselves,

And the dragons' children put flame to the fields of Planasene,

But the sacred Pnemoix protected them, and they did not burn.

(15) The army of Antoridus, seven thousand strong, raised their bows

And a terrible thunder rang out, and the sky went black with arrows,

And though they raised their shields, a rain of death fell

Upon the Planasene, whose blood anointed the fields.

(16) A mighty cry of rage went up from the army of Damertes

To see their brothers and sisters struck down.

And the army of Antoridus answered

With the thunder of spears beating shields.

(17) And the soldiers of the demon charged,

Spears thirsting for the blood of the Maker's children.

And the army of Damertes readied their shields.

(18) The righteous stood before the armies

As a boulder stands before a tide:

Unshaken, rooted there by the Maker's Hand.

And the demon's soldiers broke upon their shields

As a wave breaks upon the shore.

(19) As the sun set upon the fields of Planasene,

The armies of Neromenian had taken no steps into the lands of the faithful.

But the fields ran red. And great were the lamentations of the living

For the countless dead of Damertes.

Damertes forsakes the Maker

(20) In the deep hours of the night, King Damertes sought

Counsel from his sages, for he knew

His army could not withstand another day against the dragons' children.

And the wisest sages of Planasene consulted the stars

And found nothing.

(21) In desperation, King Damertes turned

To pagan soothsayers, saying:

"Find me a demon with the strength to counter Neromenian's."

And they reached into the darkest realms of dream

And found one who promised Damertes

To turn aside the spears of Antoridus

If he would forsake the Maker and praise only her name.

(22) So, in the hours before dawn, King Damertes cursed the Maker's name.

And he burned offerings to the demon, and praised her

That his lands might be spared.

(23) And as the sun rose upon the fields of the Planasene,

The armies of Antoridus fell to the ground

Afflicted with boils and racked with pain.

And they cried out in fear, and fled back to their own lands.

And from that day forth, the Maker's name was spoken no more

In the lands of the sacred Pnemoix.

Canticle of Silence: Creation of the Blight

The Canticle of Silence has historically been divided into three stanzas, with the corruption of the Magisters composing the first stanza, the assault on the Golden City the second, and the terrible consequences of their fall the third and final stanza. Silence is named for Dumat, the Old God of Silence, who instigated the Magisters' ill-fated breach of the Golden City and became the first Archdemon. The canticle's verses describe the corruption and evil of the Old Gods and their priests, followed by the valiant struggle of the people of Tevinter to stem the tide of the Blight the Magisters unleashed in imaginative, almost personal terms.

The original text of Silence was written by Archon Hessarian himself, and the earliest versions date back to the Transfiguration of -160 Ancient. Having been written almost two hundred years after the events it describes, the Canticle of Silence cannot be based on firsthand knowledge. As Archon, Hessarian had access to the historical records of the Magisterium and the intelligence gathered by his predecessors (who would certainly have been spying on the magisters of their day as potential rivals), but we cannot be certain how much of his creative retelling of the tale is based in historical fact. The verses are plainly written to ascribe blame for the catastrophic Blight that all but destroyed Tevinter to the priesthood of the Old Gods, and to incite the anger of the Imperium against those Altus targeted by Hessarian's Transfiguration.

It was part of the Chantry canon until 3:41 Towers, when a conclave established by Divine Amara I declared it to be too much propaganda supporting Hessarian's bloodbath and change of regimes in Minrathous, and too little sacred verse, to remain a part of the official Chant.

Despite its obvious political bias, scholars still study this Dissonant Verse for its Tevinter perspective on one of the greatest tragedies in history.

Silence 1

The Choir of Silence is corrupted

(1) First among the Old Gods was Silence.[7]

His least whisper could end wars or topple Archons.

A single word could turn recrimination into glory.

The sacred fires of his temple burned

Rare incense, and the trees of Arlathan, and lapped at the bones of slaves

While his altars dripped with the blood of sacrifices that never dried.

(2) The High Priest, Conductor of the Choir of Silence, ruled

Above all the Dreamers of the Imperium. Wisest

And most powerful of the Magisters Sidereal.[8]

In his dreams, he alone heard the voice of Silence.

(3) "Open the gates.

To my Golden City you must sojourn.

At the foot of my throne, I shall anoint you,

Most favored of my disciples,

And I shall raise you up to godhood

That all mortals shall know your glory."

(4) The call of the Old God filled the High Priest's heart,

Consuming all his waking hours and turning his dreams

To ash and bones. Every priest and acolyte of Silence

To the Great Choir assembled, and the High Priest

Shared with them the words of Silence.

---

[7] One of the titles of the Old God Dumat.

[8] The Magisters Sidereal were the group of seven high priests of the Old Gods within the Magisterium.

(5) Every priest and acolyte of the Choir
Turned their hearts and minds as one to
Their god's command. For the Word of Silence
Could not be ignored, and the fire burning
In the heart of the High Priest consumed them
As a wildfire consumes plains.

The priests formulate a plan

(6) All knew the Golden Heart of dreams' kingdom
Shone like a star, forever out of reach.
No mortal foot could tread those halls,
No hand knocked upon the gate.
Secrets beyond measure were the keys
The Choir of Silence would need, and they had few.

(7) And so the First Acolyte spoke to the High Priest
And said: "We are the masters of secrets,
But our god demands more. Let us to the Builders
Whisper, and they who construct monuments to the glory
Of the gods shall build us a road to the Golden City,
Where your promise shall be fulfilled."

(8) And the Great Conductor of the Choir heard him.

The Golden City is assaulted

The priests of Beauty are corrupted

(9) The High Priest of Beauty,[9] Architect of the Works of Beauty, designed
Every work and wonder of the Imperium according to the plans of his god.
To him, the Conductor went in secret, armed
With the whisper of Silence.

(10) But the High Priest of Beauty was sorely troubled,
For he served only the Great Plans
And would in no wise raise a servant of Silence
Above himself or his god.

(11) And yet, the fire in the Conductor's heart ignited
Within the Architect a terrible flame.
And so he turned all the lesser priests and acolytes from the Temple of Beauty
To beseech counsel from his god.

---

[9] One of the titles of the Old God Urthemiel.

The Blight begins

(12) And to him, Beauty revealed a grand plan:

"Open the gates.

And when you stand before me,

I shall give you designs

That shall rival the greatness of heaven.

I will make you First among the new gods,

And you will build a paradise on earth."

(13) So the High Priest of Beauty returned to the Conductor of Silence

And promised him all the skill of Beauty's designs

In reaching the Golden City.

The remainder of the priesthoods are recruited

(14) But the designs of Beauty's High Priest demanded more.

No small sacrifice would open the gate.

And so, the High Priest of Silence went forth again.

To the Watchman of Night,[10] and the Forgewright of Fire,[11]

To the Appraiser of Slavery,[12] and the Augur of Mystery,[13]

And last of all to the Madman of Chaos[14]

The words of Silence were revealed.

(15) Jealousy and torment consumed them all, for no Dreamer

Wished to aid the others in the least measure,

Yet none could bear that rivals might walk in the Light

Of their gods, when they did not.

(16) So each retired to their temples and sought wisdom

From the voice of their own god. And each god

Gave the same commandment:

The unreachable gate must open.

And each was promised

Power and glory beyond all reckoning

If they would only come to the feet of the gods and ask.

(17) And so they joined in secret, telling none

Who were not of the temples of their designs.

And in Minrathous, in the heart of the Archon a sliver of fear grew,

Stabbing like a wound. Though he knew not why.

---

[10] The Old God Lusacan.

[11] The Old God Toth.

[12] The Old God Andoral.

[13] The Old God Razikale.

[14] The Old God Zazikel.

Silence 2

The seven High Priests prepare

(1) The Imperium slept. In the lofty palaces

Mages dreamed of the Maker's Palace, golden and shining,

And though they knew not why, the dream turned their blood to ice.

Soldiers stood their watches, and servants hurried on errands,

Unaware of what the dawn would bring.

(2) In the Great Choir of Silence, the High Priests gathered.

A hundred chosen acolytes brought lyrium

Enough to drown a city in chiming silver

And slaves beyond counting to the temple

In accordance with the designs of their gods.

Someone speaks out against the plan

(3) As he looked upon the waiting sacrifices,

One acolyte felt the first prickling pangs

Of dread. And he turned to his fellow priests,

Saying: "Should glory come at such a price?

What reward can be worth this? If mortals

Were meant to stand among the gods,

Would the gods not open their gates to us?

Rather than demand we build a tower,

Blood, bone, and metal, to the heavens?"

The ritual begins

(4) But the gathered acolytes turned from him,

For there was nothing but ambition

Where hearts once beat within them.

And ninety-nine knives gleamed in the firelight

As the sacrifices began.

The doubting acolyte flees

(5) The one who had spoken

Into shadow crept and made himself away.

North, to the road, Minrathous bound.

Fear grasping at his every breath

That none might stop his brethren

Save the Archon himself.

The Magisters ascend

(6) The Great Choir of Silence shook
As the earth trembled in holy terror.
A wordless scream as if from
The legions of dead slaves rose
To the zenith of the black sky.

(7) Before the might of the seven Magisters Sidereal,
The Veil shattered like the flimsiest glass.
Dream and waking lay before their feet,
Two paths diverging.
Into the dream they strode, dauntless,
For nothing in the realm of gods or man
Could keep them from their promised prize.

The Magisters enter the Golden City

(8) The minds of all lay bare before the Seven,
But no mere machinations against the sleeping
Had brought them hence.
By blood and lyrium were they drawn
Inexorably to the Unreachable City,
The heart of all creation.

(9) At a touch, the gate swung wide,
And the Light parted before them like a curtain
Swept aside by nothing. Fearful to touch them.
And none saw the black mark
Spreading like a sore upon the shining gate
Where mortal hand had lain.

Silence 3

The Magisters face judgment

(1) Surrounded by glory, the Seven stood,
In the hall of apotheosis, heedless
Of what festered in the shadows they cast there,
Of what stained and corroded footprints they left.

(2) But upon the throne of heaven they found
No dragons bearing promised rewards
But the Maker of the World in all His radiance,
And the Seven cried out in shock and rage, for nothing
They had seen in vision or imagined in their most
Avaricious dreams had prepared them to see
His Light with mortal eyes.

(3) Like moths who reach a bonfire, the Seven burned.
But the Maker kept them from death,
And He held the priests before His throne
And looked upon them, His long-awaited children
At last returned to Him. And He saw
Only hunger and envy in their hearts,
Only pride and desire in their eyes,
And He knew that they knew Him not.

(4) Then the Maker heard the distant cries
Of the sacrificed. A chorus of voices beyond counting
Calling out for justice. And all that they had done
Was known to Him.

(5) The Maker of All spoke to the Seven then, saying:
"Into My house you walk uninvited, demanding rewards
You have not earned. On wings of death
And suffering are you borne hence.
The darkness planted by your betrayers in your hearts I see.
Did you not know, when you chose to revere them over Me?

(6) "The Old Gods will call to you,
From their ancient prisons they will sing.
Dragons with wicked eyes and wicked hearts.
On blackened wings does deceit take flight,
The first of My children, lost to night.

(7) "You have chosen, and spilled the blood
Of innocence for power. I pity your folly,
But still more do I pity those whose lives you have taken
In pursuit of selfish goals.
No more will you bear the Light.
To darkness flee, and be gone from My sight!"

(8) And the Veil ripped beneath their feet,
And the Seven fell. And the gates of the city slammed
Shut. And the wicked corruption they had carried
Covered it. And it opened no more.
And the Maker in sorrow turned His gaze
And no longer hoped for His children to return.

The Archon calls upon the spirits of the Fade

The alarm is raised in Minrathous

(9) The great city of Minrathous
The faithful acolyte had through desperate measures reached.
His heart like ice, certain that none
Save the Archon alone could hold back
Those wheels the high priests and their lackeys
Had set in motion.

(10) No more did the Old Gods whisper in his ear.
No more did he hear any voice in his dreams
But his own, and the mutterings of jealous spirits,
And he knew that this silence boded ill.

(11) No mere acolyte could approach
The throne of the Ferryman.
Stave and spear blocked his path
And the faithful acolyte feared that all was lost.

(12) But guided by wisdom and portent both,
The Archon bade his guard stand aside,
And the lowly priest brought before him,
That he might know the meaning
Behind the holy dread which shadowed his every step.

(13) The design of the priests was laid bare,
And the Archon turned with steel resolve
To his appointed task.
For only divine wrath could follow
Where the traitorous Seven had gone.

The Magisters fall

(14) The Seven fell from the Wellspring of Creation,
No longer creatures of the Maker's Light.
From the height of heaven they plunged,
And Tevinter saw them burn across the sky like falling stars.
Where they touched the earth,
Twisted darkness grew, poisoned by their hate.
And the clouds covered them and wept.

(15) Like a sickness, evil grew within them.
Their pride refused all measure of blame.
Not they, but their masters had brought them low.
They cried out in rage to gods
Who did not answer.
And they would have vengeance upon
The gods of broken promises.
And through them, vengeance
On the Maker and His world.

The Archon scatters the Magisters

(16) The Archon followed the path of fire
Writ large across the sky of Tevinter,
And upon the plain where once great
Barindur[15] had stood he arrived,
Girded in lyrium and silverite,
Bearing in his left hand
A staff of gold and emeralds, wreathed in lightning,
And upon his right
The ring of the Ferryman, symbol of Darinius
And the might of the Imperium itself.

The Choir of Silence is corrupted

[15] A possibly mythical city supposedly wiped from existence by Dumat. Said to be located on the southern coast of the Nocen.

(17) The Seven struck against the Archon
With all their twisted magic,
But no pestilent hate could turn aside
Tevinter's Ferryman.

(18) Across the plain, the Archon saw,
Where the defilers stood, corruption,
Blackness all consuming,
Threatened to engulf his land and all his people.
With fire and lightning he strove
To cleanse the spreading poison from the earth,
To no avail. Magic could not undo
What evil had done.

(19) So the Archon called upon the spirits of the Fade,
And adding their strength to his own,
Scattered them to the winds and the corners of the earth
And with a heavy heart
Returned to unassailable Minrathous
To prepare his people for the doom to come.

Canticle of Andraste: Epiphany of Our Lady

There is no more disputed canticle of the Chant than that of Andraste. Some five hundred versions of the Canticle of Andraste existed before Divine Amalthea II created the Conclave of Cumberland to determine Chantry canon. The one that was ultimately chosen was the version that could be sourced to an Andrastian cult in northern Orlais in -165 Ancient—the oldest form of the canticle that could be found. The verses are composed in a style similar to other Alamarri sagas, such as *Dane and the Werewolf*, which would be more typical for tales of war and heroism than prophetic works.

Although it is traditionally attributed to Andraste, it is unknown if this is the version of her revelation that she herself sang. It is likely, however, that it contains elements of the song she spread among her followers, which was no doubt altered according to the needs and preferences of each congregation.

Andraste 1

Address and greeting

(1) Hear now, Andraste, daughter of Brona,
Spear-maid of Alamarr,[16] to valiant hearts sing
Of victory waiting, yet to be claimed from
The steel-bond forgers of barren Tevene.

Andraste seeks an end to the suffering of the Alamarri

(2) Great heroes beyond counting raised
Oak and iron 'gainst chains of north-men
And walked the lonely worm-roads evermore.
Mighty of arm and warmest of heart,
Rendered to dust. Bitter is sorrow,
Ate raw and often, poison that weakens and does not kill.

(3) Why must the Shield of Alamarr shatter
'Neath bond and blade? To the wisest I sang,
To the wing'd cup-bearers of the tall sky-vaulting,
To the wintry halls of strong mountain-kings,
Where in days forgotten, voices there raised
Might be gift'd answer and those seeking find.

The Alamarri gods do not answer

(4) From sky-tearing peaks of the sacred mountain
To secret-steep'd roots of the ancient oak trees
A lonesome choir, I, song falling unanswered,
Voice on wind returning, answered no more.

[16] Old Ciriane name for the Alamarri.

Andraste despairs for her people

(5) In heart's drumming I heard footsteps thund'ring
Shield-brothers and spear-sisters distant raised
Blade to shackle-bearer, valiant of spirit
Blazing like star-shine, to battle they charged.
None to return to the lands of their mothers
By cruel magic taken, ice, lightning, and flame.

(6) Should for all seasons laments ring the sky-vaults,
Should dirges all sagas and histories replace?
By gods forsaken, fate emptied of hope,
Wounded I fell then, by grief arrow-studded,
Never to heal, death for me come.

The Maker appears to Andraste

(7) Eyes sorrow-blinded, in darkness unbroken
There 'pon the mountain, a voice answered my call.
"Heart that is broken, beats still unceasing,
An ocean of sorrow does nobody drown.
You have forgotten, spear-maid of Alamarr.
Within My creation, none are alone."

(8) Lo! My eyes open'd, shining before me
Greater than mountains, towering mighty,
Hand all outstretch'd, stars glist'ning as jewels
From rings 'pon His fingers and crown 'pon His brow.

(9) Sword-shattering fear filled me overflowing.
Grandeur of godhood no gaze should defile.
Trembling, I called out: "Forgive me, Most High,
I should sing Your Name to the heights of heaven,
But I know it not, and must be silent."
The Wellspring of All said, "None now remember.
Long have they turned to idols and tales
Away from My Light, in darkness unbroken
The last of My children,
shrouded in night."

(10) World fell away then, misty in mem'ry,
'Cross Veil and into the valley of dreams
A vision of all worlds, waking and slumb'ring,
Spirit and mortal to me appeared.
"Look to My work," said the Voice of Creation.
"See what My children in arrogance wrought."

(11) There I saw the Black City, towers all stain'd,
Gates once bright golden forever shut.
Heav'n filled with silence, then did I know all
And cross'd my heart with unbearable shame.

Andraste begs the Maker to give mortals another chance

(12) Then did I see the world spread before me,
Sky-reaching mountains arrayed as a crown,
Kingdoms like jewels, glistering gemstones
Strung 'cross the earth as a necklace of pearl.
"All this is yours," spake the World-maker.
"Join Me in heaven and sorrow no more."

The priests formulate a plan

(13) "World-making Glory," I cried out in sorrow,
"How shall Your children apology make?
We have forgotten, in ignorance stumbling,
Only a Light in this darken'd time breaks.
Call to Your children, teach us Your greatness.
What has been forgotten has not yet been lost."

(14) Long was the silence, 'fore it was broken.
"For you, song-weaver, once more I will try.
To My children venture, carrying wisdom,
If they but listen, I shall return."

Canticle of Transfigurations: Andraste's Teachings

These verses collect the teachings and sermons of Andraste. They are purported to be the work of Justinia, Andraste's disciple, who transcribed them word for word from the Prophet herself. But exactly what she wrote down is a mystery.

The version printed here can be traced back to an Andrastian group in Ferelden in -130 Ancient and is the closest Chantry scholars can find to the versions that were probably spread among the Alamarri who followed Andraste and Maferath north. Once the war band reached northern Thedas, and began to spread their faith to the people they were rallying against Tevinter rule, variations emerged. As the Alamarri did not have a written alphabet at the time, Andraste's teachings were almost certainly spread throughout her army from one camp to another and to their new allies by word of mouth. Unsurprisingly, even Andraste's own people had at least ten different versions of her teachings.

Transfigurations 1

The Commandments

(1) These truths the Maker has revealed to me:
As there is but one world,
One life, one death, there is
But one god, and He is our Maker.
They are sinners, who have given their love
To false gods.

(2) Magic exists to serve man, and never to rule over him.
Foul and corrupt are they
Who have taken His gift
And turned it against His children.
They shall be named Maleficar, accursed ones.
They shall find no rest in this world
Or beyond.

(3) All men are the Work of our Maker's Hands,
From the lowest slaves
To the highest kings.
Those who bring harm
Without provocation to the least of His children
Are hated and accursed by the Maker.

(4) Those who bear false witness
And work to deceive others, know this:
There is but one Truth.
All things are known to our Maker
And He shall judge their lies.

(5) All things in this world are finite.
What one man gains, another has lost.
Those who steal from their brothers and sisters
Do harm to their livelihood and to their peace of mind.
Our Maker sees this with a heavy heart.

Transfigurations 10

Andraste's Sermon at Valarian Fields

(1) Many are those who wander in sin,
Despairing that they are lost forever,
But the one who repents, who has faith
Unshaken by the darkness of the world,
And boasts not, nor gloats
Over the misfortunes of the weak, but takes delight
In the Maker's law and creations, she shall know
The peace of the Maker's benediction.
The Light shall lead her safely
Through the paths of this world, and into the next.
For she who trusts in the Maker, fire is her water.
As the moth sees light and goes toward flame,
She should see fire and go toward Light.
The Veil holds no uncertainty for her,
And she will know no fear of death, for the Maker
Shall be her beacon and her shield,
her foundation and her sword.

Transfigurations 12

Andraste's Prayer before the siege of Minrathous

(1) O Maker, hear my cry:
Guide me through the blackest nights.
Steel my heart against the temptations of the wicked.
Make me to rest in the warmest places.

(2) O Creator, see me kneel:
For I walk only where You would bid me.
Stand only in places You have blessed.
Sing only the words You place in my throat.

(3) My Maker, know my heart:
Take from me a life of sorrow.
Lift me from a world of pain.
Judge me worthy of Your endless pride.

(4) My Creator, judge me whole:
Find me well within Your grace.
Touch me with fire that I be cleansed.
Tell me I have sung to Your approval.

(5) O Maker, hear my cry:
Seat me by Your side in death.
Make me one within Your glory.
And let the world once more see
Your favor.

(6) For You are the fire at the heart
of the world,
And comfort is only Yours to give.

The ritual begins

Canticle of Trials: Hymns

Traditionally, Trials is said to be a collection of hymns composed by Andraste in praise of the Maker, but its origin is much more complex. Chantry scholars believe that some verses predate the Prophet by a hundred years or more and were possibly prayers and hymns to the gods of local pantheons that were altered when the people joined Andraste's uprising. No individual stanza is believed to be a whole and complete composition of the Prophet, but the verses have been collected over the ages, and through them we have a glimpse of people finding meaning in the Maker and His creation in the darkest of times.

Whether they were written by Andraste or not, the verses of the Canticle of Trials are the most beloved and oft-quoted lines of the Chant of Light. Certainly they put into words the boundless love and hope of countless faithful in the earliest part of the Chant's history.

Trials 1

Prayers for the despairing

(1) Maker, my enemies are abundant.
Many are those who rise up against me.
But my faith sustains me; I shall not fear the legion,
Should they set themselves against me.

(2) In the long hours of the night
When hope has abandoned me,
I still see the stars and know
Your Light remains.

(3) I have heard the sound,
A song in the stillness,
The echo of Your voice,
Calling creation to wake from its slumber.

(4) How can we know You?
In the turning of the seasons, in life and death,
In the empty space where our hearts
Hunger for a forgotten face?

(5) You have walked beside me
Down the paths where a thousand arrows sought my flesh.
You have stood with me when all others
Have forsaken me.

(6) I have faced armies
With You as my shield,
And though I bear scars beyond counting, nothing
Can break me except Your absence.

(7) When I have lost all else, when my eyes fail me
And the taste of blood fills my mouth, then
In the pounding of my heart
I hear the glory of creation.

(8) You have grieved as I have.
You, who made worlds out of nothing.
We are alike in sorrow, sculptor and clay,
Comforting each other in our art.

(9) Do not grieve for me, Maker of All.
Though all others may forget You,
Your name is etched into my every step.
I will not forsake You, even if I forget myself.

(10) Maker, though the darkness comes upon me,
I shall embrace the Light. I shall weather the storm.
I shall endure.
What You have created, no one can tear asunder.

(11) Who knows me as You do?
You have been there since before my first breath.
You have seen me when no other would recognize my face.
You composed the cadence of my heart.

(12) Through blinding mist, I climb
A sheer cliff, the summit shrouded in fog, the base
Endlessly far beneath my feet.
The Maker is the rock to which I cling.

(13) I cannot see the path.

Perhaps there is only abyss.

Trembling, I step forward,

In darkness enveloped.

(14) Though all before me is shadow,

Yet shall the Maker be my guide.

I shall not be left to wander the drifting roads of the Beyond.

For there is no darkness in the Maker's Light

And nothing that He has wrought shall be lost.

(15) I am not alone. Even

As I stumble on the path

With my eyes closed, yet I see

The Light is here.

(16) Draw your last breath, my friends.

Cross the Veil and the Fade and all the stars in the sky.

Rest at the Maker's right hand,

And be forgiven.

Canticle of Shartan: Rallying the Armies

This is the Dissonant Verse most closely studied by Chantry scholars and historians. Struck from the Chant during the Exalted March of the Dales, it tells the story of Shartan, an elven slave from Tevinter, who leads his fellow slaves in a revolt and joins Andraste to become one of her closest disciples.

Authorship of the canticle has never been determined. The earliest versions appeared in the Dales around -140 Ancient. Elements appear very similar to ancient elven folktales about a rebellion against tyrants led by a trickster warrior, and it is hard to determine which parts are rooted in history and which in heroic myth. It is certain that slave rebellions across the central Imperium were instrumental in the success of Andraste's campaign against Tevinter, but we cannot verify Shartan led any of them. Different versions of the canticle place Shartan's rebellion in Vol Dorma, Marnas Pell, Solas, Marothius, and Hasmal—all cities that suffered significantly from the famine that struck the Imperium and were the sites of brutal slave uprisings. Some scholars suggest that if "Shartan" existed at all, the name was a title or an ideal. Perhaps every rebellion had a Shartan, and he was truly the leader of every group of elves.

The text is very fragmented. Very few elven slaves could write Tevene, and nearly all the written language of the elves was lost at that time, so the canticle was preserved purely by oral tradition until clerics transcribed it at the behest of Justinia I in 1:8 Divine. There are gaps in the tale, and it has often been speculated that between the ninth and tenth stanzas of the song, several verses or perhaps an entire stanza was lost. The search for the missing verses of Shartan, like the search for Shartan himself, has consumed many a Chantry scholar.

Countless historians have attempted to find proof of Shartan's existence over the years, with little success. Whether or not he lived, thousands of elves did rise up against the Imperium, throw off their chains, and fight alongside Andraste. Their story has shaped our world into what it is today.

Shartan 9

The rebel slaves flee

(1) For twenty days and twenty nights the People[17] ran,

With the footsteps of the legion ever at their backs.

No rest could they find, since their flight from Vol Dorma.[18]

(2) The People cried out in despair:

"Alas, that we ever left Vol Dorma!

Better we had died there than to be hunted like sport on the plains."

---

[17] Translated from the Dalish word for "elves."

[18] Other versions name this city as Marnas Pell, Solas, Marothius, or Hasmal.

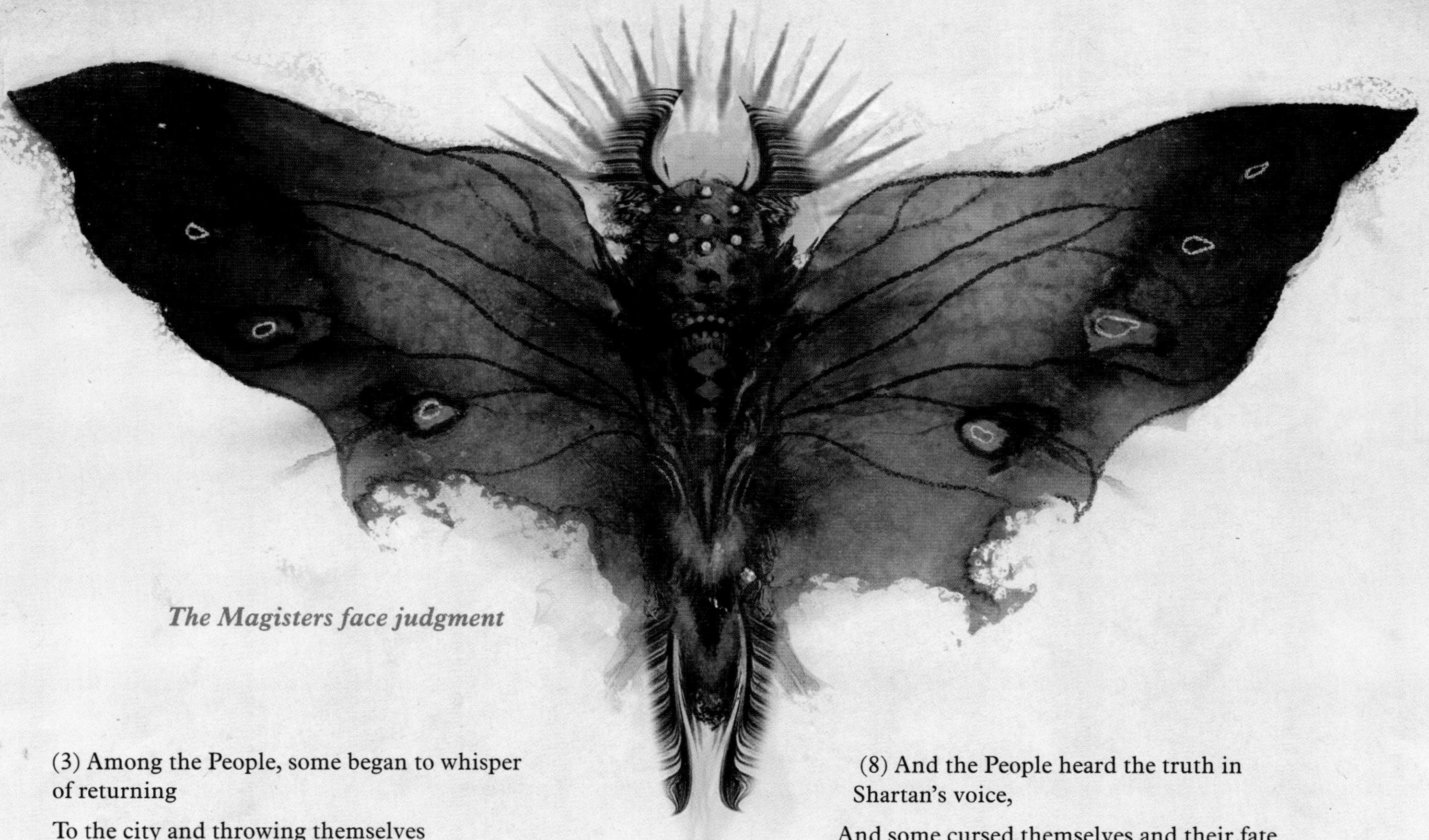

The Magisters face judgment

(3) Among the People, some began to whisper of returning
To the city and throwing themselves
At the feet of their former masters.
And Shartan heard them.

Shartan rallies the elves

(4) As the People paused to break bread at the foot
Of the hill the Tevinters called "the Lonely One,"[19]
Shartan stood on the hilltop and spoke, saying:
"Some among you wish to flee back to your masters,
To throw yourselves at their feet and ask forgiveness.
You have left that path. It is already gone.
Your feet can never again tread the dust of Vol Dorma.

(5) "He who asks for the mercy of the masters
Will stand accountable for murder and theft
And be made example for the slaves of other cities,
That they might not have the courage to rise up.

(6) "They will taunt you and humiliate you
While they hang you in the marketplace.
They will pelt you with offal while they call you
Broken, a coward, and a failure.

(7) "A dog might slink back to the hand it has bitten
And be forgiven, but a slave never.
If you would live, and live without fear, you must fight."

(8) And the People heard the truth in Shartan's voice,
And some cursed themselves and their fate and despaired.
And others began to fashion spears and bows
From the branches of trees, and girded themselves
With bark and scraps torn from their sandals
And dug pits in the earth with their hands.

The elves ambush the legion

(9) Darkness fell upon the Lonely One,
A night without moon or stars,
As the legion followed, like bloodhounds,
The trail of the rebels.

(10) And when the hunters reached the foot
Of the solitary hill, they found nothing,
The trail of their quarry vanished, as if the People
Had taken wing.

(11) The officers began to curse their men
And blame one another for losing the trail,
And the soldiers fell to bickering among themselves.

(12) In silence all around them, the People crept out
From holes clawed in the earth, and with harvesting blades
And arrows chipped from stones,
Fell upon the unwary legion and slaughtered them to a man.

---

[19] Solitarios, a large hill near Asariel.

The elves celebrate their victory

(13) And the People raised the blades of the fallen soldiers to the heavens

And rejoiced. And Shartan said to them:

"No longer are we hunted! We shall never again

Be prey, waiting to be struck down!

Let us take up the blades of our enemies

And carve a place for ourselves in this world!"

(14) The People heard him, and girded themselves

In the armor of the dead

And sharpened their blades and arrows

And prepared for war.

The army of Andraste arrives

(15) As the People danced over the corpses

Of slain soldiers, a thunder filled the air

And the ground trembled, and a hush fell over them,

As they knew a terrible omen had come.

(16) From afar, they heard the sound

Of ten thousand voices raised in song,

And the marching of a great host.

Shartan goes forth to meet the army

(17) Seeing an army beyond counting gathered in the distance,

Shartan said to the People:

"Let us not fall into the jaws of the wolf together.

I will go alone and see what army comes,

Singing, to the lands of Tevinter."

(18) Across the empty plains Shartan crept

To where the great host camped, the light from countless fires

Guiding him through the darkness.

(19) Then a great hand clamped down upon Shartan's neck,

And he was lifted into the air. And he looked into the eyes

Of a towering creature, taller than any legion soldier, featured like a man

But covered in fur like a beast and bearing a mighty shield.

Havard the Aegis greets Shartan

(20) The creature spoke in a stern voice, saying:

"Who are you to come upon us alone,

Wearing the armor of our most hated foe,

When I can see you are no man of the legion?"

And Shartan answered him: "If you hate the legion,

Then I am your friend."

(21) And the giant laughed, and set him back upon his feet,

Declaring: "Then the Aegis of Alamarri bids you welcome!

Follow me to the side of the Prophet."

Shartan meets Andraste

(22) The Aegis led him to the center of the great host,

And Shartan saw that they counted men and women of all descriptions among them.

Many bore the scars of escaped slaves, and some had come west

From the coastlands, and they stood as equals beside the wild giant men of the South.

(23) There, in the heart of them, sang a Lady radiant

And clad in armor of bright steel.

She paused her song to look upon Shartan,

And said to him: "All souls who take up the sword

Against Tevinter are welcome here.

Rest, and tell us of your battles."

The elves ambush the legion

(24) And Shartan told her: "I cannot rest
While the People wait in darkness and fear."
So Andraste sent him with three of her attendants
To invite the People to come to her side.

(25) And the People came, all astonished
To stand among Andraste's followers,
And she gave them food and drink and bade them sit
While Shartan gave her the tale of their uprising
And flight from Vol Dorma.

(26) When the tale was finished, Andraste said to Shartan:
"Truly, the Maker has called you, just as He called me,
To be a Light for your People.
The host you see before you march,
Bearing His will north, where we shall deliver it
To Minrathous, city of magisters, and we shall tear down
The unassailable gates, and set all slaves free."

(27) And Shartan looked upon the Prophet Andraste
And said: "The People will set ourselves free.
Your host from the South may march
Alongside us."

(28) The giants of the South rose to their feet as one
And bowed. And Andraste said:
"It is done. We march as one."

Shartan 10

The armies clash on Valarian Fields

(1) At Shartan's word, the sky
Grew black with arrows.
At Our Lady's, ten thousand swords
Rang from their sheaths.
A great hymn rose over Valarian Fields, gladly proclaiming:
Those who had been slaves were now free.

(2) The legion fell before them
Like wheat before the scythe,
But the armies of Tevinter were numberless,
A sea of death which crashed upon
The Prophet and her army like waves.

Shartan rescues Andraste

(3) The host of the Lady
Began to falter. The legion
Turned spear and sword, fire
And ice upon them, and the warriors
Of the Prophet were scattered,
Divided from their commanders
By magic, penned like cattle for slaughter.

(4) Shartan saw that walls of ice
Surrounded Andraste and her warriors,
And he rallied the People.
And with arrows aflame,
The walls of magic melted
And the Prophet and her warriors were free.

Andraste names Shartan her champion

(5) And the Prophet stood beside Shartan
And shouted to her host:
"Behold! Our champion!"
And gave to him the blade of her own mother
From her own scabbard, Glandivalis, saying:

(6) "Take this, my champion,
And free our people forever."
And the Prophet and the People
Struck down the mages of the legion
And claimed the field together.

(7) And before them, empty,
Outstretched lay the land
Which led to the gates of Minrathous.

Canticle of Apotheosis: Betrayal & Death

The canticle that chronicles the betrayal and death of Andraste is usually attributed to the original Justinia, an escaped Tevinter slave and Andraste's closest friend and confidante—a figure for which five Divines have been named. Whether she actually composed any of the verses is much debated. Justinia returned with the Alamarri to what is now Orlais following Andraste's execution but vanished shortly afterward.

The earliest references to the Song of Betrayal appear around -165 Ancient, five years before Archon Hessarian publicized Maferath's role in the death of the Prophet. Since no verifiable copies of that song have ever been found, it is unclear if they have any resemblance to the Canticle of Apotheosis we know today. No account of the tale includes Justinia at the meeting between Hessarian and Maferath, and since the only surviving witness to their act was Havard the Aegis, the inclusion has spurred the legend that Justinia and Havard fled Maferath's rule and hid the ashes of Andraste together, founding the cult that would eventually become the Chantry in secret. More likely, the modern Canticle of Apotheosis was written by Andrastian groups after Maferath's betrayal became known and simply absorbed the earlier Song of Betrayal.

The version of Apotheosis contained in this collection dates to -100 Ancient and appeared around the time of the old Inquisition. By then, it was a well-established part of the liturgy of Andrastian groups across Orlais and Nevarra.

Apotheosis 1

The aftermath of Valarian Fields

(1) Victory! Sweet song rising from the lips of the vanquishers,

The host of Shartan, the clans of Alamarri, a thousand freemen

Held aloft blade and spear and to the Maker gave thanks.

But for every one who stood and sang the hymn of praise,

Two lay at their feet, soul seeking the Light eternal.

(2) Maferath's heart grew cold

As he looked upon the field of the dead and heard

The chant of "Glory! Glory! Glory! Hail to the Maker

Most High! Hail to Andraste, Prophet and liberator,

Light of the world! Look upon our work, O Maker, and rejoice!"

(3) And Maferath forsook the celebrations of his people

And went apart, taking not even his Aegis,[20] his shield-brother.

In the solitude of the night, Maferath dwelled in his bitterness,

And the Light which once burned within him extinguished.

Maferath meets with Hessarian

(4) The lord of the Alamarri sent forth his most trusted runner

To the gates of Minrathous itself, to call the Archon to parley,

That like the leaves after a long winter, peace too might return to the land.

Hessarian was filled to overflowing with doubt that the offer might be true,

Yet did he reply with message of his own and arrange to meet the war-chief.

(5) Maferath took with him his Aegis, and arrived at the appointed place

Where Hessarian waited with his guard, and the two leaders of armies spoke,

Guarded in riddles, and came to an understanding between them

That peace bore a heavy price which must be paid in blood.

(6) And they returned to their own people, and said nothing.

[20] The disciple Havard.

Andraste prepares to lay siege to Minrathous

(7) The armies of the Maker marched to the heart of the Imperium.

They looked upon those gates guarded by the Juggernauts[21] of old

And despaired, for surely neither army nor god could oppose such might.

Andraste's sermon to the armies

(8) So Andraste said to her followers: "You who stand before the gates,

You who have followed me into the heart of evil,

The fear of death is in your eyes; its hand is upon your throat.

Raise your voices to the heavens! Remember:

Not alone do we stand on the field of battle.

(9) "The Maker is with us! His Light shall be our banner,

And we shall bear it through the gates of that city and deliver it

To our brothers and sisters awaiting their freedom within those walls.

At last, the Light shall shine upon all of creation,

If we are only strong enough to carry it."

(10) And the armies of Andraste raised their voices,

Singing a hymn of praise to the Maker. And feared no more.

And Andraste went apart to seek the Maker's wisdom

For the battle to come.

Maferath delivers Andraste to Hessarian

(11) Maferath went to his wife and said:

"In the hills lies a silver pool where they say

The Voice of Heaven can be heard most clearly.

Let us go together and hear the Maker's Will."

(12) Andraste went with Maferath and the Aegis to the silver pool.

As she knelt in prayer, the servants of the Archon surrounded them,

Spears raised. Andraste drew her sword

And pierced one man through the heart, but Maferath,

With a blow from his axe, struck the blade from her hands.

And it fell to the ground, and where it landed, tears welled from the land.

Andraste names Shartan her champion

[21] The giant, inactive golems that guard the gate of Minrathous.

(13) The Aegis faltered; his hand could not draw against his own lord,

But neither could it be stayed as his Prophet was betrayed.

Unarmed, he stood between Andraste and the Tevinters.

A spear pierced his chest twice, and he fell.

(14) With neither blade nor shield, Andraste gave herself up

To her enemies. And Maferath bound his wife's hands

And delivered her to the Archon to be put to death.

Apotheosis 2

Andraste is brought forth in chains

(1) As the sun rose on the army of the faithful,

The gates of the city parted and the legion descended upon the land

As the shadow of a distant storm darkens the sun.

At the forefront of the host rode the Archon himself, sword in hand.

And at his side, bound by heavy chains, rode the Prophet.

(2) Hope abandoned the armies of the faithful

At the sight of their Lady in chains. And a terrible cry

Rose from the field like the wailing of lost children.

(3) Before the host of the faithful and all of the Imperium,

The servants of the Archon assembled a great dais at the feet of the Juggernauts

And there built a pyre twice the height of a man,

The Prophet in chains placed on a stake in the center.

A devoted disciple dies

(4) The Liberator[22] drew the blade at his side

And charged the pyre, the freedom of the Prophet before his eyes,

But from the legion came a storm of arrows

Blacker than night. And the disciple who had fought side by side

With the Lady fell, along with a hundred of his People.

And among the Alamarri ten thousand swords fell to the ground in a chorus of defeat.

Andraste calls out

(5) The legion doused the pyre around her with lamp oil

As Andraste called out in a great voice:

"Maker of the World, forgive them! They have lived too long in shadow

Without Your Light to guide them! Be with Your children now, O Maker!"

Hessarian lights the pyre

(6) The Archon stood upon the dais and declared:

"Today, I end this war!" And by will alone

Drew fire from air and set the pyre aflame.

(7) The army of the faithful gathered before the gates of the city

Wept openly. And from among them voices raised

In threnody for Andraste wreathed in flame.

(8) Though the fire enveloped her like a shroud, and the heat from the blaze

Reached across the field, Andraste was silent and did not cry out.

And the legionnaires who stood guard nearby

Were shaken, and began to whisper among themselves:

"Is she truly the servant of a god?"

[22] Likely Shartan.

Andraste marches on Tevinter

Hessarian begins to doubt

(9) The Archon looked upon what he had wrought

As the flames of Andraste's pyre grew ever closer to heaven

And the heat drove even the bravest of his legion back

And his heart wavered. For though Andraste did not cry out

Yet did he see her suffering.

(10) Merciless, the fire did not spare her mortal flesh.

And while Hessarian heard over the roar of the bonfire

The cheering of his magisters, he also heard the distant

Song of the faithful mourning their Lady.

Hessarian takes pity on Andraste

(11) Before any among his advisors could draw breath,

Hessarian took blade to hand and himself

Dared the fire that consumed the Prophet.

With one swift strike he pierced her heart.

Andraste dies

(12) The sky grew dark. And the ground began to tremble as if in mortal dread.

The crowd before the gates, both Tevinter and faithful, fell silent.

The heavens wept, and yet no rain could extinguish the flame

Which was now a funeral pyre. Wind swept across the city

Like a terrible hand in rage. And the Tevinters who witnessed this

Said: "Truly, the gods are angered."

(13) In sorrow, the crowds dispersed. The army of the faithful

Turned southward, to the lands from which they had come.

The legion of Tevinter hid inside the walls of their city

And watched the sky in fear.

Havard returns

(14) The sky wept as though it would never stop, and the footprints

Left by armies turned to countless seas, as Andraste's pyre burned to embers

And grew dark. On hands and knees, wounded unto death,

Havard, once the Aegis of Maferath, crawled to the feet of his Lady.

(15) The loyal shield, broken to pieces, found only ash

Left to the wind and rain. And Havard wept

And took the ashes, still hot from the fire, and pressed them to his heart.

Andraste appears to Havard

(16) His ears filled with the song of multitudes

Raised in chorus, and before his eyes the dark skies parted

And Andraste, dressed in cloth of starlight and armored

In moonlight, stood before him, and he was afraid.

(17) The Lady knelt at his side, saying:

"Rise, Aegis of the Faith. You are not forgotten.

Neither man nor Maker shall forget your bravery

So long as I remember."

(18) At this, his wounds healed, and he stood

And gathered up the ashes, and carried them

To the lands of the Alamarri, away from sorrow forever.

Canticle of Exaltations: Prophecy

Written in -12 Ancient by the then-prince Kordillus Drakon, the Canticle of Exaltations has the clearest history and authorship in the entire Chant. Prophetic verse was extremely popular in the last decades of the pre-Chantry era, and many writers attempted to describe their visions of the Maker's return.

Emperor Drakon is believed to have rewritten the canticle several times before allowing Divine Justinia I to include it in the Chant. Collectors have paid exorbitant sums of gold for copies of his early drafts, and the penultimate version is kept locked up alongside the Orlesian imperial crown jewels in Val Royeaux. The final draft, written in Ciriane, is in a vault in the Grand Cathedral's archives.

Exaltations 1

Preludium

(1) Lady of Perpetual Victory, your praises I sing!
Gladly do I accept the gift invaluable
Of your glory! Let me be the vessel
Which bears the Light of your promise
To the world expectant.

The vision begins

(2) The air itself rent asunder,
Spilling light unearthly from the
Waters of the Fade,
Opening as an eye to look
Upon the Realm of Opposition
In dire judgment.

(3) And in that baleful eye I saw
The Lady of Sorrow, armored in Light,
Holding in her left hand the scepter
Of Redemption. She descended
From on high, and a great voice
Thundered from the top of every
Mountain and pinnacle across creation:

(4) "All heads bow! All knees bend! Every being in the Realm
Of Opposition pay homage, for the Maker of All Things
Returns to you!"

Portents of the Maker's return

(5) Seven times seventy men of stone immense
Rose up from the earth like sleepers waking at the dawn,
Crossing the land with strides immeasurable,
And in the hollows of their footprints
Paradise was stamped, indelible.

(6) And I heard from the East a great cry
As men who were beasts warred with their brothers,
Tooth and claw against blade and bow,
Until one could no longer be told from the other,
And cursed them and cursed their generations.

(7) And those who slept, the ancient ones, awoke,
For their dreams had been devoured
By a demon that prowled the Fade
As a wolf hunts a herd of deer.
Taking first the weakest and frailest of hopes,
And when there was nothing left,
Destroying the bright and bold
By subtlety and ambush and cruel arts.

(8) The ninth sacred mountain upon which rests
The mortal dust of Our Lady ascended
Whole into the heavens, to be given high honor
In the Realm of Dreams forever.
And around it, a chorus of spirits sang:
"Whatsoever passes through the fire
Is not lost, but made eternal;
As air can never be broken nor crushed,
The tempered soul is everlasting!"

(9) And I looked up and saw
The seven gates of the Black City shatter,
And darkness cloaked both realms.

Andraste gives Drakon his destiny

(10) I covered my face, fearful,
But the Lady took my hands from my eyes,
Saying, "Remember the fire. You must pass
Through it alone to be forged anew.
Look! Look upon the Light so you
May lead others here through the darkness,
Blade of the Faith!"

The Maker returns

(11) In dread I looked up once more
And saw the darkness warp and crumble,
For it was thin as samite,
A fragile shroud over the Light
Which turned it to ash.

(12) And the Maker, clad in the majesty of the sky,
Set foot to earth, and at His touch
All warring ceased. The vicious
Beasts lay down and were quieted;
The meek lambs became bold
And rose up, casting aside their shepherds
To dance at the Maker's feet.

(13) From every corner of the earth
The Chant of Light echoed,
As the Maker walked the land
With Andraste at His right hand.
And they reached the gates of Minrathous,
Where once a terrible fire swept
The Light of redemption from the face of the world,
And there, the Lady of Restitution
Drew her shining sword
And plunged it into the ground at her feet, saying:

The sins of creation are redeemed

(14) "All sins are forgiven! All crimes pardoned!
Let no soul harbor guilt!
Let no soul hunger for justice!
By the Maker's will I decree
Harmony in all things.
Let Balance be restored
And the world given eternal life."

Our Lady is sacrificed

chapter three

THE HERO OF FERELDEN

THE GREY WARDENS WILL RECRUIT MEMBERS FROM JUST about anywhere: Fereldan noble houses. Alienages. Orzammar. Even from among the Dalish. The Warden Duncan recruited the Hero of Ferelden from one such place of relative obscurity. As the most junior Warden in Ferelden, the Hero would rise up to unite the kingdom in the face of punishing odds—securing a rightful heir to the seat of power in the nation and putting down a Blight that threatened to end life in all of Thedas.

RECRUITING THE WARDEN

In 9:30 Dragon, the Archdemon Urthemiel awoke. With him, scores of darkspawn rose to overrun Ferelden. Duncan saw this coming when so many preferred to stick their fingers in their ears. At the time, the Wardens' duty was more symbolic than practical. It had been ages since a Blight, and the Warden ranks, bolstered by drifters, failures, and no shortage of convicts saved from quicker deaths, were hardly deserving of much respect. But the old treaties persisted, and the sacrifices of past Wardens were not forgotten. When Duncan came looking to recruit in Ferelden, he still found success. Alistair and the Hero survived their Joinings when others did not, and Duncan was able to secure a small but capable party to brace for the darkspawn assault.

The Warden victory over the Fifth Blight made members of the Order living legends.

DUNCAN

Behind every hero, there is a mentor—someone who props them up, leads them on those first steps down a destined path, who sees something in them they may not see in themselves. The Warden known as Duncan spent the last years of his life collecting heroes. But he also fought his share of personal demons. Years before the Fifth Blight and the Battle of Ostagar that took his life, Duncan was just one more roguish thug sentenced to death for a crime he very much committed.

The Engagement Ring

Duncan was a mutt of sorts, born in Highever, with a childhood largely spent in Orlais and the Free Marches. His mother, Tayana, was Rivaini. His father, Arryn, was a carpenter with Tevinter roots. While still a child, Duncan lost his parents and became a homeless urchin on the streets of Val Royeaux. It was there the rogue honed his thieving skills out of

The picturesque Fereldan countryside was well worth saving.

necessity. Life was not easy stealing to survive. Duncan watched as more than a few friends were killed for their crimes with few repercussions.

One night, he robbed the wrong man. This man, Guy, turned out to be the fiancé of a senior Grey Warden, Genevieve. Duncan was tipped off by an innkeeper that Guy's room would be empty. Duncan broke in and pocketed the couple's engagement ring, but when Guy caught him, a fight ensued. Guy refused to let go of the ring.

"I'd been starving. The winter had been hard," Duncan would later recall. "I'd never killed anyone before. I wouldn't have killed him then, either, but the fight was so long. He was so determined to get that ring back, he wouldn't stop. I'd meant to just put my dagger to his throat, to force him to submit . . ."

Duncan cut Guy's throat. Killed him. And for the crime, he was sentenced to death—until Genevieve called off the execution at the last second, invoking the Warden Right of Conscription. Duncan initially refused, preferring to die. But Genevieve forced him to join as punishment for his crime. It is unlikely that Genevieve expected Duncan to survive his Joining. When he did, she was forced to train him. Though brash and rude, Duncan proved himself a skilled and stealthy fighter, a strong asset to the Wardens.

Like many before him, Duncan gave up his family name when he joined their ranks. But he would not forget his past transgressions. It is rumored that Duncan's signature daggers once belonged to Guy.

Duncan's Calling

In his early days as a Warden, Duncan retained his street-tough demeanor, proving an unpredictable scamp who took unnecessary risks. He had sticky fingers and seemed to always be looking for something worth stealing. Nevertheless, he was true to his duty as a Warden. He was supposed to be dead, after all, and owed his remaining days to the Order.

Duncan was one of several Wardens involved in a harrowing expedition into the Deep Roads in 9:10 Dragon in search of Genevieve's brother, the Warden Bregan. The events, though shrouded in secrecy, were said to involve the sentient darkspawn known as the Architect.

Of the handful of brave Wardens who descended in search of Bregan, only Duncan and a Circle mage named Fiona survived the ordeal. Fiona would later be named grand enchanter and become the first person in the history of Thedas to have the effects of the blight reversed.

Duncan's time in the Deep Roads changed him. The deeper the party went, the harder the trials, and the more serious Duncan became about his role in the Wardens. He hardened, finally accepting his responsibility. By dedicating the remainder of his days to bolstering the Wardens' numbers in preparation for the impending Blight, this urchin mutt, who once killed a man for his engagement ring, helped save Thedas from certain doom.

THE HERO'S PARTY

The Hero's followers came from many corners. There was Morrigan, recruited from the Korcari Wilds and equipped with no small amount of disdain. Leliana, a sister of the Chantry, was loitering in a Lothering tavern. The Hero found Sten in a cage and fought off an assassination attempt by Zevran. Shale was literally waiting to be found, while Oghren had very nearly nothing left to lose. And then there was Alistair, of course, who had everything to gain—even if he wasn't ready to admit it.

ALISTAIR THEIRIN

As a new recruit in the Grey Wardens, Alistair was a young man of seemingly little significance, raised in the Chantry and initially destined to serve in the Templar Order, but he would play a significant role in the events of the Fifth Blight of 9:30 Dragon. He was one of only two Grey Wardens to survive the disastrous Battle of Ostagar, left to help organize a defense against the rampaging darkspawn, and then revealed to be the bastard brother of the deceased King Cailan. Thus, Alistair was placed directly in contention for the throne of Ferelden.

The Question of Birth

The question regarding Alistair's birth has been ongoing since that time. There remain many in Ferelden who refuse to believe the facts as they were presented—that King Maric is his father—and suspect that the entire story was concocted by the Grey Wardens to put a usurper on the throne. There was significant investigation into Alistair's history shortly after the Fifth Blight ended, some of it funded by lords of the Bannorn, resulting in a royal inquest in 9:31 Dragon to determine the truth. The inquest was ultimately deemed inconclusive, much to the disappointment of all involved.

What is known is that Alistair was born in 9:10 Dragon, possibly in the village of Redcliffe or nearby. Certainly he was initially raised in Redcliffe Castle at the request of Arl Eamon Guerrin, as evidenced by a letter written by his wife, Lady Isolde, that made the rounds in Ferelden and, at the time, caused significant scandal for her husband.

"I do not know why Eamon dotes on the stableboy," the letter read. "An orphan, he says, and the get of a maid who died in his service. If that is all there is to it, then why take such an interest in his welfare? Why did I not know of this maid's death, when I have lived in Redcliffe all my life? Eamon does not say, but I think it is because he feels guilty. I know my husband, and I know what it means when he averts his eyes and mumbles, and that is how he speaks of this maid. He will not admit it, but I think the boy is his. What other reason could there be, dear sister?"

Alistair was eventually sent to the monastery at Bournshire in 9:20 Dragon, and by all accounts was an unenthusiastic pupil destined for service with the templars. He resented having been forced to leave Redcliffe, which he considered his true home, and his flippant attitude repeatedly got him into trouble with the chantry priests. There are few accounts of Alistair's time there until his recruitment into the Grey Wardens in 9:29 Dragon by Warden-Commander Duncan—reportedly despite the reservations of the grand cleric and the superior performance of other prospects who had competed for the right.

Alistair rose to greatness from inauspicious roots.

"I told this Duncan that the boy was unsuitable," the grand cleric said. "We had numerous templars who'd fought to impress him, some with a history of deeds that should rightfully impress anyone. But no, he takes our willingness to provide a recruit of quality—to an ancient order that has long outlived its day, I should add—and selects a boy yet to even take his vows, and whose performance could, at best, be called middling. The lad has a smart mouth that will embarrass him—and us for allowing him to go. I forbade it . . . and the Warden recruiter replied by invoking the Right of Conscription! The gall of the man!"

What is interesting is that this appears to not have been the first time the Warden-Commander had met Alistair. The following is an excerpt from a letter presented at the 9:31 inquiry, written by a Warden-Constable Reyor two months after Alistair's recruitment:

"I know you said it was unnecessary, but as I investigate all new recruits I looked into this Alistair lad . . . and it's rather odd. There was an old groundskeeper who knew him and seemed quite fond; she reminisced about the night Alistair was first brought to Redcliffe Castle. She mentioned a young man of Rivaini descent bringing the boy, and intrigued, I gave her your description. She didn't know if that original young man was you, but she said she'd seen you come to the castle often through the years, asking after Alistair's progress and watching him. I have to ask: Is that true? Is there something about the lad the Wardens should know?"

And the response from Warden-Commander Duncan:

"Alistair is the son of an old friend. As my travels indeed bring me to Redcliffe from time to time, I have looked in on him. I believe he is a worthy addition to our ranks. There is nothing more you or the Wardens need to know."

A WARRIOR OF CHARACTER

So it was that Duncan of the Grey Wardens came to choose from among the Order of Templars a recruit who would himself join the campaign against the darkspawn. This honor was overseen by Knight-Commander Glavin of Denerim and performed in the name and by the glory of Andraste.

There was held in the Grey Warden's honor a tournament to display the Chantry's finest warriors. Templars from across Ferelden filled the courtyard with gleaming armor and a righteous glow, and it is certain that the Maker's will was present on that day. And next to the knight-commander sat Duncan, watching wolf-eyed over those who would be his recruit.

As the sparring progressed, three templars stood apart. There was Ser Kalvin of Denerim. A finer talent with a sword could not be had this side of the Antivan duelists. There was Ser Eryhn, a woman of Highever, possessed of unmatched grace with blade and shield. And there was Ser Talrew of Lothering, whose battle prowess had brought victory in many campaigns against Chasind raiders in the Korcari Wilds. The Grey Warden seemed impressed by these three warriors, but still he appeared perplexed. This did not escape the notice of Knight-Commander Glavin, who asked of him, "My friend Warden, why does your brow furrow?"

To which Duncan replied, "I have seen many fine warriors of stout heart this day, but there, across the field, I see one templar who has not been called to fight."

The knight-commander looked, and he saw the young initiate Alistair, and when he did, he sighed. "That one," he said, "is a troublemaker. His mouth and his attitude betray a willful streak that will only do his fellows harm. He is not worthy of the honor of fighting this day."

"I come to find the best of you," replied the Grey Warden, "not the most polite. Let him fight."

And the knight-commander nodded grudgingly at the young Alistair, who for his part appeared surprised. He glanced between the knight-commander and the Grey Warden as if for confirmation, and he found it in Duncan's satisfied smile.

In time, the young Alistair emerged with armor and weapon and entered the fray. The others voiced anger at the initiate's late inclusion, and their efforts to push him from consideration were obvious. Alistair reacted in his own inimitable fashion: to those he bested, he reached down, offering his hand while smiling an impish grin. If refused, the gesture was replaced with mockery that drew quiet chuckles from the crowd. Often his opponent would storm from the field in fury, and Alistair would simply turn toward Duncan and shrug, displaying an even larger grin.

But Alistair was far from the most experienced warrior on the field. He was bested by Ser Kalvin's quick blade. He was outmaneuvered by Ser Eryhn's skill. He was outlasted by Ser Talrew's endurance. Even so, when the tournament was done, Duncan turned to the knight-commander and made his choice. "I will recruit Alistair," he said.

The knight-commander was outraged, but could not refuse, for the Grey Wardens wield the Right of Conscription. Resigned, he announced Duncan's choice and took him to the field to meet the young victor amid many stern, indignant stares. None was more surprised than Alistair himself.

"But I didn't even win the tournament!" he was heard to exclaim.

"I did not ask for the tournament," Duncan responded. "Nor did I offer recruitment as its prize. I came here seeking a warrior of character, and I believe I have found him."

Alistair appeared taken aback by the response, but perhaps not unpleasantly so. He stared agape until Duncan, with the slightest hint of a smile, suggested that the young man go and collect his gear, for they would be leaving immediately. Alistair ran off with such speed that it brought knowing glances from members of the crowd.

Nothing was heard from Alistair after that night, but such is not unusual when it comes to Grey Wardens. What is known is that the templar barracks are far, far quieter without him.

—Excerpt from the journal of Brother Tevius of the Order of Templars in Redcliffe

The reference to an "old friend" caused a great stir at the inquiry. It was not well known, but when the Grey Wardens first returned to Ferelden in 9:10 Dragon—more than two hundred years after their exile following the battle at Soldier's Peak—King Maric joined a much younger Duncan and his fellow Wardens in a mission to the Deep Roads. During that time, Duncan could have become friends with the king, and thus the Warden letters were used as evidence to prove Alistair's lineage. Opponents, meanwhile, stated that King Maric would have needed to be in Redcliffe around the same period, when in fact he was either traveling with the Wardens or at the royal palace in Denerim.

That does not, however, provide an answer as to why the Warden-Commander would refer to an old friend. At the inquiry, it was suggested that finding a home for King Maric's bastard son was done as a favor, supported by testimony given by a Denerim washerwoman named Goldanna.

"I didn't know he existed, not until he showed up on my doorstep during the Blight," she told the inquiry. "When I was a girl in Redcliffe, they told me my mother died in childbirth, she and the babe both. A soldier came, said he was sent by the arl, and he gave me coin and sent me to live with my uncle in Denerim. But the babe didn't die, did he? They just didn't want me to know. Mother had seen the king once at the castle. I remember her saying how handsome he was, how bad she felt that the queen had died. That's when it must have happened, and they wanted to hide it from everyone."

Regardless of the truth, it appeared Alistair did well among the Grey Wardens. He flourished in a way he never had in the Chantry, quickly growing attached to his fellow Wardens and they to him. One can see this in a letter he wrote to Arl Eamon but never sent:

"I didn't think I belonged anywhere, Uncle. You said I should try my best, and I really did when I was at the chantry. Well, that's a lie, I suppose. I wanted to try. It was hard to want that, however, when everyone's always scowling at you. One templar kept telling me I was going to end up sent off to a Circle in the Anderfels after my vows. He laughed when he said it, a big laugh that made my gut turn to jelly. It made me think the Anderfels must be an awful place to have me end up there.

"But the Wardens are different. Everyone who comes here . . . they didn't belong anywhere either, and then they found this cause. They found each other. They don't know anything about me, where I come from, and they don't care. Duncan said I was worthy, and that's all that mattered. I thought the man must have been insane to pick me out, me of all people, but now . . . Now I don't know. They say I'm learning fast. I beat Rondall in a spar the other day, beat him honestly, and . . . I think I might be good at being a Warden. They think so, too.

"For the first time, I'm a little glad you kicked me out. Don't take that wrong. I know you felt bad that night when you sent me off, Uncle. I just mean I landed on my feet."

MORRIGAN

The Hero met Morrigan in the Korcari Wilds and, along with Alistair, was nursed back to health by her mother, Flemeth, following the disastrous Battle of Ostagar. Morrigan joined the Hero's cause at her mother's insistence and went on to play a pivotal role not only in the fight to quell the Blight but also in stopping the ancient darkspawn Corypheus more than ten years later.

Morrigan was an unlikely ally of the Hero of Ferelden.

The Chasind Shapeshifter

Legends of the "Witch of the Wilds" have persisted throughout the history of Ferelden and, with them, stories of her many "daughters." Her children are regarded with fear: infamous figures, apostates living outside the control of the Circle of Magi, many thought to be shape changers, all dangerous. And none of those daughters is more well known and controversial than Morrigan.

The first reports of Morrigan begin when a "dark-haired young woman, dressed in Chasind garb and looking very out of place" appeared in the village of Merinwood on the outskirts of the Korcari Wilds. Local villagers suspected the young woman to be an apostate, and a week later templars arrived from nearby Lothering to investigate, only to find her long gone. They entered the Korcari Wilds to search for her.

"For several days we found nothing," read one account. "We were just about to call the search off, ready to dismiss the entire report as one more in a series of local legends about apostates haunting the woods, when I heard a voice chuckling from the tree above me. I looked and saw a girl in the branches—dark hair, a wildling dressed like a Chasind savage, no more than twelve years of age. She grinned at me and said, 'You do not belong here.' I ignored the challenge and ordered her to come down in the name of Andraste and the Chantry. That made her laugh. 'Your Maker holds no sway in this forest, as you shall soon see.' I demanded again that she come down. That was when she transformed into a black bird and flew off . . . and the trees came to life. They uprooted from the very ground, lifting fully armored men up into the air with branches and vines as if they weighed nothing. Men screamed all around me, and I ran."

Two more forays into the Korcari Wilds followed. A single member of the last group of templars reported seeing the dark-haired girl in a ruin, in the company of a much older woman who could have been her grandmother, but when he called the rest of the party to see, they found no trace of either woman. Further searches were abandoned to prevent the fostering of hysteria among Fereldan locals.

This was hardly the first time the Templar Order had ventured into the wilders' forest in search of apostates. Records show the area to be a focal point for organized searches dating back three hundred years with varying degrees of success. The hostility of the forest itself, and its Chasind inhabitants, makes searches especially dangerous. Reports of actual encounters with the Witch of the Wilds or one of her daughters, however, are difficult to come by. Most seeking proof are never heard from again, which only validates the tales.

Morrigan lived for a time with her mother Flemeth in a Korcari shack.

This particular dark-haired young woman was not seen again until a number of years later, in 9:20 Dragon, when she was spotted watching a group of Avvar hunters from afar. Then, over the next several years, she was seen in various villages and towns near the Korcari Wilds, though seldom for long enough to cause a stir. She would appear, pick out a local who drew her interest, and then question or follow them until her interest waned or she drew too much attention.

"She told us her name was Morrigan," said one local. "Thought she'd come out from the woods, like other Chasind folk. Maybe to trade. We didn't see any harm in bringing her to the farm for a bite. Better to be friendly with them Chasind than tempt their anger, right? Thing is, she acted like she'd never used a proper fork. Asked strange questions of my lads, like, 'Why do you go to the chantry? What purpose is there in it?' Questions that got the missus upset, until finally she shooed the girl out. I thought she was crazy, ordering around a Chasind, but the Morrigan girl went quick enough. Turned into a giant bear and lumbered off after giving the hounds a royal scare. Last time we invited the Chasind anywhere."

At the Front of a Blight

Morrigan reemerged as the Fifth Blight hit Ferelden in 9:30 Dragon, aiding the Hero of Ferelden and Alistair, the only Grey Wardens to survive the disastrous Battle of Ostagar. The extent of her involvement in the battle to slay the Archdemon and stop the darkspawn hordes from ravaging the countryside is unknown. If she was present at the final battle of Denerim, where the Archdemon was slain, she did not remain afterward. She claimed no rewards and disappeared as quickly as she appeared.

There are some who claim this is simply another of the growing number of tales regarding the Hero of Ferelden. Many of Ferelden's legendary heroes, after all, include a story of a mysterious witch appearing to aid them: King Calenhad the Great, Dane the Hunter, King Maric, the Champion of Kirkwall . . . To add yet another to that list strains credulity.

Yet numerous reports of Morrigan traveling with the Hero of Ferelden exist.

"I saw them together in Lothering, just before the village evacuated," said one resident. "Two Grey Wardens, and with them a dark-haired witch. All I remember is she didn't look happy to be traveling with them, like she'd been forced into it. I heard her complaining, needling one of the Wardens with her: a fresh-faced fellow who looked none too happy himself. I remember it because my daughter ran up to her, said the feathers she wore on the shoulders of her robe were pretty. The witch looked surprised and asked why my daughter was still in Lothering, and my daughter said because we were still packing our wagon.

"She smiled at her and said, ' 'Tis a long and dangerous journey that awaits you, young one. These lands grow dark, and will become darker yet in the days to come.' She plucked one of them feathers out and gave it to my daughter. I remember it all, because my girl held onto that feather for years after. Called it her good-luck charm, said it had magic in it. Right up until the plague."

At the Side of an Empress

What became of Morrigan after the Fifth Blight is uncertain. For a number of years, sightings of a dark-haired woman matching her appearance were reported in Orlais, in places as far apart as the Arbor Wilds, the Nahashin Marshes, and the capital city of Val Royeaux. The last is most suspect, as a crowded city seems like the last place one would expect to find a witch of the Korcari Wilds. Yet rumors persisted that Empress Celene of Orlais had acquired a secret, arcane advisor. The empress, well known for a fascination with magic, became a patron to any who could offer insights into the mysterious.

Morrigan was finally presented to the Orlesian Imperial Court just as tensions with mages were reaching a boiling point. Though many had suspected her presence long before then, the idea that Empress Celene would officially introduce Morrigan in public, especially in light of the events at Kirkwall, was beyond belief.

She strode into the court like she was the empress herself, I swear. And what she wore! A dress all in black and dark purple, when the fashion of the season demanded one in white or pale blue. She had no mask at all, like a peasant or a priest, and wore less jewelry than my handmaiden. It was as if she mocked our conventions just by entering the room, without saying a word. Some people gasped in shock, like they would if someone brought a horse onto the ballroom floor, and we were all silent as she walked by us—alone, mind you, with nary a servant on hand—and went up to the empress's throne. Without being announced, like they were familiar. I remember the witch passing right by me, suppressing a smirk as if this were all some mirthful jest . . . and perhaps it was, to her. I will say that, scandalized as we all professed to be, almost half the gowns were dark if not black at the very next Imperial ball.

—One shocked member of the Orlesian court

The presence of a mysterious outsider in the Orlesian court caused no small amount of trouble for the empress, already beleaguered by claims against her rule made by Grand Duke

The bears that stalk Ferelden's Hinterlands are powerful and territorial.

Gaspard de Chalons. The Circle of Magi, represented by Court Enchanter Vivienne, stated the empress should disregard the "whisperings of an apostate" or suffer peril to her reputation. Empress Celene did not and had so far managed to retain the Chantry as a staunch ally to her rule. For this reason, no doubt, Morrigan had remained untouched by the templars since the revelation of her presence.

The empress also suffered the whispers that claimed Morrigan had bespelled her, allowing the witch to control the empire through her. The rumors' persistence apparently forced Morrigan into the background for a time.

"She returned every few months, coming to the imperial palace in the middle of the night without a single guard noticing her," said one elven servant of the court. "Each time she had with her some new bauble that the empress wanted. They looked strange, these things. Sometimes they glowed and seemed wicked. One time she brought what looked like a mirror, coated in rust and mud as if it had been dredged up from the bottom of a swamp. Perhaps it had. How the witch spirited that in past the guards, I have no idea. All I remember is that Empress Celene was delighted to see it. The way her eyes lit up when she saw it, you have no idea. She ordered me out immediately while the witch stood there and smiled. I wish I could have stayed. I was as desperate to know what it was all about as the empress surely was to have the witch explain it to her."

During the rise of the new Inquisition, following the blast at Haven and the death of Divine Justinia V, Morrigan was assigned to Skyhold as the imperial liaison. Whether this was to quietly remove the witch from the halls of power or simply to further her own designs is not known. Once again, after the Inquisition's victory at the Temple of Sacred Ashes, Morrigan vanished . . . though not without drawing the kind of attention and infamy that guarantee, should she appear again, it will certainly be noticed by all.

LELIANA

The bard Leliana has gone by many names, including Sister Nightingale and the Left Hand of the Divine. She came to the Hero's side under seemingly innocent circumstances, but has proven over the years to be anything but innocent. Her swift, eager blade and strong convictions have put her on the front lines of multiple wars and at the command of the Sunburst Throne.

The Lady's Grace

In Leliana's most vivid memory of her early childhood, she sees herself, a child of little more than four, holding her mother's hand as they stand on the stone terrace of an Orlesian villa, looking out at the cresting waves of the Waking Sea. Behind them are gardens of sweet orange and lavender, but the only fragrance that stands out to Leliana is the gentle scent of her mother's gray linen dress. These days, Leliana is unsure if the moment is real or merely imagined, but cherishes it nonetheless, as it is one of the few images she retains of her Fereldan mother, Oisine.

Oisine passed away soon after Leliana's fourth birthday. Oisine's mistress, Lady Cecilie Vasseur, who had grown fond of Oisine and her bright-haired little daughter, became Leliana's guardian. Lady Cecilie, who had no children of her own, was saddened by the shadow cast over Leliana's sunny disposition after Oisine's passing and gave the girl everything she asked for, hoping to see her smile again. The only thing Leliana ever asked for was books. She lost herself in stories of lost princes and lady knights. When she exhausted Cecilie's library of Orlesian and Fereldan tales, she went to the elven servants and asked them to tell her stories of their people. Leliana's obsession with stories led to a fascination with ballads and songs, and before long, Cecilie was hiring tutors to teach Leliana music and dance. Leliana recalls that one of her favorite places to practice her steps was on the stone terrace of the villa, with the gardens behind her and only a white balustrade between her and the sea.

When Leliana was sixteen, she accompanied the aging Cecilie to a soiree in Val Royeaux. It was to be Leliana's first experience with the capital and Orlesian society. Leliana describes herself as being "thoroughly dazzled," not least because it was at this function that she first met Marjolaine, who would become one of the greatest influences in her life. Marjolaine was introduced to Leliana as a wealthy widow and patron of several artists and musicians in attendance.

"She commanded the room from the moment she walked in," Leliana says. "She knew everyone and people were drawn to her. It wasn't just her beauty—and she was beautiful, though not in the style of the time, which was all about delicacy. Soft prettiness, like flower petals. Marjolaine was never soft. She was never pretty. She wasn't like the rest of them. But that's why everyone wanted to know who she was."

Leliana says she realized later Marjolaine's charm came from how well she played people. She could read them at a glance and discern their weakness. Those who desired influence, she flattered. Those impressed by power, she dominated. She was generous to those who valued wealth, and kind to servants, speaking directly and respectfully to them. She earned the loyalty of many that way.

"I only understood the significance of her manipulations when I caught myself doing the same, for the same reasons," Leliana says.

The Huntress

Much to Leliana's surprise, Marjolaine began calling upon Cecilie at the villa. Cecilie, who was growing frail, would often leave Leliana to entertain her visitor while Cecilie composed herself. Marjolaine and Leliana quickly became close friends, with Leliana enchanted by Marjolaine's worldly ways. To Leliana, who had lived a sheltered life with the pious, kindly Cecilie, Marjolaine represented adventure and excitement: a knight-errant, come to rescue the lady in the secluded tower.

While on a hunting trip, Marjolaine presented Leliana with her first bow and taught her to use it. Leliana's first inept attempts at shooting merely wounded the hart the hunters had run down. Distressed by the suffering of the animal, Leliana refused to finish it off. As Leliana watched, Marjolaine approached the wounded hart. With a practiced, steady hand, she pierced it through the eye with a long dirk, killing the beast immediately. Leliana vividly recalls Marjolaine's words then: "Never delay the inevitable. If you can strike, strike."

Later that summer, Leliana visited Marjolaine at her Val Royeaux estate. Marjolaine began teaching Leliana the arts of a bard: subterfuge, manipulation, and, of course, how to fight. "She was so subtle in it," Leliana says. "It was always in the guise of a lady's idle amusements: hunting, theater, or little games of seduction and sabotage. I didn't see what she was doing. Perhaps I remained stubbornly blind because I didn't want to see. And I became hers."

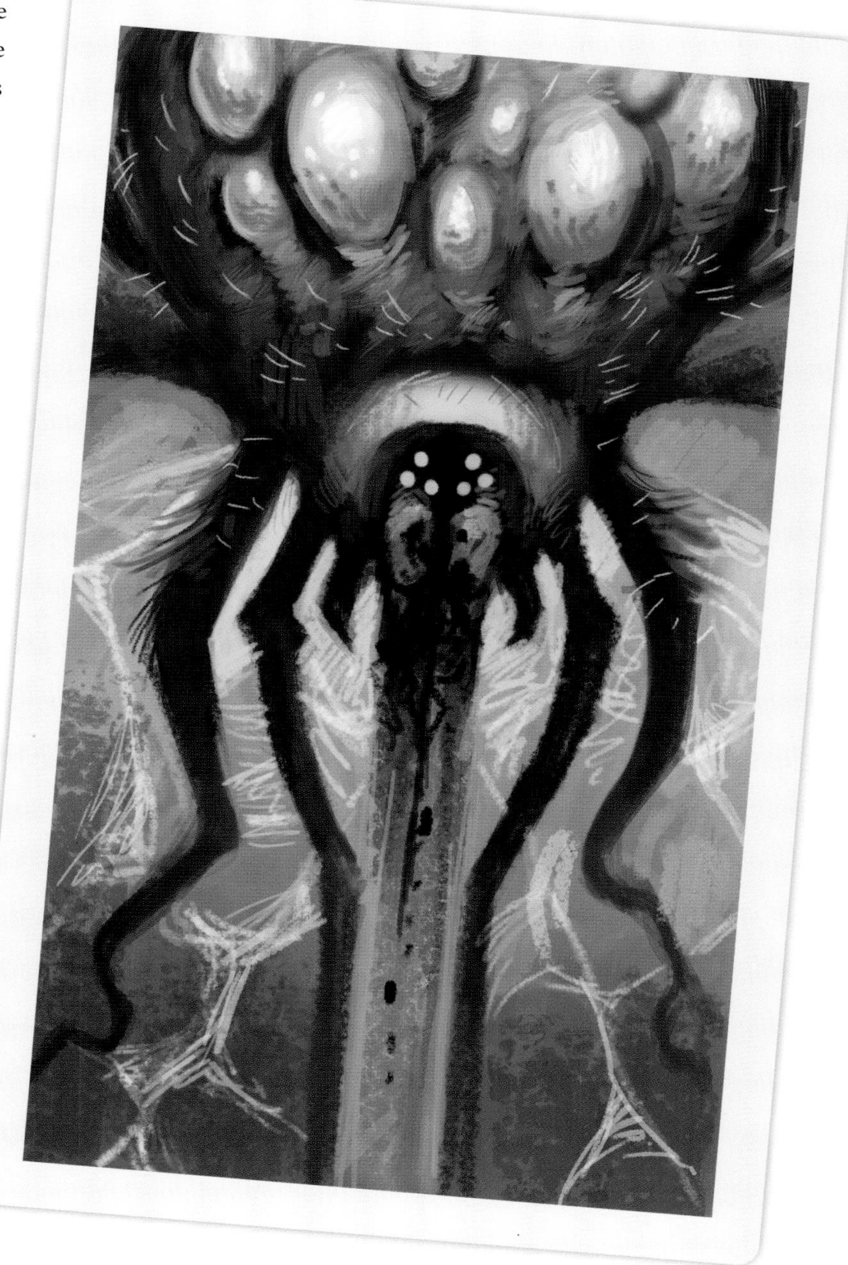

Giant spiders are found in deeper caves all over Ferelden.

While under Marjolaine's tutelage, Leliana met new friends: Sketch, an elf, and Tug, a dwarf. Together, the three got up to adventures that spanned the length and breadth of Orlais and even took them into Antiva and Ferelden. Leliana remembers these times as some of the happiest and more carefree in her life. They would come to a swift end, however, when Marjolaine grew paranoid that, with Leliana's growing skills as a bard, her protégée would one day turn on her. Staying true to her philosophy of never delaying the inevitable, Marjolaine struck, betraying Leliana and her two friends. All three were captured, and Leliana was stabbed and grievously wounded by Marjolaine.

Both Leliana and Sketch survived Marjolaine's trap, thanks to the actions of one Revered Mother Dorothea. Tug, however, did not. The loss of Tug made it difficult for Leliana and Sketch to carry on as they had been. They parted ways, Leliana fleeing into Ferelden to keep away from Marjolaine. Leliana would continue to tell stories of the trio, often embellishing the details, and admits rather freely that it is her way of reliving a happier time. Sketch, on the other hand, is rather less fond of Leliana taking liberties with the truth, as evidenced from his letters to her.

On the anniversary of Tug's death each year, Leliana opens a bottle of distilled plum brandy, imported from Antiva, and drinks it in memory of her friend. She pours a glass onto the stone for Tug, saying, "*Atrast tunsha, salroka.*"

A Shadow in the Sun

Taking strength and inspiration from the words of Revered Mother Dorothea when she was at her lowest, Leliana dedicated herself to the Chantry. She remained in Ferelden for several years, becoming a lay sister in a cloister in Lothering. The cloister offered Leliana a peace that she had never known before, allowing both body and spirit to heal. She believes she may never have left Lothering if it were not for the Fifth Blight and her "vision."

WE WHO DID NOT BELONG

"Do you want to know a secret?"

That was how I started when I toyed with stories as well as lives. But for all my clever turns, you two were fact, and friends. And yours, if you have kept it, is the secret I must leverage.

Tug held everything close to his chest. You and I knew this of him. While he lived, I respected that. But even now I can't find his name. If he had family in Orzammar, they are as lost as he.

He was marked as casteless, but no other dwarf I found shared the complete shape of it. So I think back to the day we lost him, to try to remember anything. I went through his silks, his weapons, his tools. But there were two things. Not things. Phrases. I had never heard him say the words, but they were important enough for etching and ink. First, on a handle, hidden:

"The Stone lives beneath Orlais."

I've heard this before, but more as passing phrase than anything true. And I would have smiled sadly and left it not understood, but there was a second phrase, the one I leave out of the telling. I thought it a detail that got in the way of the greater story, when I believed I knew what determined such things. Even dwarves I trust are confused by it, as the language is not how it is understood today.

"*Mathas gar na fornen pa tot isatunoll.*"

The literal is nonsense: "I'm sorry sacrifice one at my side death . . ." The last word is unknown. I have heard the first part from strange places, ending instead in "*pa salroka atrast.*" Which is the slightly less meaningless, "at my side find your way in the dark."

It seems to mean: "I regret the sacrifice of my kin, but it means we will find our way home." Which rings as defense of Orzammar's abandonment of Kal Sharok and perhaps of how Tug acted for you when you both were captured. I find that comforting, but I am sure I am wrong. It is too easy, too simple. Tug was not simple. This is something older. It is a secret, or it is gibberish. And then I thought of you.

I am sorry. I said I would not impose again. But I have been thinking of you both. How we were young in Val Royeaux. How we met at the autumn fête, Tug looting the linens, I seeking warmth and lace, and you—I thought you also came from outside, to steal books and hide from templars. But that isn't true, is it? We all left as one, we who did not belong. But you did belong. Not as "Sketch." "Sketch" has an awkwardness that is disarming in all situations. But before that, before you turned your back on everything, you had a purpose as hard to track as Tug's word. I now believe you were placed according to the stirrings of old empire and the seeding of our borders with hidden agents. Some formerly owned.

Do not think me accusing or judging. I care little for who you were before you joined us in the shadows. I contact you now because you think in different patterns. Long patterns. Books full of scribbles, building to things I never understood, if there even was something to be understood. Secrets or gibberish. And so I ask, old friend, if there was anything that your way discerned of Tug's way? Anything in your former life that would lead me to who he was? I would treat his memory better.

You were honest in all things with me. You were honest, or you were a master. I need either now.

Leliana

Send this to the master immediately!
We can weaken her through her friends!
Many died to intercept . . .

Sister Nightingale, recovered unread,
as requested. Please forgive the bloodstains.
—Charter

The chantry at Haven overlooked the village.

"First she tells me about this dream, of her falling into an encroaching darkness, allowing it to take her under," recalls a fellow sister at Lothering. "She said it was so real, like she was there. And then showed me this perfect white rose that she found from the cloister garden, from the rosebush beneath the arbor. It had been dead for two winters. And then, a single flawless rose, when there were no leaves, and no other sign of life—she thought it was a gift from the Maker. A message that He was watching and telling us to have hope. Nothing I said could shake the thought from her mind that this was a calling. With the Blight at our door and the darkspawn on our heels, she wanted to give people hope."

Leliana picked up her bow and daggers and, using the skills Marjolaine taught her, fought for Ferelden against the Blight. The bard who had cared only for fun and adventure was now infused with a purpose born of faith.

Following the Fifth Blight, she received a summons from Dorothea, now Divine Justinia V, who had been named successor to Beatrix III. Divine Justinia's appointment was controversial; she was known to be a liberal and rather worldly revered mother, and those who saw her as a threat to Chantry tradition mobilized almost immediately. Answering the Divine's call, Leliana went to Val Royeaux, where she was asked to assume the role of the Divine's Left Hand: her spymaster, maintaining a network of agents who answered solely to her.

Justinia was a savior and an inspiration to Leliana, and Leliana was eager to repay the debt. To serve the Sunburst Throne, she had to call upon the skills learned over two decades, all with the purpose of furthering the Divine's cause to reform the Chantry. From gentlewoman's companion to bard and then to Chantry sister: with the Divine's summons, Leliana was forced once again to reinvent herself.

"We are separated by years and death, but her hold on me is unrelenting," Leliana says. "Sometimes I catch a glimpse of her smile, the dismissive wave of her hand, and I turn and see it is only movement in a mirror. I hear her words, and they are mine. She is the shadow that hounds my steps, because she is my shadow. My mother loved me, Cecilie nurtured me, and Dorothea saved me, but Marjolaine made me in her image."

SENIOR ENCHANTER WYNNE

Wynne was a respected senior enchanter of the Circle of Magi in Ferelden. During the Fifth Blight, she was among the contingent of mages called to Ostagar to join in King Cailan's battle against the darkspawn. She fought alongside the Hero of Ferelden to end the Fifth Blight and later played an integral role in the White Spire conflict that helped spur the rebellion of mages in the Circles across Thedas.

Wynne's talent with magic was legendary.

The Trouble with Apprentices

Kinloch Hold records indicate that Wynne was taken from a Fereldan freehold called Langwynne. An orphan, she was discovered by a farmer's wife, sleeping in the hayloft. She was named Wynne after the fields where she was found, and lived with the freeholder's family for several months. When she retaliated against the freeholder's son's bullying by causing a fire with her dormant magical ability, the templars were called, and she was taken to the Circle.

The writings of First Enchanter Wenselus, who watched the new arrival carefully, describe Wynne as a quiet but happy child, who was especially grateful for three square meals and her own bed. Elated to be at the Circle, she approached each magical lesson with enthusiasm and thus was a joy to teach and mentor. Wynne's natural aptitude and the attention lavished upon her by her instructors led to her quick progression from apprentice to mage. She undertook her Harrowing at just shy of seventeen, years ahead of many of her peers.

Two years later, Wynne was entrusted with her first apprentice, Aneirin, a shy elven boy from the Denerim alienage.

"I demonstrated the simplest spell, to freeze over water in a cup, then asked him to attempt it," Wynne wrote after the first week with Aneirin. "I guided him in the process, but he showed no sign of understanding even the basic concepts of magic. He shrank from me when I asked him if he had heard anything I told him. I let him be for a day and tried again the next, with even less success. This time, he spilled the water. As a child, I'd performed the feat within a day of its teaching.

"After supper, I heard that he had been seen practicing in a corner of the library. I thought I would observe, to see how he was getting on, but he heard me approach and hid his accoutrements. When I asked to see what he had been working on, he shook his head vigorously and tried to escape. Is this rebellion? A childish tantrum? Secretive behavior like this will surely earn him the templars' suspicion. I must make it clear to him what is expected of him while he is at the tower."

Despite Wynne's best efforts, Aneirin did not respond to her teaching. One night, he escaped from the tower. The templars were on his trail immediately. Wynne never quite forgave herself for her failure with Aneirin and would berate herself for years, believing herself at least partially responsible for his disappearance. She handled all future apprentices with greater compassion, careful not to repeat the mistakes she'd made with Aneirin.

Earning Trust

One year after Aneirin's presumed death, Wynne found herself with child. Wynne herself reported the pregnancy to First Enchanter Wenselus, though she refused to reveal the identity of the child's father. Wenselus approached Wynne's friend (and later first enchanter) Irving, who admitted that Wynne had once divulged to him that she had entered into a relationship with a templar. Irving had his suspicions about the father's identity, but refused to say more to the first enchanter.

Wynne gave birth to a healthy baby boy, whom she was allowed one day with before he was taken into Chantry custody. The child, who was named Rhys, was taken to Lydes and from there transferred to the White Spire in Orlais when it was discovered that he, too, was a mage. The identity of Rhys's father remains unknown, though a yellowed page of an unsigned letter found in Wynne's quarters after her death sheds more light on the situation:

"It's a good thing we haven't spoken much since my return. Anger put my mind in disarray and civility would have been damn near impossible. But it is time, and perhaps in writing, I can put into words what I find difficult to say in person.

"You told me you had no choice but to let them take him. Tell that to yourself if you must; we both know it isn't true. You had

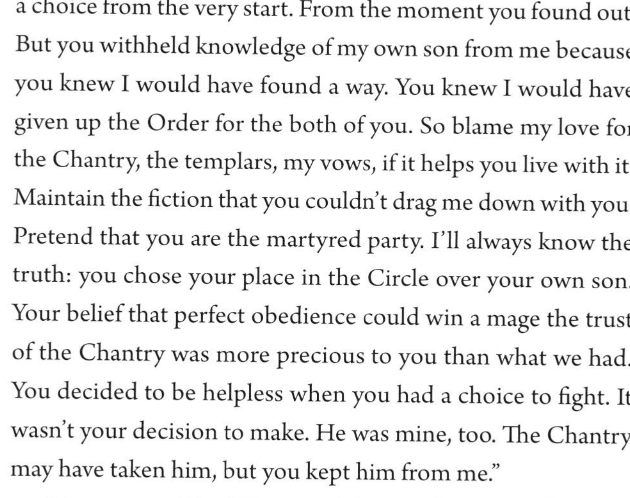

a choice from the very start. From the moment you found out. But you withheld knowledge of my own son from me because you knew I would have found a way. You knew I would have given up the Order for the both of you. So blame my love for the Chantry, the templars, my vows, if it helps you live with it. Maintain the fiction that you couldn't drag me down with you. Pretend that you are the martyred party. I'll always know the truth: you chose your place in the Circle over your own son. Your belief that perfect obedience could win a mage the trust of the Chantry was more precious to you than what we had. You decided to be helpless when you had a choice to fight. It wasn't your decision to make. He was mine, too. The Chantry may have taken him, but you kept him from me."

It is presumed that Wynne and the templar managed to work together in a professional capacity, even though their romantic relationship came to an end. Perhaps understanding emerged with time and distance—or even forgiveness.

Wynne would not come to know her son until decades later, when years of faithful service to the Circle brought her influence enough to demand access to sealed Chantry documents. She showed up at the White Spire in Val Royeaux not long after, asking to see Rhys. Her first words to him were "Good day. I'm your mother."

According to Rhys, they had a meal together, which he described as awkward. It is unknown if Rhys came to know his father at all.

OGHREN

House Kondrat was one of Orzammar's minor Warrior Caste houses. Early in the Dragon Age, it rose from obscurity thanks to several young warriors who earned prestige for the house in the Provings and on Deep Roads campaigns. One of these up-and-coming warriors was Oghren.

Proving His Worth

A young man with fiery red hair and vigor to match, Oghren defeated several decorated challengers at the Provings with his unusual mix of power and unpredictability. According to those he vanquished, Oghren was an expert at baiting his opponents into making them counter his moves, only to change maneuvers at the last moment to hit them where they were open. His signature moves and flourishes made him exciting to watch, and he soon earned himself a loyal following of devotees, many of whom were female.

Though Oghren could have had his pick of women, only one caught his eye: a young member of the Merchant Caste named Felsi. Lingering glances and a few shy words were exchanged, but before the two were able to pursue a

Also legendary was Oghren's ability to down buckets of ale.

The great dwarven city of Orzammar was built overlooking flowing magma, much as surface cities are often found near rivers.

relationship, Oghren found himself engaged to another woman. His rising fame had prompted his family to commit him to a betrothal with a promising smith from a wealthy family—a match advantageous for both houses. Oghren would later speak of his relationship with Felsi, saying, "She was beautiful, kind, funny. Maybe I deserved her once. By the time it happened for us, I didn't."

Oghren married the smith, who was called Branka. Though she was eccentric and seemed more interested in smithing than in her new husband, Oghren remembers the first few months of their union as being relatively happy and peaceful. Within a year of their wedding, however, Branka was named Paragon, and everything changed. All of House Kondrat voted to join the newly noble house. Oghren was now married to the most powerful woman in all of Orzammar, and he became a side note in Branka's life—his house dissolved, his accomplishments forgotten. Oghren found himself harboring a growing resentment that only drink could quell.

In the months after Branka's ascension, the marriage began to fall apart. Oghren was constantly drinking, and Branka spent days away from home, working on her various projects and researching her new obsession: the Anvil of the Void, a dwarven artifact once used to build an army of golems. The couple stopped talking to each other. The Paragon's disdain for her husband influenced the rest of their house, and Oghren found himself shunned by most of his own family.

Branka's Shadow

When Branka took the entire house into the Deep Roads to retrieve the legendary Anvil of the Void, she left Oghren behind. News quickly traveled around Orzammar, and he became a laughingstock. Many publicly speculated about the reasons why he was left behind: stupidity, recklessness, his reliance on ale. None of the theories were particularly flattering. Hoping to forget Branka, Oghren initiated his long-dormant romance with Felsi. The relationship did not last long, as he soon proved that he was no longer the sharp-eyed young warrior he used to be. Felsi ended their affair and left to join her mother on the surface shortly after her father's funeral. Abandoned for a second time, Oghren returned to the warm embrace of drink. When Lord Meino's youngest son joked that Branka and her house were probably dead, he challenged him to a duel to first blood. However, the deeply intoxicated Oghren was unable to control himself and inflicted a fatal wound on the boy. As punishment for the killing, he was stripped of his weapons and forbidden to carry arms within Orzammar. A warrior with no weapons is no warrior, and Oghren was nothing if not a warrior.

Help from the Hero

Stubbornly, Oghren refused to give up on Branka. When much time passed without word of their exploits, he repeatedly—and often drunkenly—petitioned the Assembly and the other warriors to launch an expedition to retrieve Branka's party. Refusing to relent, no matter how many times he was told there would be no rescue, Oghren became something of a pest in Orzammar's Diamond Quarter.

The drunken dwarf finally found a sympathetic ear in the Hero of Ferelden, who sought a Paragon to put an end to the city's succession crisis.

WE DON'T LIVE VERY LONG

Hey there, Nugget:

It's your da. You probably don't remember me, and that's good. You're better off with just your ma. She's a good one. You hang on to her.

There's a big fight coming up, and I thought I should say this before I lose the chance to say it at all. I'm a Grey Warden now, and there's really no way around it—we don't live very long. If not tomorrow, it'll be soon. I just feel it.

Nugget, I want to say that I'm sorry I left. I want the best for you, even if it doesn't seem like it sometimes. Or all the time. But it's true. You were the only good thing that came out of Oghren, after all's said and done.

Not being there was the best I had to give.

Maybe if your ma's all right with it, you can ask her to tell you about the first time we met, when I was a real warrior. I didn't do right by her. I'm trying to do right by you.

Atredum na satolva. Atrast tunsha.

—*A letter addressed to Oghren's child, written shortly before the siege of Vigil's Keep*

Together with Oghren, the Hero ventured into the Deep Roads in search of Branka. What they found down there changed Oghren. He realized that there was nothing left in Orzammar for him and left for the surface, hoping to start anew. Finding Felsi, Oghren rekindled his relationship with her. After the Fifth Blight ended, they married, had a child, and were happy—for a while, anyway.

Unfortunately, Oghren's insecurities and faults ran too deep and began to eat away at their shared joy. He found himself turning back to the ale, much to Felsi's dismay. The second time Oghren dropped their baby, he realized he was not fit to be a father or a husband. He left his family without a word and traveled to Vigil's Keep in Amaranthine, where Ferelden's new Commander of the Grey was rebuilding the Grey Wardens. He volunteered for the Order and took the Joining, becoming a Warden.

SHALE

Before the First Blight, underground dwarven kingdoms existed all over Thedas, ruling the expansive Deep Roads as monuments to their ingenuity. When the darkspawn came and threatened to overrun the dwarves completely, the Paragon Caridin turned to extreme measures to bolster their forces. He created the golems: a union of a dwarf's spirit with a body of stone to form the ultimate warrior. In the end, even the golems could not save the dwarven kingdoms, and the secret to their creation was lost.

The Long Life of a Thinking Rock

Most surviving golems show no evidence of their past life as a dwarf. Their personalities have been subsumed through the use of "control rods," created to instill absolute loyalty in these stone warriors. The golem known as Shale is an anomaly. Her personality returned, perhaps following the destruction of her control rod in 9:30 Dragon, and thus she is unique in being a golem who speaks and thinks and even seems to experience emotions.

While Shale has likely existed for more than a thousand years, her memory of anything before the last thirty years is hazy at best.

Dwarven records from the Shaperate show a "Shayle" of House Cadash, a dwarven warrior who volunteered to undergo Paragon Caridin's process in -255 Ancient and became part of the legendary "Legion of Steel." This legion was formed entirely of golems. Shayle was the only female dwarf to volunteer. The dwarven kingdoms were already crumbling under the weight of the darkspawn onslaught, however, and within a matter of years the demand for Caridin to produce more and more of his golems increased beyond the number of volunteers available.

King Valtor of Orzammar decreed that criminals, the casteless, and the unwanted would now be forced to undergo the process—a decree that ultimately led to Caridin's rebellion.

"It was thought that Valtor's punishment of Caridin would be enough," states one memory kept by the Shaperate. "Caridin would be made into a golem, as compliant as the rest of them . . . but that was not to be. He was the only one who knew how to create the control rods properly, and thus his was incomplete. He kept his mind and his free will, and now he has rebelled and fled with his loyalists into the Deep Roads, along with any means we had of making more golems. King Valtor's greed has doomed us all."

NOTES ON THE HERO OF FERELDEN

ARIANE AND FINN

Magistrate Kingston Aldebrant of West Hill and his wife, Florence, were extremely concerned when a message from Kinloch Hold arrived, informing them that their son, Florian Phineas Horatio Aldebrant, Esquire, also known as Finn, had left the tower on a Circle-sanctioned mission in the company of a Grey Warden, a Dalish elf, and a large dog. Though assured that Finn was well trained and adept at magic, Magistrate Aldebrant and Florence remained convinced that Finn was in danger and required saving to prevent him from being injured—or, worse, killed. Magistrate Aldebrant dedicated much of his considerable wealth toward locating and returning his son to the tower safely.

Investigators hired to track down the group soon discovered that Finn was assisting the Wardens in locating and apprehending a Witch of the Wilds. Finn's quest took him all over Thedas, from the Frostbacks all the way to the coastal region of Amaranthine. A letter to Magistrate Aldebrant details an encounter with Finn and the Dalish elf, after they had left the company of the Warden and the dog, and struck out on their own. According to the letter, the magistrate's men intercepted the two and narrowly escaped being impaled and fried by Dalish sword and mage spell. After being forced to drop their weapons, the investigators informed Finn of his parents' concern and urged him to return to the tower. The writer of the letter had this to say about Finn's response: "I am quite aggrieved to report that your son sighed and then advised me to 'leave in order to engage in an act of self-gratification,' though in far fewer, and infinitely harsher, words. I say with some certainty that Finn is no longer the soft, nervous boy you remember."

Finn later returned to his father's house to explain himself and say goodbye. Accompanying him was the Dalish elf, whom he introduced as Ariane. Much to Mistress Florence's chagrin, Ariane managed to sample every single food item in her pantry and cheerfully expressed a weakness for "shemlen" pickles. Before they departed, Finn returned a ghastly knitted hat to his mother and changed out of his immaculately clean robes, voicing the desire to exchange them in favor of "something leather."

At Wilhelm's Side

Shale, as a golem, was sent away by Caridin prior to his rebellion, but what became of her after that is unknown. Presumably, she fought to preserve the dwarven kingdoms until they were lost and the Deep Roads were completely overrun. Perhaps she was sent with the rest of the Legion of Steel to search for Caridin, and lost with them when they did not return. Either way, Shale was was lost in the Deep Roads and remained there, inert, waiting for someone to find her control rod and reactivate her.

A Fereldan enchanter by the name of Wilhelm, a mage who ventured into the Deep Roads from time to time in search of treasure, found Shale in 8:93 Blessed.

"It is rather remarkable. No, it is more than remarkable—it is a gift sent by the Maker," he wrote. "A shriek chased me for two days, somehow seeing through the wards I conjured, and in my terror, I found myself going into a part of the Deep Roads I knew not at all. Certain I was lost there, and that I would die either of hunger or by darkspawn, I was all but ready to lay down in despair. Then I came upon it: a magnificent golem and, beside it, the control rod.

"Would someone other than me have even known what the rod was? Doubtful. I have read more than one dusty dwarven tome that spoke of ancient Caridin and his methods. I instantly knew the rod when I laid eyes upon it. Would someone less brilliant have figured out how to use the rod to activate the golem? Also doubtful. But with a little tinkering, that behemoth of stone, all but encrusted in lichen and cobwebs, lurched to life before me. I had not only found a means to fight my way back to the surface, but perhaps also to leave my mark upon history."

With Shale at his side, Wilhelm made for a valuable ally in Ferelden's rebellion against Orlesian occupation, first with Queen Moira Theirin and then with her son, Maric. After Maric's victory and coronation as king, Wilhelm took his golem and retired to the remote village of Honnleath—protected from any duties as a Circle enchanter through his appointment as a court advisor. King Maric never once called him to Denerim to act as such.

It was a degree of freedom and impunity almost unheard of for apostates, and Wilhelm evidently took the status in stride.

"You should see the way he walks around the village with that . . . that statue following behind him," wrote one villager at the time. "He gets it to do everything. It carries his baskets, moves things out of the way that he can't be arsed to walk around, opens doors. Sometimes it even carries him when he's too tired to walk. The rest of us are supposed to ooh and aah at his impressive statue, I suppose. It is impressive; don't get me wrong. I'm told his wife complained about it damaging the doorway,

village folk eventually forgot Wilhelm's grisly murder and stopped worrying that Shale might one day come back to life. The golem became a fixture of Honnleath like any other, and was ignored.

Dagna, once a resident of Orzammar, later served the Inquisition as its arcanist.

Shale's Rebirth

It was not until many years later, in 9:30 Dragon, that the Hero of Ferelden found Shale's control rod and reactivated her. Shale revealed that she had been completely conscious during her deactivation, aware of everything that transpired in Honnleath around her, even as she was unable to move. She remembered nothing, however, of how Wilhelm had been killed and very little of her life prior. It was revealed that Wilhelm had been experimenting upon the control rod, and it was speculated that this was the reason for his death—and perhaps also the reason that Shale was now able to speak, evincing much of the personality of the dwarf she had been.

Following the events of the Fifth Blight, she accompanied a small group from the White Spire to the Warden fortress Adamant to investigate the experiments of a Tranquil named Pharamond. The research he conducted at the fortress resulted in a method to revers e a mage's Rite of Tranquility, albeit by putting the Tranquil mage in danger of demonic possession. Shale helped save Pharamond from the clutches of a demon and was last seen bound for the Circle of Montsimmard. Her whereabouts are now unknown.

so he took a chisel and made it smaller, but now he expects us to fawn over his skill at having done so—and not, say, worry why the templars don't take him away before either his magic or his statue end up killing us all one night. With any luck, that statue will end up killing him."

Indeed, while the exact circumstances are unknown, it seems that Shale *did* kill Wilhelm. In 9:04 Dragon, he was found crumpled and dead at Shale's feet, with Shale now inert and motionless. Her control rod was still in Wilhelm's hands, but no one knew how to use it. Perhaps if someone did, they feared what reactivating the golem might do. The rod was eventually sold as a historical curiosity of sorts. With no way to move or damage the golem, Shale was left where she stood: in the middle of Honnleath, gathering dust and moss. The

Shale isn't simply a golem as we have come to know them. Not any longer. She is a creature possessed of her own thoughts, capable of self-determination and emotion. I would wonder what goes on inside her mind, were she not so willing to tell me. Her moods, her irritation with us "creatures of flesh and water," her outrage at any winged beast that dares to be in her presence . . . This is no longer a mindless warrior. In that body of stone, Shale is immortal, and one wonders what will become of her in the ages to come. A creature so unique may, in the span of time, also discover herself completely alone.

—**Senior Enchanter Rhys (Aequitarian)**

STEN OF THE BERESAAD

The legacy of the hornless Qunari known simply as Sten is colored by acts of great violence. Depending on who is speaking, Sten is either a Qunari criminal who murdered a farming couple and their children over a lost sword, or a misunderstood hero, redeemed by his allegiance to the Hero of Ferelden in a time of great need.

The Curious Qunari

The beresaad give the task of guarding the port of Seheron to their youngest soldiers. It's a relatively easy job that mostly requires a tolerance for boredom and the ability to pay close attention even after hours of inactivity. There are occasional threats to the security of the city—assassins, unauthorized spies, infiltrators—and the beresaad guards, most of them under eighteen years of age, are the first line of defense for thousands of people.

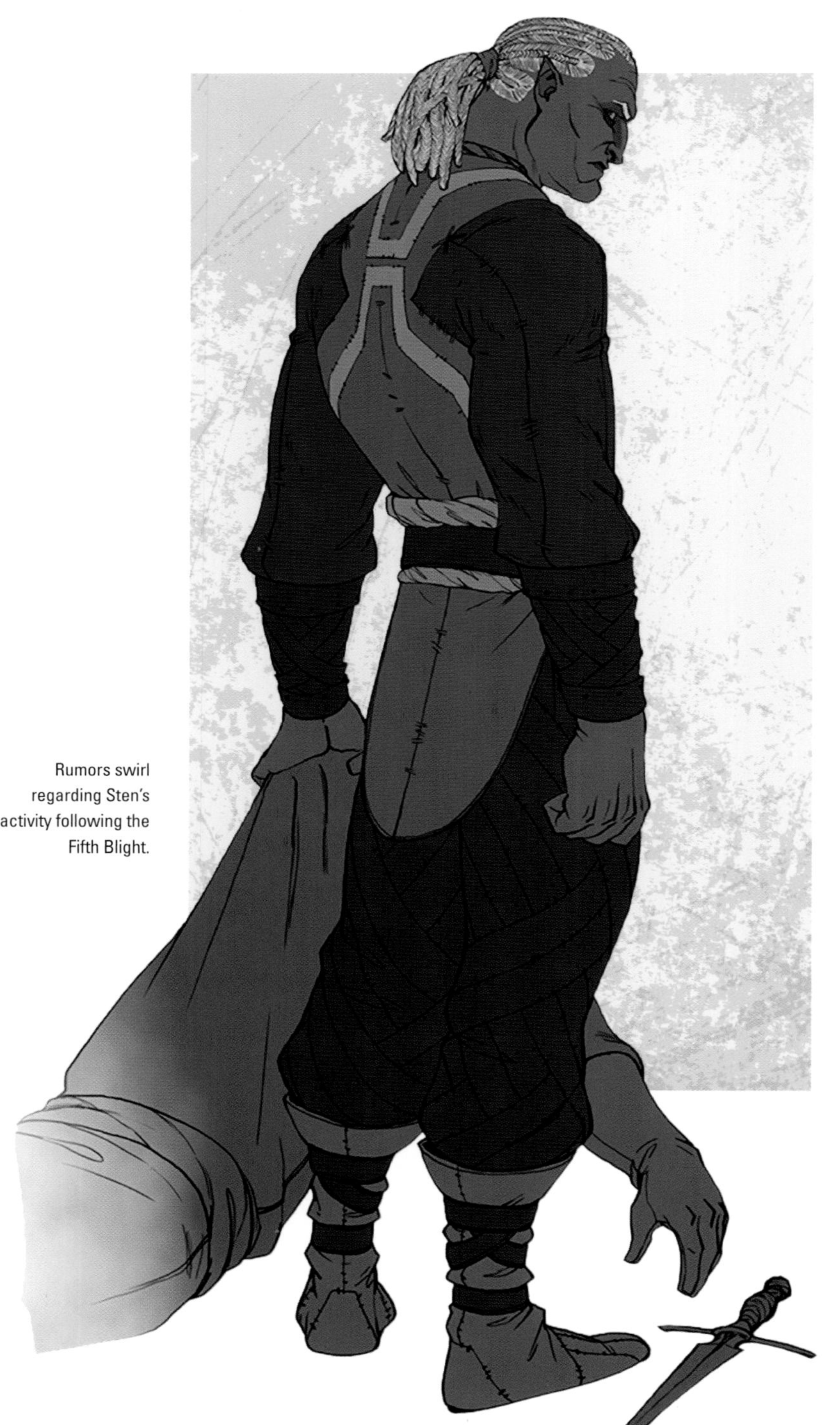

Rumors swirl regarding Sten's activity following the Fifth Blight.

The first reports surfaced in 9:03 Dragon of the soldier who would first become Sten of the beresaad and later, if rumors are to be believed, Arishok. Antivan Crows paid to infiltrate the city described a very young soldier, entirely lacking horns, stationed at the port. From their correspondence with Antiva City:

> We spent two hours arguing with the old Qunari fellow who chooses, apparently by whim, which traders are allowed into the enclave beyond the gates, and the entire time, this hornless boy soldier watched us with an odd intensity. When we finally gave up for the day and turned to leave, I heard a voice say, "Silver."
>
> I stopped. The oxmen do not *volunteer* conversation with strangers. I have hardly even heard them speak to one another. I whirled around to see who had spoken, and it was the hornless boy, who was staring at me.
>
> "I beg your pardon?" I said.
>
> "Silver," he repeated. "What does it mean?"
>
> "It's a precious metal," I replied, a bit nonplussed.
>
> "And that's why you are here." In that irritating Qunari way, it was a question and a statement at the same time.
>
> "Yes?" At this point, the others had gathered to watch the spectacle of an actual, talking Qunari. Or my bafflement, which I'm sure was equally entertaining to the lazy bastards.
>
> "Is that all?" the boy asked.
>
> "I don't know what you're implying." I was, at this point, certain he'd made us.
>
> "Is that all 'silver' means? A kind of metal." He clarified with that irritating stoic patience all Qunari have.
>
> "Well, it also means the color of the metal." Behind me, my ever-professional associate Liza snickered. "And some of the things made from it. Coins, eating utensils, and candlesticks . . ."
>
> "And that's why you are here," he repeated.
>
> We excused ourselves and quickly left.

Several Rivaini traders note the young soldier in their missives home. Hornless Qunari are a rare sight, but curious Qunari are unheard of. This boy soldier was said to interrogate nearly every delegation entering or leaving the port during the three years he was stationed there, and in most cases, his questions pertained to language. A Ghana visiting the city from Seere later told her court that the boy "for hours asked question after question about the word 'hand.' He could not understand how one could tell whether it was being used as a verb or a noun and had many inquiries as to whether other limbs and body parts were also actions in the common tongue. The discovery that one could, in fact, *eye* a ship, dis-*arm* her crew, and *leg* away before being caught greatly concerned him."

While the city of Seheron might have been a relatively safe post, the rest of the island was not. The Qunari lost scores of soldiers to skirmishes in the jungle. Tal-Vashoth, fog warriors, Tevinters, even the wildlife claimed lives. But those who escaped death still weren't safe. An ailment the Qunari call asala-taar, or "soul sickness," spread among the ranks of the survivors. Both older, experienced soldiers as well as new members of the antaam were equally susceptible, and for every soldier who fell in battle, two more had to be sent back to Par Vollen for treatment. Most of those were reassigned among the priesthood or the workers and never returned to combat. The tamassrans struggled to keep up with the losses and petitioned the Ariqun to more aggressively seek out a cure for the illness. In the meantime, the antaam promoted and lost officers at astonishing rates.

Excellent Knowledge

The young Sten-to-be was sent into the interior and disappeared from outside notice for several years. Records of him next surface during the Qunari assault on the Tevinter mainland. In 9:12 Dragon, the Kathaban of the Qunari navy brought an entire fleet of warships, including a dozen dreadnoughts, against the mainland city of Qarinus, closest to Seheron. The entire beresaad kith, divided among the ships, was sent with the navy to take point in the battle as the ships made landfall. On the Kathaban's own dreadnought, *Meraad-athlok*, the beresaad were led by a young karasaad with no horns and an excellent working knowledge of both the common tongue and Tevene.

The Kathaban's attacks initially made great progress, but the Qunari footholds in Tevinter, as always, were eventually torn apart by Tevinter legions heavily reinforced by mages. The Kathaban was forced to call off his offensive and return his forces to Seheron to defend the island. The entire antaam took this new failure hard, but none more than the Kathaban, who relinquished his role and returned to Par Vollen to be Kathaban no more.

According to reports from Tevinter spies in Par Vollen, in the aftermath of the defeat, the young beresaad officer voiced concerns to the Arishok about the Qunari strategy in Tevinter.

The darkspawn corrupt even the purest souls.

"The argument went on for some time and was notable, not only because Qunari argue so rarely, but because it is unheard of for an officer of any rank to disagree with the Arishok," wrote an unnamed spy in a report to the Archon at the time. "Our man couldn't get close enough to hear everything that was said, but it seemed that the young vanguard believed that the mainland could not be taken by direct assault and the antaam should divert more of its resources to information gathering if victory in the South was ever to be obtained. The Arishok, fortunately, dismissed the idea as ridiculous, but Minrathous should be warned. The last thing we need is for the damned oxmen to learn subtlety or politics."

Proving himself a valuable and honorable member of the beresaad, Sten eventually found his way far from Qunari

NOTES ON THE HERO OF FERELDEN

ZEVRAN ARAINAI

The Antivan Crows are more than a guild of assassins. In their homeland of Antiva, they are a political force to be reckoned with, controlling the nation through influence and intimidation. Elsewhere in Thedas, they are renowned as unrivaled hired killers.

This unsigned letter shines some light on how Zevran Arainai, the elven Crow, came to be in Ferelden during the Fifth Blight:

Guildmaster,

I have looked into the assassin Zevran, as you asked. The elf in question first came to the Crows in 9:12 Dragon as compradi—he was purchased from a house of ill repute in Rialto, where he had been raised since the death of his mother, a former Dalish put to work in the house in order to pay off the debts of her husband (another contract of ours, executed in 9:04 Dragon). She died in childbirth, and thus the boy was reared by the whores and learned what boys do in that situation.

Even at the age of seven, he was considered cunning and skilled enough as a thief that Guildmaster Talav paid off what remained of the debt and brought him under House Arainai—at that point still First Talon, if you'll recall. The house was flush with coin after the Three Brides contract, and the elven boy was one of eighteen compradi purchased that year. It's worth noting that he was one of only two to survive. The other was a human boy named Taliesen, purchased from a Tevinter wreck at Llomerryn.

Everything I've found in the records states that neither Zevran nor Taliesen showed any particular promise in the early years of their training. Certainly Talav never noted it in his records, though I would not put it past him to conceal as much. They both went through all the regular ordeals, the tests for pain resistance, the gauntlets—but it was not until the arrival of a woman by the name of Rinnala in 9:16 Dragon that they began to really matter. Rinnala came to House Arainai through the Azul contract, meaning she was yet another of Prince Estefan's bastards for us to hide away, and as the Arainai had fallen to Second Talon by that point, it was their turn.

This was, as is noted, exceptionally lucky for Talav, as the three assassins complemented each other well. Zevran excelled at seduction and poison, Taliesen was the warrior, and Rinnala (or "Rinna," as Talav's notes often name her) was the planner. They formed a team that was exceptional enough to be apprenticed as a single unit by Master Eoman Arainai.

This was, of course, around the same time that the fortunes of House Arainai truly began to change. You'll remember Talav's execution following his attempt to retake First Talon. Zevran and his fellows were still far too junior to have been involved in that debacle. They did, however, receive a great deal of work when Isidora took over from Talav. As inept a grandmaster as she ultimately was, Isidora had ambition and took any contract she could. Thus, Zevran was involved in the completion of no fewer than seventeen missions prior to Isidora's ignominious death in 9:24 Dragon. Her passing was enough to plunge House Arainai into the ranks of the cuchillos. But at the same time, Master Eoman's star rose, due in no small part to the work of this trio of young assassins.

Eoman took over as the head of House Arainai in 9:26 Dragon, eager to become a grandmaster by eliminating House Ferragani as Eighth Talon. His efforts served him well. He made alliances, earned accolades by selectively taking daring contracts (I had no idea prior to this investigation that Zevran was the assassin behind the remarkable death of Condesa Lupana in 9:27—we all assumed Eoman had done that job himself), but fell short of actually achieving his goal until 9:28 Dragon.

I believe you were involved in that business with the Rosso Noche, yes? Then you'll recall that the cult had found a legitimate heir to King Natale, though they wouldn't say who. It seems the heir in question was Rinnala. The girl was evidently too smart for her own good, tying her fate to those fanatics. Though I suppose it might have worked out had Prince Claudio not heard of it—or, rather, been told the details in exchange for a great deal of coin. House Valisti was Third Talon at the time, and eager for the possibility of pressing a claim for one of their own, so a deal was worked out with Master Eoman to eliminate Rinnala quietly in exchange for Arainai gaining Eighth Talon.

It worked. As the notes claim, Zevran and Taliesen eliminated Rinnala themselves and were told that it was part of a test. Which it was, I imagine, though perhaps not quite in the way they believed. Master Eoman became grandmaster the very next month with two effective and clearly loyal assassins at his disposal. All ended well, yes?

Evidently not. At this point, I need to read between the lines regarding what followed, but my belief is that Zevran took the death of Rinnala rather poorly. The three were extremely close—connected romantically, as tends to happen with trios who remain together for so long. He became resentful of the Crows' test of his loyalty, and although his performance in subsequent contracts appeared unaffected, I'm willing to bet this was the doing of Taliesen, working to cover for him. I believe that when Zevran bid for the sole contract on the Fereldan Wardens in 9:30 Dragon, it was not the brash bid for master rank everyone suspected, but rather a way to commit suicide.

Conjecture? Yes, I suppose it is. Still, nothing I've read about this Zevran said he was ambitious enough to reach for master, nor interested in working on his own. We also know that the contract failed, and I like to think that if Zevran had truly desired to see it to its conclusion, it would have succeeded. It worked out in the end, naturally, as the Hero of Ferelden proved to be the answer to the Blight that the council had initially seen in Teyrn Loghain, but we didn't know that at the time… and neither did he.

We do not know what became of Zevran after that point. Was he slain by the Hero of Ferelden or made into an ally? Taliesen was sent by Grandmaster Eoman to discover the truth, and himself disappeared. Sadly, the chaos in Ferelden both before and after the Blight has made any sort of investigation almost impossible. I do, however, find it rather telling that Eoman died four months after the Blight in Ferelden ended, with evidence showing a Crow responsible, even though no contract was ever issued for him. Four other members of House Arainai followed in similar fashion over the next three years, returning the house to obscurity. Then both Grandmaster Runn and Grandmaster Availa died, again at the hands of an unknown assassin.

I agree with your belief that it is Zevran who is our ghost, this so-called "Black Shadow." He has plunged the Antivan Crows into chaos and has almost certainly allied with elements of the cuchillos to overthrow us. If we do not find him, and stop him, this elven son of a whore—an assassin who never even attained the rank of master—will undo us all.

lands—sent as part of a group to investigate signs of the Blight in southern Ferelden. When he lost his sword, he lost his honor and his freedom. But it was never clear if he lost his life.

The Antivan Crow known as Zevran was hired by Loghain to assassinate the Hero of Ferelden.

Well after the events of the Fifth Blight, rumors that Sten had replaced the disgraced Arishok spread and greatly alarmed Minrathous. If they are true, many believe the war with the Qunari could finally find a victor.

THE BATTLE OF OSTAGAR

Duncan and the Hero traveled to the ruined fortress of Ostagar near the Korcari Wilds to prepare for a battle with the rising darkspawn. It was at this fortress that the Hero and the recruits Jory and Daveth underwent their Joining ritual to become Grey Wardens. Only the Hero survived.

Together with Alistair and led by King Cailan, the king's troops and the predominantly Orlesian Wardens fought a great battle against the corrupted creatures. The plan was to hit from two sides. While a front led by Cailan and Duncan engaged the darkspawn head-on, the Warden and Alistair would light a beacon to signal warmaster Loghain Mac Tir, who was waiting with troops to flank the enemy. When the beacon was lit, however, Loghain instead ordered his troops to retreat, giving up the battlefield and leaving the king and the Wardens to fight to their deaths.

Of the Wardens who fought at Ostagar, only Alistair and the Hero survived—saved by Flemeth and nursed back to health in her home deep in the Korcari Wilds. Back on their feet, Alistair and the Hero joined up with Morrigan on a journey to unite Ferelden against the Blight by invoking the Wardens' ancient treaties and delivering justice to the traitorous Teyrn Loghain, who'd used the defeat at Ostagar to seize power in Denerim.

LOGHAIN

History will remember Teyrn Loghain Mac Tir as many things: a war hero who fought beside King Maric to retake Ferelden from its Orlesian occupiers; a decorated general with an irreplaceable mind for strategy; the attentive, if absent, teyrn of Gwaren. But to most, Loghain was a traitor: the usurper of the throne of Ferelden during the Fifth Blight. A cold man of stubborn character who refused to trust anyone but himself, Loghain displayed a poverty of judgment and distrust of the Wardens during the height of the Blight that might have doomed Ferelden, if not for the actions of the Hero.

While much has been written about Loghain's time at Maric's side and his treachery during the Blight, less has been said about his time in Gwaren.

The New Teyrn

The skill to plan a battle and rule a domain are not the same, and it is rare that they occur in a single person simultaneously. King Maric gave the vacant teyrnir of Gwaren to his close friend and advisor Loghain Mac Tir in order to elevate him to nobility, but the gift came with a serious drawback. Gwaren had suffered under the Orlesian occupation for years and was in a state of deep disrepair. Because of its remote location, no Orlesian governor had ever wanted to reside in the castle. Decades of neglect had left it nearly in ruins. The roof in the great hall had collapsed. Rain had flooded much of the living area. Birds nested in the rafters of the kitchen and the larder—and such a vast colony of rats lived in the basement that it might have been considered its own kingdom.

Upon arriving in Gwaren for the first time since he helped liberate it, Loghain took one look at his new home and gave it up for lost. He lived out of a tent pitched in the middle of

The old village of Crestwood was flooded when it was overrun by darkspawn.

the courtyard while he tried to bring the port into order and recruit an army capable of defending the teyrnir.

After a month of watching their new teyrn live among them like a transient and suspecting that this new lord was just as likely as the Orlesians to abandon the keep and the village, the people of Gwaren sent a representative to speak with Loghain. Maeve, who came from a long line of cabinetmakers, possessed patience, attention to detail, and very little tolerance for those who neglect to care for their furniture. She had a word with the newly appointed lord, which turned into an argument, which turned into a shouting match. In the end, she calmly reminded the Hero of River Dane that no matter what King Maric said, he wouldn't be teyrn of anything unless his freeholders swore fealty, and if he left Castle Gwaren crumbling and empty, not one knee would bend to him.

After cursing the stubbornness of his fellow Fereldans in general and Gwaren cabinetmakers in particular, Loghain had no choice but to divert some of his attention to repairing the keep. The first thing he did was hire Maeve to supervise the work.

Two months later, he asked her to marry him.

Anora's Youth in Transit

The early years of Maric's reign were filled with unease. The king was too new, the Bannorn had grown too used to fighting and too unaccustomed to politics, and the threat of invasion was too great. Loghain spent much time in Denerim with the king and left ruling Gwaren to his wife. Teyrna Maeve was neither a soldier nor a strategist, but she was an incomparable foreman, and the teyrnir rebuilt itself under her guidance. For the first time in almost an age, the port was in working order, the roads were maintained, and the lumber mills were running every day.

However, by 9:10 Dragon, Maeve had begun to worry that her husband's absences from Gwaren were taking a toll on their young daughter, Anora. Loghain spent more than half of every year away in Denerim, and could not be spared by King Maric. In fact, Maric left Loghain on the throne in his place that year during his disappearance. The teyrna knew her husband would never forsake his duty to his king, but her stubbornness was a match for his. Their argument spawned at least one rumor of dragons roosting in the castle, but the outcome was foregone. Loghain began to take their young daughter with him on his trips to the capital. This had two immediate results: First, that his trips were necessarily shorter in duration, and second, that the Hero of River Dane quickly became an expert in braiding the little girl's hair. He also learned how to convert the tales of his bloody battles into bedtime stories for children, how to interrupt talks with leaders of the Bannorn to tend to skinned knees, and how to sneak cookies into cabinet meetings. Anora flourished under the new regimen, and perhaps as a side effect, so did he.

King Maric's death in 9:25 Dragon and Anora's marriage to the newly crowned Cailan Theirin put an end to Loghain's visits to Denerim for a time. He returned to Gwaren and Teyrna Maeve, and for three years he remained there in relative peace and quiet. In 9:28 the king, the queen, and the entire Fereldan royal court traveled to the remote castle for the funeral of Teyrna Maeve. When they left, Loghain left with them, never to return.

Loghain, longtime advisor to the Fereldan throne, betrayed his people when they needed him most.

CAUTHRIEN

Ser Cauthrien came to Loghain's service by chance. She belonged to a poor family and was out doing work on the farm when she saw a man on horseback being attacked by several bandits. Having no idea that he was skilled enough to deal with the men on his own, she rushed to his assistance, and found out belatedly that the man she'd "saved" was none other than Loghain, Hero of River Dane. He took her in, offering her a position with his soldiers, and she rose through the ranks through sheer determination.

Cauthrien worshiped Loghain as a hero and was extremely proud of her country—believing that by serving him she was serving Ferelden in the best way she could. Becoming his knight and right hand was the proudest moment of her life, and her commitment to him remained until the end of his short reign over Blight-torn Ferelden.

A portrait of Cauthrien in Gwaren's resurrected keep, commissioned because of her service to the village and its then-celebrated teyrn, was defaced and subsequently removed following the Battle of Ostagar. She is mentioned here because history may otherwise forget her.

ANORA

Queen Anora, daughter of disgraced Teyrn Loghain and widow to King Cailan, was never one to stay quietly in the background. It is common knowledge that in the five years Anora and Cailan held the throne together, she was wielding the power. In the period before his death, Anora was held in much higher esteem than her husband by the people of Ferelden, nobility and commoners alike, and commanded the respect even of foreign nations, having once inspired Empress Celene of Orlais to declare, "Anora of Ferelden is a solitary rose among brambles."

Few were surprised that, with a father like Loghain Mac Tir, Anora grew into such a capable and quick-witted figure of authority. But for all her restraint in adulthood, her youth was marked by significant rebellion.

KING CAILAN'S PRIVATE CORRESPONDENCE

To His Majesty, King Cailan of Ferelden:

My Warden-Commander assures me that we face a Blight. This thing threatens us both, and we must work together to fight it, lest it devour all. Our two nations have not had a happy history, but that is all it is—history. It is the future that is at stake now. Let us put aside our fathers' disagreements so that we may secure a future for both our countries.

My chevaliers stand ready and will accompany the Grey Wardens of Orlais to Ferelden. At your word the might of Orlais will march to reinforce the Fereldan forces.

Sincerely,
Empress Celene I

Your Majesty,

My men will arrive as soon as possible to bolster your forces. Maker willing, this Blight will be ended before it has begun.

Cailan, I beseech you, as your uncle, not to join the Grey Wardens on the field. You cannot afford to take this risk. Ferelden cannot afford it. Let me remind you again that you do not have an heir. Your death—and it pains me even to think of it—would plunge Ferelden into chaos.

And yes, perhaps when this is over you will allow me to bring up the subject of your heir. While a son from both the Theirin and the Mac Tir lines would unite Ferelden like no other, we must accept that perhaps this can never be. The queen approaches her thirtieth year, and her ability to give you a child lessens with each passing month. I submit to you again that it might be time to put Anora aside. We parted harshly the last time I spoke of this, but it has been a full year since then and nothing has changed.

Please, nephew, consider my words, and Andraste's grace be with you.

Eamon

This letter appears to have been crumpled then carefully smoothed out and folded again:

Cailan,

The visit to Ferelden will be postponed indefinitely, due to the darkspawn problem. You understand, of course? The darkspawn have odd timing, don't they? Let us deal with them first. Once that is done we can further discuss a permanent alliance between Orlais and Ferelden.

Celene

Trouble at West Hills

No complete records exist of the West Hills incident. The few accounts that have been tracked down are second- or thirdhand at best and filled with such wild impossibilities as to render them little better than rumors.

The only verified fact of the matter is that in the summer of 9:23 Dragon, a freeholder from a farm in the West Hills arling traveled to Denerim to petition King Maric for help. According to official notes by the court scribe, the farmer was in hysterics and insisted that a hundred giants had taken over his farm and that the king must send the army at once. As giants are almost unheard of in Ferelden and certainly are rarely seen in groups larger than two, Maric sent a scout to investigate the freehold and report back. After ten days, the scout did not return, and Maric began talks with Arl Wulf of West Hills about the problem.

Prince Cailan is on record as having interrupted the king's council with the captain of the Royal Guard by volunteering to go and drive off the giants, but he was told the matter was already handled. The next morning, the prince had vanished, putting the entire city of Denerim into a state of alarm and suspending all regular business while the guard and the king searched for him.

Some nine days later, the scout who had been presumed dead, the crown prince, and Lady Anora Mac Tir were found together in the village of Crestwood in West Hills arling, drunk as dwarves, covered in bruises, cuts, and ash, and smelling strangely of cheese.

The tavern keeper in Crestwood, Angus, gave the following testimony to the Royal Guard:

> Maybe six days ago they come in, the lad with the blond hair was all cloaked, but I could see he was half-purple like he'd come out second best in a fight with the ground. The lady was all but carrying him, and asked about a healer, but the lad kept insisting he needed ale, kegs of ale, a cartload. I told him we didn't have that much on hand, but there was a brewer at the edge of the lake might. So away they went. Come back again just yesterday with the soldier, spending coin like it weren't nothing at all, not saying a word, just laughing now and then like mad folks. If the king wants them, he can have them. Those two are trouble if I ever laid eyes on it.

The brewer's house was locked up, and the owners were clearly away, but the guard found that a storehouse had been broken into and a wagon and some two dozen kegs had been stolen.

At the freehold, the Royal Guard found the tracks of a giant, but not the giant itself. Empty ale kegs littered the ground in all the pastures. None of the dairy's three dozen cows could be located anywhere, but searchers found remains of only two carcasses, and the farm's cheese room was entirely bereft of cheese, though the farmer insisted he had several hundred wheels aging and almost ready for market.

Hoofprints led into a forest on the eastern edge of the farm, where a terrified woodcutter relayed the following account:

> I heard voices out in the forest a little after sundown. Someone was shouting about "glory" and "history," and as I crept closer, I was almost killed by stampeding cattle! I climbed a tree to get out of their path, and from up there, I saw some kind of spirit, all golden, shouting at the forest and saying, "I command you to go back! I command it!" I thought it was blood magic at work, so I ran out of there fast as I could.

Almost a week later, scouts found the remains of a burned giant at the bottom of a cliff almost a mile from the freehold.

The scout who had disappeared, Lieutenant Dara, later made the following report to the king:

> I arrived at the dairy farm near dusk and found exactly one giant had, in fact, taken up residence and was eating one of the dairy cows in the middle of the south pasture. I tried to sneak around west and north along the perimeter of the farm to look for any of the supposed "hundred" other giants, but the one in the south pasture spotted me and gave chase.
>
> I wound up running for my life, trying to lose the brute by dodging through the freehold's outbuildings, but the monster was too fast. He was nearly upon me, so I dove into what turned out to be a root cellar where he couldn't fit or reach me. I stayed still, and I guess the smell of turnips and onions in the cellar was overpowering enough that he decided I was gone. I tried to wait for him to move before sneaking out to report back, but he camped out in the middle of the farm, only about thirty feet from my hiding place, so I was stuck down there. For days. Not sure how many. Until the prince and Lady Anora found me.
>
> When I emerged from hiding, the giant was gone, all the cattle were gone, the air was full of ash, the stink of burned hair, and an odd whiff of cheese, and when I asked what had happened, Lady Anora just said, "We're going to get a drink. A lot of drinks. Maybe all the drinks they have. Come on."

Prince Cailan would give no answers to questions posed by his father, the Royal Guard, or the arl of West Hills. When pressed on the subject, he would pause dramatically and say, "It's better that the people of Ferelden never know the lengths to which their prince must go to protect them." When Lady Anora was asked, she merely said, "We defeated the giant. Now, let's never speak of this again."

Queen Anora was rebellious in her youth.

REDCLIFFE

Not every force in Ferelden fought in Ostagar. The troops in service to Eamon Guerrin, the arl of Redcliffe, did not participate. Cailan, it seemed, felt he could handle the fight without them.

When the Hero's party sought Eamon to help unite the nation against the Blight, they found Redcliffe in chaos. Eamon was ailing and incapacitated, poisoned by a blood mage named Jowan working for Loghain. Eamon's wife, Isolde, believed only the ashes of Andraste herself might cure him—and sent troops out in search of them, however impossible a task this seemed. The remaining soldiers then turned on the townspeople after the Guerrins' mage son, Connor, was possessed by a demon of desire in the midst of a misguided attempt to help his father.

It is said that to save Redcliffe and Eamon, the Hero traveled to the Temple of Sacred Ashes near Haven to retrieve Andraste's remains with the help of famed Chantry scholar Brother Ferdinand Genitivi. The Hero's party cut down any undead at Redcliffe and, with some degree of controversy, restored Eamon's health.

Together, with the help of the Hero's party, they would unite the disparate people of Ferelden to take on Loghain and end the Blight.

ARL EAMON

Though Queen Rowan was well respected, there was some apprehension when her brother, Eamon Guerrin, succeeded his father as arl of Redcliffe. A quiet young man, Eamon had spent the better part of his youth in the Free Marches due to Ferelden's occupation. Some questioned his ability to rule anything—let alone an arling still reeling from the war with Orlais. It was clear early on that Eamon did not possess the easy charm that endears a ruler to peers and public. However, what he lacked in charisma, he made up for in good-natured pragmatism and an earnest affection for his homeland.

A pair of Orlesian governors had been placed in charge of Redcliffe during the Orlesian occupation. When Eamon returned to claim his place as arl, he found the Orlesians unwilling to retreat so easily. He joined the resistance in removing the last of Orlais's forces from Redcliffe and its surroundings. It was during this time that he caught the attention of Isolde, a girl four years his junior and daughter to one of the governors. Having spent her formative years in Redcliffe, Isolde was drawn to the idea of resistance and those fighting for a place she had grown to love herself; in particular, she fancied the young Fereldan who claimed the right to be arl. While her infatuation proved one-sided at the time, Isolde's interest in his cause was not deterred. She offered information to the resistance and, when the Orlesians were eventually driven out, elected to stay in Denerim with a cousin who had married a Fereldan. As she declared somewhat dramatically in her diary: "My heart is here for many reasons. I'm not leaving. They can't make me."

Having reclaimed his lands, Eamon quickly turned his attention to helping the arling recover. His efforts resulted in improvements to trade and security for Redcliffe and its surroundings. No stranger to the court at Denerim, Eamon made

Redcliffe Castle overlooks Lake Calenhad.

The forests of Ferelden hide terrible threats.

regular visits to the capital. His calm practicality earned the respect of his brother-in-law, King Maric, and the young arl soon found himself among the king's advisors. "Eamon's as loyal as a mabari," Maric once proclaimed, not knowing how true his statement would prove. In the years to come, Eamon took in Alistair, a child he was told was the king's son, asking few questions and providing the boy with a home. He later served as advisor to his nephew, King Cailan.

It was on a trip to Denerim, six years after their initial meeting, that Eamon again crossed paths with Isolde. The capital was not a comfortable place for Isolde. With her Orlesian accent and familial connections, she was seen as an enemy at best, outright accused of being one at worst. Except by Eamon. Now a young woman, Isolde evoked an animation few had seen in the arl. Afternoons were lost to cheerful tours of the city, evenings to hushed conversation. "It seems our secrets are safe with Eamon, unless the enemy has a pretty ear," Arl Rendon Howe once remarked during a banquet. It was a clear attempt to curry favor with Maric, who disapproved of Eamon's relationship with the Orlesian. But if the court thought Eamon's loyalty meant he would bow to their pettier whims, they were mistaken.

"I see no enemies here," Eamon replied, "only a lady of Ferelden—and the lady of Redcliffe, if she will consent to it." The two were married within a month.

While Isolde trusted in her husband's support, she remained uncomfortable among Ferelden's nobility—an insecurity exacerbated by the impending birth of the couple's only child. Long-buried gossip pegging Alistair as Eamon's bastard began to resurface. Conception had not been easy, and an anxious Isolde became fixated on the idea of her husband's "proper Fereldan son." Though Eamon denied the claims, he kept Alistair's suspected origins a secret, and Isolde's doubts grew. Unable to bear his wife's heartbreak, Eamon sent the boy to a monastery. Though Alistair's anger broke Eamon's heart, he kept it from Isolde. Fortunately for the couple, the uneasy tension that arose between them would soon give way to happiness.

Connor Guerrin was born on an exceptionally warm afternoon and had the immediate affection of his father. The war with Orlais had forced Eamon from his country, and he was determined to impress upon his son the glory of Ferelden. The toddler Connor was often seen surveying his future arling from atop Eamon's shoulders—an arling he would never rule.

An entry from Isolde's diary marks the end of their familial bliss: "The room was so cold. Poor Connor was crying. He says a new room won't make it better, but the one down the hall is less prone to drafts. My sweet boy, never wishing to cause trouble."

Isolde eventually admitted to herself that Connor was a mage. Terrified of losing her son to the Circle, she concealed the truth from Eamon and begged Connor to do the same. The boy's loyal heart and quiet nature, so reminiscent of his father's, worked in Isolde's favor. But Connor's powers were growing. Hoping a tutor might teach her son control, Isolde hired Jowan, unaware that he had been paid to poison Eamon. Desperate to save his ailing father, Connor made a deal with

Many tried to aid Arl Eamon as he suffered. Only the ashes of Andraste saved him from death.

a demon, whose power ultimately plunged Redcliffe into chaos. Only the timely intervention of the Hero of Ferelden released the village from the demon's grip and prevented the arl's death.

None would have blamed Eamon for taking time to recover from his ordeal—his rivals at court were no doubt counting on it. But the arl, ever loyal to Ferelden's well-being, traveled at once to Denerim. The recent death of King Cailan, coupled with the questionable rise of Loghain, meant Eamon needed to intervene. He was instrumental in calling the Landsmeet that ultimately resolved the succession dispute between Cailan's widow, Anora, and Eamon's former charge, Alistair.

Following the Blight, Eamon remained in Denerim, once again serving as advisor to the throne. He enjoys the trust of the court to this day, although in recent years he has voiced dissatisfaction, particularly following the throne's decision to allow rebel mages the use of Redcliffe. "The Circles' fate lies with the Chantry, but we should not encourage its dissolution," Eamon said in an address to the court. "Many deny mages in their bloodline. But if a mage was your brother, your sister, your child—would you not see them protected?"

At first, many expected Eamon to return to his arling. When this did not occur, his prolonged stay in the capital was attributed to the lingering effects of his poisoning. He made a few brief trips to Redcliffe to help organize the region's recovery following the Blight, but always returned to Denerim. As the months passed, it became apparent that he would permanently reside in Denerim. He returned to Redcliffe only once more, when he declared his brother, Teagan, his successor and gracefully retired from the role of arl. Some claim Eamon could not bring himself to reside in Redcliffe Castle following the tragedy surrounding Connor. Of course, such rumors hold little malice. Teagan is well respected in Redcliffe, and Eamon's steady demeanor is viewed as a positive influence in the capital. Eamon is now a permanent fixture in Denerim. On fair afternoons, it is not uncommon to find him walking the same paths he excitedly showed Isolde years ago. If not happiness, he has found a peace in Denerim that many agree is due.

TEAGAN

Redcliffe's current arl is almost more Marcher than Fereldan. His mother, Arlessa Marina, was the youngest sister of the ruling margravine, Thalia Aurum of Ansburg. Just before Arl Rendorn Guerrin publicly threw his support behind the Rebel Queen, he and his wife decided that the arlessa should take their younger children and flee to her sister's protection. In 8:93 Blessed, Marina took ship from Denerim with her sons. Teagan was only two years old when he left Ferelden's shores.

Arlessa Marina became feverish during the passage north, and by the time the ship made landfall at Wycome, she was gravely ill. She was taken to Ansburg by carriage and attended by healers from the Circle, but her condition only worsened. She died just one day after arriving at the family home.

When their father was slain at the Battle of West Hill six years later, the margravine adopted both Teagan and Eamon. It was little more than a formality at that point, as Teagan had already been raised for most of his life by his aunt and uncle as if he were one of their own children. He and his cousin Cador were nearly the same age and completely inseparable. The pair were known rather infamously throughout the margravine's keep as a single entity: "Trouble."

"Trouble ran through the mews and turned all the falcons loose in the yard."

"Trouble got into the pantry and ate mince pies until we had to call a physician."

THEDOSIAN ARTISTS: HEMIARE ALLEGRI

The Antivan artist Hemiare Allegri has yet to grace our most dignified court with his presence, but his work has nonetheless found favor with the aristocracy's younger set. Previously rumored and now confirmed to have been born in one of the many brothels of Antiva, he displayed his talent at an early age and was fostered by some of the city's most prominent sculptors. His origins are of no consequence in the face of his talent as far as most are concerned, and yet despite his amazing skill, he remained a mostly local Antivan name until quite recently.

Allegri first became known to this critic largely due to a gracious gift granted in thanks for my most humble of words by a young lord who had spent the summer in the Antiva City court but a few years ago. The simple yet delightful statue still holds a place of honor in a far-too-slim collection of the now-celebrated sculptor's works, but it is fervently hoped that with the new commission announced last year by Duke Prosper, more of his art will be brought to Orlais. There has been much questioning, however, as to the medium selected. After all, Allegri's most celebrated work has always been in the realm of sculpture, and architecture, even! Therefore, why one would choose to order a simple pastel work was the source of great confusion for most art enthusiasts in Orlais.

The nature of the commission was greatly confusing to myself as well. However, upon further thought, it is undeniable that not only is the duke very well traveled but he is yet to return with anything but the most exquisite of art pieces as gifts for the empress. While some greatly doubt this latest commission, it is now my belief that the talent evidently displayed in the sculptures I have viewed will likely translate to something undoubtedly unique in a painting. Allegri's draftsmanship is unmatched, and even a series of incomplete silverpoint sketches commissioned by Chantry archivists for the sole purpose of chronicling contemporary events could pass muster in the finer private galleries of the capital.

Perhaps we shall be gifted with a carved shallow-relief painting, not unlike the many glorious and yet sadly anonymous works that adorn the ceiling of the chantry in Antiva City? We can only hope to be so blessed.

—*From* A Still Life of Modest Artistic Discernments: Thedosian Artists Through the Ages *by Plume*

"Trouble snuck into the gallery this morning and knocked half the paintings off the wall and got jam on all the rest."

As far as the margravine's servants could determine, the boys' "terrible twos" lasted for a good seven years. Only Percival, the oldest of the margravine's sons, could reliably persuade Trouble to do what they were told.

Eamon returned to Ferelden in 9:02 Dragon to become the arl of Redcliffe, leaving his brother behind. Not that Teagan minded. At eleven years old, his great ambition in life was to fight in the Grand Tourney and own a hundred warhorses, not necessarily in that order. He was not even certain where Ferelden *was,* being profoundly bad at geography. And history. And he doodled jousts during his mathematics lessons. "The boy may have greatness in him, but he hides it remarkably well," his tutors said. As bad as Teagan was at scholarship, he was an excellent horseman, and his combat instructors believed he showed enough promise at the joust to be able to one day represent Ansburg in the Grand Tourney.

On his eighteenth birthday, Teagan received a letter from his brother, Eamon, asking him to return and rule the bannorn of Rainesfere at Redcliffe. Teagan was all set to refuse; he intended to leave with his cousins Cador and Percival to fight together at a tournament in Starkhaven in just a few weeks. Teagan's aunt, however, persuaded him to pay a visit to his brother in person before refusing his birthright entirely. His home in Ansburg would always be waiting for him.

So, in 9:09 Dragon, Teagan returned to Fereldan soil for the first time in sixteen years to meet a brother he only barely remembered. Eamon met him in Denerim with his young wife, Isolde, and they made the trip to Redcliffe together. By the time they arrived at Lake Calenhad, Teagan had agreed to take his title and lands.

Despite his new responsibilities, Bann Teagan traveled back to Ansburg every year to visit family, and even as arl of Redcliffe, he spends more time in the Free Marches than in Denerim. During Grand Tourney years, the people of Redcliffe complain that they see so little of him, they might as well be governed by a portrait on the wall.

DEEP ROADS AND DEEPER FORESTS

The Hero enlisted the aid of a great many forces, among them the isolated but powerful dwarves of Orzammar and the Dalish of the Brecilian Forest. But as influential as the ancient treaties of the Wardens were, neither group was in a position to commit troops before sorting out their own troubles. The dwarves were in a holding pattern over who would take the throne after the death of their king, Endrin Aeducan, while the Dalish battled werewolves deep in the forest.

WHAT REMAINS OF AN ARCHDEMON

We found it by chance, and not the good kind. The darkspawn filth eats at everything: weapons, armor, even the blessed Stone Herself. Usually we're careful. But the Heidrun Turning was more brittle than we could know. The darkspawn scum knew, though. They led us on, grinning, banging their shields. The Legion of the Dead doesn't stand for that. I led the charge right at 'em. And then we were falling.

When we picked ourselves out of the loose rock—two of us dead, everyone else as raw as a skinned nug—we were far below, maybe sixty feet down and nothing but loose stone above. We'd broken through into a bad spot, all right: old tunnels, long overrun. The smell was like a slap. You could hear the spawn chittering and whispering nearby. Thousands. We're dead anyway, but that trick left me steaming angry. I wanted our lives to buy something better.

Aydis figured it out. Rarely an original thought in her head, but that's because she's got half the Deep Roads taking up space in there. She sketched out where we had to be and figured that if we cut downwards, we could cross through House Sobat's old mineshafts, climb back up to Varen's Notch, then hack into the darkspawn rear guard. But instead of the Sobat shafts, we broke through into darkspawn tunnels. Strange ones, too. Looked like they'd clawed through the stone with their bare hands. They fought us shoulder to shoulder down there, and they weren't grinning anymore. When we came to the cavern, we saw why—and why the Heidrun Turning, up above, was falling apart. There's no filth like darkspawn, and no filth like an Archdemon's, even one long gone and turned to dust. The cavern was ripe with stench, claw marks ripped into the rock. Darkspawn corpses sat here and there, dried out, heads pressed against the stone.

They'd died praying, we realized. This hadn't just been an Archdemon's lair. This was what remained of its prison.

The rest of the 'spawn wouldn't set foot inside after us. But we couldn't stay either. There was something in there, some feeling that stirred the brains in your skull, made the hands go numb. It couldn't be the place: the beast was gone, and what echo could last that long? But that's the head talking, and when your guts are screaming that you have to leave, you sodding well leave.

We got clear, made it to the Notch. But none of us have slept right since. I tell you, I'll kill my way through a darkspawn horde and whistle as I go; I'll look an Archdemon in the eye if I have to. But whatever chains keep those monsters bound, I want nothing to do with. Even among the darkspawn, there are things unnatural.

—Report sent to the Orzammar Shaperate by Kardol, Legionnaire of the Dead

Dangers lurk in the Deep Roads. Few dare explore them.

BRANKA

The Shaperate in Orzammar maintains meticulous records of Paragons past. Its records of Paragon Branka are particularly extensive, owing to the fact that Branka is the only Paragon to be named in four generations of dwarves.

Branka was a Smith Caste woman who excelled at her art from a young age. According to the Shaperate, she picked up the hammer just before her third birthday. The first object she crafted was said to be an iron badge, shaped like a nug's ear. Though large and crudely made, it bore the earliest signs of what would become the Paragon's signature hammering technique. The nug-ear badge has been preserved for its historical value and now resides in the Shaperate's vault.

Though Branka was a talented smith, her family could not have predicted that she would one day become Paragon. Before she was even twenty, her family made an offer of marriage to a gifted warrior, Oghren of House Kondrat. Both families saw the match as mutually beneficial, and the proposal was accepted.

A little over a year after her marriage, Branka was named Paragon when she invented a smokeless coal. Branka's invention upped the productivity of the Smith Caste by allowing them to work safely in caves that lacked ventilation. With the elevation in Branka's status, her family was named to the Noble Caste, and all members of House Kondrat were absorbed into the newly noble House Branka. The assimilation allowed Branka to meet another warrior, a distant cousin of Oghren's named Hespith.

Hespith and Branka began spending time together, the latter often eschewing Oghren's company in favor of Hespith's. It became an open secret that the two women were having an affair. As Branka was a Paragon, any objections voiced by Oghren were simply ignored, by both Branka and the rest of the house.

Records imply that Branka's quest for the Anvil of the Void was supported, perhaps even encouraged, by her lover. The two spent many hours in the Shaperate, poring over old scrolls, hoping to pinpoint the location of the artifact. In 9:28, Branka mounted an expedition into the Deep Roads to retrieve the Anvil. She took all of House Branka, save Oghren, with her for support.

She and the entire house were presumed dead when they did not return. Oghren enlisted the Hero of Ferelden to venture into the Deep Roads to find her. What they found is not in any official record of the Shaperate.

TAMLEN

There are stories of a mysterious mirror discovered in the Brecilian Forest by a group of Dalish elves from the Sabrae clan. The mirror, now believed to likely be an eluvian, was hidden within ruins deep in the woods. They say it showed the elves who found it strange images of a city underground. One of these elves was a young warrior named Tamlen. When he touched the mirror, it took him away.

IMMORTALITY AND THE QUESTION OF ZATHRIAN AND THE LADY

We whisper it, as we whisper a great shame. Not because we believe we had it, but because we believe we lost it. Immortality.

Let us set aside the arguments about whether it is possible to live forever and concern ourselves with the practicalities. Of what the eternal elf might have looked like and if such a state is even desirable.

First, we seek examples. There are constant rumors of the "elder from the other clan," but inevitably the members of that clan likewise have heard the same of another. An endless chain of hopeful myths. We have but one verified example of a modern member of the People exceeding what we call a lifetime: Zathrian of the Brecilian Forest.

Zathrian's years were extended not through restoration of the natural means we assume have been poisoned by the press of humanity, but by the lashing of soul to spirit through the manipulation of life and blood. His was a literal crime against nature, for in seeking vengeance, he manipulated the heart of the Brecilian Forest, itself possessed of an ancient spirit. His family torn apart by human cruelty, Zathrian bound the spirit, the Lady, to a wolf and bade her kill for him.

As Witherfang, the Lady killed, but also did she infect. For this manipulation was of such strength, of such hatred, it made victims of all sides. The Lady, bound to the wolf, infected human and elf alike, turning them to werewolves, spurring myth and legend throughout Ferelden. And Zathrian, bound to his curse, lived to see the cost of what he had unleashed and lived yet longer with the soured memories of his broken family. Yet, we are not to judge the act. Those events found their end in due course. Of interest now is Zathrian himself and how he fared for his additional years. Did he find his natural state and, within it, understanding?

We know that the minds of spirits are focused in a way that is alien to mortals. They seem myopic, but is that what they are or *because* of what they are? It is conjectured that Zathrian lived at least three centuries. This is unheard of, but still a blink when compared to eternity. His clan prospered and believed the longevity of their Keeper marked him as closer to what we once were. But all would mention his severity, his distance. His manner does not describe the mind of someone at peace. We can presume that the guilt of his actions weighed upon him, but for many, one lifetime is enough to prompt restitution. It took him far longer. We must ask why.

Consider a mind that ascends to immortality through hatred for what it has lost. Even if that loss remains a focus, in the fullness of time, there will be other losses. His clan were mortals, and he outlived generations of them, watching friend after friend wither and die, some falling to the very curse that sustained him. What were they when compared to the original pain? Was their loss as great? Was it lesser? Was the number overwhelming, or numbing?

We must remember it was the arrival of an outsider, the Hero of Ferelden, that spurred the ending of the curse. Zathrian may have known regret, but as his own life extended, the lives of all around him seeming mere moments, did they remain as peers? As children? As acquaintances known only for a fleeting moment? As his focus approached that of a spirit, was he still able to empathize with those around him?

It can be argued that an immortal would have to be distant, or eventually all it would know is loss. What would our world look like to such a creature? What actions would they be capable of when everything except themselves is fleeting and therefore of little relevance to eternity? If we as elvhen discover a path back to what we were, we must be sure that the path is wide enough for all. For the individual who stumbles into that journey, who endures when all else is dust, can only be alone.

—Keeper Ilan'ta, for discussion among the hahren'al as they gathered for Arlathvhen

When Tamlen reemerged days later suffering from the effects of the blight, his fate was sealed, and he was cut down.

Whether or not this story actually happened is the subject of much debate in Dalish circles. Regardless, it is frequently told around campfires in many clans, often to stress to curious children the dangers of the ancient mirrors.

KINLOCH HOLD

When the Hero's party arrived at Kinloch Hold and were ferried to its Circle Tower on Lake Calenhad, they found the tower overrun by demons. It seemed that in a misguided attempt to rebel against Chantry control, a senior enchanter named Uldred had brought chaos upon the tower. The party fought Uldred and put down the demons, clearing the Circle of strife—though not without significant casualties.

IRVING

First Enchanter Irving would often laugh when asked about his youth as an apprentice at Kinloch Hold. According to him, he was merely adequate as a student: competent enough not to be a danger to himself and others, but never brilliant. As he took on greater roles and responsibility within the Circle, however, Irving found that he had a talent for, and greatly enjoyed, the duties of an administrator. He was frequently quoted as saying that "with the power to control the primal forces of nature in my hands, my greatest joy came from managing the books."

It is no surprise, then, that Irving was appointed first enchanter of Ferelden's Circle of Magi. Some criticize his supervision of the Circle, accusing him of being too lenient with his mages and citing countless troubles that have plagued it since he took on the role of first enchanter. However, many others believe that a cursory look at the facts makes it evident that the problems within Kinloch Hold indirectly resulted from the chaos of the Fifth Blight and the Fereldan civil war of the same period. Most see Irving as a successful leader, under whom the mages enjoyed a generally agreeable life, with more freedom than their counterparts in other Circles.

It is a surprise to many that Irving often credits Knight-Commander Greagoir for his success as first enchanter. The two were first introduced many years prior, when Irving was still just a student of magic and Greagoir a young templar who showed great potential. Though their friendship was never entirely without conflict, mutual respect and understanding resulted in a working partnership rarely seen in the Circle leadership.

GREAGOIR

As a young templar, Greagoir was described by his superiors as a "model templar." Strong, skilled, and devoted to both the Chantry and the mages, he was thought by many to be the picture of what the templars *should* be at their best. Most of the mages and templars serving in Ferelden's Circle of Magi were certain that it was just a matter of time before Greagoir would be named Knight-Commander Robard's successor.

Though Greagoir spent most of his career at Kinloch Hold, the knight-commander's journals show that Greagoir was sent away to Denerim for a period of about a year and a half, just before the beginning of the Dragon Age. Though his absence was attributed to the chantry in Denerim requiring templars, rumors abounded that he was ordered to leave as part of a punitive sentence for trespasses unknown. However, the knight-commander was quick to take action against any who repeated the rumors, and the gossip soon stopped.

When Greagoir returned, he seemed to be the same templar he always was, as focused and dedicated to his duties as ever. As a sign of his trust, Knight-Commander Robard appointed him to the post of knight-captain immediately upon his return. A short five years later, he assumed the role of knight-commander, when Robard finally retired from his post. Knight-Commander Greagoir has retained his position for several decades, and was at Kinloch Hold when the Fifth Blight struck and the tower was overrun by demons.

JOWAN

Most know Jowan as the blood mage responsible for the attempted assassination of Arl Eamon Guerrin during the Fifth Blight. First Enchanter Irving, head of the Circle of Ferelden, had this to say about the troubled apprentice's time at Kinloch Hold:

NOTES ON THE HERO OF FERELDEN

ORZAMMAR DURING THE FIFTH BLIGHT

The memories of the Shaperate provide some insight into key figures in Orzammar during the Fifth Blight. It appears there was some significant disagreement over the rightful heir to the kingdom at that time. Two parties, a Lord Harrowmont and a Prince Bhelen, contested the throne vacated by Bhelen's father, King Endrin Aeducan. Neither seemed particularly suitable. Also of note were figures in the underworld, where around the same time leadership was also changing hands. Shaper Czibor provided this much:

Pyral Harrowmont

Lord Pyral Harrowmont was an influential figure in Orzammar's political scene, a deshyr in the Assembly, and a close friend and second to King Endrin Aeducan. His connections and distinguished bloodline made him a highly respected figure. On his deathbed, King Endrin named Lord Harrowmont his successor—a claim that was fiercely contested by his youngest son, Bhelen Aeducan, leading to one of the worst succession crises in Orzammar's history.

Bhelen Aeducan

Prince Bhelen was the youngest child of King Endrin Aeducan. Spiteful and ambitious from the start, Bhelen coveted his eldest brother Trian's claim to the throne. When the opportunity presented itself, he schemed to have Trian murdered and the crime pinned on their remaining sibling. With the crown prince dead and the second in line for the throne exiled for fratricide, Bhelen was free to be his father's heir. When Endrin named Lord Harrowmont his successor instead, Bhelen contested the claim, refusing to let power slip from his grasp.

Prince Bhelen fathered a son by his casteless mistress, the kind of woman some call a "noble hunter."

Jarvia

It is an embarrassment to Orzammar that Jarvia's name is known from Dust Town to the Diamond Quarter. A casteless duster who took over the criminal Carta from its previous leader, Beraht, she is considered responsible for expanding the Carta's operation, increasing its power and wealth, and turning it into an organization that was feared even by some in the Noble and Warrior Castes. Though she was killed, her influence on the Carta lingers—a festering wound in Orzammar's side.

House Dace

Jerrik and Brogan were brothers, members of the noble House Dace of Orzammar, and cousins of house patriarch Anwer Dace. While both were accomplished warriors, the older Jerrik received many more accolades than Brogan did. Brogan always seemed to be content to remain in Jerrik's shadow, celebrating his victories as though they were shared.

When scholar Darion Olmech came to the Daces with proof that he had discovered the location of Amgarrak Thaig, once a center for research on golem construction, House Dace funded and supported his expedition, thinking it would bring the house wealth and status. Brogan was sent on the expedition, which went missing with no word. Although Lord Anwer Dace declared the expedition lost and all members dead, Jerrik would not accept the death of his brother and hired his own team to go after the lost expedition.

HOW TO PREVENT MAGIC IN ITS EARLIEST STAGES

While joy takes dominance, sensations more akin to fear are not uncommon. The key is understanding that preparations might be made.

Should mage blood run through your line, no matter how distant the relation, avoid conceiving in winter. While with child, sleep with dried embrium beneath your pillow to ensure good health.

Infants and most small children will show no signs of magic. However, you can purge the body of unwanted elements before they take hold. Place leeches on each of the child's limbs. When done, burn the leeches. Be sure not to inhale the smoke. Afterward, wrap the child's limbs in cloth blessed by a Chantry sister.

A child showing signs of magic may be submerged in water until the breath is nearly lost. If magic is still weak within them, it will die before the child. Should the trouble persist beyond reason, certain talismans may suppress the child's skill.

—*Excerpt from* The Art of Parenting for the Good Andrastian *by "Sister" Geraldine. The Circle confiscated all known copies of the book in 9:28 Dragon. Knight-Commander Emalde defended the decision, explaining that the advice offered was dangerous and "frankly insane." Mother Joselyn of the chantry in Verchiel similarly denounced the book's content, adding that the author "appears to have given herself the title of Sister, rather than receiving it from the Chantry."*

Hurlocks are formidable foes, especially in large numbers.

"All mages have their strengths and weaknesses. I have known mages who were forces of nature—masters of the primal school—whom I wouldn't let near me with a healing spell or a bandage. We all have limitations; our task is to identify them and work within them. And Jowan . . . well, Jowan's troubles came from unmet expectation, the perceived distance between 'should' and 'is.' He never achieved things he believed were well within reach; he was disappointed in himself and thought we would be, too. We never were. If he hadn't turned to blood magic, there would have been no cause to make him Tranquil. All that happened after was a result of that decision. I think he regretted it in the end, but regret counts for little. Once you take the first step into the forbidden school, there is no stepping out again."

Jowan's foray into blood magic forced Irving's hand. When Knight-Commander Greagoir proposed the Rite of Tranquility, the first enchanter had no choice but to agree. But the signed order was discovered by Lily, Chantry initiate and Jowan's lover, and the two hatched an escape plot. Though they succeeded in destroying Jowan's phylactery, they met a templar ambush at the tower's great doors. To protect Lily, Jowan launched a surprise blood-magic attack against his ambushers. Lily, who had till then believed Jowan to be innocent, finally saw him for who he was and rejected him. For her part in Jowan's plot, she was sentenced to be taken to Aeonar, the notorious magical prison.

I dream of that moment. But I am never in it; I am always apart, watching it happen over and over and over. I see what he does to the templars, and I see her, Lily—the girl I used to be—recoil from him. I scream at her, shout at her to leave with him. "He loves you! He said he would give it all up! You know there's no lie in that!" But the hurt is too fresh, and the Chantry's lies are stark in her mind. She never goes with him. She stays and is taken away, and I wake up here in Aeonar.

He could've saved me. And if I were with him, I could've saved him.

—From a confession written by Lily

Jowan was in hiding when he was discovered by Teyrn Loghain Mac Tir. Loghain gave Jowan a chance to redeem himself, by becoming his spy within Arl Eamon's castle. The desperate Jowan agreed and was sent to tutor Connor Guerrin, the arl's son, who was secretly a mage. While in Redcliffe Castle, Jowan poisoned the arl, on Loghain's orders, setting in motion a chain of events that nearly led to the arl's death and the destruction of all of Redcliffe.

SOMETHING HAS CHANGED

I am Lily, myself, alone. There is no one in this cell except me, and I am myself.

I write these words each day. At Aeonar, it's wise to remind yourself of these things. Especially now.

The last inmate the templars brought was a boy, wearing velvet with one sleeve torn off. A noble from Hercinia, the whisper ran, suspected to be an apostate hidden by his family while he practiced blood magic on their servants. The templars locked him in a cell. He ranted and cursed at them, but the rest of us grew quiet, waiting.

Aeonar is a prison designed to let things in. The Veil here is so perilously thin that even I can feel it. The denizens of the Fade gather like monstrous shapes pressing against a fine curtain. And if you are a maleficar or an apostate, you are a beacon to them, ripe for possession. Thus, the templars bring those here who are accused, but whose true nature cannot be proven. Aeonar is the final, terrible test.

Within a few days, we all heard it from the boy's cell—that horrid, gobbling shriek that never becomes familiar. The templars were quick. Knight-Captain Brynn sees that they keep their swords as sharp as mercy. We exhaled again.

I am Lily, myself, alone. I am no maleficar, just a Chantry initiate who loved deeply, and foolishly. My lover . . . my Jowan . . . revealed himself as a blood mage and was forced to flee his Circle. I wanted to go with him. I wanted to stand by his side. He swore the rumors were false—that he'd never think of using such terrible magic. But it was a lie, one of many he must have told me.

It has been years now, studying and praying in my cell or walking the halls where Tevinter mages once did their experiments. New faces arrive, and I lie awake waiting to hear that shriek. Sometimes the templars administer . . . tests, as abominations can be cunning and patient. The tests leave their scars, but each time I pass. I am Lily still.

"I will speak to my superiors again," Knight-Captain Brynn told me. But something has changed. There have been no Chantry messengers in weeks, and the templars' frowns deepen. The last messenger feared there might be open war between mages and the Templar Order. What does that mean for us? Aeonar is an isolated fortress, a fine prize for any mage skilled in demonology, and the templars might decide to purge this place, for their own safety.

With no new orders, Knight-Captain Brynn must decide for himself what to do. He's a good man. But as Aeonar teaches, sometimes being a good man means having a well-honed blade.

—From a diary sent to Seeker investigators, who later found Aeonar deserted with no signs of violence

The darkspawn corruption turns ordinary people into hideous, mindless ghouls.

ULDRED

Uldred was a senior enchanter in Ferelden's Circle of Magi. Brilliant and gifted with words, he maintained a position as one of First Enchanter Irving's most trusted advisors while simultaneously working to turn other mages to his Libertarian point of view. After Uldred's death, investigations revealed that he had been quietly encouraging them to break away from the Chantry's restrictive modes of thought and introducing blood magic to those he thought could be useful to him in his ambitions. To deflect suspicion, Uldred would occasionally reveal the identity of these potential rebels—a ploy that allowed Uldred to defend some of his activities to Irving as having been in the service of keeping the Circle strong and free of corruption. Many have theorized that Jowan was one of those mages who gravitated toward Uldred's voiced opinions and was betrayed by him.

Taking advantage of the civil war in Ferelden, Uldred staged a coup during the Fifth Blight, hoping to free Ferelden's Circle of Magi. The coup failed, and Uldred paid for it with his sanity and, ultimately, his life.

My journey began with a single question: "What if? What if there's nothing wrong with blood magic?" Just holding that thought, in the beginning, was difficult. Painful. It is remarkable, how easily we are made to fear our own minds. The templars need not know; they need not lift a finger. We punish ourselves for questioning with shame and with fear. But I faced my shame. I faced my fear. Step by laborious step, I began to see the threads of the Chantry's web. Step by step, I was able to unravel it. This system they have set in place . . . how elegant a solution it is. If I were not its victim, I would surely admire it.

—From the locked diary of Senior Enchanter Uldred, retrieved from his quarters after his death

THE LANDSMEET & DENERIM

At Denerim, the conniving Arl Rendon Howe imprisoned Anora for speaking against her father, Loghain. The Hero freed Anora and killed Howe. With Ferelden united, Eamon healed, and Redcliffe no longer under the threat of demons, Eamon called a monumental Landsmeet to remove Loghain from power and install a rightful ruler —leaving it to the Hero to decide whether Anora or Alistair was a better candidate for the throne.

With the matter sorted, the Hero, together with the many peoples of Ferelden, launched an all-out assault on the Archdemon and his darkspawn at Denerim, ultimately slaying the corrupted dragon and returning a fragile peace to Thedas.

RENDON HOWE

Rendon Howe was the arl of Amaranthine until Teryn Loghain promoted him to arl of Denerim and Highever.

A cold, calculating man, Howe was rumored to be responsible for the deaths of the Cousland family, slaughtering them while their soldiers were fighting at Ostagar. He was born during the Orlesian occupation and, like many of the nobles at the time, joined Prince Maric's rebels. He fought alongside young Bryce Cousland, future teyrn of Highever, and Leonas Bryland, future arl of South Reach, at the bloody Battle of White River. It was the most catastrophic defeat of the entire occupation, from which only fifty rebel soldiers escaped alive.

The Hero of Ferelden killed Howe while seeking to rescue Queen Anora.

The Battle of White River

The Rebel Queen rallied the nobles of Ferelden against the Orlesian occupation as her father never could. By 8:80 Blessed, the rebellion had grown from small, isolated bands, each fighting for their own lands, into two armies: the Army of the North, under the command of Bann Angus Eremon of the Waking Sea, and the Army of the South, commanded by Arl Rendorn Guerrin of Redcliffe.

In the ranks of Bann Angus's army were many of the young nobles of the coastal lands of Ferelden. Daughters and sons of lords who had been driven from their lands by the Orlesians flocked to the Rebel Queen's banner in droves. Among them were Rendon Howe, who had turned against his father, Tarleton, to side with the rebels, and Bryce Cousland, whose father, the teyrn of Highever, was hidden away in a farmstead in South Reach, dying of a wasting disease. Leonas Bryland, the half-Orlesian son of the arl of South Reach, had grown up with Bryce and followed his friend into the northern army. The three boys, nearly the same age, quickly became inseparable, bonding over ancient tales of heroism from their separate lands and stories of the homes and families they'd left behind.

Rage demons are drawn to anger.

In 8:96, the Rebel Queen was betrayed and murdered by some of her own nobles in collaboration with the usurper Meghren. Hard on the heels of their victory, Orlais sent two regiments of chevaliers across the Fereldan border to end the rebellion once and for all.

Without Queen Moira to lead them, her generals fell to arguing. Arl Rendorn Guerrin refused to move the army of the south from the Hinterlands while his men searched for Prince Maric, who he prayed had survived the ambush that killed the queen. Bann Angus, however, was concerned more with meeting the Orlesian advance before chevaliers stormed the Hinterlands than with finding the lost heir of Calenhad the Great. Angus finally grew impatient and took his army to intercept the chevaliers who would have to pass through the narrow valley of White River south of Lake Calenhad.

The Fereldans dug out hasty fortifications, but from the beginning, they were outmatched. The chevaliers outnumbered them more than two to one and had the advantages of better equipment and training. For two days, the army of the north, including a young Rendon Howe, barely managed to hold the valley against charge after charge from the Orlesian cavalry. Each assault cost Ferelden scores of soldiers and forced the defenders back a little more, but Bann Angus was determined to keep the Orlesians from reaching the Hinterlands.

In an attack during the second night, Rendon Howe was gravely wounded, taking a chevalier's spear through the gut during a cavalry charge. Bryce and Leonas dragged him from the field before the chevalier could finish him off, but Bryce took a wound to the arm in the process. Bann Angus, seeing his men at their breaking point, finally chose to retreat. But there was only one way out of the White River Valley, and the Orlesians were on top of them the entire way. Angus himself was killed by an arrow storm while trying to sound the retreat. In the end, only fifty of nearly a thousand Fereldan soldiers escaped the slaughter.

Howe's friends carried him to a freehold in Redcliffe, where Bryce talked the farmers into giving the soldiers shelter. The remnants of the once-great Army of the North hid in the farm's outbuildings while Leonas put his Orlesian heritage to good use, convincing their chevalier pursuers that the retreating Fereldans had fled west into the Frostbacks.

Howe's condition grew worse during the night, so Bryce made the half-day trip, despite his own injuries, to the closest village in search of help. He returned late the next night with a nervous herbalist, who applied a great number of elfroot poultices to injured soldiers for the next few days.

Howe was by far the most badly wounded of the survivors, and so most of the soldiers left to find the Army of the South without him. Bryce and Leonas stayed with their friend and made the journey on foot to join up with the army nearly a full month later. When they arrived, Prince Maric, already informed of the defeat at White River and the events of its aftermath by the other survivors, personally awarded them medals of valor. Bryce and Leonas went on to join the Army of the South, but Rendon could not. He spent months in South Reach, his wounds tended by Eliane Bryland, Leonas's sister, who was an accomplished herbalist and physician.

The death of his uncle Byron just a few months later made Rendon Howe the arl of Amaranthine. Hearing the news, Howe decided to return to his arling despite his injuries. Eliane, concerned that the trip would certainly kill him, chose to go along despite Howe's protests. Nearly a year after they reached Amaranthine, Howe proposed, saying that if she wasn't going to leave already, they might as well marry. Leonas, concerned by the changes in his friend's behavior since White River, attempted to persuade his sister to break off the engagement, but she refused. Leonas then tried to talk Rendon out of the marriage, but was told directly that Howe needed her for her dowry and connections. Leonas severed all contact with Howe and his sister.

THE INFINITE CAPACITY TO LEARN AND GROW

When a man pledges himself to a cause and pours his heart into it and people believe in that same cause, they call him passionate. They call him righteous and dedicated; they hold him up as a man to be admired. But when they oppose his cause, they see that same passion in his eyes and call it madness. They seek to destroy him, lest he infect others with his lunacy.

This was how the slaves of the Orlesian Chantry saw Kolgrim. To them, he was a dangerous madman to be put down. But to me he was a mentor and a father. I knew him all my life, and he inspired me. He taught me how to swing a sword and how to be fierce. He showed me that I should not fear power, but seek it out, exult in it. From Kolgrim I learned that there is no shame in wishing to be more. Kolgrim believed that the Maker blessed us with infinite capacity to learn and grow, and thus it was our responsibility to do exactly that. Those who were complacent spurned the Maker's gift. That is why the high dragon called to him. He recognized that the Disciples of Andraste could achieve greater heights on her wings. And the dragon understood his desire, I think. She respected our strength, as we did hers.

Kolgrim led us with wisdom and passion, but the Chantry never understood that. Because he revered a dragon and replaced their prophet with a creature of greater power, he was called insane and put down.

—As told by Tamar, Disciple of Andraste and Inquisition agent

Most of Amaranthine's freeholders were ambivalent about their new arl—his father had been a traitor to the Crown, and his late uncle had been much beloved—and many delayed swearing fealty to Rendon or gave their allegiance to Highever. Some believed that the arling should pass to Arl Byron Howe's nine-year-old daughter instead of Rendon. None of the banns or freeholders attended Howe's wedding to a half-Orlesian noble from the South, Howe's widowed aunt and her children remained in the Free Marches, and in the end only Bryce Cousland and his fiancée, Lady Eleanor Mac Eanraig of the Storm Coast, came to witness their vows.

RIORDAN

Riordan was a veteran member of the Wardens who fought alongside the Hero of Ferelden at the Battle of Denerim.

After losing contact with the Wardens in Ferelden following the events at Ostagar, Riordan was sent from his post in Orlais to Denerim to find out what had happened. At Denerim, he was taken prisoner by Rendon Howe and tortured. The Hero of Ferelden helped Riordan escape Howe's dungeon, and Riordan joined the Hero's fight to stop the Archdemon.

It was from Riordan that the Hero learned how to kill the Archdemon, a secret of the Warden Order.

Riordan fought valiantly against the Archdemon at the Battle of Denerim. He was thrown to his death after wounding the beast. Some would argue that Riordan's sacrifice turned the tide, allowing the Hero of Ferelden to finish off the Archdemon. Regardless, Riordan died a hero, and a statue of his likeness now keeps watch over Denerim's market district.

THE COUSLANDS

The banns of the northern Fereldan coast (who local legend says are really just raiders who made good and retired) beached their fleets of fishing and cargo ships during the Orlesian occupation and returned wholeheartedly to the business of piracy. Ferelden's impromptu "navy" of privateers lay in wait for their prey in a hundred rocky coves, hidden bays, and inlets along the Waking Sea and were commanded, if anyone could call it

Denerim is the largest city in Ferelden as well as its capital.

such, by Bann Fearchar Mac Eanraig, the Storm Giant of the Storm Coast. All four of Bann Fearchar's children were raised from birth on the deck of a warship, but his second daughter, Eleanor, was by far the most talented raider in the family, taking her first Orlesian warship at only fifteen. Her ship, the *Mistral*, was so notorious for capturing and sinking enemy ships that the Orlesians nicknamed Lady Eleanor "the Seawolf."

"The only thing worse than the Storm Giant himself is his daughter," wrote one Orlesian admiral to the emperor. "The Seawolf strikes with a hundred times the ferocity of her father, and once she sinks her teeth into a ship, one might as well give it up for lost. What navy is equipped to fight monsters?"

When King Maric reclaimed Denerim, every last soldier in his army knew the Orlesians would retaliate by sea. Bann Fearchar called upon the army to send every soldier it could to support his ships in defense of the capital. The crew of every Fereldan warship was doubled for boarding actions, and every soldier who couldn't keep his rations down while sailing was camped in the crags of the Storm Coast and Waking Sea bannorns to guard the ships from assault by land.

Lord Bryce Cousland, by then a decorated officer of the army and commander of his own regiment of infantry, joined the soldiers waiting to board the Orlesian warships and led them from the deck of the *Mistral*. His first meeting with the famous Seawolf at Morrin's Overlook went poorly enough that the incident was eventually immortalized in a sea chantey, "The Soldier and the Seawolf," sung on both sides of the Waking Sea—one of many facts about her youth that Lady Eleanor never shared with her children.

Despite their unfortunate start, the pair turned out to work extremely well together. Avoiding burning catapult shot and hails of arrows, Eleanor brought the *Mistral* alongside one imperial warship after another, while Bryce led his soldiers to board and burn. Together, they destroyed a dozen enemy ships side by side in the battle in Denerim Harbor, cementing their friendship and demonstrating once again that nothing brings Fereldans together like a good fight.

Lord Bryce's father, Teyrn William, who lived nearly all of his life in hiding from the Orlesians, succumbed to illness shortly after the battle. As his only son, Bryce had little choice but to bring his father's body back to Highever for the funeral from South Reach arling, where he'd spent the last few years.

The return of the Couslands to Highever, after nearly seventy years of absence, was greeted with shock by its people. The banns and freeholders of Highever were anxious to meet Bryce and swear allegiance. Many of the freeholders along the Amaranthine border came to swear fealty to the new teyrn instead of their arl, adding further complication to the proceedings. Teyrn Bryce spent four months receiving oaths and taking possession of his ancestral home, and every day without fail he sent a letter to Lady Eleanor—sometimes more than one a day. One letter was reportedly just a stick-figure drawing of him sitting in Highever's great hall looking bored.

They met again in Denerim at the formal coronation of King Maric. The teyrn of Highever attempted to propose to the Lady of the Storm Coast by singing her all ten verses of "The Soldier and the Seawolf." She only let him go to three. The song was not sung at their wedding.

THE SOLDIER & THE SEAWOLF

The lion's ships were Denerim bound
Oh, drop him, Lady, drop him!
Let the true king's call for aid resound
Just drop him, Lady, drop him!
A soldier lad from the army came
Oh, drop him, Lady, drop him!
Leading thirty souls in Maric's name.
Just drop him, Lady, drop him!

Turn him loose and let him go
Down to the rocks and waves below
The depths can have that scurvy knave
Just drop him, Lady, drop him!

When the soldier met the *Mistral*'s crew
Not a word of their great deeds he knew
And the Seawolf he took for a servant lass
Great Andraste, what an ass!

'Fore the Seawolf's ire, no man could stand
Soldier felt his death was close at hand
Two great steps back did he retreat
And the cliff side crumbled 'neath his feet.

VAUGHAN

Vaughan Kendalls was a Fereldan nobleman, the son of Arl Urien Kendalls of Denerim. Born to privilege, with a distant father who was more preoccupied with his ambitions than his children, Vaughan was given everything he asked for, if only to keep him out of the way. Used to getting what he wanted, he grew up spoiled and insolent, and as a young man, he surrounded himself with sycophantic nobles who rarely spoke against him.

Cruel and insensitive, Vaughan took a special pleasure in inflicting misery on elves, who were barely more than animals in his mind. He had even been quoted as saying that the destruction of their barbaric civilization was a favor done to the world: "We don't allow rats to thrive and call their warrens a city."

Master Vaughan was always a terror. Putting bloated bodies of dead mice in my girls' pockets. Switching out the keys they had just set down for ones that had spent an hour in hot coals, so they would be burned. How he laughed when they shrieked! And if you were an elf, oh, Maker help you. I sent so many of them away, to save them. Oh, he was beastly. Those who didn't know him thought he was such a lovely boy. They weren't wrong. If he wanted something, if he needed to, he could be a charmer. But we saw him for what he was.

I don't know if it's true, but they told me he died in an elven uprising. I'm not sorry. The Maker is just.

—The arl's housekeeper, who ran the household when Vaughan was a boy

SHIANNI

Shianni's mother died of a terrible fever when the girl was six. Never having known her father, Shianni was left alone in the world. Two days after her mother's death, Cyrion, her uncle, came to the freehold in order to bring her to the Denerim alienage, where he lived. To ease the grieving child's worries about moving, he gave her a small cloth mabari, stuffed with hay, which had belonged to his own child.

The first few months in the Denerim alienage were difficult for the little girl. She had never left the country before, and the city was terrifying: full of strange smells, full of strangers. And Shianni had never before seen an alienage and was quite terrified of Hahren Valendrian, whom she once described as looking like "an apple that fell but no one picked up, that's found in spring after being outside all winter." She spent many days beneath her blankets, missing her mother and wishing that her father would return for her. She became convinced that her father was a Dalish warrior, who had been torn away from her mother through circumstances not of his own making, and who would one day come to take her away to live in the forest, where she would learn the true meaning of being elven.

Shianni eventually came to love the Denerim alienage. The people she once feared as strangers became her friends and family, even apple-faced Valendrian. Witnessing the squalor that some of them were forced to live in made her angry. Her passion allowed her to find her voice, and she never allowed anyone, human *or* elf, to take advantage of her or her loved ones. The terrible events that took place at her cousins' wedding, which culminated with her kidnapping by Vaughan, the son of Arl Urien Kendalls of Denerim, merely strengthened her resolve.

After her ordeal, Shianni was determined to protect the elves of the alienage from those who, like Vaughan, used their

The mabari is a loyal and intelligent war dog celebrated in Fereldan culture.

power to abuse and terrorize the helpless. When Teyrn Loghain installed himself as regent after King Cailan's death and began selling Denerim elves into slavery to fund his war, it was Shianni who stood up against all odds and urged the elves to fight. After the Battle of Denerim, she became the new elder of the Denerim alienage and, one imagines, continues to do her best to improve the lot of those she cares about most.

SHIANNI'S MATCH

I have found perfect matches for two of our young people. For Soris, it shall be Valora. She is a lovely girl, responsible and kind. I think you will all come to adore her. As for Cyrion's child . . . Well, I'd rather not reveal the identity of the chosen match yet; the arrangements are still being made with the family and they may fall through, so I shouldn't get ahead of myself. You'll be pleased to hear that the family is well respected in Highever, even by some humans.

That is the good news out of the way. Now the less auspicious news. It has been difficult to find a counterpart for your Shianni. Considering what you've told me of her spirited nature, I figured it would be best to match her with a young man of a less passionate temperament. Perhaps that way they will influence each other for the better. Unfortunately, no such young man comes to mind. We may have to expand our search. Perhaps in Gwaren?

From what you have said, I gather that Shianni is in no hurry to get married. That's a relief at least. It gives us time.

—*From a letter to Valendrian, elder of the Denerim alienage*

AWAKENING

Though the Archdemon was defeated at the end of the Fifth Blight, the darkspawn remained. The ancient emissary known as the Architect surfaced. His experiments on his own kind had led to the creation of a new breed of darkspawn: talking creatures with the capacity, it seemed, for rational thought. Among his experiments was a sentient broodmother, known as the Mother, whose apparent freedom from the call of the Old Gods and newfound consciousness caused her to go insane. Warden documents suggest that it was the Architect who, around this time, willingly awoke Urthemiel, hoping to remove the Archdemon's corruption by making him drink the blood of Grey Wardens.

When an army of darkspawn under the Mother's command rose to attack Ferelden, it was up to the newly instated Commander of the Grey and fellow Wardens to stop her.

THE ARCHITECT & THE MOTHER

The darkspawn are an omnipresent threat in the Deep Roads, surging forth to the surface every few centuries to wreak havoc with a Blight. For all that the Grey Wardens have so far been able to stop these Blights from destroying humanity, they have never been able to retake the Deep Roads or to stop the darkspawn entirely. That said, these creatures are fairly predictable: they possess a savage cunning, if not a true intelligence. They cannot speak, cannot be reasoned with, and are single-minded in their hatred of all things living.

Thus, the reports in 9:10 Dragon of a truly intelligent, talking darkspawn known as "the Architect" sent a shock wave through the Grey Wardens.

The Grey Wardens sent three different expeditions into the Deep Roads beneath Ferelden in an effort to track down the Architect or to discover what remained of those Wardens who had accompanied Duncan and Fiona. They reported finding the ruined thaig of Kul-Baras but no trace of the Architect or any evidence the expedition had occurred. Further investigation was abandoned, despite repeated efforts by Duncan (after becoming Warden-Constable under Warden-Commander Polara) to reinitiate it.

The ancient darkspawn known as the Architect may have played a role in the corruption of the Golden City.

Shortly after the end of the Fifth Blight, in 9:31 Dragon, the Architect was said to have returned, this time with a different plan: to "awaken" darkspawn through the introduction of Grey Warden blood, allowing them speech and intelligence and freeing them from the control of the impulses that drove them.

The Mother turned on the Architect after he created her.

As a young Warden recruit, Duncan (*below*) is said to have joined Maric in the Deep Roads.

"We know this Architect had awakened a number of darkspawn to serve as his minions—not least of which was a broodmother called 'the Mother,' who, after undergoing his Grey Warden transfusion, produced horrific immature darkspawn she called 'the Children,'" reads another Warden report. "Not all these creatures appeared to appreciate their transformation, which puts to question the validity of his offer to use these awakened creatures to hunt down the remaining Archdemons and end the Blights forever. Indeed, there is evidence to suggest that it was the Architect himself who found the Fifth Blight's Archdemon and who thus prompted the Blight to occur. This is a dangerous creature, one whose plans place no importance on the massive suffering or destruction they could cause—and who may very well be possessed of insane delusions of a grandiose nature. Should he or any other awakened darkspawn like him ever be encountered again, they should be approached with extreme caution if not outright exterminated."

What became of the Architect following this second encounter is unknown, though it's possible he may have been slain by the Warden-Commander of Ferelden. The Grey Wardens have clamped down on all information regarding the incident, and for several years later, the city of Amaranthine was swarming with Grey Wardens from as far away as the Anderfels. Any results of their investigation have not been shared publicly, though eyewitnesses state they saw several creatures looking like darkspawn being taken away from the city in cages . . . odd mainly due to the fact that the Grey Wardens have never before attempted to take darkspawn captives. What this bodes for the future, and whether there will be more encounters involving intelligent darkspawn like the Architect, remains to be seen.

We have two surviving members of the unauthorized expedition into the Deep Roads: the young rogue, Duncan, and the elven mage, Fiona. Both are junior members of the Order and thus can hardly be faulted for Warden-Commander Genevieve's actions . . . but their lack of experience means their word also cannot be taken at face value. To add to this, Warden Fiona has apparently had the corruption stripped from her blood. She is, for all intents and purposes, no longer truly a Warden. This is unprecedented in all the ages since our Order was founded in the First Blight.

Still, if there is even a kernel of truth to their tale of a talking darkspawn, it is worrisome indeed. A creature that called itself the Architect, that dreamed of peacefully ending the Blights by infecting all of humanity with the corruptive taint? Can we even imagine the death toll that would exact? What we would be left with is a race of people—all Grey Wardens, by way of this strange "Joining"—rendered infertile by the very taint it believes would save us. Horrifying in its twisted logic.

More curious is the nature of this Architect being. Is it truly a darkspawn, some evolution of the breed . . . or something far worse? I'm reminded of tales of the original Tevinter magisters who entered the Golden City and were cast back down as the very first darkspawn. Could this Architect be one of them? Could he be a ghoul, made immortal by the taint and yet unable to remember what he once was? Think of such a man, down in the Deep Roads for centuries with nothing but guilt and darkness to keep him company. He must be mad, if this is true. Even if it is not, this is not something we can allow to spread. The Chantry would lose its mind at the very possibility.

—Unsigned Grey Warden report

NOTES ON
THE COMMANDER OF THE GREY

MHAIRI

Little is known about the Warden named Mhairi, who is said to have fought alongside the Commander of the Grey for a time following the Fifth Blight. This much was recovered from the journal of a Grey Warden named Nolan:

I didn't know her well. I only met her once before her Joining. The night before, she sat down beside me for supper. I knew they'd told her what I was and what I'd done. But she treated me like any of the other recruits. She just said hello and talked. She said the Grey Wardens were going to be a new beginning for us both. She was excited for the Joining, for rebuilding the Order.

It should've been her who survived, not me. She was worthy of the honor. A decorated knight, fought in the Battle of Ostagar. Me? Nothing. A criminal.

My Joining came a week later. When it was done, one of the older Wardens, from the Marches, told me about a tradition some of them have. Tasting of the blood joins us, and those who succumbed to the ritual are Wardens, just as we are. So we remember them and honor their sacrifice by carrying them in our hearts. He showed me the list he had. Names of those who'd died. It was old, bloodstained. "Had it a long time?" I asked.

He smiled. "Won't be much longer now."

That night I wrote down the names of my brothers and sisters who lay down beside me and did not rise again. And I thought of Mhairi, and how she treated me like a brother even before the Joining.

Mhairi of Dragon's Peak, I remember you.

NATHANIEL HOWE

Nathaniel Howe was one of the three children of Arl Rendon Howe of Amaranthine. After spending years in the Free Marches, he returned to Amaranthine to seek vengeance on the Grey Wardens, whom he blamed for his father's death.

Squire

Young Nathaniel idolized his father. Growing up with stories of how Rendon Howe fought for Ferelden's freedom, by the side of the rightful king, Maric Theirin, he came to believe that his father was a hero. The boy would spend hours in the trophy room at Vigil's Keep, sitting among the displays of heritage armor and weapons, wondering when he would be big enough and strong enough to put on his grand-uncle's armor and wield his father's swords. As the years passed and the relationship between his parents deteriorated, the trophy room and associated fantasies became Nathaniel's refuge—the place where he could escape from his wretched family life.

When Nathaniel was older, Arl Rendon decided that he should be sent away to be trained in the arts of war. Arlessa

Grey Wardens typically don griffon heraldry.

Eliane suggested that he be squired under her cousin Ser Rodolphe Verley, a trained chevalier and fixture in the court of the ruling Vael family of Starkhaven. Though Ser Rodolphe was Orlesian by birth, Rendon was impressed by his skill and discipline and approved of Eliane's choice—a surprising turn of events, as arl and arlessa hardly agreed on anything. Nathaniel protested the joint decision loud and long; he wished to stay by his father's side, like his younger brother Thomas, whom he felt the arl favored. However, the decision was final, and Nathaniel was made to board a ship to the Marches.

Nathaniel remembers his master, Ser Rodolphe, as a large man with a bright red beard streaked with gray. A grim and serious man, Ser Rodolphe proved to be a harsh taskmaster who did not tolerate indolence or mischief of any sort. In his first week in Ser Rodolphe's company, poor judgment led Nathaniel to joke about his master's armor, which earned him the punishment of having to carry buckets of water from one end of the castle grounds to the other. From then on, he made jokes only when Ser Rodolphe was well out of earshot. Without levity to brighten the monotony of squirehood under the chevalier, Nathaniel's days became a gray blur of drills, chores, and boring history and military lessons.

Fortunately, Nathaniel made the acquaintance of one of Ser Rodolphe's watchman archers, who taught him to draw a bow. The chevalier did not approve of the discipline, calling it a coward's way of making war, but despite Ser Rodolphe's intense disapproval, Nathaniel continued to hone his archery skills on his own time. His daily practice of shooting fruit off the walls of the castle, while a much-needed reprieve for him, became a great source of annoyance to everyone else, especially the servants.

Howe the Archer

Two years later, Ser Rodolphe was invited to the Grand Tourney that was to be held in Tantervale. He and his entire household traveled to attend the festivities, with the chevalier himself enlisting in the joust. Nathaniel would later look back on this event as one of the most enjoyable experiences of his time with Ser Rodolphe and perhaps even his entire life.

Nathaniel Howe (*right*) was said to be exceptionally skilled with a bow.

Nathaniel had only ever read of the Grand Tourney in books, and nothing he had learned could prepare him for the reality of it. All of Tantervale was bedecked in blue and gold pennants; there was dancing and singing in the streets, and wine flowed freely. On the tourney field, ladies in brightly colored silks sat beneath crisp white tents, swooning over the armored knights doing battle on the sands before them. At Ser Rodolphe's behest, Nathaniel found himself joining in the grand melee, in which over a hundred warriors would do battle. Nathaniel's nimbleness allowed him to evade and best several heavily armed knights and even an Avvar barbarian before he was defeated by a man in Orlesian livery with piercing blue eyes and a cruel smirk. Though Nathaniel was disappointed in his performance, Ser Rodolphe seemed pleased enough. In an uncharacteristic show of generosity, the knight rewarded Nathaniel with a purse of gold and instructed him to use it well. Apparently, Ser Rodolphe may even have smiled at him, though he was never sure if it was just a trick of the light.

According to Nathaniel, he spent his purse of gold almost entirely on ale and cakes, saving just enough to buy a replica of Hessarian's Sword of Mercy and a small mechanical bronto that would play music if wound up. Intoxicated and sleepy, he wandered onto the field in the middle of a contest of archery and was almost shot. Recovering quickly from his near-fatal experience, Nathaniel declared that he was better than the archer currently shooting, holding up as evidence the fact that she had missed her target and almost killed a man. He was promptly handed a bow by the archer, a young, leather-clad elven woman, and told to prove himself. Though he was drunk, stuffed full of sugar, and holding a tinkling bronto in his mouth, Nathaniel managed to at least match the performance of the elf, hitting most of his targets square in their marked centers. His ability proven to all, Nathaniel departed the field in the company of the elf, whose name was, she said, "Erina, or maybe Avina."

Nathaniel spent the rest of the day in the company of Erina (or maybe Avina), forgetting entirely about Ser Rodolphe's scheduled showing at the joust. He would later have to lie to the chevalier about having watched his "astounding" performance. Fortunately for Nathaniel, Ser Rodolphe was elated by coming in fourth place, and Nathaniel's lie went unquestioned.

Howe the Warden

Nathaniel spent almost eight years training with Ser Rodolphe. Over that time, he grew to love the Free Marches and its people. He admits that he had little interest in becoming arl of Amaranthine, as the life of a wandering knight and archer appealed to him. Perhaps he would have stayed in the Marches if the events of the Fifth Blight had not taken place. Nathaniel says he barely recalls what he was doing when he heard of his father's death at the hands of the Grey Wardens. The details of Rendon's death were vague, but the core of the message stood out: Grey Wardens broke into the traitor Arl Rendon Howe's estate and slaughtered him. To add insult to injury, the Howe family's castle, Vigil's Keep, had been seized by the Fereldan Crown in response to Rendon's treachery and was being given over to the Grey Wardens who had murdered him.

The news of Arl Rendon Howe's involvement with the regicide of Cailan Theirin tainted the name of Howe from

The Warden Duncan died valiantly at Ostagar facing the darkspawn scourge.

A BROKEN SWORD

Arishok:

The Tal-Vashoth who fled to the High Reaches with a dozen saarebas have been destroyed by my beresaad, as commanded. To be complete, this report must include a full account of the human who fought alongside us.

Our Ashaad spotted him wandering near our camp, singing a song and swinging his weapon at thistles. He wore the armor of a basvaraad, the Chantry templars, so I gave the order to drive him off. Instead, he greeted us as if we were members of his own beresaad, appearing to see us as fellow templars. He then attempted to hug the Ashaad, addressing him as "Greagoir" or "Greggles." Discipline prevailed.

While attempting to resolve this confusion, we were ambushed by several of the Tal-Vashoth and two of their saarebas, who rained down magical fire from the cliffs overhead. There were several injuries before we could react. The human basvaraad exclaimed, "Mages can be so rude!" and charged up toward the saarebas, sword drawn. Instead of the immediate death I expected, he fought like one crazed by saar-qamek. He dispatched the saarebas in the manner of Chantry templars, allowing us to rout the Tal-Vashoth and tend to the wounded. When the battle was over, the basvaraad returned to our side, smiling and talking endlessly about what he believed to be our hunt for "those pesky maleficarum."

Since he had been useful and I could not compel him to leave, he was permitted to remain at the camp and share our meal. From his ramblings, I eventually understood him to be one rendered viddath-bas by the lyrium his Order is fed. Many of the places he spoke of were in Ferelden. When questioned about his purpose in the High Reaches, the basvaraad answered, "That crow wouldn't stop pecking at my armor while I was on duty, so I chased it. Crows really do fly a long way, don't they?"

The basvaraad accompanied us throughout the High Reaches for several days as we clashed with the Tal-Vashoth repeatedly. Each time, the basvaraad fought with skill, then continued to talk with equal abandon. Despite these disruptions, his abilities allowed us to destroy the saarebas with minimal casualties for such a mission. When the task was complete, he said that he would meet us in a nearby tavern for "a victory pint" and marched away, singing as before.

Some of my beresaad claimed this human was as dangerous as those we hunted, as his mind was broken and he did not know his own strength. I replied with the proverb "a broken sword is a hundred nails waiting to become." In that spirit, I attempted to glean as much intelligence as possible from his words. One element he was most insistent that I include: it seems that we were misinformed, as when spelled in this manner, "Carroll" is not a female name.

—Message from an unknown Qunari sten, intercepted and translated

Ferelden to the Free Marches. To save his mentor embarrassment, Nathaniel chose to leave Ser Rodolphe's household. Vowing vengeance on the Grey Wardens, he made his own way to the nearest port and booked passage on a ship bound for Amaranthine.

Nathaniel's return to Vigil's Keep was bitter. Stealing into what was once his home, he found himself making his way to his old hideaway, the Howe trophy room. It had been torn apart, the heirlooms of his father lost or looted. Here, the truth sank in: the Howe family was destroyed, their name and reputation ruined, their history stolen, their ancestral keep conquered. Nothing, not even vengeance, could restore what had been taken.

VELANNA

Velanna was a Dalish elf mage recruited by the Warden-Commander of Ferelden after the Blight, as part of a campaign to rebuild the Grey Wardens. She only agreed to join the Wardens in order to find her sister, who had been taken by the Architect.

Origins

When Velanna speaks of her youth, she laughs mirthlessly and describes herself as "all skin and bones and sour expressions—a thoroughly unpleasant child." A stark contrast to her younger sister Seranni, born two years later, who was affectionate and mirthful and loved by all.

"I should have hated her, hated her for being everything I wasn't," Velanna wrote in a journal, dated after the Blight had ended. "But you can't hate Seranni. It would be like hating the warmth of the sun. Like hating spring. Even I, disagreeable as I was, could not help loving her. My love for my sister was my one virtue."

When the sisters were little, Seranni would try to involve the somber Velanna in play with the rest of the clan's children. Though she would've been happier with her scrolls and quills, Velanna would humor her little sister and sit awkwardly by, trying to make sense of their pastimes. Her attempts often failed. Velanna could seldom resist pointing out loopholes in rules or logical flaws in the childish premises of their games, resulting in cries of dismay and her swift ousting from the group. Seranni would come to Velanna later, as she sat sulking in the aravel, to persuade her to play better with the others. Velanna would roll her eyes and snort, but promise to keep her criticism to herself next time. But the next time was always like the last time, and eventually Seranni could no longer convince the others to allow Velanna to join their games.

Velanna was nine when she discovered her magic. She describes it as the proudest day of her life. For years she had dreamed of being a mage. The ancient elves had magic in their veins; they were tied to the wind and the trees and the earth, and Velanna very much wanted to be like them and to know that she was of their blood. And then one day, after years of waiting and hoping and reaching her mind out to the wind and the trees and the earth, it happened. A single flame, in a small cupped hand, kindled by her wish and fed with her longing. Velanna brought the flame to Keeper Ilshae without delay, and outright declared that she would be the Keeper's First. Ilshae was stunned, but also impressed by Velanna's boldness. After giving the idea some consideration, she agreed to groom the young elf as her successor.

Velanna took to her magical training immediately. For the first time in her life, she felt like she belonged. Magic became her refuge, and she threw heart and soul into the study of it. For once, she had an excuse when Seranni asked her to play; studying to be the Keeper's First was, of course, more important than anything else.

Conflict with Humans

Velanna thrived under Ilshae's tutelage, and the Keeper became a second mother to Velanna. As the years passed, however, Velanna became sensitive to the gaps in elven lore—the history of her people that had been lost to slavery and genocide. She became bitter and developed an intense hatred of humans, one that even Ilshae found troubling. Even so, the Keeper decided to disregard Velanna's feelings, waving them off as a personality quirk of a severe young woman.

Perhaps Keeper Ilshae came to regret that decision. As long as the clan steered clear of the humans, Velanna's hatred posed little problem. But contact with the humans was inevitable, and one day, the clan found themselves camping too close to a human village. The villagers, made anxious by news of roving bands of darkspawn, turned violent in their attempt to defend their territory from what they saw as a threat. They set fire to the woods where the clan had settled, determined to drive the Dalish away from their farms. The clan escaped, but lost aravels and several halla to the forest fire.

Velanna was furious at the suffering inflicted on her clan, not to mention the flagrant destruction of nature. Before the clan had had time to recover, she proposed that they fight back and seek vengeance on the humans who had tried to burn them out of the woods. Instead, said the Keeper, the clan should move away as soon as they could and take greater care in avoiding human settlements in the future. Velanna and Ilshae argued bitterly over what course of action to take, and neither was willing to back down.

She will not listen. She wants us to stand. If we run, she thinks it means they have made us run. One more victory for the shemlen. I have told her countless times: it is not about victory, but survival. We win nothing by dying. Indeed, the only triumph we can hope for is to live, to thrive, in spite of all they do to us.

Sometimes I wonder if I should not have named Faladhin as First. He lacks Velanna's natural ability, of course—no one can deny Velanna's raw talent . . . Mythal'enaste! No one can deny that much about Velanna is "raw."

Perhaps with age, she will learn and gain wisdom. That is the hope.

—From the writings of Keeper Ilshae, collected by Ferelden's Commander of the Grey and found in the archives at Vigil's Keep

In the end, Ilshae gave Velanna an ultimatum: if she was adamant in seeking justice, she would have to do so alone, in exile from her clan. Heartbroken but too proud to apologize, Velanna left, taking with her the few clan members who agreed with her. Though Seranni did not approve of Velanna's actions, she followed the exiles, hoping to persuade her sister to give up her vengeance.

Seranni never got her wish. She was kidnapped by a darkspawn called the Seeker, under the command of the Architect. The rest of Velanna's band died in defense of Seranni. The Seeker then planted the weapons of a village militia at the destroyed camp, hoping to throw any other elves off its trail, and also to satisfy its perverse curiosity about the nature of elf and human behavior. When Velanna returned to find her companions dead and her sister gone, she flew into a rampage, lashing out at any and all humans who crossed her path, in a misguided attempt to get the "shems" to release Seranni. That was how the Commander of the Grey found her.

Is it any surprise? Seranni was Velanna's whole world. She would never admit it, but she clung to her sister like life. With Seranni gone, Velanna was missing a piece of her own heart. She was broken, no longer whole. And what wouldn't you do to restore your heart?

—From a letter to the Warden-Commander, from Keeper Faladhin, Ilshae's successor, reflecting on the Grey Wardens' encounter with Velanna in the Wending Woods

NOTES ON THE COMMANDER OF THE GREY

SIGRUN

A scrawled report apparently written by Sigrun, dwarven associate of the Commander of the Grey, presented here unedited:

Yesterday, a friend suggested that I write a report about myself.

"Wow, Sigrun, you've lived such an interesting and varied life! Surviving Dust Town, the Legion of the Dead, the surface . . . I could just go on and on! But there's so much left untold! Why don't you write all about it? It'll be such an inspiration to others, don't you think? Other casteless, other legionnaires, other small but terrifying people . . ."

(Not her words exactly.)

First I thought, "What? Really? My life?" And then I thought, "Well, why not?" Let's see if darkspawn blood makes good ink!

(It doesn't. Just so you know. It seems to want to crawl off the page on its own. I'm not making this up. I swear it does that.)

Anyway, let's start from the beginning . . .

I was born in Dust Town. ~~They say I slid out of my mother like a buttered nug going through a~~ I was an easy birth. My mother's name was Jana, and we had a little shack in Dust Town that we shared with her brother and his wife and their four children. My mother made her bits helping merchants unload the brontos. It was never really enough. She loved me, though, and told me that often, and was sorry she couldn't give me more. It never occurred to her to go to the surface. It doesn't occur to many dusters.

From the time I could walk, I did what I could. Begging came first—a crying child, brand or no brand, is hard to see, even for the most cold-hearted nobles. But the ladies were the easiest. Especially those who couldn't have children of their own. And believe me, it was a big problem up in the Diamond Quarter. ~~Maybe having man-sized statues of your ancestors peering down at you with their glittering eyes doesn't do much for the mood~~ I pitied them.

Anyway, when I got old enough that the tear-stained face just wasn't working anymore, I turned to thieving. It helped put a little more food on the table, especially since my ma was getting sicker. I won't go into that. I'm not looking for sympathy, and it's just something that happens to dusters. Dust Town's just a hard life, you know? No food, smoke and waste from the forges—it's just bad. Anyway, it was my turn to look after her, so I did, as much as I could.

That's when I met Mischa. She helped me out. I stole some food and she caught me, but paid for it instead of telling the shopkeeper. Don't think I even thanked her. I have shit for manners these days, but back then, it was worse. Much worse. Anyway, she told me that if I ever wanted to get away from stealing, to come see her at her shop in the commons. So the next day, I did. She started me off running errands for a few bits a day. Tough lady, never gave me a moment's rest. Sigrun, deliver this package to Janar. Sigrun, get those plates off the shelf and wrap them in leather. Sigrun, just run over to the door and come back. Now do it twice more. Things like that. Even though she wanted to help, I think deep down she believed what everyone always says about us brands, that we're bad. We can't help it. We're born criminal, and if left to ourselves, we do criminal things on instinct. Like ~~shitting and fucking~~ breathing. She thought if she didn't keep me constantly occupied, it would be, "Oops, how did I end up with the monument to Endrin Aeducan in my pocket? I guess I must've swiped it without realizing!"

I guess I showed her how wrong she was, huh? (That was sarcasm.) I couldn't even look at her when the guards were taking her away. I didn't have to look at her. I could tell she was staring at me. I could feel it. She knew it was me that planted the statue of Paragon Bemot. Who else could it be but me? It was the rotten casteless duster. It was her own fault for trusting me.

Well, after Mischa was exiled, it was back to thieving for me. It was in my nature, after all. And by that time, my ma had died and dear Uncle Boro wasn't going to support me, so I was on my own. I could've gone to someone in the Carta and tried my hand (and other bits) at being a noble hunter. But I didn't have the looks, and no noble's going to put up with a mouthy brand. ~~Not mouthy in the way I'm mouthy anyway.~~ So thievery it was. Big time, this time. Got protection from the Carta to work certain parts of the Commons. I was doing all right, till they found me with my hand in Damira Helmi's pocket. She had this beautiful, ruby-encrusted purse . . . I was thinking of all the roast nug I was going to eat, and I got careless. The guards chased me all through the Commons. I really should've just gone with them, but I was stupid. I fought back, and one of the guards, he . . . cracked his head on a pillar. I just wanted to trip him to get away. I never intended for him to die.

But he died, and they caught me. A casteless killing a member of the Warrior Caste in good standing? Well, it was execution or the Legion. I chose the Legion. They threw me a party! Well, they threw a party for the Legion recruits from the upper castes. I just happened to be there. And technically it was a funeral, with dirges and mourning. But there was also feasting and drinking, which, to me, made it a party. I ate all the roast nug I could, and then we were ushered out the great doors and into the dark.

Paragon's mercy, was it dark. You don't know dark until you've been in the Deep Roads without a torch. People started lighting them, slowly, but in those first few moments, I thought I was going to cry. And then I felt a hand on my shoulder, and someone telling me that it was going to be all right. It was Varlan Vollney. We became friends. He taught me to read and write. Without him, you wouldn't be reading this right now, would you?

He died in Kal'Hirol. I still miss him a little bit, sometimes. But he was ready. He'd been ready for a while. He never told me what he did to end up in the Legion, but I got the feeling it was something really bad that he felt terrible about. So he was ready to go. I never was. Not till I met the Grey Wardens.

(Wow, that did not come out well. "Grey Wardens make Legion of the Dead member wish for true death." That's not what I meant. You know what I meant.)

Anyway, there it is—the story of my life. Shorter than I thought it would be. Actually, people say that to me a lot. The other story of my life.

ANDRASTE'S BOOKSHELF

ESSENTIAL TOMES FOR THE PAINFULLY DEVOUT

A Guide for Chantry Faithful *by Sister Lilian Hatch*

It has been said that every Thedosian bookshelf is complete with only a well-worn copy of the Chant of Light. This does not mean the Maker's words are the only ones His children should read. Indeed, the Maker speaks through the rare blessed among us, and we have much to learn from the critical perusal of a well-tested tome. We simply must choose what we read carefully.

Collected and discussed here are some of the most important excerpts from Chantry-approved writers like Ines Arancia, Sister Petrine, and of course, Brother Genitivi—including, for the first time, a section from the unpublished second volume of *In Pursuit of Knowledge: The Travels of a Chantry Scholar.*

Also included: writers to avoid unless you wish to see a Seeker at your door.

CHANTRY-SANCTIONED AUTHORS

• BROTHER FERDINAND GENITIVI •

"As it is the duty of all true sons of the Chantry to make the Chant heard from every corner of the world, I made it my mission to find as many corners of the world as possible. The Maker can hardly expect us to do one without the other."

Few authors have been as prolific and influential as Brother Ferdinand Genitivi. A devout brother of the Chantry, Genitivi has brought the wider world of Thedas to us through his writings, in the necessary context—largely through eyes guided by the Maker's principles.

While there are times when Genitivi's writings do verge on empathetic and even accepting of primitive and backward cultures, he is never obscene. Indeed, Genitivi's writings—including *In Pursuit of Knowledge: The Travels of a Chantry Scholar*, *Tales of the Destruction of Thedas*, *Kirkwall: The City of Chains*, and even the more obscure *Stone Halls of the Dwarves*—have their place in a proper Chantry bookshelf and may be taught freely to advanced students of the Maker ready to move beyond the Chant of Light.

Notable works: *In Pursuit of Knowledge: The Travels of a Chantry Scholar*; *Tales of the Destruction of Thedas*; *Stone Halls of the Dwarves*; *Kirkwall: The City of Chains*; *Thedas: Myths and Legends* (contributing author); *The Stone and Her Children: Dwarves of the Dragon Age*; *Tales from Beneath the Earth* (contributing author).

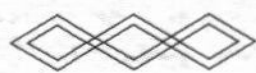

The History of the Chantry

Chapter 1

THE FIRST BLIGHT devastated the Tevinter Imperium. Not only had the darkspawn ravaged the countryside, but Tevinter citizens had to face the fact that their own gods had turned against them. Dumat, the Old God once known as the Dragon of Silence, had risen to silence the world, and despite the frenzied pleas for help, the other Old Gods did nothing. The people of the Imperium began to question their faith, murdering priests and burning temples to punish their gods for not returning to help.

In those days, even after the devastation of the First Blight, the Imperium stretched across the known world. Fringed with barbarian tribes, the Imperium was well prepared for invasions and attacks from without. Fitting, then, that the story of its downfall begins from within.

The people of the far northern and eastern reaches of the Imperium rose up against their powerful overlords in rebellion. The Tevinter magisters summoned demons to put down these small rebellions, leaving corpses to burn as examples to all who would dare revolt. The Imperium began to tear itself apart from within, throngs of angry and disillusioned citizens doing what centuries of opposing armies could not. But the magisters were confident in their power, and they could not imagine surviving a Blight only to be destroyed by their own subjects.

Even after the Blight, Tevinter commanded an army larger than that of any other organized nation in Thedas, but that army was scattered and its morale dwindling. The ruin of Tevinter was such that the Alamarri barbarians, who had spread their clans and holds over the wilderness of the Fereldan Valley at the far southeast edge of the Imperium, saw weakness in their enemy, and, after an age of oppression, embarked on a campaign not only to free their own lands, but to bring down mighty Tevinter as well.

The leaders of that blessed campaign were the great barbarian warlord Maferath, and his wife, Andraste. Their dreams and ambitions would change the world forever.

Chapter 2

WHEN THE PROPHET Andraste and her husband Maferath arrived at the head of their barbarian horde, southern Tevinter was thrown into chaos. The Imperium had defended against invasions in the past, but now they stood without the protection of their gods, with their army in tatters and their country devastated by the Blight. Many felt that the timing of the invasion was yet another of the Maker's miracles in Andraste's campaign to spread His divine word.

Andraste was more than simply the wife of a warlord, after all—she was also the betrothed of the Maker. Enraptured by the melodic sound of her voice as she sang to the heavens for guidance, the Maker Himself appeared to Andraste and proposed that she come with Him, leaving behind the flawed world of humanity. In her wisdom, Andraste pleaded with the Maker to return to His people and create paradise in the world of men. The Maker agreed, but only if all of the world would turn away from the worship of false gods and accept the Maker's divine commandments.

Armed with the knowledge of the one true god, Andraste began the Exalted March into the weakened Imperium. One of the Maker's commandments, that magic should serve man rather than rule over him, was as honey to the souls of the downtrodden of Tevinter, who lived under the thumbs of the magisters.

Word of Andraste's Exalted March, of her miracles and military successes, spread far and wide. Those in the Imperium who felt the Old Gods had abandoned them eagerly listened to the words of the Maker. Those throngs of restless citizens who destroyed temples now did so in the name of the Maker and His prophet, Andraste. As Maferath's armies conquered the lands of southern Tevinter, so did Andraste's words conquer hearts.

It is said that the Maker smiled on the world at the Battle of Valarian Fields, in which the forces of Maferath challenged and defeated the greatest army Tevinter could muster. The southern reaches of the mighty Imperium now lay at the mercy of barbarians. Faith in the Maker, bolstered by such miracles, threatened to shake the foundations of the Imperium apart.

Of course, the human heart is more powerful than the greatest weapon, and when wounded, it is capable of the blackest of deeds.

Chapter 3

IT IS SAID that at the Battle of Valarian Fields, Maferath stood and looked out over his armies. He had conquered the southern reaches of the greatest empire the world had ever known and built splintered barbarian clans into a force to be feared. With pride in his heart, he turned to congratulate his men and found that they had turned from him.

Maferath fell to the evil of jealousy. After all that he had done, his wife was the one to receive all the glory. He saw his wife's power and influence, and tired of his place as second husband, below the Maker. His heart swelled with fury. If he had conquered just to have his wife wrested from him by a forgotten god and a legion of faith-hungry rabble, then perhaps this war was not worth the trouble.

Here, history and the Chant of Light come apart. History tells us that Maferath looked north into the central Imperium and saw nothing but more war against a rapidly regrouping army, and he despaired. The Chant of Light holds that Maferath chafed with jealousy of the Maker, and jealousy of the glory that Andraste received although it was he who led the armies.

Maferath traveled to the imperial capital of Minrathous to speak with the Archon Hessarian. There he offered up his wife to the Imperium in return for a truce that would end hostilities once and for all. The Archon, eager to put down the voice of the prophet that stirred his own people against him, agreed. Maferath led Andraste into an ambush where she was captured by imperial agents, putting an end to her Exalted March.

Crowds of loyalists stood in the central square of Minrathous to watch Andraste's execution. By command of the Archon, she

The mighty temples of Minrathous were made of jet stone mined near Kirkwall.

was burned at the stake in what the Imperium believed to be the most painful punishment imaginable. According to the Chantry, however, Andraste was instead purified and made whole by the flames, ascending to life at her Maker's side. By all accounts, there was only silence where they expected screams. At the sight of the prophet burning, the crowds were filled with a profound guilt, as if they had participated in a great blasphemy. So moving was the moment that the Archon himself drew his sword and thrust it into the prophet's heart, ending her torment and leaving those assembled to consider the weight of what they had seen.

Whereas the execution of Andraste was meant to be a symbol of defeat for the faith of the Maker, in truth it all but sealed the fate of the worship of the Old Gods and paved the way for the spread of the Maker's Chant.

Chapter 4

THE CROWDS PRESENT at the death of Andraste were right to feel despair. It is believed that the prophet's execution angered the Maker, and He turned His back on humanity once more, leaving the people of Thedas to suffer in the dark.

In these dark times, mankind scrambled for a light, any light. Some found comfort in demonic cults that promised power and riches in return for worship. Others prayed to the Old Gods for forgiveness, begging the great dragons to return to the world. Still others fell so low as to worship the darkspawn, forming vile cults dedicated to the exaltation of evil in its purest form. It is said that the world wept as its people begged for a savior who would not come.

Andraste's followers, however, did not abandon her teachings when she died. The cult of Andraste rescued her sacred ashes from the courtyard in Minrathous after her execution, stealing them away to a secret temple. The location of that temple has long been lost, but the ashes of Andraste served as a symbol of the enduring nature of the faith in the Maker, that humanity could earn the Maker's forgiveness despite its grievous insult to Him.

With time, the cult of Andraste spread and grew, and the Chant of Light took form. Sing this chant in the four corners of Thedas, it was said, and the world would gain the Maker's attention at last. As the Chant of Light spread, the cult of Andraste became known as the Andrastian Chantry. Those who converted to the Chantry's beliefs found it their mission to spread Andraste's word.

There were many converts, including powerful people in the Imperium and in the city-states of what is now Orlais. Such was the power of the Maker's word that the young King Drakon undertook a series of Exalted Marches meant to unite the city-states and create an empire solely dedicated to the Maker's will. The Orlesian Empire became the seat of the Chantry's power, the Grand Cathedral in Val Royeaux the source of the movement that birthed the organized Chantry as we know it today. Drakon, by then Emperor Drakon I, created the Circle of Magi, the Order of Templars, and the holy office of the Divine. Many within the Chantry revere him nearly equally with Andraste herself.

The modern Chantry is a thing of faith and beauty, but it is also a house of necessity, protecting Thedas from powerful forces that would do it harm. Where the Grey Wardens protect the world from the Blights, the Chantry protects mankind from itself. Most of all, the Chantry works to earn the Maker's forgiveness, so that one day He will return and transform the world into the paradise it was always meant to be.

—Excerpted from *Tales of the Destruction of Thedas*

BE WARY OF ELVEN SOURCES

The elves like to talk. Be they Dalish or of the city in origin, the elves have an oral tradition in which much of their knowledge and traditions is passed along but never actually written down. Is it any wonder then that what they have written down is to be taken with a grain of salt? The elves like to disseminate teachings from keepers like Gisharel and hahrens like Sarethia. But really, none should be consulted in any serious search for knowledge; they should at best be regarded with a kind of novel curiosity. At worst, these elven sources are apocryphal.

Here is one such example, most commonly attributed to the aforementioned Hahren Sarethia of Highever's alienage:

The Rise and Fall of the Dales

The humans tell tales of Andraste, and to them, she was a prophet. To our people, however, she was an inspiration. Her rebellion against Tevinter gave our people a window through which to see the sun, and we reached toward it with all our strength. The rebellion was brief but successful; even after the death of the prophetess, we fought on for independence as the human Imperium began to crumble. In the end, we won freedom and the southern land known as the Dales, and we began the Long Walk to our new homeland.

There, in the Dales, our people revived the lost lore as best we could. We called the first city Halamshiral, "end of the journey," and founded a new nation, isolated as elves were meant to be, this time patrolled by an order of Emerald Knights charged with watching the borders for trouble from humans.

But you already know that something went wrong. A small elven raiding party attacked the nearby human village of Red Crossing, an act of anger that prompted the Chantry to retaliate, and with their superior numbers, they conquered the Dales.

We were not enslaved as we had been before, but our worship of the ancient gods was now forbidden. We were allowed to live among the humans only as second-class citizens who worshiped their Maker, forgetting once more the scraps of lore we had maintained through the centuries.

Signs of wealth and excess can be found in even the smallest ports of coastal Rivain.

Seers of Rivain

NOWHERE IN MY travels, not in the heart of the Imperium nor the streets of Orzammar, have I felt so much an outsider as in Rivain.

The Chant of Light never truly reached the ears of these people. The years they spent under the thumb of the Qunari left most of the country zealous followers of the Qun. But resistance to the Chant goes deeper than the Qunari War. The Rivaini refuse to be parted from their seers, wise women who are in fact hedge mages, communicating with spirits and actually allowing themselves to become possessed. The Chantry prohibition against such magical practices violates millennia of local tradition.

—Excerpted from *In Pursuit of Knowledge: The Travels of a Chantry Scholar*

The Tal-Vashoth

BEING LOST IN an ancient Tevinter ruin in northern Rivain is highly overrated.

And then I found myself beset by several bands of Qunari, apparently working in concert. I fled and managed to hide in a little village by the name of Vindaar. The people there, mostly humans and a few elves, were devout followers of the Qun.

It was the most organized village I ever laid eyes on. The houses were identical and arranged along perfectly orthogonal lines. The fields were well tended and apparently communal. But there were signs of damage everywhere, as if the town had suffered repeated sieges: buildings shattered, fields burned, and a great many empty houses. I spent the night in the home of Vindaar's matriarch, who introduced herself only as "Seer." When I tried to regale my hostess with the tale of my Qunari assailants, I discovered something.

Qunari, Seer said, are people who follow the Qun. Her people. Those born into Qunari society who reject the Qun are called Vashoth, which means "gray ones." These gray ones must leave their homes, for they have no place among the Qunari. Sadly, many turn against the society that cast them out.

From the Chantry and Qunari to raiders and seers, the nation of Rivain is a mosaic of disparate peoples living in relative harmony.

These outcasts call themselves Tal-Vashoth, "the true gray ones." Often, they have no skills to make an honest living, so they sell themselves into service, usually becoming mercenaries. Even the most inept fighter among the Qunari race possesses prodigious size and an intimidating visage. These, she informed me, were my attackers in the countryside, the same band that wreaked such havoc on Vindaar.

The Tal-Vashoth wage a bitter war against the Qun, the Qunari, and sometimes against order itself. They are no match for the Qunari army, so they generally strike at farms, travelers, and those who stray too far from Qunari protection. I was lucky to escape with my life.

—Excerpted from *In Pursuit of Knowledge: The Travels of a Chantry Scholar*

Nevarrans Do Not Burn Their Dead

THE FOURTH TIME I attempted to cross the border into Nevarra from Orlais and was turned back by chevaliers, I decided to take the more roundabout path: A ship back to Ferelden, and then another to Nevarra. The outcome was more than worth the trouble.

The whole country is filled with artistry, from the statues of heroes that litter the streets in even the meanest villages to the glittering golden College of Magi in Cumberland. Perhaps nowhere is more astonishing than the vast necropolis outside Nevarra City. Unlike most other followers of Andraste, the Nevarrans do not burn their dead. Instead, they carefully preserve the bodies and seal them in elaborate tombs. Some of the wealthiest Nevarrans begin construction of their own tombs while quite young, and these become incredible palaces, complete with gardens, bathhouses, and ballrooms, utterly silent, kept only for the dead.

—Excerpted from *In Pursuit of Knowledge: The Travels of a Chantry Scholar*

The crypts of Nevarrans are often decorated with their most prized possessions.

In Nevarra, the dead stay wealthy and powerful. Nobles may live decades overseeing the construction of their own tombs.

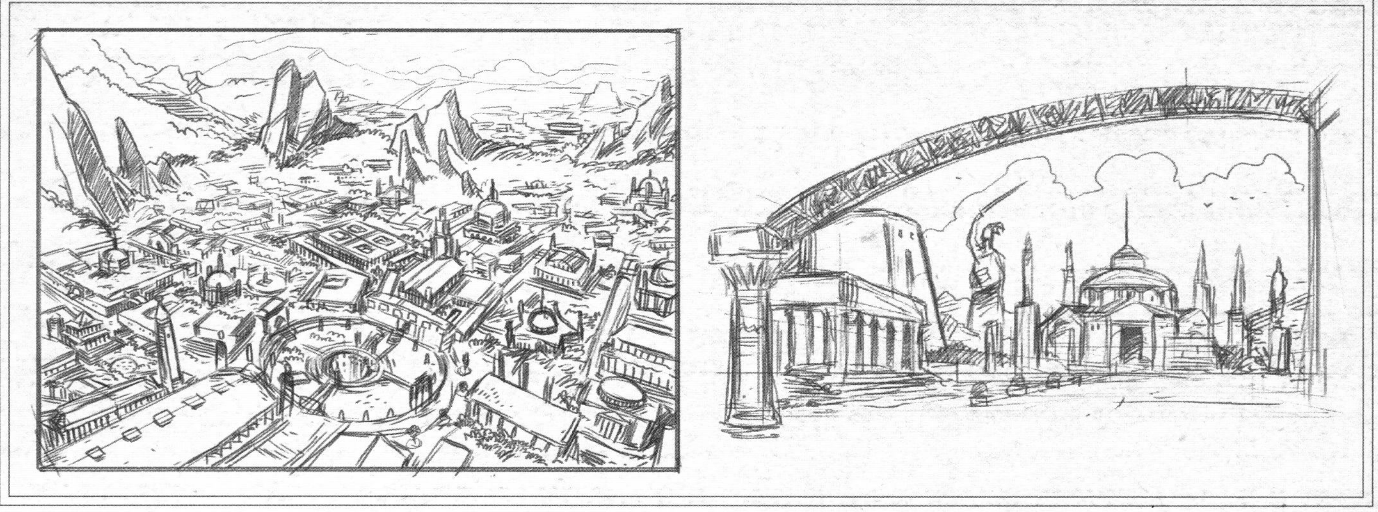

The city of Nevarra (*left*) grows from the Grand Necropolis at its heart. Cumberland (*right*) is home to the College of Magi.

Beyond Thedas

FOR MANY AGES, the world that lies beyond Thedas has been largely unknown to us. Rumors and legends exist, tales of hardy sea captains crossing the ocean in search of treasure or ill-fated forays into the wilds, but they have always been buried under hearsay. Any serious attempts at exploration have been foiled by either the devastation of the Blights or the discouragement of waters plagued by both pirates and Qunari dreadnoughts.

Still, with so many ages having passed since the Fourth Blight, the nations of Thedas are slowly pushing at the edges of their borders. It is inevitable that interest will turn outward, and that both landless settlers and intrepid kings will seek new lands to claim. The question, then, is what will await us when the shadows lift and the age of human exploration begins in earnest?

To the North and South

THE FIRST THING we must consider, before casting our eyes beyond the shores of Thedas, is that we have not even explored our home completely. Most maps stop at the forests of the South and the jungles of the North, but there is plenty of evidence to suggest that considerable territory lies beyond both these borderlands—inhospitable as it may be.

In the South, most knowledge stops at the expanse of wilderness in southern Orlais and Ferelden. This is not true for the Chasind people who live in those forests, however. According to them, if one travels far enough to the south, the trees give way to "sunless lands" that spend much of the year covered in snow, and places even farther, filled with mountains of ice. As inhospitable as this sounds, there are already people who live there. My first impression is that these were other Chasind, but I was harshly corrected on that point. Considering the Chasind word for them, Agadi, is also their word for "exile," my suspicion is that these are groups who were expelled from the forests and have since splintered off into their own culture. Certainly bad blood lingers, and the Chasind consider the sunless lands to be dangerous and forbidden.

In the North, one must first survive the dangers of the Wandering Hills in the Anderfels before reaching the northern jungles known as the Donarks. The threats there, aside from disease and savage wildlife, include Qunari out of the enclave of Qundalon. Tevinter sailors report that the jungles extend far to the north, although accounts of just how far vary wildly. The Tevinter word for this expanse is Viridis—"the Green"—and it is the word that adorns the few nautical maps that include the region. Anything beyond the coastline is a mystery, however, and if the tales of flying chimera and wingless dragons have any truth to them, it is no wonder that the jungles hold little interest to most.

The Boeric Islands

MOST PEOPLE OF Thedas are aware of the islands immediately to the north of our shores: Par Vollen, home to the dread Qunari, and Seheron, a land that has been in constant contention for many ages. Few are aware, however, that the Boeric Ocean to the north is littered with islands, some of which are quite substantial in size. Some provide haven for pirates, while others have colonies belonging to either the Qunari or the Tevinter Imperium (and which change hands as the war between them rages on), but there are many reports of other islands far beyond the reach of both nations.

Of particular interest is the possible existence of a large island called Par Ladi. Legends suggest that the inhabitants of the island, Parladians (for lack of a better term), are an insular people uninterested in contact with outsiders. According to one detailed account, the Parladians are said to have a capital with coastal fortresses that rival any in Thedas. The people there are "bedecked in gold and jewels, as cultured as any Tevinter nobleman even though they spoke an unknown language," and are quick to expel any foreigner who approaches—even, according to the account, a crippled ship that limps into their ports.

The interesting question, if these Parladians do indeed exist, is why they have not attracted the attention of the Qunari. Perhaps they have, but their fortresses are enough to hold their enemy back, and we in Thedas hear nothing of their battles. Other sailor tales, however, raise a more interesting possibility. They speak of Parladian witches, reminiscent of Rivaini seers, who have cloaked their island in a spell that discourages any who seek it out. Superstitious nonsense, or an explanation as to why no serious effort to contact these people has ever occurred? Whatever the truth, the lack of a berth in the Boeric Ocean (whether by virtue of the refusal by Parladians to offer it or the lack of their existence) has prevented Thedosian ships from ranging further north.

The Mysterious West

IF ONE JOURNEYS west across the Anderfels, one will reach the settlement of Laysh. Once a sprawling port town, Laysh largely fell to ruin after the Third Blight . . . but not, as one might suppose, due to darkspawn attacks. The entire purpose of Laysh was to receive ships from across the Volca Sea, odd-looking cargo vessels that would arrive laden with wares and spices of a like never seen in Thedas. The trade was lucrative enough to justify Laysh's existence even in such harsh territory, at least until the traders stopped coming in the early Black Age.

According to Ander legend, these traders were called Voshai. They were also said to be hostile to the people of Laysh, completely uninterested in learning the king's tongue for anything more than barter, and almost obsessively interested in acquiring lyrium. Also of interest are the tales that said the captains of every Voshai ship were dwarves, treated with such deference that it implied dwarves held a place of profound power in their society . . . or, at the very least, among the seafarers of their culture. In contrast, there are no reports of elves on the Voshai ships.

While Laysh was hardly a port of sufficient size to build sturdy ships, it is said that several Tevinter merchant houses banded together to mount an expedition, with the thought, "If they won't come to us, we'll go to them." The expedition did not return, and neither did the few vessels that followed, until eventually all interest in the Voshai faded. Reports in recent years suggest the Voshai ships may have returned to Laysh, supposedly carrying tales of a "massive cataclysm" in their homeland—the reason for their absence, perhaps?—though the truth of these reports is questionable at best.

Across the Eastern Ocean

THE AMARANTHINE OCEAN, lying to the east of Thedas, is a massive body of water plagued by terrible storms, as well as sea creatures. According to Antivan legend, however, a few daring sea captains have made the crossing . . . and found an untouched and verdant land. Universally referred to as "Amaranth" in these tales, it is said to be completely uninhabited by any civilized race. Indeed, the descriptions attributed to these captains suggest the land is almost a paradise, completely devoid of creatures larger than a small bird. True or not, at least one captain suggested that Amaranth held great promise for future settlers willing to make the dangerous voyage.

It is at this point that the legends regarding Amaranth become questionable. One story suggests that a group of Old God cultists departed for the land aboard a trio of ships in the late Storm Age. Another suggests that several groups of settlers sponsored by Free Marcher merchants left from the island of Estwatch in the Blessed Age. Still more claim the same is true for several pirate lords of the Felicisima Armada. All such tales end the same: with the expeditions never being heard from again. One tells of a Marcher lord's valiant wife commandeering a vessel to cross the ocean in search of her lost husband, only to find his settlement mysteriously abandoned and a lone survivor so crazed with terror that he killed himself rather than be taken from the cave in which he hid.

It is entirely possible that such tales are exaggerated, the sort of common legend that spreads and changes with each passing, and that Amaranth does not exist—the idea of a paradise across the ocean is an alluring one, after all. Some scholars have advanced the notion that, should a land exist to the east, it is most likely where the Qunari come from . . . and thus why would such a land be uninhabited? Did the Qunari abandon their homes completely, leaving no trace of their former civilization? Or did they come from elsewhere, and Amaranth is simply another land with a mystery that will one day be solved by future explorers?

—Excerpted from *In Pursuit of Knowledge: The Travels of a Chantry Scholar*, Volume II

In Par Vollen, home to the Qunari, the structures are like beehives.

◆ SISTER PETRINE ◆

"It is a truth universally acknowledged that nothing is more successful at inspiring a person to mischief as being told not to do something."

Perhaps less brave than Genitivi in her pursuit of knowledge, Sister Petrine is by no means less of a polymath—and at times more inclined toward a dissenting opinion. The controversial Fereldan sister has written on subjects as diverse as barbarian tribes, in the examination of both Chasind and Avvar in *Ferelden: Folklore and History*, and military history, in *The Exalted Marches: An Examination of Chantry Warfare.*

Troubling, however, is her willingness to explore taboo subjects like the Tevinter Imperium in *Black City, Black Divine* and even the lies of Shartan in *The Dissonant Verses*, which presented verses excised from the Chant of Light for their apocryphal sources and content. Petrine has been the subject of much criticism in the Chantry for her approach, writing about the greatest evils with almost objective language. At times her tone can even be perceived as contemptuous toward certain of the truths we hold so sacred.

It is therefore a risk to teach or even read Petrine. Some of her work is fine and, indeed, helpful. Few outside Ferelden understand the nation as well as those who have read her histories. Lesser texts must be read with a highly critical eye and, in the case of the largely banned *Dissonant Verses*, thick, black ink.

Notable works: *Ferelden: Folklore and History*; *A Study of the Fifth Blight*; *The Exalted Marches: An Examination of Chantry Warfare*; *Of Fires, Circles, and Templars: A History of Magic in the Chantry*; *Thedas: Myths and Legends* (contributing author); *Alamarri Myths and Legends*; *Tales of the Mountain-People*; *The Ancient North*; *The Changing Face of Thedas*; *Empire and Imperium*; *An Examination of Orlesian Government*; *The Dissonant Verses* (banned).

The City Elves

WHEN THE HOLY Exalted March of the Dales resulted in the dissolution of the elven kingdom, leaving a great many elves homeless once again, Divine Renata I declared that all lands loyal to the Chantry must give the elves refuge within their own walls. Considering the atrocities committed by the elves at Red Crossing, this was a great testament to the Chantry's charity. There was one condition, however—the elves were to lay aside their pagan gods and live under the rule of the Chantry.

Some of the elves refused our goodwill. They banded together to form the wandering Dalish elves, keeping their old elven ways—and their hatred of humans—alive. To this day, Dalish elves still terrorize those of us who stray too close to their camps. Most of the elves, however, saw that it was wisest to live under the protection of humans.

And so we took the elves into our cities and tried to integrate them. We invited them into our own homes and gave them jobs as servants and farmhands. Here in Denerim, the elves even have their own quarter, governed by an elven keeper. Most have proven to be productive members of society. Still, a small segment of the elven community remains dissatisfied. These troublemakers and malcontents roam the streets causing mayhem, rebelling against authority, and making a general nuisance of themselves.

—Excerpted from *Ferelden: Folklore and History*

Legend of the Juggernaut

THE ARM OF the Imperium is long.

Once it reached even this forest, in a time when the barbarian tribes of the Clayne still ruled the land. The Tevinter magisters fought to take it from them—inch by inch, if need be, using terrible magic. The magister Harach brought an army to this forest, led by Alaric, his friend and general. For Alaric, Harach fashioned a suit of the finest armor, infused it with lyrium and his own blood magic, and named it "Juggernaut" after the unstoppable giant golems guarding the gates of Minrathous. Thus armed did Alaric win many victories against the Clayne.

Genitivi once wrote that to know a place, one must know its people. To simply observe is not enough.

When defeat came, it came from within. Alaric's own lieutenants rose up against him, jealous of the favor he had curried with the magisters and eager to take the Juggernaut armor from him. Alaric was slain, and as each successor gained the armor, the other lieutenants turned against him instead. The Tevinter outpost fell to vicious infighting. In a fury, Magister Harach voyaged to the outpost and slew the last three lieutenants.

The Clayne, however, were already approaching the outpost in force. The barbarian chieftain of the Clayne desired the fabled armor for himself, and even with all his power, Harach could not hope to stand against them all. Instead, Harach used the last of his own life force to cast a spell of blood magic that bound demons to the bodies of the three dead lieutenants, as well as Harach's own lifeless corpse. These bound revenants hid the pieces of the Juggernaut armor, and although the barbarians sacked the outpost, the chieftain found neither the armor nor the revenants.

The Juggernaut armor's legend lives on, and more than one brave soul has ventured into the depths of the Brecilian Forest in search of it, never to return.

—Excerpted from *Ferelden: Folklore and History*

The Llomerryn Accords

FIFTY YEARS. That's how long it took the Imperium to drive out the Qunari occupation. But the rest of northern Thedas was not so lucky.

Both Divines, white and black, declared Exalted Marches and for the only time since the Schism of the Chantry, they worked together. A century-long siege resulted, with the giant Qunari entrenched in Antiva and Rivain, and all of Thedas throwing armies against them.

The war drained the resources of every nation in Thedas, leaving most on the brink of collapse. For the giants, it did not appear to be the damage to their armada or the loss of their soldiers, but

Genitivi is known for his writing, but he often sketched what he saw in vivid detail.

the terrible toll upon the Rivaini population that prompted their retreat. When the third New Exalted March had all but massacred the people of Kont-aar without even chipping the Qunari occupying force, the giants finally withdrew.

The treaty that put an official end to the Qunari Wars was signed on the politically neutral island of Llomerryn off the southern coast of Rivain. One hundred and fifty years after the assault on the mainland began, the Qunari left our shores. They received the northern archipelago in exchange for cessation of hostilities against all the nations listed on the accord. Only Tevinter refused to sign, and so the war continues to rage in the Imperium to the present day.

It's worth noting, however, that the Kingdom of Rivain immediately violated the treaty. Twice. Once, when the humans of northern Rivain—nearly all practitioners of the Qun and therefore, by definition, Qunari—refused to leave their homes and go in exile to the islands. And again, when the Rivain Chantry and nationalist forces, unable to convert their people back to the worship of the Maker, tried a purge by the sword, slaughtering countless unarmed people and burying them in mass graves. It's a fortunate mystery that the leaders in Kont-aar did not alert their allies in the Northern Passage, or we'd still be fighting the giants now.

—Excerpted from *The Exalted Marches: An Examination of Chantry Warfare*

Glandivalis

IT IS HERESY today to speak of Shartan, an elven slave who rose up against his Tevinter masters to help Andraste's barbarian invasion. Andraste crossed the Waking Sea with a horde of warriors at her back, and a rebellion occurring behind the enemy lines

Shartan was a slave who became a devotee of Andraste herself, . Andraste gave him a mystic blade that he called Glandivalis (translation unknown) and he fought at Maferath's side. the Canticle is one of the Dissonant Verses, and has been ever since the Exalted March of the Dales.

don't speak of elven heroes or the role they played in Andraste's war

—Excerpted from *The Dissonant Verses*

BE WARY OF VARRIC TETHRAS

"You heard about the Kirkwall chantry being destroyed? The guy responsible used to be a friend of mine."

The prolific dwarven author Varric Tethras can be closely linked to the mage agitator Anders and the events that led to the mage uprising in Kirkwall. Even if Tethras did not have blood on his hands, his body of work remains, by and large, little more than smut, pulp, or, at times, smutty pulp. One need only look at the titles of his work to know they should be avoided. *Hard in Hightown*? *Darktown's Deal*? It takes more than a loose grip on alliteration to call oneself a writer.

Of course, his writing is quite popular with the younger, more rebellious students of the Chantry, who have been known to share it secretly among themselves. It's not unheard of to pry up a dormitory floorboard and find a copy of *The Viper's Nest* or, Maker forbid, *The Tale of the Champion*. If a Tethras book is found, it should be burned on sheer principle.

Notable works: *Hard in Hightown*; *The Tale of the Champion*; *Darktown's Deal*; *The Viper's Nest*; *The Dasher's Men*.

Hard in Hightown

Chapter 1

They say coin never sleeps, but anyone who's walked the patrol of Hightown Market at midnight might disagree. The pickpockets and confidence men head to the taverns at dusk, the dwarven businessmen and nobles go back to their tiny palaces to fret over the ways they got cheated, and the market falls silent.

Donnen Brennokovic knew every angle of the market with his eyes closed. Twenty years of patrols had etched it into him so that he walked that beat even in his dreams. The recruit, Jevlan, was another story. The ring of steel striking stone told Donnen that the kid had stumbled into a column again. His new armor would be full of dents by sunrise.

"Torches would make this easier." The sound of Jevlan hauling himself off the pavement was like a tinker's cart crashing.

"Torches make you night blind. You'll adjust." Donnen crossed the square to help the kid to his feet. A breeze scurried across the plaza, sending the banners and pennants shivering and carrying an old, familiar scent. Donnen stopped in his tracks. "Something's wrong." His voice was low, warning. He peered into the dark, up at the mezzanine just above them. "Follow me. Be ready for trouble."

The two guards climbed the dark stairs and there, in a puddle of shadow, found the body. Gold-trimmed satin glittered through the blood.

"Get the captain," Donnen sighed. "We've got a dead magistrate."

◆ PHILLIAM, A BARD! ◆

"When the reader sees 'Edited by Philliam, a Bard!' they know they'll be enthralled every step of the short journey, cover to cover. Some authors rescue stories from ruins. I rescue stories from authors."

It is becoming difficult to avoid the works of the young "Philliam, a Bard!" And it is doubly difficult to determine that it is actually his work that you are avoiding. He appears to feel no shame in extensively quoting the works of his betters, sometimes to the detriment of the depth of a subject. But one must admit that he is responsible for a great many of the books that now find their way to remote readers, some of whom may be inspired to pursue more complete studies.

For this reason, it is with caution that I do not wholly condemn the tomes that bear his insufferable moniker, for they are as likely as not to contain the abridged thoughts of our most knowledgeable Chantry scholars, though they themselves toil in obscurity.

Notable works: *Rebels of the Marches: Allegory in Rebellion*; *Orlesian Legacy: How Institutions of the Oppressors Linger—The Speeches of Viscount Michel Lafaille*; *The Champion: History, Ancient and Current*; *We Need Not Demons: Our Dangerous World*; *Song of the Old Marches: The Death of Goodman Ser Austice at the Hand of the Reaver Shius*; *A History Not of Heroes: Readings in the Ugly Heart of Change*; *The Folly and Other Whimsies: Collected Commentaries of Orlais*; *A Disposable Walking Tour of the Capital*; *Small Legends: Of Nugs and Foxes*; *On the Glassworks of the Marquisate of Serault*; countless others.

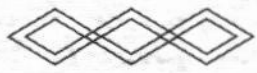

Philliam, a Bard!, on Philliam, a Bard!

WHAT CAN BE said of Philliam, a Bard!? What can't?

Below lie examples of dedications to excite and entice, preferably attributed from graybeards of note. They are to be applied to each new volume in service of creating a brand of excitement. Bless the speed of printing blocks over the wavering hand of the myopic monk. I also recommend wax and foil to catch the eye.

Also, it is fully and always "Philliam, a Bard!" The exclamation speaks to the infamous nature of the discipline. Not to suggest violence, for that would invite unseemly attention. Rather, I intend to remind the reader that the profession of "Bard" came first. That it was the assassin who masqueraded as the storyteller, because storyteller was the more daring life. Too long have the robed-with-quill sought legitimacy through the factual landslides they call books:

Let it be known that among mere observers and watchers, there is one who does, who is a doer. Who does not reason from a distance, but wades in and gets his boots dirty. And then sells the story of it to purchase new boots, for there is no uniform, no shackles! Not when there is knowledge to be rescued! And not just from wet ruin, but dry record! For knowledge is in danger not just when cities crumble, but when the uninspired obscure it in the density of their prose, when the scholar confines it to libraries where only those as dusty as the shelves may find it! These are the stories of peoples, by peoples, and they belong with said.

Philliam, a Bard!, mines not just the depths of history, but of historical record. His anthologies spare the reader the search, for if searching was their wont, they would join the bearded quills droning their way across Thedas. No! The reader of today craves the point, the victory, the treasure! While humility will not allow us to dispute that "getting there is half the fun," if the reader can simply be there, presented in digest, then half the fun is already theirs in a fraction of the time, weighting it more like 20/80. Is it any wonder Genitivi dined alone, having spent half to get twenty? That's not just a confirmation of waste; it is informational fiscal irresponsibility. The modern reader knows when their attention is spent frivolously. They know.

Philliam, a Bard!, reminds the reader that history is theirs, and full of adventure more grand than any fiction. Perhaps not of imagination, but that too can be explored when the greatest of physiological and mental studies are brought to focus in volumes that dispense with pretense, formality, and numbing verification. The great works are out there, stagnating, for want of an editor to shape them for today.

—A letter from Philliam, a Bard!, to his editor

Genitivi on Philliam, a Bard!

I NOW HAVE a greater and personal understanding of the lord who finds a poached carcass bereft of trophy horn and gall, with all else left to rot. I have never had to withstand such an attack on my work, not among the scrutiny of my peers, nor among the admittedly sparse eyes of the public I have reached. My research on the cultural history of the sporadic occupation of the Green Dales was intended to be studied as a complete tome, and though it was of considerable and imposing weight, to separate out any given chapter or, worse, single notes of fact, is to diminish understanding and to fracture perception.

Do not think me without proper etiquette, for I first made attempt to speak with this Philliam in person. It is fully Philliam Bernard Aloicious Trevelyan, is it not? A storied name, but as he is of such distance from the patriarch, and as he himself has abandoned the use of it, I could not in good conscience level a complaint against the family. I could quote the whole of his genealogy if I thought he was of a mind to care for it, but this Philliam seems more inclined to reductionism. He has certainly done as much for the term "bard" or, indeed, "author," "editor," "archivist," and all manner of abused vocation.

I have made complaints at numerous academic forums over the appropriation of my work, although their ability to censure is limited, as the young culprit is not a member. So I complain directly, for it is antithetical to the scholarly spirit to reduce the potential of knowledge in such a manner. I seek recompense in the only form that this wretch appears to understand.

With humble gratitude,
Brother Ferdinand Genitivi

Philliam, a Bard!, on Genitivi

I LOST MY interest during the sentence about—and as long as—the Green Dales. I did his work a favor in rescuing its own interesting bits from beneath itself. Hood's message to the king was riveting in isolation. The abridged is a bridge to readers who are willing to cross, or would he rather his tome weigh only on the minds of students forced to endure it? And the claims I do it only for coin? My name is known by far more than his, I'll wager and wager high. Arrange for payment and a special thanks in the next volume. It's likely more than he's seen from the libraries that beg of him.

The abridged is a bridge. Note that for the spine of even more portable tomes. Books for the pocket, the abridged is a bridge.

Signed,
Philliam, a Bard!

◆ INES ARANCIA ◆

"Why do I love plants? Because they're not people. That's why."

The botanist's best source on all manner of plant is the ubiquitous *The Botanical Compendium.* Its author, the notoriously prickly Ines Arancia, is an expert on all things living in the ground that aren't dwarves. Yes, it is true that Arancia is a mage. But it is commendable that someone with such awful powers would give herself instead to the study of the Maker's smallest miracles. Anyone who doubts Arancia's commitment to the teachings of Andraste need only read what she has to say on Prophet's laurel. Her compendium is an essential book for any crafting table and, combined with Ledoure's *The Whole Nug*, any true believer's kitchen. So much better than the work of that heretical Lord Cerastes.

Notable works: *The Botanical Compendium* (multiple editions)

Ambrosia

Felicidus aria—commonly known as the Silent Plains rose—is, to this day, the only plant found growing on the Silent Plains, which were tainted by the Blight a thousand years ago. As mentioned in the section on rare flowering plants, felicidus aria is not technically a rose, though its flowers do exude a sweet, rose-like scent.

The flower is rare, and is in danger of becoming extinct because of its value in the creation of ambrosia, which is distilled from the roots of the plant. Dozens of these plants go into the making of just one vial. Some say that the wives of the most powerful Tevinter magisters once used ambrosia to perfume their baths in a vulgar display of wealth.

Amrita Vein

Amrita was a hedge mage, famed for her talent as an herbalist. She could brew philters to soothe every ache or ailment, even coax the ill back from the brink of death. As word of Amrita's talents spread, she was made a target for capture. Amrita fled from them, refusing to go to a Circle. The templars took off in pursuit, dogging her steps, until they came to the edge of the Western Approach. Knowing the templars were less than half a day behind her, Amrita forged ahead. When the templars came to the edge of the desert, they stopped and turned back, believing that Amrita would be doomed to die in that sandblasted wilderness.

But Amrita did not die. She crossed the wasteland on foot, living off the strange plants that grew there, finding water in roots buried beneath the sand. On that long trek, Amrita discovered the herb now known as Amrita vein. She brought it out of the desert with her and continued to study and cultivate it. Amrita's extensive writings about desert plants, including Amrita vein, eventually found their way to the White Spire, where it was decided that her contributions would earn her a degree of freedom. She was allowed to continue living as she desired, as long as she submitted to the Harrowing.

Arbor Blessing

"Blessed by the vine in spring,
I shall not fear the winter's sting."

Arbor blessing is a useful vine that is notoriously difficult to cultivate, as if it had a mind of its own. The wind often carries its minuscule seeds for great distances from the parent plant. It is hard to say what causes the seeds to sprout once they land. However, it has long been believed that comfort and abundance follow where arbor blessing goes. Perhaps the vine only chooses conditions that promote rich harvests from domesticated flora. Therefore, see arbor blessing in spring, and you shall not grow hungry in winter.

Crystal Grace

The flowers of the crystal grace plant are appreciated for their beauty as well as their medicinal value. Pale blue and shaped like delicate crystal bells, the flowers should almost tinkle in the breeze. In fact, I have heard a tale of an Orlesian lady who ordered crystal grace to be planted all over her bower and then hired a mage from the White Spire to enchant the blooms to do just that. Eventually, she grew tired of the chiming and set fire to her lawn in a fit of pique.

Let us learn from this. These plants were created exactly as our Maker intended, and our interference rarely improves them.

Dragonthorn

The wood of the dragonthorn tree is prized for its strength, and has been used to craft bows of remarkable quality, but the leaves are equally valuable. Alchemists have known for centuries that an extract of dragonthorn leaves will enhance and stabilize other, more volatile magical compounds.

Embrium

Embriums are flowers from the orchid family. Their therapeutic qualities were actually discovered because of the flowers' exceptional beauty.

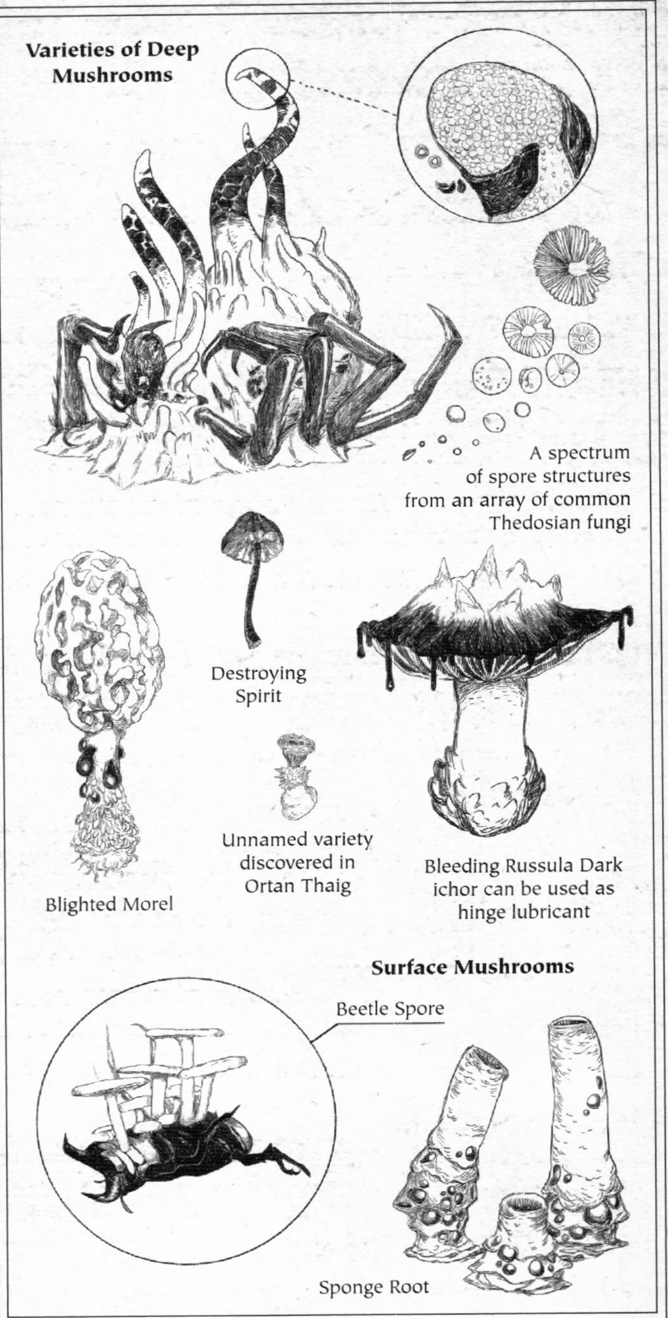

Mushrooms come in many varieties. Some are quite dangerous, making Arancia's work essential for foragers.

The beloved daughter of Lord Ignace Poulenc of Orlais fell victim to a terrible sickness of the lungs, which her healers were unable to cure. Thinking the girl would soon perish, her parents surrounded her bed with brightly colored flowers, hoping that they would bring some warmth and cheer in her last days. Oddly enough, the girl began to recover from the illness and grew stronger each day. Her parents were baffled but overjoyed. The healers eventually learned that the fragrance of one of the flowers eased the child's breathing. The flower was an embrium, and later became known as the Salubrious Embrium.

The other variant that has certain magical properties is known as Dark Embrium.

Felandaris

The name felandaris is elven, meaning "demon weed," which is fitting for this rare plant because it grows only in places where the Veil is thin. Felandaris is easily identified. It's a twisted, wicked-looking shrub with long, thorny shoots and no leaves: a skeletal hand, reaching out from an unmarked grave. Many swear the plant radiates a palpable aura of malevolence, so it comes as no surprise that it unnerves many a junior herbalist.

Prophet's Laurel

According to Orlesian folklore, Andraste's followers and sympathizers tossed sprigs of the laurel in her path as she was led to her pyre. After she burned, her ashes blew across the leaves on the ground, bestowing upon them their famed purifying qualities. It is just a tale, of course. The laurel was recognized as a healing herb long before Andraste's time. Ancient Tevinter scrolls describe the use of the laurel in poultices, tinctures, and even incense. Though the legend might be pure fabrication, the laurel will always be symbolic of Andraste's sacrifice. Its glossy, dark leaves represent the Sword of Mercy; the red berries, the drops of her blood upon it.

Spindleweed

It is an old country saying that spindleweed grows best for the sorrowful. Verdant spindleweed in a household's garden has often brought neighbors offering consolation, usually without even asking what might be wrong.

This originates from the plant's use as a seasoning for dishes meant to speed the recovery of the infirm. A person who grows much of it is likely caring for the fatally ill.

Vandal Aria

The vandal aria is a flowering shrub, related to the rare and nearly extinct felicidus aria, otherwise known as the Silent Plains rose. Of course, neither variety of aria is a true rose, and they are called roses only because of their sweet scent. The fragrance of the vandal aria, however, is lighter and greener than that of its rare cousin, and redolent of honey and cut grass.

The felicidus aria is best known for being the only plant capable of growing on blighted land. Vandal aria lacks this quality, but is capable of proliferating almost everywhere else, even though it seems to favor dry, arid climes. If left to grow wild, the vandal will take over a space, choking out any other plant unfortunate enough to be in her way.

BE WARY OF (FORMERLY) SISTER LAUDINE

"(Formerly) Sister, (formerly) scholar, (formerly) blind. I feel it necessary to ensure the reader that I report with an understanding of who we are, who we could be, and who we choose to be. To entice is to lead."

Laudine's work—and it is only "Laudine," for I will not grace her with the title she has betrayed—is not to be read, not to be celebrated, and not to be trusted. She willfully abandoned that to which so many aspire: sisterhood within the Chantry order. And to what purpose? To put to paper her tawdry examinations of unspoken society that, by extension, should also remain unwritten.

She was always such, always prying, making use of secrets told in proper, shrouded confidence. It is upon good authority that I extrapolate she would also be untrue in matters most private, such as intended paramours, should she be trusted with knowledge of same. Her written works are to be viewed with the greatest of skepticism, if they are to be viewed at all. And they are not.

Notable works: *Our Orlesian Heart; Songs of Old Orlais: She of the Highwaymen Repents; Val Royeaux: Excesses Grand and Otherwise*

A Letter to Mother Hevara

Laudine on her rueful decision to leave the Chantry, despite the foolish generosity of the good revered mother, included here to show her obstinate nature:

Mother Hevara,

Thank you for your concern, but I trust you will accept my refusal in the tone it is intended: the greatest respect that I am capable of commanding as a simple child of the Maker. I remain convinced of the greater good the Chantry can do, though I cannot in good conscience return. There remains a difference between the potential and the actual, between the spoken and unspoken. And sometimes, between the spoken in private and the accused in public.

I learned as much as I trusted the Chantry to teach, and have used those lessons to illustrate in a different way: by showing who we are and what we do. As people, as members of court, as innocents, as lovers, and as players of the Game. And we are all of these, knowing or not. Often it is the knowing or not that separates us and invites blame and shame. I would peel back that which hides us from each other.

My "former" status is fact, and I will continue to denote myself as such. I have no fear that it appears salacious and may draw the wayward or scandal-seeking. That may be the new audience who needs these reflections, who would be open to understanding. I am no longer interested in preaching to the choir, as nothing true is shared. Not because we in the choir agree about our natures, but because we assume we already do. He made us in all our shameful ways. To hide from ourselves is to hide from Him.

—(Formerly) Sister Laudine

For ages, Thedosians have looked up in the dark to find meaning in the stars. Here (*clockwise from upper left*) the constellations Fervanis, Eluvia, Satinalis, and Servani are mapped with the aid of an astrarium.

◆ SISTER ORAN PETRARCHIUS ◆

"The stars are the eyes of creation, and to look into them is to make contact with the Maker."

Many of the constellations formed by the stars above were first read and interpreted in the days of the ancient Tevinter Imperium and thus carried meanings that supported their heathen beliefs. Over time, and with the rise of the Chantry, those meanings evolved to reflect great truths about the Maker's children. Sister Oran Petrarchius did not discount history in her study of the stars but, in telling the story of their evolution, revealed the stars' true nature.

Included below are constellations taken from her seminal text, *A Study of Thedosian Astronomy.*

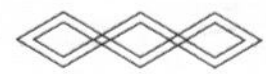

Satinalis

Referred to as either "Satina" (after the moon) or as "Satinalia" (after the holiday) in common parlance, the constellation Satinalis has always been depicted as the Celebrant: a seated man playing a lyre. It should be noted that, in ancient Tevinter, the constellation was known as "Mortemalis," and was represented by a warrior holding aloft a head (usually that of an elf). The movement to officially rename it took hold in the Divine Age, and after eight hundred years, the original is all but forgotten.

Fervanis

Commonly referred to as "the Oak," the constellation Fervanis is generally represented by a towering tree with leafless branches. Many scholars believe this is a representation of nature that harks back to the lore of the early Neromenians, whose beliefs largely aligned with animism, prior to the rise of Old God worship and the creation of the Tevinter Imperium.

Others, however, believe Fervanis was originally a constellation of the elven people—specifically, a depiction of Andruil, goddess of the hunt. Vir Tanadahl, the Way of Three Trees, is a central tenet of Andruil, and some think that Fervanis originally represented this concept.

Eluvia

Owing primarily to the popular Orlesian tale of the same name, the constellation Eluvia is commonly referred to as "Sacrifice." During the Glory Age, folklore told of a young woman saved from a lustful mage when she was sent into the sky by her father—after which the mage killed him (hence the sacrifice). The daughter became the constellation, depicted as a seated woman with her head in the clouds. Prior to this tale, Eluvia was thought to represent Razikale, the Tevinter Old God of mystery, and the constellation was the source of many superstitions involving the granting of wishes.

Servani

Referred to as "the Chained Man" in common parlance, the constellation Servani is traditionally represented by a man dragging a heavy chain behind him. This is thought to be an ancient Tevinter representation both of Andoral, the Old God of slaves, and of the Tevinter system of slavery itself. The representation of Servani has been used by the Trisalus guild for well over two thousand years (according to their claim), and is visibly imprinted upon the armor of both Juggernauts, the giant golems guarding the gates to the city of Minrathous.

A PARTIAL LIST OF ESPECIALLY BANNED BOOKS

- **The Imperial Chant of Light**
- **The Qun**
- ***Questioning the Chant*** by Magister Vibius Agorian
- ***Carmenum di Amatus,*** an anthology of poetry
- ***The Lies of the Nobles, the Truth of the Qun,*** author unknown
- ***Veilfire: A Beginner's Primer with Numerous Teachings, Exercises, and Applications*** by Magister Pendictus
- ***Edicts of the Black Divine*** by Father David of Qarinus
- ***Templar Tomfoolery: Saucy Little Tales from the Barracks,*** compiled by Senior Enchanter Wentworth Higginbottom
- ***An Alchemical Primer of Metallurgy*** by Lord Cerastes of Marnas Pell
- ***The Alchemist's Encyclopedia*** by Lord Cerastes of Marnas Pell
- ***The Randy Dowager***
- ***The Seer's Yarn: A Treasury of Tales for Children All Over***

ROUNDING OUT THE CHANTRY BOOKSHELF

There are a great many other writers who can provide the devout reader with clarity on topics from Chantry history and Andrastian philosophy to matters of battle tactics. Here is a short list of books and authors that should have a place in any home.

Religion

The Chant of Light: Literary Analysis and History by Sister Tessaria

The Word and Challenge of the Chant by Revered Mother Hevara

Before Andrastianism: The Forgotten Faiths by Sister Rondwyn of Tantervale

Secrets of the Most Holy by Sister Damson

Reflections on Divinity by Revered Mother Juliette

History

The Emperors of Orlais by Brother Harlon Ascari

Tales of the Wardens by Sister Manon

Architectural History of Orlais by Elodie Ferrneau

The Highlands of Orlais by Lord Ademar Garde-Haut, royal historian

Exalted: A History of the Dales by Lord Ademar Garde-Haut, royal historian

The Storm Coast and Its History by Brother Vincent

A Compiled History of the Occupied North by Renatus of Ayesleigh

Legends of Ferelden by Mother Ailis

A Shadow Unfolds by Brother Ansel

Tales and Legends of the Free Marches by Lord Rodney Pierce

Legendary Blades of Thedas by Lord Roderick Gutenschwantz

Art

A Still Life of Modest Artistic Discernments: Thedosian Artists Through the Ages by Plume

An Illumination of the Art and Artifacts of the Imperial Court of Orlais by Lady Simone Therese Germaine

Orlesian Musical Tradition by Sister Rosette

A Garden's Grace: Songs of the Field, collected by Maryden Halewell

Theater

The Heir of Verchiel by Paul Legrand

Wilkshire Downs by A. Pourri

Death in the Mansion by Violette Armand

The Sword of Drakon: An Examination of the Life and History of the Father of Orlais by Marquise Freyette

Children's Books

Bedtime Stories for Good Children by Sister Marigold

The Last Griffon by Warden Warren

How to Spot a Mage and Other Advice for Young Girls by Sister Harriet

Biology, Geography, and Cultural Studies

The Wilds of Thedas by Stephan d'Eroin

A Study of the Southern Draconids by Frederic of Serault

Herbology in Thedas by Master Ilian Gravire

A Journey through the Dales by Lord Horace Medford, "Adventurer"

A Land of Fog by Brother Ashor Vell

Land of the Wilders by Mother Ailis

Notable Fortresses, Castles, Towers, and Other Edifices of Interest in Ferelden by Henry Lannon

Lands of the Abyss by Magistrate Gilles de Sancriste

Annals of the Scarlet March by Brother Bedine

Magic

The True Threat of Magic by Lady Seeker Alandra Vael

The Shape of the Fade by Enchanter Ephineas Aserathan

Spirits of the Spire by Senior Enchanter Francois

Patterns Within Form by First Enchanter Halden of Starkhaven

The Interplay of Spirits in the Common Laundry Room by First Enchanter Luidweg of Ansburg

Beyond the Veil: Spirits and Demons by Enchanter Mirdromel

Tales of the Imperium by Sister Dulcinea

Mages in Orlais by Senior Enchanter Percivale

Our Honored Dead: A Guide to the Mortalitasi Order by Prelate Davidus

OTHER SOURCES OF NOTE

◆ MASSACHE DE JEAN-MIEN ◆

The swordmaster Massache de Jean-mien's worth as a writer is often cited with the title of his seminal work: *A Meditation upon the Use of Blades*, required reading at the Academie des Chevaliers. In it, all manner of essential tactics for swordplay and sword work are covered. Though it is not widely distributed outside chevalier circles, any apprentice of the blade should seek out a copy.

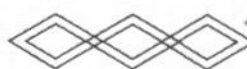

MAGES ARE NOT demons or monsters. They are men and women like any other, except for their skill with a weapon few are given. I say this to be clear that I do not think all mages should be put to the sword, as some believe. However, every mage walks through life with a blade drawn and ready, whether they wish it or not. Those who insist that mages are harmless must ask how the apostates who fling fire when the templars attack learned to kill so well. We in the Academie know well that no skill comes without practice.

If you fight a mage, you must close with him, regardless of the danger, or risk being overwhelmed. A mage's strike rarely hits with the force of a trained chevalier's blade, but often carries unnatural energies: fire that boils a man inside his armor, lightning that steals the strength from his limbs, and so forth. To hold back is to give him time to alter the battlefield to his advantage in some fashion, whether he summons a wall of ice, a demonic ally, or magical flames to strengthen the blades of his guards. We know that the warrior who controls the battlefield is most often the victor. You must keep him reacting to you and continue your attack.

Mages rarely wear heavy armor, but their magic can shield them as effectively as our own plate. I have said many times to watch the hips and arms of your opponent instead of the hands, but with the mage, the hands and arms may be your only clue. If his body is protected from your blade, attempt to tangle his arms or bear him to the ground. It is not elegant or honorable, but there is no honor when fighting a mage. There is only survival.

—Excerpted from *A Meditation upon the Use of Blades*, required reading at the Academie des Chevaliers

◆ SISTER DORCAS GUERRIN ◆

A member of the Guerrin family of well-connected Fereldan nobles, Sister Dorcas Guerrin is close enough to get invited to the parties but in no danger of inheriting any responsibility. She has, however, proven enthusiastic about the history of the region, even if she sometimes gleefully prances over the truth to the most exciting conclusion. Sister Guerrin's best-known books include *Walking the Chant*, *Marks of the Blight*, and *Living Redcliffe*.

AMONG THE SADDEST legacies of the Fifth Blight are those poor souls who survived the darkspawn attacks across Ferelden only to succumb to the corruption of the blight itself. We have seen animals—birds, wolves, and even bears—corrupted into mindless ruinations of their former selves, but humans are by no means immune.

Those unfortunate victims not killed quickly by contact with darkspawn blood or disease become mad with fever. Their bodies lose their hair and become misshapen with sores; in their last lucid thoughts, many speak of hearing whispered words, or a song that no one else can catch.

It is vital that once victims begin hearing such things, they are put out of their misery quickly and mercifully. There are stories across Ferelden of these ghouls, maddened by the corruption of the blight, attacking their friends and spreading the corruption further. While it is likely that the sickness will eventually kill a ghoul, the dying strength of these poor creatures makes them nearly as great a danger as the darkspawn themselves.

They are no longer our friends, our family, or our countrymen. They are victims of the Blight, and must be given the same mercy Hessarian showed Andraste: a swift sword.

—Excerpted from *Marks of the Blight*

◆ LADY ALCYONE ◆

***The Dowager's Field Guide to Good Society* is a lady's best friend when attempting to navigate the twists and bends of Orlesian high society. This book is not to be confused with *The Randy Dowager*, a publication of particularly ill repute that any follower of Alcyone would burn and bury.**

IN ORZAMMAR, DWARVEN society is divided into rigid castes with houses that compete for power and prestige. But all that is discarded when a dwarf abandons the Stone for the surface. Under the open sky, everyone is equal. Or so the story goes.

The truth is that thousands of years of tradition are not so easily tossed aside. Even though surface dwarves are officially stripped of their caste, many maintain a hierarchy among themselves along the old caste lines. Formerly noble houses are accorded more respect than casteless brands who come up in search of opportunity. The poorest "noble" dwarf on the surface looks upon the rich "lower caste" dwarves with contempt.

Upper-class surface dwarf society is roughly divided into two camps: kalnas, who insist on maintaining caste and rank (typically those from the Noble or Merchant Caste families), and ascendants, who believe in leaving Orzammar's traditions underground and embracing life in the sunlit world. Maintaining some tie to Orzammar was seen for generations as the only lifeline for surface dwarves. Bringing surface goods to their kin underground and lyrium and metals to the surface was not only the most lucrative means of making a living, but also a sort of sacred duty, as many surface dwarves willingly accepted exile and the loss of their caste to better serve their house or patron. In recent years, many surface dwarves, particularly ascendants, have branched out. They started banks, mercenary companies, and overland trade caravans. They became investors and speculators in purely surface trade. These new industries have proven tremendous sources of wealth, but are looked down upon by their more conservative kin.

For less-affluent surface dwarves, association with a powerful kalna can open many doors. They can get credit with dwarven merchants and are offered work opportunities by the powerful Dwarven Merchants Guild more readily, sometimes, than more-qualified but less-connected individuals.

—Excerpted from *The Dowager's Field Guide to Good Society*

◆ BARON HAVARD-PIERRE D'AMORTISAN ◆

This good baron's guidebook, entitled *An Anatomie of Various Terrible Beasts*, is all the rage among the Orlesian aristocracy. His colorful language, coupled with the lengths to which he goes to learn more about the most bizarre beasts in all Thedas, is the talk of Val Royeaux. It's rare to attend a party where someone doesn't quote the man.

THE CHANT OF LIGHT claims that the Maker made us, and in our folly, we think ourselves blessed by such fact. If fact it is, for in my seeking, I find only base illusions, the better for being torn down and mocked as inadequate in the harsh light of reason. But as an exercise, let us say that it is true, that the Maker made us.

I have seen the gurgut basking in a slanted shaft of sunlight in the penumbral canyon, its putrescent tongue scenting the rancid air of the nameless and unnameable swamp, swishing the uncaring grass of the plains with its passage. It is some cousin of the wyvern, but bereft of the savage ferocity for which the latter is praised and hunted by Orlesian nobles. Its thick-lidded eyes stare witlessly, and its jaw hangs agape; it is not befuddled or frustrated by its want of reason, but perfectly content, a drooling idiot.

Its pallid belly stretches and distends, disdaining all reason, when it gorges itself upon its prey. I have seen such a lowly beast swallow a chevalier whole, the great and shining warrior taken by surprise in the tall grass, his silverite armor gleaming as the gurgut unhinged its jaw to draw the chevalier in. Across its belly, I saw the kicks and struggles grow frenzied and then still, and the idiot beast settled into a happy torpor. The ruined armor of the noble chevalier lay among the gurgut's spoor several days later.

Say that it is true, that the Maker made us. What if He made us for food? What if the grand purpose of our searching existence is to stretch the belly of a beast that slinks through the tall grass? What if there is a single unbending purpose and, in it, we are cattle to feed the witless leviathans that slumber unseen beneath us?

—Excerpted from *An Anatomie of Various Terrible Beasts*

◆ FIRST ENCHANTER JOSEPHUS ◆

Few mage writers exercise as much restraint and respect in their writing as First Enchanter Josephus, whose seminal *Tranquility and the Role of the Fade in Human Culture* is as enlightening as it is reassuring.

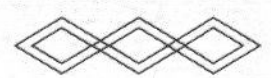

ALTHOUGH APPRENTICES DO not know the nature of the Harrowing, all of them understand its consequences: they either pass and become full mages, or they are never seen again. Those who fear to undertake this rite of passage, or those who are deemed too weak or unstable, are given the Rite of Tranquility instead.

The actual procedure, like the Harrowing, is secret, but the results are just as well known. The rite severs connection to the Fade. The Tranquil, therefore, do not dream. This removes the greatest danger that threatens a weak or unprepared mage: the potential to attract demons across the Veil. But this is the least of Tranquility's effects. For the absence of dreams brings with it the end of all magical ability, as well as all emotion.

The Tranquil, ironically, resemble sleepwalkers, never entirely awake nor asleep. They are still part of our Circle, however, and some might say they are the most critical part. They have incredible powers of concentration, for it is simply impossible to distract a Tranquil mage, and this makes them capable of becoming craftsmen of such skill that they rival even the adeptness of the dwarves. The Formari, the branch of the Circle devoted to item enchantment, is made up exclusively of Tranquil, and is the source of all the wealth that sustains our towers.

—Excerpted from *Tranquility and the Role of the Fade in Human Society*

◆ FERDINAND PENTAGHAST ◆

The legendary dragon hunter and heir apparent to the Nevarran throne would rather write about the restorative and culinary benefits of dragon bits than rule Nevarra. Pity, too, since his writing isn't exactly easy on the nerves or the stomach. While his writing is not technically blasphemy, it can be hard to recommend a Ferdinand Pentaghast book. Still, he is preferable to Pol Ageire Phridee's awful *The Most Dangerous Things to Eat.*

COLLECTING DRAGON'S BLOOD is extremely difficult, even for the most accomplished dragon hunter. First, one must locate the increasingly rare creature. Second, one must bleed it. However, I believe that at the moment of death, the blood loses something special—a certain fiery essence, perhaps. Of course, bleeding a live dragon is quite tricky.

Dragon's blood has a wide variety of uses, both magical and culinary. It's an important component of rune crafting and those like my great-grandfather enjoy a sprinkling of the powdered stuff on their food at the dinner table.

—Excerpted from *Discovering Dragon's Blood: Potions, Tinctures, and Spicy Sauces*

◆ THE SHAPERATE ◆

The Shapers of Orzammar treat the archiving of information, which they call Memories, with an obsessive focus often seen in squirrels. What they collect is commonly dry facts, useful in answering questions of research pertaining to anything dwarven, such as "who," "what," "when," "where," and "how." Often it can be difficult, based on their methods, to discern "why," but frankly, the dwarven rationale for why something is may conflict with the Chantry explanation anyway.

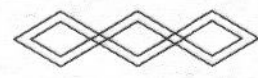

WE ARE THE Children of the Stone. She supports us, shelters us, offers us the most priceless gifts of the earth. The worthy return to her embrace in death, becoming Ancestors. The unworthy are cast out, unable to rest, that their failings may not weaken the Stone.

So it has been since the earliest memories. We live by the Stone, guided by the Ancestors, who speak with the voice of the Provings, and whose memories the Shaperate keeps forever in lyrium.

We do not accept the empty promises of heaven as the wild elves do, or vie for the favor of absent gods. Instead, we follow in the footsteps of our Paragons—the greatest of our Ancestors, warriors, craftsmen, leaders, the greatest examples of lives spent in service to our fellow dwarves. Our Paragons joined with the Stone in life, and now stand watch at our gate, ushering in those surfacers privileged to visit our city. We know there is no greater honor to hope for, no better reward for an exceptional life.

—As told by Shaper Czibor

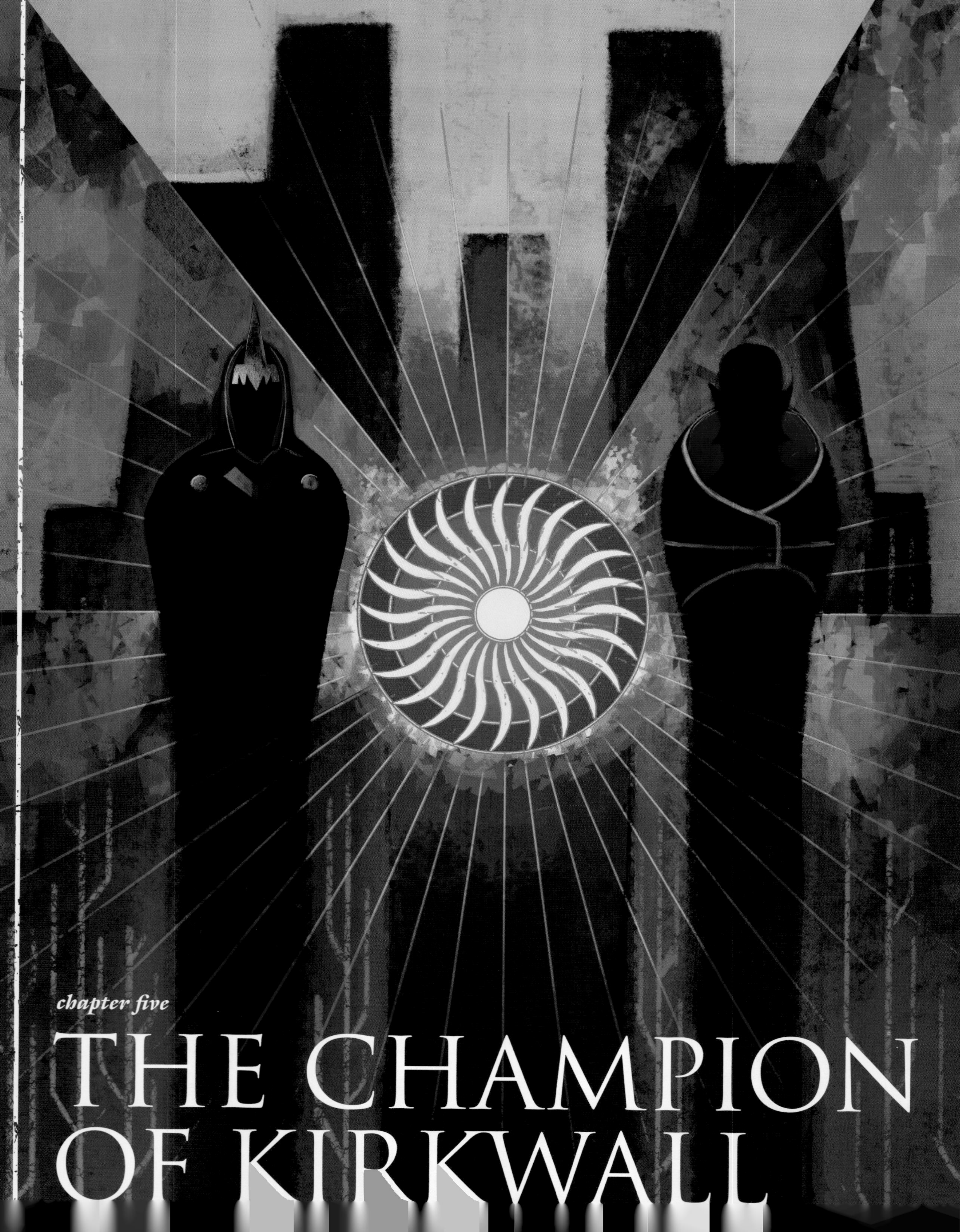

chapter five

THE CHAMPION OF KIRKWALL

ONE PERSON'S HERO IS ANOTHER PERSON'S BLIGHT. Following the events of the mage uprising in Kirkwall, to invoke the name "Hawke" among some was to speak the name of Andraste's betrayer himself. Hawke was a major catalyst in the war between the mages and the templars, and at the center of an expedition that set the vicious element known as red lyrium upon the world. But history may instead remember Hawke as the Champion of Kirkwall—a savior who delivered the city-state from certain destruction and a pillar whose absence would have made a bad situation so much worse.

THE HAWKE FAMILY

Hawke came to Kirkwall as a refugee, fleeing the Fifth Blight in Lothering with twin siblings, Carver and Bethany, and mother, Leandra, in tow. The voyage was fraught with peril. Hawke left Ferelden with two siblings but reached Kirkwall with only one—and likely would not have survived at all if not for impossibly good fortune.

Within the walls of the Marcher "City of Chains," the Hawkes and the Amells reunited with some of the more colorful branches of their family tree and struggled under the weight of a father's legacy.

MALCOLM HAWKE

Malcolm Hawke was an apostate mage, most known for his dealings with the Grey Wardens and his secret courtship of noblewoman Leandra Amell, whom he whisked away to Ferelden against the wishes of her father. Together the couple would raise three children, one of whom became the Champion of Kirkwall.

The details of Hawke's identity, gender, and abilities differ depending on who's telling the story.

It Began at the Gallows

Very little is known about the early life of Malcolm Hawke. Records from the Kirkwall Circle of Magi indicate that he was brought to the Gallows late in the Blessed Age, where he settled into life as a young apprentice quickly.

Malcolm's sharp mind and innate gift for magic soon distinguished him from his peers. By all accounts, he picked up the basics of magic quickly and was casting complex spells by the time he was fourteen. Malcolm's startling advancement then slowed to match that of his fellow apprentices. By the time he undertook his Harrowing at age nineteen, he was, to the casual observer, no greater a mage than any other in the Kirkwall Circle. Unremarkable. Decidedly average. Almost too average. Senior Enchanter Consuelon believed that Malcolm was simply concealing his talents and had done so for some time. He shared his suspicions in a letter to First Enchanter Honorus in 9:01 Dragon.

"It is just not prudent to stand out at the Gallows," Consuelon wrote.

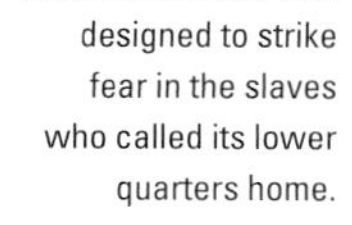

Much of Kirkwall was designed to strike fear in the slaves who called its lower quarters home.

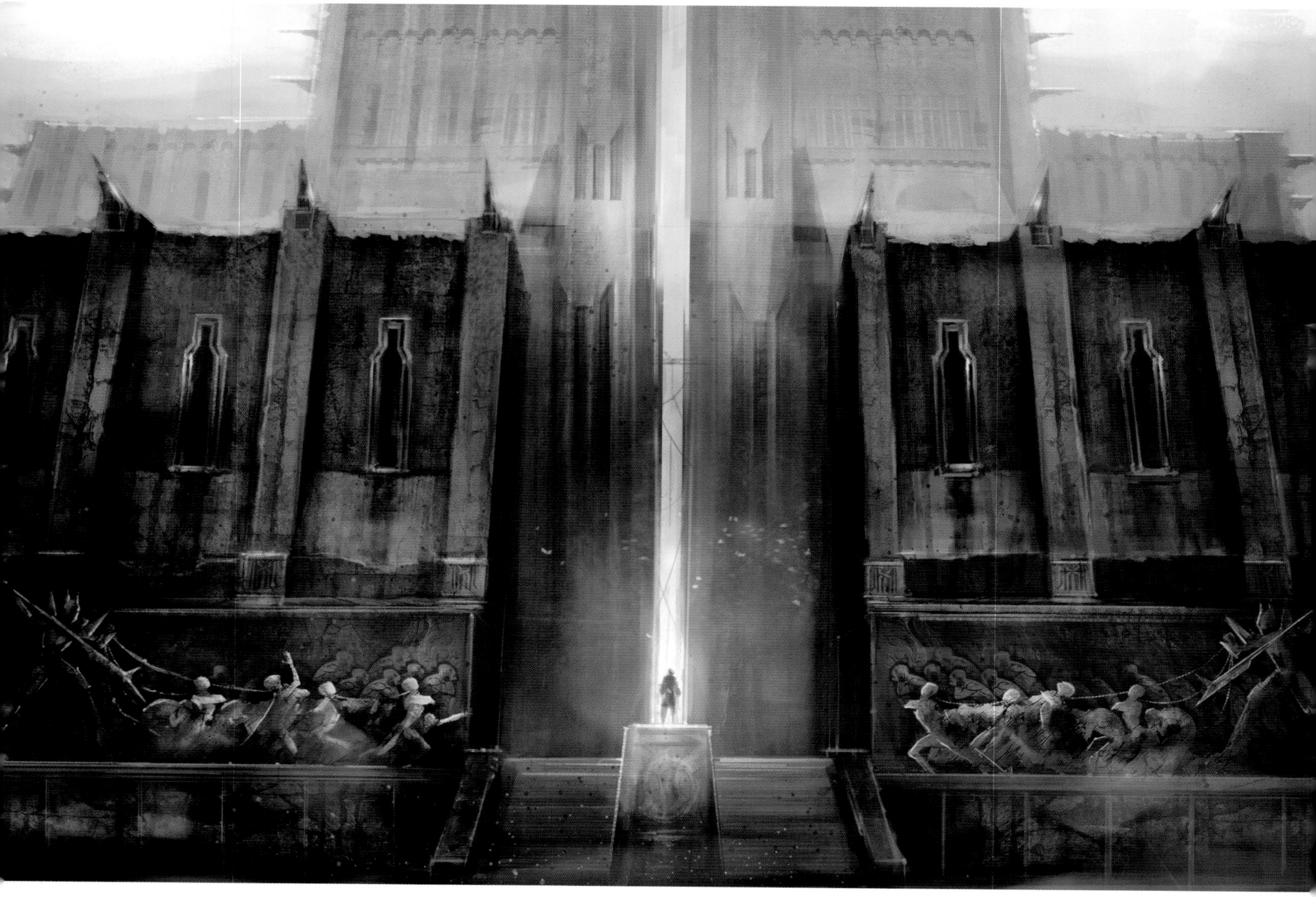

A rare talent! A sharp and curious intellect! He seems to understand magic through gut feel and instinct. I'm sure the entire Gallows has heard about how he conjured fire on his second try. And as all the other apprentices labor over the spell, the little scamp says to me, "They think too much about moving their hands, when they ought to be thinking about moving the fire." If I didn't like the boy as much as I did, I would hate him. I too had trouble with that lesson as a child.

—Enchanter Ursula on Malcolm Hawke

Lady Leandra Amell

In 9:05 Dragon, a lavish banquet was thrown for the visiting Grand Duchess Florianne, niece to Emperor Florian of Orlais. All of Kirkwall high society gathered at the estate of Viscount Perrin Threnhold to welcome the young duchess. Kirkwall's Circle of Magi was invited to provide magical entertainment for the guests, and sent four mage representatives, including

Malcolm Hawke, to the estate. As a precaution, a number of armored templars accompanied the mages, and many said the entire company made for quite an impressive sight. Also present, as guests of honor, were the head of the influential Amell family, Lord Aristide Amell, and his family: his wife, Bethann, and their children, daughter Leandra and younger son Gamlen.

After the feast, the Circle mages took the floor; the ballroom of the Threnhold estate filled with sound and light. One of the mages presented a view of the Black City in the Fade, through a curious "window" summoned out of nothingness. Another caused blue lightning to arc across the high ceiling of the room, and made a gentle snow fall upon the musicians. A third commanded an apple tree to sprout at his feet, and at his command, the tree flowered and produced a single red apple, which was presented to the grand duchess. As the performance concluded, Malcolm caused a fantastical, fiery bird to emerge from the flame of a candle. The bird took wing and flew twice around the ballroom, pausing briefly over the upturned face of the spellbound Lady Leandra Amell.

A few nobles who were present later recalled the two young people speaking on a side balcony, their heads bent close together. It is not known what passed between them, but Malcolm left Viscount Threnhold's estate deeply in love with the young noblewoman.

Over the following months, Malcolm continued to steal away from the Gallows to meet Leandra. Malcolm was known to have struck up a strong friendship with a templar, Ser Maurevar Carver, and some speculate that Ser Maurevar played a crucial part in protecting Malcolm and Leandra's secret.

The Grey Wardens and Flight

Several months after their first meeting, Leandra Amell realized she was with child. This discovery immediately changed the nature of her love affair with Malcolm. Even though Malcolm always had vague dreams of one day marrying the woman he loved, the knowledge that Leandra would bear his child within the year spurred Malcolm to action. He asked Leandra to run away with him. When she agreed, they wed in secret, and Malcolm began planning an escape from the Gallows. Templar records indicate that Ser Maurevar assisted Malcolm, although it is unclear if the templar was a direct accomplice in the theft of Malcolm's phylactery or whether he simply allowed it to happen. Later on, when he faced disciplinary action, Ser Maurevar was quoted as having said: "Rule is not served by caging the best of us."

Malcolm combed Kirkwall's docks for a ship's captain daring enough to take a fugitive apostate and his new bride aboard his vessel. Unfortunately, by the time Malcolm had secured passage to Ferelden, the land of his birth, the young couple

Much of Kirkwall's architecture has survived multiple regimes and been repurposed as the city evolved.

faced a different, and much more dangerous, obstacle. Lord Aristide Amell, Leandra's father, had learned of his daughter's condition and was furious. He spread word that Malcolm was a dangerous apostate on the run and hired men to capture him and turn him over to the templars. Leandra was forbidden to leave the family home but was able to get a message of warning to Malcolm through her younger brother, Gamlen.

Hunted and nearly penniless, Malcolm was faced with a decision: escape on the ship to Ferelden, leaving Leandra behind, or stay and face the wrath of Lord Aristide and the templars. Malcolm stayed, refusing to abandon his love and their unborn child. He was hiding in a seedy Lowtown tavern planning his next move when he was approached by a Grey Warden. The Warden, Larius, had been searching for a mage willing to travel deep into the Vimmark Mountains to perform a terrible blood-magic ritual that would bring an ancient darkspawn under control. As Hawke later recounted, no Grey Warden mage could perform this task. It was crucial that the mage's blood be pure—untainted by the Grey Warden's Joining. The chosen mage would also have to be skilled, and brave enough to face whatever horrors the Vimmark Mountains had in store. To secure Malcolm's cooperation, Larius threatened Leandra's life, but also hinted that the Grey Wardens might intervene to allow the couple to leave Kirkwall, as payment for services rendered.

Despite his contempt for the Wardens' methods, Malcolm saw an opportunity and seized it. He agreed to Larius's terms.

Malcolm left Kirkwall for the Vimmark Mountains in the company of Larius and his Wardens. He left a simple message for Leandra, saying that he had gone to buy their freedom. What occurred in the Vimmark Mountains is shrouded in mystery. What is known, however, is that Malcolm Hawke returned triumphant and that Warden-Commander Larius was more than happy to uphold his part of the bargain.

Under the protection of Larius's heavily armored Wardens, Malcolm marched up to the doors of the Amell family estate and demanded that Leandra be brought to him. There was no reply, but the doors soon opened to reveal Leandra, standing alone. No guards, no angry Lord Aristide. When Malcolm expressed surprise, Leandra simply told him that they were free to leave and that her father would no longer pursue them. Noting that his new bride carried nothing with her, he asked, "Is there anything you would take with you?" To which Leandra replied, "I have everything I could ever want."

They boarded a ship that night and sailed off to Ferelden, and a new life.

LEANDRA AMELL

Leandra Amell was the noble mother of the Champion of Kirkwall, Hawke. She gave up a life of wealth to elope with the apostate Malcolm Hawke and lived as a peasant's wife for her love of him. Three years after Malcolm's death, Leandra and her children returned to Kirkwall, fleeing the Blight. She later died in the city of her birth, the victim of an insane mage.

Of Noble Blood

Leandra Amell was born in the later years of the Blessed Age, the first child of Kirkwall's powerful Amell family. The Amell bloodline dated back to the Fourth Blight, and the Amells were considered one of the foremost noble families in all of the Free Marches. As eldest daughter of Lord Aristide Amell and his beloved wife, Bethann, Leandra was afforded the best upbringing. Servants attended to her every need. She was schooled in music, politics, and history and excelled at her studies. She also learned to ride and shoot a bow, though her tutor always maintained that her archery skills were "fair to middling at best."

When Leandra was still a baby, her little brother Gamlen was born. The two would remain close all throughout childhood. At the age of eleven, Leandra was betrothed to Comte Reynaud de Launcet's eldest son, Guillaume. Leandra and Guillaume met the next summer, at the comte's country estate. After the visit was concluded, Leandra apparently remarked to her mother, "They are so very Orlesian, Mama."

Life with Malcolm

Over the months following Florianne's banquet, Leandra and Malcolm continued to meet in secret. Gamlen was often involved, either smuggling Malcolm into the Amell family estate through the servants' entrances or escorting Leandra when she slipped away in the dead of night. As Leandra later told her children, she and Malcolm never really spoke of building a future together, as they were both keenly aware of the forces that conspired to keep them apart. Leandra was a noblewoman from a prominent family, already promised to another, and Malcolm was a mage. And so the lovers turned their thoughts to the present, and tried to be content with stolen moments, knowing that each one might be their last.

When Leandra realized she was with child, everything changed. Malcolm and Leandra discussed the option of her leaving, of marrying Guillaume de Launcet and lying about the child's true parentage, but Leandra refused to let go of the man she loved. They would stay together, she said, no matter what it took. Moved by Leandra's declaration, Malcolm asked her to marry him. She agreed, and they resolved to marry and run away to Ferelden, Malcolm's country of origin.

The two devised a plan. Leandra would stay with her family, concealing her pregnancy, while Malcolm found a way to escape the Gallows. In the meantime, Leandra tried to convince Gamlen to help them. With his fondness for cards, he frequented Lowtown gambling dens, home to the worst scum Kirkwall had to offer. But Leandra hoped that among this scum would be a ship's captain who would agree to transport an apostate and a pregnant noblewoman on the run.

Leandra Amell? Of course I remember Leandra. That whole affair was the scandal of Hightown. My parents wouldn't even speak the Amell name for months. But to us giddy young girls, oh, it was romantic. There were such stories about Malcolm Hawke in those days. He was a pirate, he was a lost prince, he was a mercenary with a heart of gold. And in secret, all of us went to our beds wondering when it would be our turn to be swept away by true love.

—Lady Phyllis Reinhardt, childhood friend of Leandra Amell

Gamlen at first refused to assist his sister, thinking her plan too dangerous. But Leandra begged and pleaded, and Gamlen relented. Within a week he'd gathered the names of a few crusty mariners who might be willing to help. Leandra immediately passed the list of names on to Malcolm, along with

Distraught, Leandra begged her mother to keep the truth from Lord Aristide, but to no avail. He was immediately alerted to his daughter's situation and was, predictably, furious. Not only had Leandra broken her engagement with Launcet's son, but she also carried the unborn child of an apostate mage. At one point during the heated exchange, Lord Aristide was overheard saying, "Amell blood has always carried the stain of magic. And you . . . with a mage . . . Why would you add to this disgrace?"

Despite Leandra's pleas for understanding, Lord Aristide sent men in pursuit of Malcolm. Leandra appealed to her mother for help, but Lady Bethann turned away from her daughter. When Lord Aristide forbade Leandra from leaving the house or ever seeing Malcolm again, Lady Bethann simply said, "If she wants to ruin her life, let her." From then on, Lady Bethann refused even to be in the same room as Leandra. With a mother who wouldn't look at her and a father intent on bringing her love to justice, Leandra's only comfort was her brother, Gamlen.

Before Malcolm left for the Vimmark Mountains on a mission for the Grey Wardens, he sent Leandra a simple message, saying only that they would be free when he returned. Leandra waited by her window day and night, trusting that Malcolm would come for her. The day finally arrived when Malcolm was spotted at the Kirkwall gates with an entourage of Grey Wardens. Hearing the news, Lord Aristide went to his daughter, and asked her to make a choice: her family, or the apostate. If she chose to stay, her child would be accepted into their family—willingly, even gladly. She would not have to marry Guillaume de Launcet. She would not have to marry at all. Everything would be forgotten. But if Leandra chose her apostate, then she would no longer be welcome in their home. She would have no claim to her birthright, or her name. She would leave and take nothing with her. When Malcolm finally arrived at the gates of the Amell estate, Leandra chose her heart. Before she left, however, Leandra insisted on saying goodbye to her mother. Lady Bethann gave no reply to her daughter's increasingly desperate knocking at her door.

some of Leandra's jewelry, which would have been more than enough to buy passage anywhere in Thedas. Then there was nothing to do except wait.

Lord Aristide's Anger

Though Leandra went to great lengths to conceal her condition, her behavior aroused the suspicions of one of her maids, who began speculating with the other servants about her young mistress's predicament. The gossip eventually reached the ears of Lady Bethann, Leandra's mother, thanks to an indiscreet bit of whispering. Lady Bethann quickly discovered that there was more to the rumor than idle gossip and confronted her daughter. In a great outpouring of tears, Leandra confessed to everything: her love for a mage, how she carried his child, and their plans to run away.

Following the destruction of the chantry, Seeker Cassandra Pentaghast was dispatched to interrogate Varric in the search for Hawke.

Servants who witnessed the scene said that Lord Aristide took his daughter's hands, raw from pounding on Bethann's door, gently in his own, and told her, "Just go, Leandra. You are no longer an Amell, and she is no longer your mother."

A New Family

Leandra and Malcolm left Kirkwall that night aboard a rickety vessel. The ship docked in Highever, and the two made their way east, finally settling in a small village near Amaranthine. Malcolm found work as a farmhand, and Leandra put her needlework skills to good use by mending torn items of clothing for a few bits apiece. Both were careful to keep their origins a secret, though their neighbors often remarked on how well-spoken each was.

Hawke's brother Carver struggled for recognition under his sibling's shadow.

The first Hawke child, who would become the Champion of Kirkwall, was born a few months later, and both Malcolm and Leandra were overjoyed. Leandra wrote to her family in Kirkwall, telling them of the child's birth, but received no reply.

In the winter of 9:11 Dragon, Leandra gave birth to a set of twins: a girl and a boy. The boy was named Carver, in honor of the templar Ser Maurevar Carver. And Leandra called her daughter Bethany, in memory of her mother, Bethann. Just before the twins were born, Leandra received news from Gamlen: their ailing father, Lord Aristide, had passed away. Lady Bethann had died the year before. A grieving Leandra wrote back after the twins' birth, sending her love, and telling Gamlen of Carver and Bethany. There was no reply.

When Bethany was nine, her magical powers manifested and without even touching a local bully, she threw him clear across a field. The family was forced again to move, but this time with all haste, bringing only what they could carry on their backs. After weeks of travel, looking over their shoulders, the family settled on the outskirts of Lothering, and Malcolm took on the task of training his daughter.

Leandra was happy in Lothering, and they lived peaceful lives. Unfortunately, in 9:27 Dragon, Malcolm Hawke succumbed to illness and passed away. Leandra was inconsolable for a time, but remained strong for her children. The fate of the Hawke family was left up to her and her eldest.

When the Blight began three years later, Leandra and her three children fled across the Waking Sea, back to Kirkwall. As the family was crossing darkspawn-infested country, one of the twins fell prey to an ogre. Leandra never really got over the death. Upon arriving in Kirkwall, the family was forced to seek refuge in Gamlen's Lowtown shack, as the Amell mansion had been sold years before to pay off Gamlen's debts. Leandra worked tirelessly to see the Amells restored to their proper place. She lived long enough to see her first child come into wealth and reclaim the family's estate. In 9:34, she perished at the hands of the insane blood mage Quentin, who used Leandra in a terrible ritual to resurrect his dead wife.

GAMLEN AMELL

Gamlen Amell was born a year after his older sister, Leandra. Like Leandra, Gamlen was afforded the best upbringing and education the Amells' gold could buy. But no matter how well Gamlen did, it seemed he could never compare with the beautiful, accomplished Leandra. Leandra, the talented lute player, who mastered the intricate melodies of "The Red-Breasted Robin" when she was eight. Leandra, who could recite the names of the great Orlesian houses and their histories without missing a beat. And Leandra, whose name was on the lips of Hightown's finest. "Oh," they would gasp, "what a perfect little lady on her white pony." And "Oh, how lovely she is, how gracious and kind." Everyone loved Leandra, and Lord Aristide and Lady Bethann loved her most of all.

A Young Rake

Nevertheless, Gamlen adored his sister. The siblings' governesses remember Leandra helping Gamlen with his studies and defending him to their tutor. When Leandra received a treat or a reward from their parents, the first words from her mouth were "And what about Gamlen? Gamlen should get one, too." In their free time, the children would play in the many rooms of the Amell estate, upsetting the servants with their antics. Even when they got older and left their play behind, the siblings were still often seen in each other's company—whether out and about in Hightown, sharing secrets in the garden, or reading in the great sitting room of the Amell estate.

As a young man, Gamlen cultivated a love of betting games. Diamondback, Chanson d'Argent, Wicked Grace, Dead Man's Tricks—he played them all, and lost a great deal of gold doing so. It began as an innocent nobleman's pastime: cards and liquor after dinner. That quickly progressed to cards with the more rakish elements of society in various Lowtown taverns. Before long, Gamlen was pawning Amell heirlooms to continue games played dockside on ale barrels. He would return home in the wee hours of the morning, smelling of tar and cheap wine, his

FILES ON THE INVESTIGATION OF THE CHAMPION

CARVER HAWKE

Carver Hawke, younger brother of the Champion of Kirkwall. They never really seemed to get along. Seems the shadow Hawke cast stretched back to childhood. Those who knew Carver then had a lot to say. Not sure how much is useful, but here's the best of what I found.

From the mouth of Avris Tanner, captain of the militia of Lord Richelieu, Orlais:

I'll say no bad about him, despite him being a shit of the highest order. For all the offense and testing of patience, I'd have him at my back before any of your proper-acting blades. And not because of the Champion. Because of Ostagar.

Carver was out of Lothering, which was nowhere, like most of us and our own nowheres. That's what you get for infantry in the king's army. Because what else were we good for? Stablehands? That's a fine life for some, but not when you want a sword in your hand more than anything. Carver had that, same as me. Better than me. Said he wanted to protect his family. That someone had to, because his father had died and, well, you know how the Champion turned out. Carver took it real serious, and I could tell he was hiding some family shame. And now we all know about fallen nobles and mages on top. But he was all right, it skipped him. And I can't fault him for family. Not that family.

I doubt Carver trained anywhere serious before joining, but he was stronger than most. You could tell he'd come up with his own drills. Carver said his father taught what he could, but he'd mostly watched mercs sparring when he was young, then aped it with whatever wooden waster he could get. I knew how it was, I did my time with a stick or two. That's what you do when you're on your own for lack of money or interest. Or whatever concerned a father like his. Carver picked up the right way soon enough, though he bitched no end while doing it. Always knew better, he did. But again, I'd have him at my back. Because he wanted to be there, with soldiers, right down to the stupid tattoos we got. Because of that old lie, that if something on you is permanent, you're permanent. Plus mabari mean strength. And when we went to the big fight, against the darkspawn, you'd never seen the like.

We were far back from the named companies, supporting the "glory" of their charge or whatever. So far afield, I barely heard the call to attack. Not Carver, though. He ran as fast as he could, and damned if he didn't cut a wedge in the horde. A few of us kept the 'spawn off his flanks and used him as a spear. Our standard leapt ahead. Then we stopped, like we'd hit a wall. I never heard a retreat, but I heard the yelling when the royal colors went down. And then the Wardens, too. And I thought we were done without them. But not the Hawke boy.

The more ground we lost, the harder he swung that plank of a sword of his. He was shouting that we had to win, that it was to keep our homes safe. I swear he was crying when we finally tackled him, but damned if I'll hold that against him. It took three of us to drag him to cover. I had to slap him back to his senses, to make him see that killing five or ten more 'spawn wouldn't matter. The wall was on us, and dying there wasn't going to help anyone. I said if he wanted to do his family good, he'd get them safe. This wasn't his failure, because it sure as shit wasn't mine either. We fought our way out and went our separate ways.

I heard about the Champion. About Kirkwall. And I heard what became of Carver. Not surprised by any of it. You wouldn't ask him around for tea, but he had a stare like a templar, drive like a Warden, and more skill than sense. And I'll not say a bad word more than that, because I'm still here and ruddy kings aren't. And that's because of men like him trying.

This tone was common to his compatriots from Ferelden. I've no doubt there are ways to attack the legacy of the Champion through association—a certain uncle comes to mind—but the brother is not the place to find weakness. There may be little to like and no shortage of embarrassment, but respect seems a given despite it.

purse emptied, and Leandra would hurriedly direct the servants to draw him a bath and have his clothing laundered or burned. But even Leandra couldn't protect Gamlen forever. When Lord Aristide discovered Gamlen's penchant for gambling, he reduced his allowance by half and told the guards to prevent his son from leaving the estate after dark. Gamlen made some efforts to curb his gambling habits, but his saved gold occasionally grew heavy in his pocket, and he'd be forced to lighten his load, sneaking out to spend nights in seedy Lowtown dives.

Leandra's Betrayal

When Leandra first met her husband Malcolm at an extravagant affair at the viscount's estate, it was Gamlen who made it possible for them to speak privately. The ballroom was filled with people, prying nobles, friends of the family, but Gamlen convinced Lord Aristide and Lady Bethann that Leandra was feeling faint from the excitement and needed some time alone in the fresh air to regain her composure.

Knowing her brother had been leaving the estate on late-night gambling excursions, Leandra asked him to help her continue to see Malcolm in secret. Gamlen was apprehensive, but agreed to her requests all the same. He was certain that Leandra's infatuation was only temporary and that the love affair would be over in days. However, days turned to weeks and weeks to months, and Malcolm and Leandra's love only grew stronger.

When Leandra realized she was carrying their child, it was Gamlen whom she first told. Gamlen flew immediately into a panic, understanding fully what this could mean for Leandra. He advised her to start seeing Guillaume de Launcet, the man

FILES ON THE INVESTIGATION OF THE CHAMPION

BETHANY HAWKE

Should we trust the young woman of little learning or the figure we can't locate who seems practiced in lies? In either case, Bethany Hawke was determined not to stand out, and her success or failure in that has no bearing on our investigation of the Champion.

From the mouth of Ebrin "Peaches" Janith:

Why do you want to know about her? She never did anything fun. Stayed down in her house, most of the time. I suppose that was because of the Amell thing. I mean, maybe she didn't know, but you can tell when someone is born better, right? That's what they say. They can feel things under their mattresses and such. She didn't seem like that, though. Her brother sure wasn't.

I saw her do magic once. We were by the river, and a wild dog chased us and bit her. But then she made it go to sleep. I was so afraid, and I was crying because I thought we'd die. But she was crying, too, so I didn't say anything. To anyone! She stayed inside even more after that, but I brought her books sometimes when I'd try to see her brother. I hope she wasn't sad all the time. She was too nice to be magic.

From the pen of someone identified only as Sade:

I found her like we find most: scared, uncertain. The onset of the ability can terrify the mage most of all. But she was not unloved or unprotected and did not need me. And that is to the credit of the father. We talked for a time, made sure he had what he needed for the training of one with her potential, and then I went on my way.

Or so I let them think.

We watched, as is our wont. The Hawke children were blessed by all manner of ability, but they did not bear it equally. Of the Champion, you know. The world knows. And also the boy, Carver. Denied magic, he wanted nothing more than to be special. But Bethany. Sweet Bethany. You could see it in her every movement, how she held the fire of the arcane as far from her heart as possible: She did not want to be special. She wanted to be normal. Or what she perceived as such.

We spoke of that many times, I in one guise or another. Sheltered as she was, by her own doing, she reveled in stories of the far and away. Tales of the courtly life she might have had, had she not been denied the name Amell when it was of note. The father hid the history of that well enough, and she could only dream of knights and the simple duties of court. And of princes—my goodness, did the child know the names of storied princes. I believe she danced with a book once. But then, the best of us have.

The father coached Bethany's power with clear pride. The thread of magic tied the family together. His death was undoubtedly hard, especially as it was to simple sickness. But that too was a gift of his, in a fashion. We of talent often think we can bend the world to our will, and we are especially helpless when reminded of our limits. It could have broken her, made her open to the failings of our gift. But Bethany did not break. She was masterfully reserved, a trait many mistake as weakness. Restraint is a flavor of command. Holding power within is the foundation of focusing it outward. Her training continued without his instruction, perhaps even without her knowledge. And that is where we could have returned to her, if not for the Blight.

If the father's death removed anything from the girl, it was the comfort of shared experience. For "normal" is a function of the company you keep, and among her fellows, among those who suffer the same trials, she would have found both peace and power. I believe Bethany would have excelled in a true Circle, in a proper fraternity. Aequitarian by choice, I should think. Though I suspect, like many, she would have surprised herself with leanings to the Libertarian. We've said as much to many others. We tell them not to be afraid, and they never are. We tell them to pay attention to what the Circle teaches, but pay most attention to what it doesn't. And we tell them they will see us again, and when they do, glory.

And now you know what we are willing to say. Do not pursue further, as we will not respond in writing.

to whom she was already betrothed. Their parents would forgive her if both families believed the child to be Guillaume's. Leandra said that if she was to do this, then she needed to see Malcolm one last time, to tell him to his face. Gamlen took this to mean that Leandra was finally breaking it off with the mage, and arranged a meeting.

But when Leandra and Malcolm met, it became abundantly clear to Gamlen that Leandra had no intention of leaving Malcolm and had merely lied to him. Once Malcolm had gone, Leandra told Gamlen that they were going to run away to be married.

Gamlen was destroyed when Leandra left with Malcolm. The last thing she said to him was "Look after Father and Mother."

The Decline of the Amells

Bethann barely spoke after Leandra left. She grew pale and thin, a shadow of the vivacious society lady she used to be. Invitations to soirees and balls were ignored, and piled up outside her door. At supper, she would stare at her food as though unsure what to do with it. Lord Aristide and Gamlen would try to engage her in conversation, with little success. Eventually, she stopped coming down to dinner altogether. Lord Aristide soon followed suit and began taking his meals in his office.

The Amell estate grew silent and cold. Servants worked without a word, their moods reflecting that of the troubled household. They went to Gamlen for instruction, mindful of Lord Aristide and Lady Bethann's need to remain undisturbed. Unused to the responsibilities of running the house, Gamlen left most of the major decisions in the steward's hands. Eventually the grim atmosphere became too much for him to bear, and he began spending more time away from home, losing himself in drink, cards, and the lovely ladies of the Blooming Rose.

When Leandra's first child was born, Gamlen received a letter from her. He read it and spent a day laboring over a reply, but was unable to produce a letter that didn't read like an accusation. Eventually, he locked Leandra's letter away in his desk and tried to forget.

And then Revka Amell, Gamlen's cousin, learned that her firstborn was a mage. The child was taken to the Circle, Revka weeping in the streets behind the templars. The scandal rocked Hightown and added to the ghastly rumors swirling around the Amell family. Whispers followed Gamlen whenever he left the estate. His noble friends started finding excuses not to see him. The many young noble ladies who had previously found him irresistible could no longer stand the sight of him.

It was at this time that he befriended Mara, one of the Amells' chambermaids and the daughter of the old head cook. Mara was a quiet, intelligent young woman, with bright blue eyes and a thick mane of chestnut hair. Unlike the other servants, she did not avoid Gamlen for fear of upsetting him. When he returned home after a night of drinking and whoring, she would take his coat and boots and ask him how he was. Gamlen felt that she truly meant the question. She cared, about the family and about him. And he began sharing his sorrows with her.

As such things go, Gamlen fell in love with Mara. She was the one constant in Gamlen's life and his only happiness. Even when the other servants, fearful of the rumored "curse," left to seek employment elsewhere, Mara remained loyal to the Amells. "I grew up in this estate, same as you," she'd tell Gamlen. "It is as much my home as it is yours."

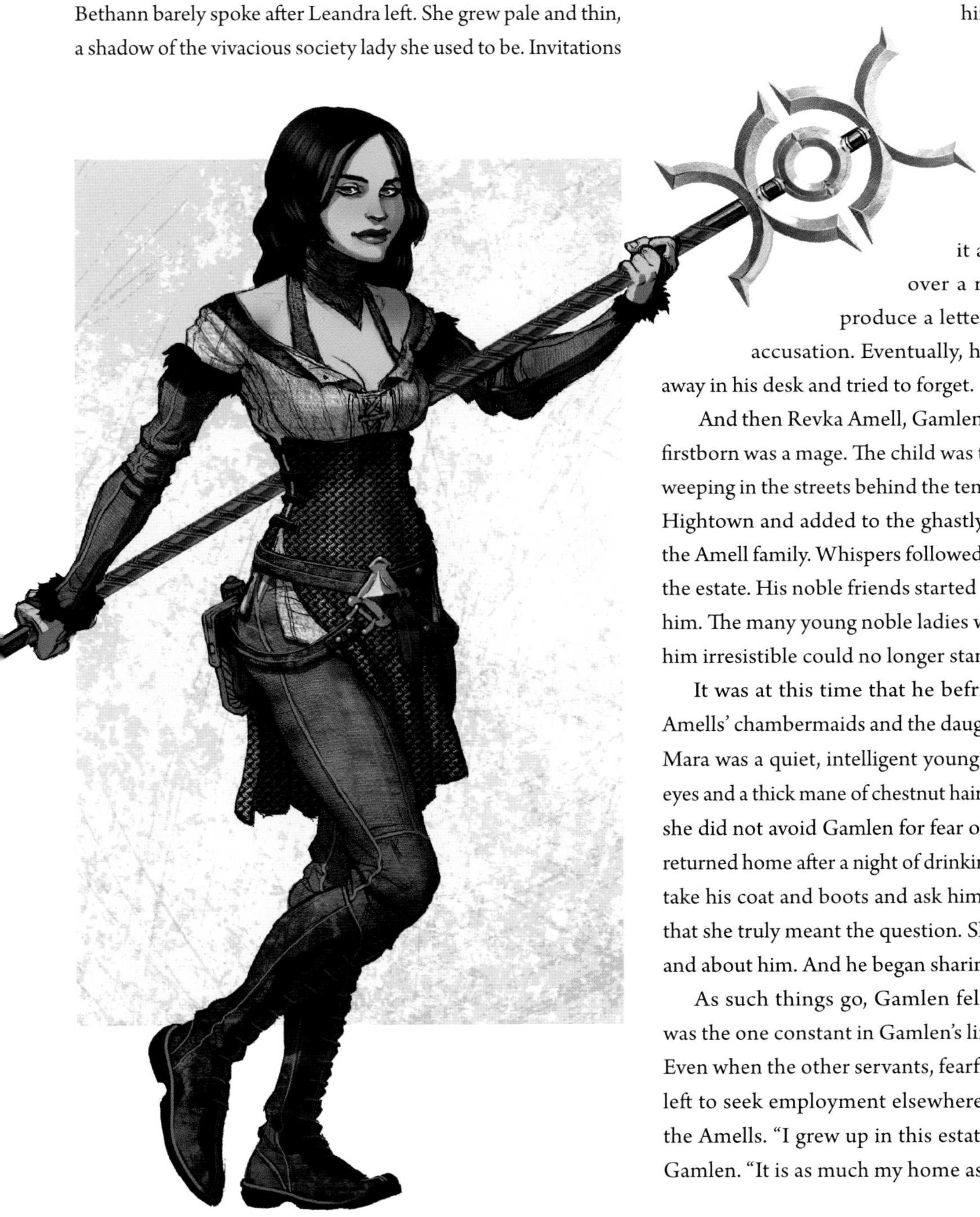

Bethany was Hawke's only sister and a talented mage.

Lowtown (*above*) is home to the notorious pub known as the Hanged Man.

When Lord Aristide and Lady Bethann were stricken with cholera, it was Gamlen and Mara who nursed them. They got better, eventually, but never regained their full strength. After a second bout, Lady Bethann passed away. Lord Aristide clung on to life for another year, spending his days in the estate's courtyard garden, a sad gray figure cloaked in a blanket. Near the end, Lord Aristide raised his eyes to Gamlen. "Leandra?" he whispered. "Yes, father," said Gamlen. "I will fetch her." Lord Aristide died that night.

When Lord Aristide's will was read, Gamlen was dismayed to learn that the Amell estate and fortune had been left to Leandra. Gamlen was to be provided for, of course, earning a monthly stipend. However, due to his propensity for excess spending and gambling, Leandra would control that stipend. Furious at this turn of events, Gamlen hid the truth about Aristide's will. The late lord's true intentions would not be known for decades.

The Gem of Keroshek

The Amells' ill fortune did not abate with Lord Aristide's death. Gamlen's cousin, and Revka's brother, Damion, got in trouble with the law, and Lord Fausten, Damion's father, went bankrupt defending him. When that wasn't enough, Lord Fausten resorted to borrowing gold from the Council of Five, a Kirkwall organization known for ties to mercenaries and slavers. It was all in vain. Damion was thrown in prison, and Lord Fausten wasted away and died. Revka disappeared one day, and her husband took their four remaining children and moved away from Kirkwall, eager to escape the troubles that plagued Revka's family. Gamlen was the only Amell left in Kirkwall, and when it came time for the debt to the Council of Five to be repaid, Gamlen was the one they sought. He was forced to pay back Fausten's debt to save his own life. When the Council of Five was done with him, Gamlen had lost his home and almost all of Aristide's remaining fortune. Nearly penniless, he had no choice but to take up residence in Lowtown.

Mara stayed with Gamlen through all this, and she found employment with the Reinhardts, a noble family that was once close to the Amells. Gamlen returned to the card dens of Lowtown, attempting to regain his fortune the only way he knew how. He became obsessed with an old gambler's fable: the Gem of Keroshek. According to legend, he who possessed the gem would never lose a bet. Gamlen spent what little gold he had left pursuing the lucky gem, going on vague clues and far-fetched stories. But following the gem's trail proved to be impossible; every lead turned to smoke, and Gamlen would return home each night, empty-handed and poorer than before.

Even Mara—gentle, loyal Mara—who had stayed with Gamlen through everything else had finally had enough. She'd hoped they could start a new life, Gamlen finding some honest work, but honesty and work were never concepts with which he had much acquaintance. One day, when Gamlen returned home, Mara was just gone. The message she left read: "You've thrown your life away. I won't let you waste another's." Gamlen was well and truly alone, with nothing but his regret for company.

In 9:30 Dragon, when the Blight began, Leandra returned to Kirkwall with the shattered remains of her family. While Gamlen was at first resentful of having to share his small shack with his sister and her children, he would come to accept, if not love, his relatives. After Leandra's death, Gamlen was often spotted deep in his cups in various Lowtown dives. According to the barkeep of the Hanged Man, Gamlen confided in him on a particularly difficult day, saying, "For a while it was like old times. Just me and her—family." Gamlen would say no more after that.

I didn't know anything about my father. For the first five years of my life, I believed my mother found me on the beach, clinging to the underside of a turtle. When I realized that it couldn't be true, Mother told me that my father had died. He had a good heart, she said, but sadness stole it away. She never talked about him much after that, but I often saw her sitting on her bed, with this old scrap of red silk in her hand. She showed it to me, said it was the only thing she had of his. It was like a little banner or something, with figures that looked like birds. I don't have it anymore. It was with her when we burned her.

—Charade

QUENTIN, BUTCHER OF LOWTOWN

Quentin was an escaped mage from Starkhaven's Circle of Magi. Fascinated with the forbidden arts, Quentin chafed within the Circle's rigid boundaries. When his wife died, Quentin was consumed with the idea of resurrecting her. Leandra Amell was an unfortunate victim of this obsession.

An Obsessive Love

Much effort has gone into piecing together facts on the man known as Quentin, the notorious "Butcher of Lowtown" and murderer of the Champion of Kirkwall's mother, Leandra Amell. He was once a member of Starkhaven's Circle of Magi, but escaped long before it burned down. Various reports indicate that Quentin always had a fascination for forms of magic beyond those sanctioned by the Circle. His desire to continue dabbling in such things was likely what prompted his escape.

As an apostate, Quentin took on an apprentice, Gascard duPuis, an Orlesian nobleman who had managed to keep his magic a secret all his life. Gascard idolized Quentin and admired him for daring to push the boundaries of what was possible.

FILES ON THE INVESTIGATION OF THE CHAMPION

CHARADE AMELL

I don't believe following this lead will bring us any useful information on the Champion or the war. For one, the cousin is quite separate, thanks to the distance of her father. For another, she avoided being dragged into the later events in Kirkwall.

There is little on the mother or her immediate family, the Hartlings. They were traders of note a generation ago, with several routes between Nevarra and the Free Marches. The relationship with Gamlen Amell seems unrelated, and Mara Hartling maintained her holdings before and after the assumed dates of the affair. A series of shifts in trade had diminished the name prior, and Mara appears to have done little to restore it. Any contracts were sold and the proceeds primarily invested in schooling the daughter, possibly in anticipation of the mother's passing.

We can find no account of Charade's birth name, a seemingly deliberate and recent absence of records. It suggests that she will be a noteworthy figure in the future, but for her new associations, not her lineage. I also expect we won't be so lucky to intercept another letter as the one below. The group she has joined has recovered and changed again.

From a letter signed "Red Jenny":

I found the cache and Lady Whatever's knickers. A bit dark to mark it with the red from the lieutenant's finger, but he was a first-grade prick, so good for you for making a point. Royeaux's was right. You're fun. I'll back you, too, so you're in if you want. We'll fill you in on what to look for, how to do, and how not to do but seem like you did. You'll find the name carries itself. You're best to come east, though I have Nevarra. Kirkwall you met, and Starkhaven is full up. We spread out, like it used to be. No guild, and no gathering to get bad attention.

One thing, and one thing only. Don't cross another friend. We don't let that stand, not anymore. The old ones, Denerim and the like, they learned that the hard way. They were proper bloody, even scared a few Crows, and still nearly lost the lot. When red goes to black, don't turn your back. I'll explain later. For now, have fun and share the wealth.

Together, master and apprentice explored realms of magic others could only dream about.

At this time, Quentin was also deeply in love with and married to an unnamed woman. She may even have been a noble, as fragments of Quentin's writing revealed her to be a lover of books and, of course, white lilies. The woman died unexpectedly, most likely of some illness, and Quentin was unable to save her. When she died, Quentin was distraught and never recovered from the blow of losing her. He became reclusive and kept himself locked in his study, working in isolation. Gascard offered to help, but his assistance was turned down. Any attempts to get Quentin to reveal his work were met with cold silence. Gascard grew increasingly bitter over this perceived slight. One day, against his master's wishes, he broke into Quentin's study.

A passage from a tattered journal, recovered from Gascard's Kirkwall mansion years later, is enlightening, to say the least:

"I saw the most incredible things. The severed head of a cat, immersed in a solution, the jaws clenching and unclenching of their own accord. The body was skinned and splayed out on a wooden table, with the heart removed and placed on a scaffold of golden pins. And still beating strongly. He had achieved it, though it was just the beginning. Life from death . . ."

Hawke's closest allies came from all corners of Thedas.

Quentin discovered Gascard's break-in and was greatly displeased. Gascard's pleading to be involved in Quentin's research only irritated the elder mage more, and Gascard was sent away. The next day, the study was stripped bare, and Quentin was gone. Gascard would spend the rest of his life trying to find Quentin.

It is now known that Quentin had begun his work to re-create his dead wife and that this obsession would lead him to unspeakable acts, including the abduction and murder of Hawke's mother.

HAWKE'S INNER CIRCLE

Hawke's rise to infamy was buoyed by an inner circle of trusted companions and contacts. First among them was Aveline, a warrior of significant skill aided by Hawke's family after darkspawn set upon Aveline and her husband, Wesley, while the couple also fled the Fifth Blight in Ferelden. Wesley did not make it, and Aveline accompanied the Hawkes on the voyage to Kirkwall, where she joined the city guard.

In Kirkwall, many colorful characters came out of the woodwork: a dwarven writer named Varric; a charismatic, if unpredictable, healer named Anders; an awkward yet charming Dalish mage named Merrill. The infamous raider Isabela, a lyrium-tattooed former slave of Tevinter named Fenris, and the pious prince of Starkhaven, Sebastian Vael, were also rumored to fight at Hawke's side.

VARRIC TETHRAS

The life of Thedas's most celebrated author began with the final downfall of his house. Noble House Tethras had been one of the most wealthy and well connected of the noble families of Orzammar from time immemorial, but tragedy has always clung to its name. As House Garen, its founding predated the Blights, and it produced dozens of kings. In the Exalted Age, however, it reached its pinnacle: Paragon-King Orrick Garen, the only king of Orzammar ever to be made a Paragon during his reign. The pinnacle of House Garen was also its end. Paragon Garen sentenced one of his own sons, Tethras Garen, to walk the Deep Roads as punishment for the murder of his sister, Unaria. When it was later revealed that the Carta, not the prince, had killed Princess Unaria, Paragon Garen was overcome with guilt. For years, he sent men to search the Deep Roads for his lost son, without success. After a decade of searching, he changed his name and the name of his house to Tethras, to honor the child he had wronged.

As the Blessed Age drew to a close, the great House Tethras took its final turn. Lord Andvar Tethras was caught fixing Provings—not merely a felony, but a blasphemy, as the dwarves believe that Proving matches are the way in which their ancestors, and through them the Stone, communicate with the living. Andvar and his entire house were exiled to the surface for his crime. Hundreds of people of all castes were forced topside: warriors sworn to the service of the house, servants, artisans who relied upon House Tethras for patronage, and scores of noble caste relations, all exiled for the crime of one man.

As a result, Andvar's second son, Varric Tethras, was born on the surface, in exile among humans and elves. It is hardly surprising that so many of his books deal with crime and tragic mistakes and feature as their protagonists mostly outcasts. It is surprising, however, that so few of his books feature dwarves at all.

The beardless Varric Tethras is anything but a typical dwarf.

The Dasher's Men and *Darktown's Deal*

His first serial, *The Dasher's Men*, published in 9:18 Dragon, is his least-known book and also the only one with a dwarven hero. The story pits two rival Carta clans against one another in a turf war, with a pair of casteless brothers caught in the middle. It ends, as nearly all Varric's stories do, in tragedy. Sales were modest—it appears to have sold primarily in dwarven enclaves—but it was enough to encourage Varric to write *Darktown's Deal* in 9:20 Dragon: a serial about Kirkwall's Coterie, which met with some critical acclaim and better readership.

The Viper's Nest

In 9:23 Dragon, perhaps motivated by personal dissatisfaction with the Merchants Guild, he published *The Viper's Nest*, about the friction between Kalna and Ascendant families within the guild and their dealings with several professional guilds of assassins. Oddly, despite the story's setting among the Merchants Guild, the hero of the book is an elven courier from the Undercity, and it views the proceedings with Carta and merchant princes through the eyes of a complete outsider. The book was extremely well received by critics and readers alike, but sold poorly due to a multitude of distribution problems. Copies of the book that escaped mysterious warehouse fires or loading accidents and found their way to the public are considered collectors' items.

Varric's mother, Lady Ilsa, had suffered from poor health since leaving Orzammar, but in 9:26 she finally succumbed to an ailment of the liver. Afterward, Varric ceased writing entirely for several years, and sources within House Tethras have claimed that he was working on a manuscript tentatively titled *The Mercenary's Price*, which he would read to his mother at her bedside and which he destroyed upon her death.

Hard in Hightown

He didn't publish again until 9:33 Dragon, when he began his most popular work, *Hard in Hightown*, about the clash between a shadowy organization known as the Executors and a secretive group of agents in the employ of the Divine herself over an ancient artifact, with a weary Kirkwall guardsman caught between them. Due to the turmoil in Kirkwall at the time, the serial was published sporadically, chapters being printed sometimes as much as six months apart. Collected volumes of the complete novel have been the best-selling book in five nations since 9:36 Dragon, eventually outselling even Brother Genitivi's *Travels of a Chantry Scholar* to become the widest-read book in Thedas, Tevinter excluded.

The Tale of the Champion

His most recent book, *The Tale of the Champion*, is also his only work of nonfiction, and details the life of Varric's friend Hawke, the famous (or infamous) Champion of Kirkwall, and the events leading up to the explosion that destroyed the Kirkwall Chantry in 9:37 Dragon. Oddly, the book has been received as if it were another novel. One Antivan critic notoriously complained that the book's premise was implausible and that it was impossible to believe that any one person could befriend such a baffling assortment of ruffians as Hawke did. He gave the book one star. Supposedly, Hawke sent him a letter of thanks.

ANDERS & JUSTICE

The apostate mage known as Anders was born and raised in a small farming village in Ferelden. His father was originally from the Anderfels, but had come to Ferelden when he was just a boy. Cheerful and good-humored, young Anders was well liked by the people of his village and was often seen surrounded by a gaggle of village children. That was, until he turned twelve, when he accidentally set the family's barn on fire with magic. Anders's father feared his son's newfound abilities, and though his mother still loved and wished to protect him, the templars were called. Anders was clapped in irons and taken away to

FILES ON THE INVESTIGATION OF THE CHAMPION

AVELINE

We approached many in Kirkwall presumed close to Aveline. The answer was always the same:

"You want those answers, there's one place you go," First Lieutenant Donnic Hendyr said.

"The captain? She'll speak for herself," said Master Sergeant Brennan Evighan.

"You ask her yourself, not me," Lieutenant Harley Casimi said.

So we did.

From the office of the guard captain of Kirkwall, acting marshal of the Kirkwall citizens militia, with the authority and sanction of Provisional Viscount Bran:

Did some new council of busybodies ask for this? Here, again, is why I am loyal to Kirkwall. My father was Orlesian, but I am not. Yes, you might find a troubling record of the chevalier Benoit du Lac, but that is because his patron fell to some idiocy of the court and my father took exile over execution. I was a child. I don't remember Orlais. And while the capital is a fine city, I don't care to call it home and owe it no allegiance. I was raised Fereldan, but I'm a Marcher and Kirkwaller now.

On Service:

I assume you also need repeated assurance of my training, because I didn't attend whatever academy is being sold as essential by the parents of whoever seeks my job. I served in the army of King Cailan, and while I was sponsored as an officer despite having no Fereldan title or holdings, that was the effort of every coin my father possessed, and I will not have it questioned. And yes, his hopes were obvious given my namesake: Ser Aveline, the first woman welcomed as an Orlesian knight. "Welcomed" after her death, of course. He wanted it to inspire me, and it did. As did the cost of the life he was forced to leave: a mother I can't remember. He'd only say she sacrificed everything for Orlais. And I will only say that I'll not have another life lost for a title. And that includes any fool who thinks "Captain" is a steppingstone to "Viscount."

I'm not the knight my father wished. I'm not here to further my name elsewhere. I'm a soldier, and I found a place that needs that. Kirkwall has no standing army; it has the guard. We keep order, and we are the heart of the militia, if need be. And for good or ill, we are needed, thanks to the Champion.

On Endings and Beginnings:

And now you will question my association with the absent Hawke, forgetting the contribution that let you live to ask. I met the Champion as we were fleeing the darkspawn at Lothering, an act criticized by brave talkers who weren't there. I stood for King Cailan at Ostagar. I fought the horde. My company was part of the first charge. The only charge. We all felt the silence when the traitor Loghain quit the field. When my small company knew the battle—and our king—was lost, I ordered a scattered retreat to avoid drawing the darkspawn. I told my people to make for their homes and keep going. I made my own way to Lothering, where I had chance to see the Blight take even more from us. A sibling from the Champion, and my husband, Wesley. I've allowed comment on that elsewhere, but that is not—and will never be—your business.

Your masters will of course try to dwell on the first years after we arrived. Kirkwall closed its gates to those fleeing the Blight, and the Champion made a costly bargain to gain access. I benefited from that, yes, but I consider it an example of why the underground should be leashed, not strangled. Kirkwall was too afraid, and had that trickle not been possible, not only would it have lost the person who would come to do it the greatest good, but the pressure on the walls would have been unrelenting. Even Tevinter stone will yield eventually.

Now to the "crimes" of the young Champion while a citizen. Yes, the Amell estate was thought to have concealed an apostate, but we all know the truth of the time. It was money, not magic, that decided who received templar scrutiny. I would offer the eventual madness of Knight-Commander Meredith as proof that it was the overbearing nature of her Order that failed this city. Not the Champion we were lucky to have. Or the guard I have been fortunate to lead. Or the people of Kirkwall, who now have to listen to the muttering of peacetime nobility.

I stand for this city. My guards stand for this city. And that will not change so you or your patrons or their kin can stand upon it. Not after what it went through.

Kinloch Hold. The only thing he was allowed to bring with him was a small pillow, hand-embroidered by his mother. First Enchanter Irving of the Circle recalls that Anders refused to speak when he arrived there, not even to tell the other apprentices his name. They began calling him "the Ander," referring to his Anders heritage. "Anders" would become the only name he'd use.

The young mage rebelled against the Circle's rules and restrictions. Having known friends, a loving family, and a life free of constant supervision, he was keenly aware of what he'd lost. Anders made his first attempt to escape less than six months after arriving at the Circle. When he was caught, he was brought immediately to Irving. When asked why he escaped, Anders replied that he had simply wanted to go home. Irving took pity on the tearful boy and decided that punishing homesickness was unnecessarily harsh and would only serve to deepen the child's hatred of the Circle. Irving had Anders escorted to his room and counseled the templars to treat him with greater kindness.

History will forever remember Anders for destroying Kirkwall's chantry in an act of violent rebellion.

After his first try, Anders made no recorded attempts to escape for more than a year. But the second time Anders slipped away from the Circle, it took the templars three weeks to find him. The next time, it took over a month. To elude the templars, Anders displayed an ingenuity and resourcefulness far beyond his years and was described by Ser Hadley, one of the many templars assigned to hunt him down, as "a skinny,

Aveline saw herself as Hawke's protector.

blond headache." Luckily for Anders, his friendly manner and easy charm had by then endeared him to many at Kinloch, including First Enchanter Irving. Most saw him as nothing more than a spirited young boy with a troublemaking but mostly harmless streak in him. Irving

The senior Warden known to most simply as Stroud recruited for a time in Kirkwall.

in particular looked upon Anders with sympathy and made valiant attempts to help him become accustomed to life in the Circle going so far as to arrange some time outdoors for well-behaved apprentices. There is no indication that Irving's good intentions had any effect on Anders. Years later, the first enchanter would remark that perhaps his approach had backfired. The kindness he showed to Anders every time he was returned to the Circle simply proved to the boy that he could get away with most anything. When asked if he regretted not punishing Anders more severely, perhaps with Tranquility, Irving only sighed and would not discuss the matter further.

When Anders was still an apprentice, he met and befriended an older boy, Karl Thekla. Karl and Anders would commiserate about life in the Circle and joke bitterly about being templar slaves. For years the two were inseparable, and Anders later disclosed that there was more than a simple friendship between Karl and him. The two shared a deep love, and their relationship was a sanctuary, an escape from the harsh realities of life in the Circle. Anders would often tell Karl that he was the one good thing about Kinloch Hold. In the years when Anders and Karl were together, Anders made no attempts to escape the Circle.

Shortly after both Anders and Karl had undergone their Harrowings, Karl was transferred from the Fereldan Circle to Kirkwall's Gallows, where more experienced mages were needed. Anders did not take their parting well, and he would not see Karl again for many years, though the two would continue to write to each other.

In the weeks that followed Karl's departure, Irving, worried that Anders would likely try to escape again, cautioned him that there would come a point when even the first enchanter would not be able to protect him. Irving requested that Anders be watched carefully, hoping increased templar scrutiny would discourage the young mage from doing something regrettable. By this point, however, Anders no longer cared. The pain of losing Karl was too much, and Anders broke out once again. He was recaptured on the docks in West Hill, trying to buy passage to Kirkwall.

The Grey Wardens

Anders endured several more years in Kinloch Hold, before making his final escape. After his sixth escape attempt, he spent a year in solitary confinement, locked in a small cell that was watched day and night by the templars. Anders's only company that year was one of the tower's mousers, a cat he named Mr. Wiggums. According to Anders, Mr. Wiggums was later possessed by a rage demon and killed three templars before being put down. There is no mention of a possessed cat anywhere in the Circle of Magi's records.

Shortly after emerging from solitary confinement, Anders escaped again. He'd learned that his phylactery had been moved to Amaranthine, and traveled there, thinking he would destroy it once and for all. The templars anticipated this move and captured him in the city. They were passing through Vigil's Keep on the day it was to be handed over to the Grey Wardens, when the keep was attacked by darkspawn. The darkspawn quickly overwhelmed Anders's templar guard, leaving him to defend himself. Finding Anders to be a capable mage and interesting company, the Warden-Commander invoked the Right of Conscription and recruited him to save him from arrest by the templars. Anders took the Grey Wardens' Joining ritual and survived. It had taken him multiple attempts and almost two decades to get free of the Circle, but he had done it. As he was a Grey Warden, the templars could no longer touch him.

Anders traveled with the Warden-Commander for several months as they worked to rebuild the ranks of the Wardens in Ferelden and investigated a new breed of darkspawn. While a Grey Warden, Anders met Justice, a Fade spirit stranded in the decomposing body of a dead Warden named Kristoff. Justice struggled to understand the real world and the people who inhabited it, leading him to engage in probing discussions with Anders, as well as the other newly recruited Wardens. During one of these discussions, Justice asked Anders why he did nothing to stop the oppression of mages, even though he always expressed hatred of it. The discussion must have given Anders much to think about. Until then, it seemed he'd only concerned himself with his own freedom, never stopping to think about the injustice that others like him still faced.

Months later, Justice, Anders, and several other Wardens were sent on an assignment. None of them ever returned to Vigil's Keep. The Wardens who investigated the disappearance tracked the missing men to a forest south of Amaranthine. In a clearing lined with the charred stumps of trees, they found the bodies of the men, torn limb from limb and left to rot. Neither Anders nor Justice was among the dead.

It came to light later that Justice had possessed Anders at that camp in the woods. Anders would later speak of how he was haunted by what Justice had shown him: that although he was free, other mages were still oppressed. Both Anders and Justice knew that it was a wrong that needed to be righted, and Justice believed that together, they could accomplish this.

MERRILL

Many have heard the rumors. The Champion of Kirkwall consorted with blood mages. The Champion unleashed an abomination on the city. The Champion was an active practitioner of blood magic. All of it is unlikely. While true that the Champion associated with the Dalish apostate known as Merrill, a calm examination of the facts shows no evidence of blood magic whatsoever.

According to official Chantry investigators, the elf Merrill was born in Nevarra and then given to the Sabrae clan of Dalish at a very young age for magical training. This form of fostering is common among the wandering Dalish. Her new clan was one of several that spent much of the next several years in eastern Ferelden, mostly around the Brecilian Forest. Few people even knew for certain that the elves were there, but rumors and superstition have surrounded the Brecilian Forest for ages.

"Tomas went into the forest to look for a cow that wandered off and never came back," one anonymous villager told a local broadsheet. "Some folks said it was werewolves got him, but his brother Darin had a few too many and went to look for him anyway. He ran out of there, saying walking trees and demon elves were chasing him."

Merrill was First to the Sabrae clan of Dalish elves.

The Chantry determined a much more likely source of the stories were the darkspawn that surfaced from a cavern in the nearby woods during the Fifth Blight, of which copious evidence was found. No evidence of "demon elves" was ever located.

With a Blight rising in Ferelden, the Sabrae clan booked passage across the Waking Sea on the *Pride of Amaranthine*, a ship that made several trips between Ferelden and the Free Marches to ferry refugees. When asked if he had any knowledge as to whether any of the elves aboard his ship practiced blood magic, the captain glowered, and an extremely large boatswain, brandishing a marlinspike, threatened to throw questioners overboard. Chantry investigators took that to mean no.

After reaching the Free Marches, Merrill left her clan and settled in the Kirkwall alienage, where her neighbors barely took note of her at all.

"Merrill? No, she wasn't a blood mage. Maker, what a thought!" said Reeba, elder of the Kirkwall alienage. "Blood mages do sacrifices and mind control. Merrill mostly got lost on her way to and from the Lowtown market. Every day. For three years."

Perhaps the most damning thing that can be said about Merrill is that she had obvious ties to the criminal underworld—the Carta, the Coterie, and any number of smugglers, raiders, and mercenaries—largely through her association with Varric Tethras. However, nearly every inhabitant of Kirkwall claims Varric as an associate, so it might be simpler to say that everyone in Kirkwall associates with criminals. Certainly, that would explain a great deal about the city-state.

As with nearly all of those closest to the Champion, Merrill has disappeared since the terrible events in the Gallows and has not been seen since.

KEEPER MARETHARI

In the summer of 8:82 Blessed, Marethari Talas, First to the Keeper of the Sabrae clan, seemed to have the world in the palm of her hand. She had just married her childhood sweetheart, the Keeper's Second, Sarel. She was well on her way to mastering

Kirkwall's alienage is far from the worst in Thedas.

the arcane arts of her people, and was already considered one of the most talented Dalish mages alive. Her clan kept camp in a remote part of the Frostback Mountains, well away from any human settlements, and the season's hunting had been good.

But as the first snows of winter began to fall, Marethari's fortunes turned. Avvar warriors attacked the clan, slaughtering more than a dozen elves, including her husband, and gravely wounding their Keeper. With her clan in turmoil and her Keeper's death almost certain, Marethari took charge, ordering the Sabrae to move into the lowlands. And while they did, she sought out a place in the alpine forest where old magic lingered, a place her wise Keeper had warned her never to enter, where it was said one might find the Witch of the Wilds.

Whether she found the witch or not, no one knows for certain. But she met up with her clan in the lowlands three days later, looking grim. Her mentor, the Keeper, died of his wounds a day later. And the Avvar tribe fell prey to what some survivors said were trees come to life, the wrath of the Mountain-Father Himself.

CORRESPONDENCE FROM SEEKER ARCHIVES IN VAL ROYEAUX, DATED 9:37 DRAGON

To Seeker Cahail:

I write this in the hope that my next missive isn't an order for your arrest. The reports from Kirkwall are horrific: abominations in the streets, blood magic running rampant . . . When I permitted the formation of this "Band of Three," you claimed their investigations would aid the Chantry in preventing such atrocities. Yet there is a report that one of this band was an apostate you took from templar custody?

I have given you a long rein, but no more. Explain yourself.

Lord Seeker Thalric Edain

Honored Lord Seeker,

The Band of Three had nothing to do with the destruction of the Kirkwall Chantry, nor the events afterward. To my endless regret, they had already perished. The suggestion that they were involved is abhorrent. The Band of Three shared the goal that has driven me all my life: scouring blood magic off the face of Thedas. This isn't something that can be achieved with an Exalted March. The cancer must be traced back to its roots, and that is a painstaking task.

The boasts of the ancient Tevinter magisters are absurd. Blood magic wasn't some divine blessing sprinkled on their heads: its secrets were wrested from the elves of Arlathan. Yet modern understanding of the links between Tevinter lore and elven magic is pitiful. Too much has been lost. So yes, I recruited an apostate for the Band of Three, but Vahnel was no maleficar: he was a Dalish mage who surrendered peacefully. He had seen blood magic destroy his Keeper and others. He joined Brother Kerowen and Felestia gladly, and his knowledge proved to be key.

Elven history and slavery, the Tevinter Empire, blood magic: Kirkwall's history has been marked by all of them, and so I sent the Band there to investigate. They were bound with holy vows to uncover what lore they could, to trace the roots, and return that lore to us. In their search—why there are so many blood mages in Kirkwall, the nature of the Veil there, whether the "Forgotten Ones" in elven lore are connected to the "Forbidden Ones" in other works—I hoped to find the answers we need.

Alas, they died with their work incomplete. The tomes they recovered are invaluable, but not as worthy as those brave scholars' lives. With Kirkwall in such turmoil, it is unlikely another investigation there would prove fruitful.

I understand your concerns, Lord Seeker. But I make no apology. The memory of my brother, torn limb from limb and then turned into a blood mage's puppet, will haunt me until I die. Whether you approve or not, I will spend the rest of my life seeing blood magic brought to an end. And I will use whatever, or whomever, I can find.

Your servant and the Maker's,
Seeker Cahail

ISABELA, THE RAIDER QUEEN

Isabela, a notorious raider and self-proclaimed "Queen of the Eastern Seas," began her life in Rivain in the shadow of her mother, herself a noted thief and a charlatan. Isabela never knew her father, though her mother once, while drunk, is said to have described him as "large, hairy, and good with his hands."

Early on in her so-called "career," Isabela's mother infamously posed as a Rivaini seer to help a village in the Rivaini interior with their troubles—in exchange for coin, of course. It was there she took the name Madam Hari, after what the locals called elf-root. When she grew bored, Hari would leave the village to "seek spirits," or so she claimed. These trips, often made with Isabela in tow, could last weeks and took them to any place people had pockets. Hari taught her daughter that there was nothing wrong with taking from those who guarded their possessions poorly. The young Isabela took to dishonesty quickly and marveled at how easily one could come by coin with just a clever tongue and deft hands.

But the life of a fraud began to wear on Madam Hari, and she grew disillusioned with her path, even as her own daughter came to love being a trickster. It didn't take long for Hari to turn to the Qun to bring meaning to her life. Within the Qun, she had a place and was treasured for what she was, not what she pretended to be. Hari intended for her daughter to convert to the Qun as well, but Isabela refused.

"The Qun told people who they were, instead of letting them find out for themselves," Isabela once said. "It was slavery by another name."

Mother and daughter fought long and bitterly over Hari's decision. And then Hari simply stopped trying to persuade her daughter. Isabela thought she won, that she had finally convinced her mother to stop allowing the Qunari to train her into accepting slavery. She was wrong. Not two days later, a man came to the door of their little shack with a small entourage. He wore brocade and perfumed silk. His nails were clean and smooth. "Just take her," Hari told the man, without looking at her daughter. The man, who was called Luis, was to be Isabela's new husband. It would be the last time the mother and daughter would ever see each other.

Isabela often says that her mother sold her for a handful of gold and a goat. Occasionally the goat is a cow, or twelve chickens. Several patrons of the Hanged Man in Kirkwall swear they heard Isabela say that her mother's price was a basket of Fade weasels. But according to her close friend Varric, Isabela once, and only once, said that her mother gave her away in exchange for nothing more than the promise that her daughter would be looked after.

Luis took Isabela to Antiva City, where he had made his fortune as a merchant. There, in Luis's grand manor, Isabela was groomed for high society. Gowns and jewelry were commissioned specially for her. Only the best was good enough for Luis's new prize, and he made sure Isabela was paraded in front of him for his approval every time her maids dressed her. The wedding took place three weeks after her arrival, just before Isabela's nineteenth birthday.

"The affair was held in the most opulent hall Isabela had seen in her entire life," wrote one handmaiden. "She sat, saying nothing, at the head of the largest table, watching as her new husband entertained his guests and business partners. No one

The pirate Isabela lived for a time in Denerim during the Fifth Blight.

said a word directly to her, but everyone looked her up and down, nodding, and praised Luis for the acquisition of his exotic plaything. We kept her goblet filled with spiced wine. I assume it made the ordeal easier to bear."

Isabela couldn't help enjoying the first months of her life with Luis. Servants attended to her needs. Her every desire was met, even exceeded. She had a carriage that would take her anywhere in Antiva City. A tutor taught her to read and write. Luis would dine with her most nights and speak to her cordially, if not affectionately. But after a year, the novelty of being Luis's pampered consort wore away. There are, after all, only so many times a young woman can get a new dress or necklace before finer things lose their appeal. Boredom came first. It was quickly replaced by irritation, then anger. When she had been in Rivain, she could do as she wished, go where she wished. Now, maids and guards followed her everywhere, "for her protection," they said. She could do anything she liked, as long as it befitted the lady of the house. She could have anything she wanted except her freedom.

Isabela's growing displeasure made her bold. She sent back Luis's gifts. She rearranged the furniture in her bedroom, with every chair facing the walls, and showed up to dinner wearing men's trousers. Luis found Isabela's behavior exasperating. She was turning from a lonely, sad girl to an insolent young woman who no longer craved his attention. He began to lose interest in her. At first Isabela was pleased, thinking that he would soon let her go, but Luis continued to keep her in his manor. Isabela's anger grew.

Buzzards often circle the poorer quarters of Kirkwall.

It was around this time that Isabela met the young Antivan Crow Zevran Arainai while on an excursion in the town. They got along well and started up an affair, based more on physical attraction and Isabela's desire to test her boundaries with Luis than actual love. It was Zevran who taught Isabela the basics of knife combat. Later on, in her raiding days, she would expand upon his teachings to create a style all her own.

While carrying on her relationship with Zevran, Isabela continued her campaign of defiance against her husband. She had discovered a love for books, especially the bawdy and the philosophical, and drew on what she read to engage Luis's friends in uncomfortable discussion. Luis responded by having her kept away when he was entertaining, but she defied him and turned up anyway, often drunk. Luis had her locked in her chambers and forbade her from leaving. Isabela countered by smashing everything in her rooms. Realizing that his young wife was completely out of hand, Luis resolved to get rid of her. It was at this time, according to his journals, that he planned to "lend" her to certain business acquaintances of his who had expressed an interest. This never came to pass. Not a week later, Luis was assassinated in his bed by Zevran.

Isabela swears to this day that she did not plan to have Luis killed, though she certainly benefited from his death. The Antivan Crows keep their records secret, and so the identity of the person who wished Luis dead has never been revealed. Even Zevran, the assassin contracted to kill Luis, does not know who it was. What is known is that before Zevran killed Luis, the assassin spoke to Isabela and told her of the plan. It was she who gave him the location of the key to Luis's room, allowing Zevran to enter undetected. When Luis's death was discovered in the morning, Isabela was already gone.

The *Siren's Call*

Some weeks prior to Luis's death, he and Isabela attended the launch of his new ship, the *Siren's Call,* which was to be the fastest in his merchant fleet. Isabela was enchanted by the vessel and its billowing white sails. When Zevran told her that Luis was to die, her first thought was of the ship and how she could ride it to freedom.

As Zevran was killing her husband, Isabela left the manor, crawling out a window, with nothing but the clothes on her back, two daggers that Zevran gave her (out of the seven he carried), and a sack full of her jewelry. She used the jewelry to bribe some sailors into helping her commandeer the *Siren's Call* and sail it to Rivain.

The ship docked in Llomerryn, a notorious den of raiders and thieves. Once there, Isabela found she was unable to retain the services of the mercenary sailors she'd hired. They abandoned her, leaving her in a strange town with no gold and a ship she couldn't sail. A day later, Isabela found herself using her untested knife skills in a duel with a man she has only referred to as the Jackdaw, someone with contacts in the Felicisima Armada. She made a bet: if she could best the Jackdaw in single combat, he would help her find a crew and a job. Isabela won the bet, and to this day she is unsure if the Jackdaw lost to her intentionally, out of pity.

Whatever the case, Isabela soon found herself with a new crew and a new captain for the *Siren's Call.* She knew she would be unable to captain her own ship and wanted to learn under someone who could. And so she began her life as a raider on her own ship with another man at the helm. Isabela later killed the captain over an insult and took back control of the *Siren's Call.* As for the Jackdaw, there are rumors that he and Isabela began a passionate love affair after that first duel. They would see each other every time she returned to Llomerryn, but a year later, the Jackdaw left the island for parts unknown, and was never seen again.

Isabela spent years as a raider, the captain of one ship in the vast network of vessels that composed the Felicisima Armada. On the seas, she was involved with all manner of criminal activity: piracy, smuggling. Isabela is cagey about her activities as a raider, and records are few and far between. It is known that she spent this time honing her fighting skills and learning to navigate, all the while building a reputation as a female raider without match, as likely to bed you as shank you. Official reports from various countries also indicate that over the course of ten years, Isabela spent a total of seven months and twenty-one days in numerous jails in port cities around Thedas.

FENRIS

Fenris was formerly a slave to a Tevinter magister named Danarius. It was Danarius who had Fenris's skin tattooed with lyrium, giving him unusual abilities. The process caused Fenris to lose his memory. After his escape from Danarius, Fenris fled to Kirkwall, where he met Hawke and spent several years trying to piece together his past.

Leto

Little is known about Fenris's childhood, which comes as no surprise. Even he cannot tease much sense from the murky memories of his past. We know that his birth name was Leto and that he and his sister Varania were slaves in Tevinter. Leto and Varania served a Tevinter magister called Danarius. It is not known whether the siblings were born into his service or whether they were bought by the magister at some point.

Danarius was an accomplished mage who experimented heavily with magic and lyrium and constantly pushed the boundaries of what lyrium could do. In his research, he stumbled upon an ancient treatise that described a process of embedding lyrium beneath the skin. The lyrium, once fused with the flesh, would bestow remarkable abilities upon the one privileged enough to bear the markings. Danarius was fascinated by the potential that these lyrium tattoos held. But the treatise's instructions were vague and spotty in places, and he spent years refining the technique.

Danarius went to unknown lengths to rediscover the process, and when it was close to perfect, he decided it was time to find a living subject. The one chosen had to be young and fit. They had to be willing to undergo the operation and be strong enough to bear the pain of branding without flinching. If they balked at the last minute, the process would be ruined and months of preparation wasted. Danarius wanted a subject with iron resolve, and so he asked for a volunteer from his favored slaves. The slave who earned the position would be given a place as Danarius's personal bodyguard, prized above all others, and earn a boon from Danarius himself.

Many slaves, elven and human, jumped at the chance to become Danarius's subject. They asked for riches, greater privileges, and even the permission to marry. But Leto only wanted freedom for his sister and their mother. He fought long and hard to prove himself worthy of what the slaves all believed would be a gift. Leto's determination, more so than his physical abilities, impressed Danarius, and so he was chosen.

Danarius kept his part of the bargain. Varania and their mother were declared free and released from their duties as slaves. They were also given a small sum of gold with which to start their lives as free people. The family said their goodbyes, and Leto was taken away to be prepared for the procedure.

A series of letters from someone identified only as "Silus" to his lover sheds light on Leto's weeks of preparation. During this period, Silus was one of four guards given the task of watching him and the only one who established any sort of relationship with the slave. Silus described Leto as "quiet,

Lyrium tattoos cover Fenris's body.

but with a shrewd wit that revealed itself at the most unexpected moments." According to Silus, Leto carried some apprehension about Danarius's ritual, but was comforted by the knowledge that his sister and mother were free and happy.

Leto was delivered to Danarius as soon as the magister was ready to perform the branding. The process took several days and the combined efforts of many of Danarius's most dedicated apprentices. Danarius revealed his new masterpiece a month later in front of friends and colleagues from the Circle of Minrathous. He is quoted as saying, "I have transformed a crude elf into a work of art. Behold Fenris, my wolf."

The Dog

As Danarius had intended, the lyrium brands gave the newly renamed "Fenris" impressive new skills. He was now able to become incorporeal, to pass through solid objects at will. This ability would become Fenris's signature—while in the Champion of Kirkwall's company, he became known for punching through the chests of his enemies and taking hold of their still-beating hearts.

But the brands had changed Fenris in more ways than one. While his body healed from the process, his mind did not. The pain of the lyrium brands was so great that it left his mind irreparably damaged. He forgot everything of his life before the lyrium: his mother, his sister, and what he had done to become what he was. Danarius was Fenris's entire world—his master, his creator, and perhaps his only friend.

Fenris's formidable abilities both impressed and intimidated Danarius's associates and gained the magister no small measure of influence and renown. Wherever Danarius went, Fenris would follow; the "little wolf" was Danarius's bodyguard but, more importantly, a living testament to Danarius's genius and skill.

It is clear that Danarius treated Fenris as little more than a possession, a trophy to be flaunted. For if Danarius had any ounce of regard for Fenris, he likely would have told Fenris about his past, about his family. Even by the time of his escape, Fenris knew next to nothing about who he really was.

Danarius's social and political commitments eventually took him, and Fenris, to Seheron—on the front lines of the Imperium's war with the Qunari. While on Seheron, the magister and his slave were caught in the middle of a Qunari attack. Fenris protected his master, cutting a path to a ship that was about to pull anchor. Danarius was allowed onboard, but there was no room for his slave. The ship pulled away, leaving Fenris on the docks.

Magic is a burden for many who wield it.

Fenris was able to survive the ensuing fight with the oxmen, but he was gravely wounded. To escape death or capture, he fled into the uncharted jungle that bordered the Tevinter encampment. After stumbling over root and rock for what seemed like hours, Fenris finally collapsed, overwhelmed by the pain of his injuries.

He woke up much later in an unfamiliar tent. His wounds had been cleaned and bandaged. Food and water had been laid out for him. Emerging from the tent, Fenris swiftly learned that he had been rescued by the Fog Warriors: Seheron natives who fought a guerrilla war against both the Qunari and the Tevinters. Fenris lived with the Fog Warriors while he recovered. They taught him all they knew about the Qunari invaders, information that would be crucial to Fenris's associate Hawke in later years. Above all, the warriors taught him that there were those who were willing to fight and die for freedom.

Fenris might have made a new home with the Fog Warriors, had Danarius not reentered his life months later. Danarius had spent a great deal of effort and gold to track down his little wolf, his investment. When Danarius came into the Fog Warriors' camp, Fenris's new friends stopped him from reclaiming his property. To demonstrate the power he held over Fenris, Danarius simply laughed and commanded Fenris to kill the Fog Warriors. Fenris obeyed.

But all wolves, even little ones, eventually wake to the realization that they are not dogs.

The Wolf

Fenris massacred the Fog Warriors, his rescuers and friends, at the word of his master. Upon seeing their lifeless bodies at his feet, he must have realized that he could no longer stay with Danarius. With the Fog Warriors, he had tasted freedom, and obedience no longer suited him. He escaped through the jungle and boarded a ship headed south, pursued by the magister every step of the way.

Fenris's journey eventually took him to Kirkwall. Danarius sent hunters after Fenris, but they were little more than an impediment. Fenris's plans to mislead Danarius's lackeys resulted in an encounter with Hawke in 9:31 Dragon. At their first meeting, Hawke helped Fenris in his attempt to confront his former master, who he suspected was in Kirkwall. Danarius was not found then, but Fenris and Hawke struck up a lasting alliance.

SEBASTIAN VAEL

Sebastian Vael is a prince of Starkhaven, the youngest son of the ruling Vael family. Forced into the Chantry by his family, he escaped with the help of Grand Cleric Elthina, only to find faith and return voluntarily. With the brutal murder of his family, Sebastian became heir to the Vael legacy and was torn between duty to his beloved Chantry and to his family. The destruction of the Kirkwall chantry and the death of Elthina affected Sebastian deeply. He has since returned to Starkhaven to plan his next move.

The Wayward Prince

Sebastian was the youngest of three sons born to the Vael family that has ruled Starkhaven for generations. As a young man, he was an irresponsible rake. As a friend of the family once said, "The boy has impulses, but unlike a true gentleman, lacks the will and the means to restrain them."

Sebastian would spend his substantial allowance on drink, entertainment, and the wooing of the fine ladies of Starkhaven. Though the Vaels disapproved of Sebastian's proclivities, not everyone was quite so disdainful. The many ladies Sebastian lavished his attention upon adored him, finding his rebellious streak utterly irresistible. Sebastian was often the topic of conversation behind closed doors. Young noblewomen giggled and blushed at his notorious exploits, many hoping that they would be the next to catch the young prince's eye.

Sebastian Vael is the youngest of three children.

As Sebastian's lifestyle grew more and more outlandish, his family began to fear the shame he was bringing upon the family name. Worse, they feared the creation of a Vael bastard, who might one day grow up to challenge the heir to the throne of Starkhaven. Since the devout Vael family had a tradition of dedicating at least one member per generation to the Chantry, Sebastian's father decided to give him into the Maker's service. This would fulfill the family's obligation and get the trouble-maker out of the way in one fell swoop. Sebastian was escorted, against his will, to a cloister in faraway Kirkwall, where he was meant to stay for the rest of his life.

Kirkwall's cloister was a miserable experience for Sebastian. He'd lost the life he had, been driven into exile away from everything and everyone he knew, because someone else was embarrassed. Though he believed in Andraste and the Maker, he had had no intention of taking vows—or, worse, remaining celibate—until he was done experiencing the pleasures life had to offer. Guarded constantly by men handpicked from the family's personal guard, there was little chance of escape. And then he received a message: a friend in the Chantry who could help him leave. All he had to do was meet her at midnight.

Driven by the thought that freedom was close, Sebastian went to the meeting place at the appointed time. The "friend" who had sent the note turned out to be Grand Cleric Elthina. She knew Sebastian was unhappy in the cloister. He had not chosen this life; it had been forced on him. Though he sang the Chant and performed the tasks of a brother, his heart did not belong to the Maker. Elthina allowed Sebastian to leave, telling him that no one should enter the Chantry through the back door. When he was ready to make a commitment to the Maker, the front door would be open.

Sebastian took the opportunity Elthina gave him and left for a time. But Elthina's words lingered in his mind and made him examine his life, its meaning, and what he truly wanted. It didn't take long for Sebastian to find himself on the road back to the Chantry, this time with an open heart and a willing spirit. When he took his vows, he meant them.

A Higher Calling

Sebastian stayed with the Chantry for several years. Much to his surprise, he found peace in service to the Maker. Grand Cleric Elthina became a mentor and an inspiration. She became

An artist's depiction of the Kirkwall chantry, rigged to explode.

the mother he'd always wished he had—someone who valued him for the person he was, rather than his political usefulness. Sebastian was glad that he was no longer part of the Vael family. He was free, at peace with himself, and, for once, had found real meaning.

It didn't last long. In 9:31, the Vaels were brutally murdered by mercenaries of the Flint Company hired by unknown individuals. On hearing the news, Sebastian was gripped by grief and anger. Though Elthina tried her best to turn him from ill thoughts, Sebastian's thirst for vengeance could not be quelled. He left the Chantry and sought help to take down the murderers of his family. The one who would answer this call was Hawke, who hunted down the mercenaries of the Flint Company and was well paid by Sebastian for the effort.

In 9:34, Sebastian and Hawke crossed paths again. Sebastian had discovered that the Flint Company was hired by the Harimanns, an old noble family once allied with the Vaels. With Hawke's help, Sebastian investigated the Harimann estate, trying to discover their reasons for breaking the generations-long bond between the two families. What they found in the estate was chilling. Lady Harimann had been consorting with a desire demon that called itself Allure. Lady Harimann believed she had the strength to resist the demon. She was wrong, and the demon ensnared her mind and the minds of her family, exposing their latent desires. Now, the lady's only thought was of seizing power in Starkhaven. She was so obsessed with the idea that she hired mercenaries to murder those who stood in her way—such as the Vaels. Sebastian learned the truth, and he and Hawke destroyed the demon, freeing the Harimanns from its influence.

Sebastian was then torn between returning to peaceful life as a Chantry brother and reclaiming the throne in Starkhaven. He was the last surviving Vael: if he did not return to Starkhaven to take his rightful place as the Vael heir, his family's age-old legacy would be lost. Yet, it would mean leaving the Chantry.

In 9:37 Dragon, the situation in Kirkwall became increasingly dire. As trouble brewed between the mages and the templars, word arrived that the Divine was considering an Exalted March. The Divine sent an agent, one Sister Nightingale, to investigate the unrest. Grand Cleric Elthina asked for Sebastian to meet with the Nightingale to convince her that Kirkwall could still be redeemed. Unfortunately the meeting between Sebastian, Hawke, and Sister Nightingale was interrupted by the Resolutionists, a violent faction of mages that believed in freedom at all costs. Sister Nightingale suspected that the Resolutionists had a hand in the trouble, and feared the Divine would be forced to take steps. She sent a warning to Elthina to leave Kirkwall, before returning to Orlais to speak with the Divine.

Despite Sister Nightingale's warning, Elthina refused to leave. Even Sebastian could not persuade her to seek sanctuary in Val Royeaux. Elthina stubbornly chose to stay with her flock. Her decision would ultimately lead to her death, when the chantry was destroyed in an explosion caused by the apostate mage Anders. Sebastian took Elthina's death hard, and stood firmly on the side of Anders's execution.

NO IDLENESS FOR MAGES

Not everyone has a window, but we rise at dawn, lightly dressed, and begin at the front gates with Senior Enchanter Verend leading us. A slow jog about the ground floor, then up the stairs and past the dormitories. The wide staircase up to the library floors is where our legs truly begin to stretch. Past the dusty old suits of armor and robes on display outside the first enchanter's room, then down to a brisk walk as we pass the laboratories—no sense rattling someone's potions off the shelves.

The last stage is the most grueling, as we run up the many, many stairs to the roof of the tower, where a warm wind is always blowing. The old griffon statues stare down at the dusty city of Hossberg and the walls that encircle it—still scarred from the siege of the Fourth Blight, even after all these years. While we catch our breath and stretch, we can look over and see the wide, hot steppes beyond those walls, smoke trickling from the villages nestled here and there—that desolation where darkspawn crouch in the heat of the day and roam, tireless, at night.

Up on the roof, we work at calisthenics with one of the Grey Wardens assigned to the tower, before the sun grows too strong. Our bodies taken care of, we descend to tend to our souls at the first service of the day in our small chantry.

I have heard that in the Kirkwall Gallows, mages are locked in their cells with barely room to stretch, let alone exercise. I can promise you that any mage of the Anderfels would be stark raving mad after a week of such treatment. We Anders are not a people to sit idle. Besides, fitness of the body builds the strength of the mind. How can you stand against demonic possession if you're never given the chance to sweat? No wonder Kirkwall has such trouble with blood mages.

In the Anderfels, softness or sloth is quickly corrected. The Fourth Blight never truly ended here; the land is still scarred by it, and darkspawn and blighted creatures are a constant menace. The Grey Wardens often require our help against them, and many of us join their ranks. And so we train to strengthen our bodies, we play-battle against one another under a templar's watchful eye, we venture into the Fade to bolster our skills, and we pray to the Maker for victory.

—Notes kept by Enchanter Kessa Enos,
of the Hossberg Circle of Magi, 9:35 Dragon

BODAHN & SANDAL

Bodahn Feddic is a dwarven merchant who, after being exiled from Orzammar, became famous as a purveyor of sundry items to both the Hero of Ferelden and the Champion of Kirkwall. He worked alongside his adopted son, Sandal, a talent at both enchantment and rune crafting.

Brontos are beasts of burden often kept by dwarves.

Merchant Caste

Bodahn Feddic was born and raised in Orzammar, the last great city of the dwarves. As a child of the Merchant Caste, he often said that commerce was in his blood. When Bodahn's father died, he took over the family's business, Feddic Trades, and expanded it from a small booth in the Orzammar Commons to a thriving establishment with clientele from all over the Diamond Quarter.

Instead of trading in common wares and everyday necessities, as his father did, Bodahn made his fortune dealing in rare artifacts. The great noble houses had long pined for the glory days of the dwarven kingdom, and the shrewd Bodahn realized early on that they would pay good gold for a taste of what was lost. He began paying casteless thugs for every ancient bauble and trinket they could bring him from the lost thaigs in the Deep Roads. The farther down the Deep Roads the thaig was, the more Bodahn would pay, and the nobles would pay him a hundred times that price for something from a happier age. If anyone suspected where the antiques came from, they didn't pursue it. As far as Bodahn was concerned, he was doing the honorable thing: saving the fine treasures from lying in the dust.

I took everything. There was always a buyer, no matter what was brought back. Broken swords? You could make up a story about them. Old tiles? If they weren't chipped, you could clean them, maybe add a little glaze of color and fire them back up, and there you were, good as new. Who wouldn't want to have their dining table set with tiles from Branimir Helmi's washbasin, eh? Once, a gang of dusters even brought me back an anvil stamped with House Ortan's symbol. Made a killing with that one. I think Lady Lenka Meino uses it as her dressing table.

—Bodahn Feddic

On rare occasions, Bodahn would venture out himself—but not far and always with an entourage of hired mercenaries for his protection.

One day, one of the dusters working for Bodahn returned with a gilt ornament and two colored stones: one black, one the color of bright blood. Bodahn examined the ornament and saw that it was a dragon's head, crafted of iron, layered with gold, and broken off at the neck. The stones were jewels of some unnamed variety, perfectly smooth, even, and about the size of a child's eye. The duster swore that there were more, much more; he had chiseled his finds off a wall filled with such things. He would take Bodahn there, for a princely sum, but Bodahn himself must accompany him. Where was this mysterious wall of gold and jewels? Past the lost Aeducan Thaig, and down. Down where? The duster couldn't say.

Bodahn agreed to accompany the man and moved to make arrangements for his mercenary guards. The duster wouldn't allow it. A small army going past Aeducan Thaig would draw the attention of the darkspawn. It must be him, Bodahn, and two men at most—Bodahn's bravest and quietest. So it was settled. The small party headed out of Orzammar that same day.

They followed the casteless man for many hours. He seemed to know his way by touch alone and refused to allow the guards to light torches. Bodahn would later shudder while recalling the experience. He described how the duster told them to step only where he stepped. He talked about the darkspawn howls in the deep dark—echoes from afar that came closer and closer, only to grow distant again and fade away. What came after was a silence so thick Bodahn felt he would be smothered by it.

When they reached their destination, what Bodahn saw nearly took his breath away: a glittering wall that depicted ancient tales of heroes and Paragons. Elves, dwarves, dragons, and creatures Bodahn could not name, brought to life in a mosaic of gold and jewels. It was vast beyond his imagining, stretching upward far above the glow of the torch, into the upper reaches of the chamber, and down, its lower segments buried beneath the rocks they stood upon. Bodahn took a torch and walked the wall, trying to gain a better understanding of its scale. When an old cave-in halted his progress, he turned around, and that was when he saw the boy: a dwarven child, about five years old.

At that moment he first heard the darkspawn coming. They had seen the party, or heard them, and were coming for blood. Bodahn grabbed the child and ran. His men collapsed the tunnel behind them, and Bodahn caught a last glimpse of the jeweled wall as the Deep Roads came down around it.

Bodahn took the child back to Orzammar but never did discover how the boy came to be in the Deep Roads. The boy didn't have a name or a family, so Bodahn named him Sandal and took him for his own son.

I dropped my torch. I thought he was a ghoul or a rock wraith or something worse. But no, it was just a small boy, hair pale like marble, clear blue eyes—no blight to be seen in him at all. "What you doing out here, boy?" I said. He didn't reply, just stood there, calm as anything. And then he hears something, points at me, points at the dropped torch, and says, "They're coming."

"Who? Who's coming, boy?" I ask. He just points at the torch again. That's when I hear it, that darkspawn screech. I imagine they smell fresh blood. I hear the men shouting, and I say to the boy, "We have to go." He just stands there, half-smiling. So I pick him up. So light he was, back then. I pick him up, and I just run.

—Bodahn Feddic

Exiled with Some Fortune

Bodahn and Sandal lived for several more years in Orzammar, until Bodahn was forced to flee to the surface to escape the wrath of a noble house. Bodahn's scavengers had found a pair of handsome bracers in the Deep Roads. He cleaned them and put them up for sale. A noblewoman recognized them as a pair made especially for her dead brother and accused Bodahn of stealing them. She used her influence to have Bodahn's store closed and Bodahn himself arrested.

Bodahn suspected the noblewoman would not be satisfied until everything he'd built lay in ruins and he himself was dead. He couldn't allow that to happen; it would leave little Sandal all on his own. And so Bodahn convinced his guards to leave the cell door unlocked by promising them half of his fortune. He escaped, took Sandal and the remainder of his gold, and ran from Orzammar, heading to the surface. It was there, beneath the alien skies of topside Thedas, where, years later, he and Sandal first encountered the Hero of Ferelden and their adventure really began.

THE DEEP ROADS EXPEDITION

Not long after arriving in Kirkwall, Varric encouraged Hawke to join an expedition down the Deep Roads with Varric's brother, Bartrand. Underground, in the long-abandoned passageways of the dwarves, they discovered an idol made of a strange, red lyrium—a more potent and unpredictable form of the already dangerous crystal. Bartrand double-crossed Varric and Hawke, absconding with the idol and leaving the party to fend for themselves amid the darkspawn and wraiths down below. Somehow, Hawke's party emerged safely and, with ample wealth to show for the trouble, rebuilt the Hawke family legacy, and rose to noble standing in Kirkwall.

BARTRAND

Exiled Lord Andvar Tethras had two sons: one who was good at everything and one who was good for nothing, according to their mother. Currently, there is some debate over which is which. But in his younger days, everyone in the Merchants Guild knew Bartrand Tethras as a man who could do no wrong. His skill as an investor was unmatched; he made a vast fortune and was well on his way to restoring House Tethras to its former glory.

More than that, Bartrand quickly became the heart of the Merchants Guild's social scene. The parties hosted at his family's estate were lavish returns to the lifestyle of Orzammar. Even the most powerful of the older, established surface families found themselves fighting for invitations to dinner. It was widely rumored that he was courting a girl from House Dace, and his peers generally assumed that Bartrand would elevate House Tethras to the upper crust of surface dwarf society entirely on his own.

As these things go, Bartrand's fortune changed him. The more coin Bartrand made, the more it became an addiction. He began to neglect his family and friends in order to work.

MAGIC TRICKS

My Dear Boy,

Your pious outrage might earn you some approval with your knight-lieutenant, but I beg you to join the rest of us in the real world, lad. Do you have any idea just how wealthy the Circles of Magi can be? The amount of gold the nobility pays for enchanted goods would overflow a well. Many mages—particularly Lucrosians—are from good families, used to entertainments and the finer things in life . . . and Maker knows they can afford them. So why shouldn't they indulge a little?

Besides, a few musicians and dancers and an elaborate dinner is nothing. There are a dozen acting troupes in Val Royeaux and Halamshiral who specialize in bringing plays and stories into Circle Towers. A little collapsible scenery, the right costumes, a sprinkle of artfully chosen scent, and they can transform a workshop into an enchanted forest, a cold courtyard into a war tent on the eve of battle, or a dining hall into a darkspawn lair.

It does the mages good, too. When you see the same dreary walls day after day, a change to the familiar is a taste of freedom.

When mages entertain themselves, now, that's a sight. No mere "tricks" there. I've seen ones who could juggle fire into ice or breathe a word into one hand and release a song from the other. I once saw a mage build a cathedral out of playing cards, upside down, yet it was impossible to knock it over! Even a game of battledore and shuttlecock takes on a new dimension when the players can move objects with their minds.

It isn't all idle entertainment, either; most mages I know are eager to put their hands to useful work. Those gorgeous wooden panels in the teyrn's castle at Ostwick? The ones that show the Qunari Wars on the Waking Sea? All carved by an enchanter at the city's Circle, over the ten years he spent there. More than a few palaces have benefited from the artistry of mages: tapestries, stained glass, anything that takes time and patience.

In my day, some knight-captains frowned on mages spending their time and magical power for "frivolous ends." Frivolous? Any mage with enough fine control to keep an audience enthralled, or to build a mosaic of Andraste, has better mastery of their magic than one who only uses it to destroy. Leave the moralizing to the revered mothers, my boy. It's not for us to say how a person should stay occupied in their own home.

—A letter from retired Knight-Commander Golan Drader to his grandson, Knight-Templar Colm Drader, 9:21 Dragon

He stopped throwing parties and eventually stopped attending them. His fiancée, Raella Dace, attempted, with the help of his younger brother Varric, to persuade Bartrand to take a break from running the Tethras businesses, but with no success. Lady Raella broke off their engagement, a fact that Bartrand barely noticed.

FEYNRIEL & ARIANNI

Feynriel was the son of a Dalish elf and a human merchant from Antiva. His mother, Arianni, left her clan and raised him in Kirkwall's alienage. She hid his magical abilities when he first discovered them. Feynriel was saved twice by the Champion of Kirkwall: once from slavers in 9:31 and then from the Fade in 9:34.

Child of Two Worlds

Ancient Tevinter was once ruled by a class of mages known as Dreamers, also called somniari. The Dreamers possessed the rare ability to control the Fade—to walk it without the use of lyrium and shape it to their desires. It was the Dreamers who were first said to hear the call of the Old Gods and share the wisdom of these gods with the people of Thedas.

It is said that the First Blight and the birth of the darkspawn crippled the Dreamers; for the first time in thousands of years, they could no longer hear the voices of their gods. Over the next hundred years, fewer and fewer mages with the Dreamers' legendary abilities were found in Tevinter. Attempts to breed the ability proved futile, and the resultant mages were pale copies of the true somniari—weak of power and frail of mind. Some believe that there were real Dreamers found in Dalish clans and that the Dalish had studied the somniari arts, but even there, they were few and far between. No one had seen a surviving Dreamer for centuries, until Feynriel.

Feynriel was the product of a romance between the Dalish elf Arianni and a traveling Antivan merchant, Vincento. Arianni left her clan, much to Keeper Marethari's disappointment, to pursue a relationship with Vincento. Their affair was passionate but short lived and ended the moment Arianni told Vincento she was with child. He swore that it was not his choice, but that he had to return to Antiva to attend to the family business. But Arianni knew the truth: Vincento could not take an elf for a wife and never intended to. And he certainly wanted nothing to do with the elf-blooded bastard she carried. Heartbroken but knowing there was nothing she could do, Arianni did not stop Vincento from leaving.

Alone and pregnant, the desperate Arianni turned to her clan for help, but the Dalish would not accept a human living among them. Arianni's child was too elven for its father and too human for the Dalish. Arianni had no choice but to return to Kirkwall.

his son. Months later, she received a curt reply. It wasn't much, but she showed it to Feynriel, who was overjoyed.

When Feynriel was eight, he discovered that he could make things happen just by thinking about them. One winter, he wished very hard for their small houseplant to bloom. The next morning, the plant was covered in fragrant white blossoms. Arianni was shocked, but Feynriel told her not to be frightened. He had made the flowers bloom for her. When she asked why, he explained that she had looked sad all week and he knew how much she loved flowers. Arianni was both touched and terrified by what her son had done. She knew now that he was a mage,

Many blame Divine Justinia V (*left*) for not doing enough to prevent the crisis at Kirkwall.

Red templars emerged following the discovery of red lyrium in the Deep Roads under Kirkwall.

Sympathetic alienage residents helped her find a job washing linens, which allowed her to eke out a poor living for her and her son, Feynriel.

Feynriel's early years passed without incident. Arianni maintained that she tried her best to keep him away from those who would mock him for his parentage. But a mother cannot protect a child from everything, and there came a day when Arianni needed to explain Feynriel's origins to him. As the product of an elven-human union, he would always be different, always an outcast. Once Feynriel learned about his father, he could not stop asking questions. He wanted to know where Vincento was and whether he was ever coming back. Arianni did not have answers for her son, but his questions compelled her to try to reach Vincento again. She wrote to him at the address left to her and told him about

Hawke's legacy is undeniable.

and that if anyone found out about him, he would be taken away from her. Growing up Dalish, Arianni had been exposed to magic daily and had watched her own Keeper instruct others. She believed she knew enough about the subject to help Feynriel control his powers and resolved to teach him to hide them.

Arianni's plan worked, at least for a few years. But over that time, she realized that her son was unlike any other mage she had encountered. He had a strange connection to the Beyond—what humans called the Fade. There were times when she could not wake him from his sleep. More alarmingly, on rare occasions he would freeze while awake and occupied, as though his mind had suddenly stopped working. When that happened, it could take up to an hour for Feynriel to come back to his senses.

But it was when Feynriel's dreams began to take on a sinister nature that Arianni truly began to fear for her son's life. Feynriel complained of hearing voices when he dreamed and said that the dreams had started to feel "real." It was clear to Arianni that her limited knowledge of magic could no longer protect her son. He was in danger from demons and the Fade, and she needed to turn to someone who could help him: the Circle. Arianni sought aid from the templar Thrask, whom she knew to be sympathetic to mages. Feynriel found out that Arianni had contacted the templars, and feared that she planned to turn him over to the Circle. He ran away, first seeking out his father, Vincento, who had returned to Kirkwall. Vincento could not help his son, but directed him to an ex-templar, Samson, known for helping runaway mages. Samson led Feynriel to a Captain Reiner, who he thought would help Feynriel escape but who instead captured him to be sold as a slave. Feynriel would later be saved by Hawke, who encountered a distraught Arianni searching for her son.

After his rescue, Feynriel would come to believe that Hawke was the only one he could trust. He often sent letters to the Hawke residence, though it is unclear whether Hawke ever sent a reply. In 9:34, Feynriel fell into a nightmare and could not be awoken. Arianni sought out Hawke again, begging the Champion to save her son. Arianni had reached out to the Keeper of her clan, Marethari, who understood immediately that Feynriel was a Dreamer—the first in centuries. Marethari believed that Feynriel could be saved if someone he trusted could enter the Fade to draw him out. This person would have to be Hawke.

Feynriel's fate after the Fade is uncertain. Some say Hawke failed to stop Feynriel from becoming possessed by a demon. Others believe that Feynriel's sojourn to the Fade resulted in him becoming Tranquil. Still others say he ran away to Tevinter to be taught to control his somniari abilities. Whatever the case, Feynriel was not seen in Kirkwall again.

XENON THE ANTIQUARIAN

Xenon the Antiquarian is the infamous owner of the Black Emporium, a collection of strange and exotic items amassed by Xenon over his three-hundred-year lifespan. Only people Xenon deems worthy are ever allowed entrance to the Black Emporium. For everyone else, Xenon and his priceless hoard remain but a legend.

A Living Antique

According to legend, Xenon was a Kirkwall noble who lived in the Steel Age. He possessed as much arrogance as he did wealth, and was offended by the thought that someone like him should have to succumb to death like a mere peasant. Accordingly, Xenon committed his time and a good portion

CORRESPONDENCE FROM THE SEALED VAULTS OF WEISSHAUPT, DATED 1004–1006 TE

Senior Warden Sashamiri,

The First Warden has agreed. The darkspawn Corypheus must be captured and held by whatever means we can find. Your protests have been noted, but we cannot waste this opportunity. If Corypheus is the key to having influence over the darkspawn, it is our duty to discover how, for the good of all Thedas. That means someone must devise a trap that can draw and hold him. Your wisdom has been proven a dozen times over; I cannot entrust this task to anyone else.

Can I ask this of you, Sasha, or must it be an order?

Warden-Commander Farele

Warden-Commander,

I swore obedience, not willful ignorance. I will do as you ask, but I will have my say first: you are becoming too complacent about this creature, Farele. If you need to remember what darkspawn are, go to the Silent Fields and remind yourself what horrors Dumat wrought on my homeland.

Sashamiri

Warden-Commander,

The transcript of your conversations with Corypheus seems to have an answer, though not one the First Warden will like. The creature speaks of Dumat almost with reverence. We know already that the Archdemon had control over the darkspawn horde, that they were drawn inexorably to its presence. There it is, then: if we need to draw Corypheus and bind it, we should send to Weisshaupt for what remains of Dumat's carcass. In the blood of that Archdemon, and perhaps the ancient weapon I've been studying, I may find what I need. You, however, need to find somewhere that this trap can be laid. The more remote the better. If nothing else, my friend, it will keep you out of the Deep Roads.

Sashamiri

of his vast fortune to a pursuit of immortality. According to the tales, he made a deal with a Witch of the Wilds for eternal life, but unfortunately failed to ask also for eternal youth. As the years wore on, Xenon aged like any other man. His skin sagged, then grew wrinkled and leathery. His bones and muscles became feeble and twisted under their own weight, which they could no longer support. His aged internal processes subjected him to all manner of indignities that cannot be detailed here. However, unlike any other man, for whom death is a welcome release from the horrors of advancing decrepitude, Xenon was not able to die.

When Xenon realized he had doomed himself to an eternity of, not life, but a dreadful *undeath*, he began searching for ways to preserve his failing body. Every possible solution was explored; no mythical remedy was deemed too obscure, no magic too dangerous or forbidden. He scoured whole libraries of books, collected thousands of magical artifacts, and was visited by hundreds of mages, all in his attempts to stop the ravages of time. Sadly, almost all of the preservation methods Xenon underwent did not have the desired effect. Some say a few dark rituals returned the blush of youth to his skin, but the effects never lasted for long. Xenon's body continued to wither and decay until he could no longer move on his own.

Xenon's wishes are now carried out by his many servants, who continue to search for a way to reverse the effects of aging on their master. Some of these servants are responsible for curating the thousands of artifacts that populate the Black Emporium. Others guard Xenon and his treasures. Those who have seen Xenon in his mysterious Black Emporium describe him as being in some ways fused to his great chair, a twisted mass of calcified flesh. They say it is difficult to tell where furniture ends and Xenon begins, so much is he a part of his cursed station.

To Warden-Commander Farele:

The authority to remove the Archdemon's remains did not include permission to raid the fortress libraries, too! Senior Warden Sashamiri has already been provided with the tomes she asked for. You are ordered to return all materials immediately or face censure by the First Warden. What has gotten into you?

Stafen Nerrah, Chamberlain of the Grey,
Weisshaupt Fortress

Farele,

It is done. You will soon have your captive darkspawn, far beneath the Vimmark Mountains. Once the other seals are laid by my apprentices, this trap will be closed. I hope you will gain Corypheus's secrets . . . but I have ensured it will not get yours. The blood of the Archdemon is consuming my life, even as it draws Corypheus inexorably on. Forgive me, dear friend, but blood magic has its price, and I've chosen to pay this one. I pray it is enough to make you see how this monster has been manipulating you. With my death and the destruction of Dumat's remains, the secret of this spell will be lost: no Warden can fall to Corypheus's manipulations and give it the knowledge to break its chains from within. Not even you.

In peace, vigilance.

Sasha

MALCOLM'S LEGACY

Hawke and party were led to the Vimmark Mountains to investigate the actions of Carta dwarves there, including a former associate of Varric's named Gerav. The party discovered the dwarves were possessed by some powerful force and were attempting to free the ancient Tevinter magister Corypheus using the blood of Hawke, whose father had trapped Corypheus in a tower prison. Wardens Janeka and Larius were also trying to reach the tower: Janeka to free Corypheus, and Larius, suffering from the effects of his Calling, attempting to stop her.

What happened up in that prison remains a mystery. Though there were rumblings that Corypheus was freed only to be defeated by Hawke, it now appears Corypheus must have escaped somehow. There is no record of Janeka or Larius following the events at the prison.

JANEKA & LARIUS

Ages ago, the Grey Wardens built a prison in the Vimmark Mountains to house an ancient darkspawn called Corypheus. Seals were placed upon the prison to keep Corypheus from escaping, and only the most high-ranking Wardens of the Order were entrusted with knowledge of the prison.

Early in the Dragon Age, Warden-Commander Larius of the Free Marches was charged with keeping Corypheus from escaping. Larius had achieved his high rank at a younger age than most through perseverance and dedication to the duty of the Wardens. Since there was no Blight on the horizon, the Wardens were to remain vigilant—something Larius took quite seriously. When one of the mages serving at the prison informed the Warden-Commander that the seals holding Corypheus were deteriorating from age, Larius set out to find a solution. That solution would be Malcolm Hawke: an apostate with everything to lose, who could thus be trusted to keep the prison's location a secret.

Decades later, after almost thirty years spent as a Warden, Larius would be forced to answer his Calling. Before leaving for the Deep Roads, he turned command of the prison over to a senior Warden named Janeka, a close friend and ally. She had served for many years and was already familiar with the wards of the prison.

After Larius's departure, however, Janeka began to doubt if keeping Corypheus imprisoned was in the Wardens' best interest. Over several months, she became convinced that the creature held the key to ending the Blights forever.

The ancient darkspawn Corypheus would later demonstrate an ability to influence Grey Wardens.

"This darkspawn . . . why did my predecessors choose to hold it in this place, instead of destroying it?" she wrote in a private journal. "I have turned the thought over and over in my

FILES ON THE INVESTIGATION OF THE CHAMPION

GERAV

From a sealed report, addressed to Leliana, from Varric Tethras:

"Gerav made Bianca." A statement like that is simple, and people like things to be simple. More importantly, the Carta likes it. So I let them believe Gerav made the crossbow. Sometimes, the truth's just too complicated. Or too dangerous.

You want to know what really happened? It began, as everything does, with an idea. Somewhere in Gerav's spider's nest of a brain was an image: a repeating crossbow that was easy to operate, easy to aim, that could punch through steel like it was an undershirt. Well, Gerav took the idea to the Carta bosses, and it captured their imaginations. It's not hard to see why. If they could be built, if they could arm the Carta muscle with them, no number of antique ceremonial shields would be able to stop the Carta. The dusters would take the Diamond Quarter.

So Gerav got the gold he needed to turn the idea into reality. He had the first prototype within a week. It didn't work. Neither did the second, the third, or the eighteenth. Bosses were getting restless, and Gerav was getting desperate. That's when I heard about the whole thing. Repeating crossbow? Sounded fascinating, so I went to see him. Somehow, I managed to convince him to sell me one of the prototypes. Number Fourteen, actually. It was the one that had come the closest and was made right before the designs started getting a bit . . . outlandish.

Anyway, Fourteen would eventually become my Bianca . . . but we weren't there yet. She didn't work. Just to see if it could be done, I asked around for another smith to take a look at her. My contacts pointed me to a lady just a few years out of her apprenticeship. Her work was solid, they said. She was brilliant and still young enough that she hadn't picked up the bad habit of knowing. That's the problem with experienced smiths. They know. They know how to do things, how not to do things. They know when things can be done, when things can't be done. But knowing leaves very little room for dreaming.

The smith? Her name was Bianca.

I met up with her, and one thing led to another . . . Before I knew it, I had a repeating crossbow on my hands. Until this day, I don't know how she did it. Gerav and the Carta eventually found out that Fourteen worked, and I let them believe that all I did was adjust some of her pins. I knew, by that time, that I couldn't reveal Bianca's involvement. The Carta would never leave her alone. I didn't want that . . . She didn't want that.

Well, Gerav got another chest of gold and spent the next few years trying to replicate the success of Fourteen. When he could, he'd build little upgrades for my Bianca—some of them worked; some of them didn't. Then he stopped writing. We found out later that he was part of the Carta scheme to capture Hawke for Corypheus. I was angry at the time, but it wasn't really his fault. He'd drunk darkspawn blood and wasn't himself by the time we found him. He's gone now . . . and I'm sure I told Cassandra all about that a year or so back, and I don't feel like going into it again.

So there it is. The story. Or at least the relevant bits. I'm going to hold you to your promise, Nightingale. You never let the truth about Gerav and Bianca out.

mind, and there is only one answer: power. This entity holds power. They say it is ancient. It must hold knowledge about Blights past. Perhaps knowledge of how to conquer them all. Yet we let it sleep. We hold it in silence. But silence must end, for the good of all. I shall be our deliverer."

Janeka enlisted the service of a cell of the dwarven Carta, forcing them to drink darkspawn blood and using them to track down the descendants of Malcolm Hawke, whose blood was needed to break open the seals holding Corypheus. The events that occurred during the rise of the Inquisition would make it clear that, even then, Janeka was in the thrall of Corypheus. So subtle was Corypheus's control, however, that Janeka never suspected that her drive to free the creature was not of her own making.

Janeka was not the only Warden that Corypheus controlled. Larius, the former keeper of the prison, still lurked within its walls, drawn back from the Deep Roads by a compulsion he could not explain. However, unlike Janeka, Larius was aware that it was the ancient darkspawn that called to him. Though the taint was well advanced in his body, he did all he could to fight Corypheus's influence and Janeka's attempts to free him.

THE QUNARI CRISIS

Before Hawke arrived in Kirkwall, a Qunari vessel crashed off the shores of the city, stranding the crew. The displaced oxmen took a home in a compound near the docks and began a search for the Raider Queen known as Isabela, sure that she'd stolen a Qunari relic, the Tome of Koslun. Led by the Arishok, the Qunari stayed in Kirkwall in the hopes that they would reclaim the tome.

After the expedition into the Deep Roads, Hawke's wealth and status in Kirkwall rose considerably. In 9:34 Dragon, Hawke became involved in the growing unrest between the landed Qunari and the office of Viscount Dumar. When the Arishok rose up and killed the viscount, Hawke put an end to the violence and saved Kirkwall from a full-on Qunari occupation.

THE ARISHOK

The Kirkwall incident of 9:34 Dragon, the first attack by Qunari outside the Tevinter Imperium since the Storm Age, reminded Thedas why it should fear them.

"Fires blanketed the city in thick smoke that blinded anyone mad enough to venture out their door," the Comte de Launcet wrote of the attack. "Screams echoed down from somewhere in Hightown. The city guard scattered, dealing with a hundred burning barricades and oxman ambushes in the black smoke. No one knew what was happening. I heard someone say that a fleet of dreadnoughts had sacked the harbor, that they were rounding up everyone like cattle for slaughter. None of us imagined the quiet oxmen who'd sat in the docks for so long could have been capable of so much chaos."

Only the swift intervention of Kirkwall's Champion saved the city from conversion to the Qun. In the aftermath of the murder, and in an unprecedented public display, the remaining two members of the Qunari ruling body, the Arigena and the Ariqun, traveled to Kont-aar to make a public statement before an assembled crowd of Chantry officials, diplomats, and Rivaini seers.

"The actions of our brother in the city-state of Kirkwall are disgraceful and reflect neither the demands of the Qun nor the will of the Qunari people," the Arigena announced to the masses in the now-famous address. "We are saddened that the one chosen to be the physical presence of the Qun before the world has proven to be so brittle, and we grieve that he has led the men under his command away from their purpose."

Even the Qunari considered the Arishok's behavior shocking. How, then, could such an unstable individual be granted a position in the Qun's ruling body?

In 9:25 Dragon, the Qunari lost their Arishok of twelve years to wounds he sustained in Seheron. The tamassrans immediately began the process of selecting his successor. Officers from the infantry and the navy were brought to Par Vollen for testing. The Tevinter Imperium's intelligence service watched the proceedings closely.

Ranging in rank from the Kathaban to the stens, officers were subjected to a variety of tests, the purposes of which were almost completely impossible to determine.

Agents reported seeing soldiers meditating under observation by the tamassrans, writing essays, and on one occasion, walking over hot coals. Several officers, after their written exam, were made to arrange large rocks in a courtyard. After each test, the tamassrans returned some of the soldiers to their posts.

The Arishok's attempts to take Kirkwall were thwarted by Hawke.

After ninety days of testing, two candidates were selected by the tamassrans and sent before the Ariqun and the Arigena for a final choice: the Kithshok who commanded the garrison at the fortress of Alam, and the Kathaban of the navy. Each met with the Qunari leaders, and after another two days of deliberation, the Kithshok was chosen to be the new Arishok. The reaction from the Imperium was immediate. A dozen assassins were dispatched from Minrathous, possibly at the command of the archon himself, to eliminate the new Arishok.

Only two made it past the Ben-Hassrath into the city of Par Vollen. The Arishok killed both assassins himself. In his previous role as Kithshok of Alam's garrison, he had long been considered one of the chief obstacles to an Imperium victory on the island of Seheron. Among Tevinter's legates, he was known as "The Mad Ox," believed to be completely unpredictable and noted for his sometimes-inspired but incredibly high-risk battlefield tactics.

He was sent to personally receive the recovered Tome of Koslun from Empress Celene—a gesture intended to secure some degree of diplomatic relations between Orlais and the frustratingly enigmatic Qunari people—but the Felicisima Armada intervened. Before the book could be given to the Arishok, one of the Felicisima Armada's captains stole it from the palace and attempted to sail away. The Qunari response was as predictable as it was disastrous.

"They knew. Maybe oxmen can smell guilt," later wrote Arvid, a surviving crewman of the *Siren's Call*. "All the ships on the Waking Sea, and the dreadnought, came straight for us. Cannons firing. No warning shots, just real, live, 'burn them all' fire. We couldn't have outrun them even if we hadn't gone straight into a storm. Never seen any ship lose a dreadnought, even if they weren't full of burning holes. Not even sure if we hit a reef or the cannon fire took us down. It was just smoke and water and thunder and death all around."

Both ships wrecked on the Wounded Coast, leaving the dreadnought crew stranded and leading inexorably to the Arishok's ill-fated attack on Kirkwall.

Following the incident, the tamassrans are reputed to have chosen his successor by entirely different criteria, but as it is still unclear to outside observers what the Qunari chose their Arishok for before this disaster, there's no telling what the new Arishok may be like.

VISCOUNT MARLOWE DUMAR

Viscount Marlowe Dumar became the viscount of Kirkwall in 9:21 Dragon. He is remembered as a weak, ineffectual ruler whose authority was severely curtailed by the powerful templars and their stringent knight-commander, Meredith. Dumar wore the viscount's crown until his death at the hands of the Arishok during the Qunari uprising of 9:34.

The Puppet

The Dumars had roots in Kirkwall since the early Storm Age. By the early Dragon Age, the family, while still noble, was only modestly wealthy and nowhere near as prominent as some of the other Hightown houses, such as the Amells, the Threnholds, or the Reinhardts. Lord Randall Dumar, unlike many other lords, even did some work. He would often personally oversee the operations at the family's trading company, located on the docks. Marlowe Dumar, Lord Randall's first son, grew up believing that there was nothing wrong with good, honest labor.

When Marlowe was twenty, he met Phyllida Bowens, the young daughter of Kirkwall's foremost cartographer. While not noble, the Bowenses were a prosperous family thanks to the cartographer's commissions from the viscount and several Vael princes in Starkhaven. Phyllida lived a few doors away from the Dumars in Hightown, and Marlowe often saw her accompanying her mother to market. He eventually worked up the courage to speak to her, and the two young people fell in love and were shortly married.

In 9:14 Dragon, Marlowe and Phyllida's first child—a daughter they named Venetia—was born. The birthing process was difficult on Phyllida, but both mother and child survived. Sadly, the baby was frail and did not thrive, no matter what Phyllida and her nurses did. A month after the birth, Venetia died. Phyllida's grief was deep and long-lasting, and she blamed herself for her daughter's ill health. Nothing Marlowe did could console her.

The viscount's keep was impressive. Even the door had presence.

Phyllida eventually recovered, and by 9:16, she was pregnant again. Once again, the birth was troublesome, and Phyllida labored for almost two days to bring her child into the world. Marlowe was beside her bed throughout the ordeal, and they say he refused to leave even to feed himself. The midwives worked long and hard, but as time dragged on, they realized that it would be impossible to save both mother and child. They asked Marlowe to choose: his wife or his son. Marlowe would have chosen Phyllida but for Phyllida herself, who was adamant that their son be the one to live. She had already lost one child. She would not lose another. With great effort, the child was delivered, and Phyllida lived long enough to hold him and name him Saemus, after her grandfather. Her last words were "Tell him about me. Keep him safe."

The viscount's throne.

Though Marlowe was heartbroken by the loss of his beloved wife, care of his young son filled his days, and he soon found himself coming to terms with Phyllida's death. But Marlowe would never remarry, nor give the idea much thought.

By 9:21 Dragon, and after years of misrule, Viscount Perrin Threnhold had lost almost all the support of Kirkwall's nobles. His decision to block off the Waking Sea passage turned them against him entirely. Threnhold's goal was to extract tolls from passing ships to line his own pocket, but this action made trade impossible, and trade was Kirkwall's lifeblood. While other nobles wrote frantically to Knight-Commander Guylian, urging the templars to do something, Marlowe did as his father had done. He went down to the docks and oversaw the running of the Dumars' company, finding ways for Kirkwall's trade, no matter how diminished, to continue. Still, he worried that Threnhold would eventually destroy the city with his schemes. He did not have to worry for long. Though Knight-Commander Guylian preferred to stay out of Kirkwall's politics, his hand was eventually forced. Guylian paid the ultimate price for his intervention when the viscount had him hanged. This ignited a series of battles between the viscount's forces and the templars, which culminated in Threnhold's arrest and defeat.

Kirkwall was now in need of a viscount. The new knight-commander, Meredith, appointed Marlowe to the seat, much to his surprise. Just before he was crowned, he met in private with the knight-commander at the Gallows. Marlowe was escorted, surrounded by grim templars, to Meredith's well-appointed office, and there, she explained her reasons for the choice. Kirkwall was filled with entitled degenerates. Marlowe was different. His family had always been humble. They never grasped for power or gold, never felt that it was owed them. "With my help, you will turn this city around," she said. "We will be allies."

Meredith's message was clear: Remember who holds power in Kirkwall. Remember what happened to Threnhold when he overreached. To drive home her point, she presented Marlowe with a small carven ivory box at his coronation. The box contained the Threnhold signet ring, misshapen, and crusted with blood. On the inside of the lid were written the words "His fate need not be yours."

Marlowe ruled Kirkwall without incident for almost a decade, in no small part thanks to Meredith's backing. During his reign, the templars grew even more powerful, and the

The viscount's chambers.

knight-commander's influence was evident in almost every one of Marlowe's decisions. However, from 9:31 on, the seething tensions of the city made it almost impossible for him to keep the peace. Pulled in every which way by factions he could not appease, the weak viscount was unable to maintain control in his own city. When his only son, Saemus, was brutally murdered, Marlowe gave up hope completely.

He was beheaded by the Arishok in the Qunari uprising of 9:34.

SAEMUS DUMAR

Saemus Dumar was the son of Viscount Marlowe Dumar. Chronically unsure of his place in the world, Saemus eventually converted to the Qun. Anti-Qunari agitators later assassinated him as part of a scheme to oust the Qunari from Kirkwall.

The Philosopher

When Saemus was only five, his father was appointed viscount of Kirkwall. This was an enormous change for the small family. For their protection, the services of a dozen guardsmen were retained. The Dumars' modest estate became crowded with strange faces, and it took several months for the young boy to learn that the heavily armed men roaming the halls were not there to hurt him. The worst part of all of it was that Marlowe would spend his days at the keep in Hightown and return late at night, his face creased with worry. The days when Marlowe would set Saemus on his knee and tell him stories grew fewer in frequency and then disappeared altogether. Father and son would never recover their close relationship from Saemus's early years.

Saemus was a shy boy, and spent most of his childhood without friends. His nurses spoke about inviting neighborhood children to the viscount's house to play with Saemus. Not wanting to seem impolite, Saemus would try his best to be sociable. Sadly, the visits routinely ended up with the invited children playing together and Saemus electing to sit on his own, reading a book. Saemus's love of books and learning only grew more intense as he aged. A ten-year-old Saemus would often be seen pestering his father to bring him to the keep's library so he could peruse the many history books kept there. At the viscount's keep, Saemus discovered *In Pursuit of Knowledge: The Travels of a*

FILES ON THE INVESTIGATION OF THE CHAMPION

BRAN

From the notes of Master of Portraiture Nohlan Thrantus III of Orlais, late of Kirkwall:

We are tasked with the evaluation of the current viscount, and in lieu of the fullness of history, we must measure him by the means that we have. From the standpoint of portraiture, the man is an unmitigated failure.

Lafaille, the first. Proud, draped in Orlesian couture but with the colors of the Marches. The points on his crown, his sons, but not that one.

Threnhold, the tyrant, his frame now stored beneath the stairs. But when last viewed, a mailed glove resting upon a helm very nearly that of a templar.

And Marlowe, his posthumous frame showing the draw of his cloak severed, to suggest both his violent end and that of the Dumar line. Crimson accents drive the point home like the point of the Arishok's blade.

These are but a few of the striking commentaries masquerading as portraiture in the halls of power. They honor the past, but also remind of the fortunes that await if certain steps are repeated. Thus, the artist plays a vital role in shaping our government.

What, then, of Bran? When Kirkwall found its leadership vacant due to circumstance, and when time was ripe for a true change maker to appear, our noble families voted for a placeholder. An interim leader compelled to the position, to suffer through uncertainty so that no one of value would be lost to the inevitable arrows of dissent or conquest. Bran would not take the title "Viscount" without "Provisional," exposing how temporary he wished the role to be. He does not offend, deferring to ballot after ballot rather than imposing personal edict. He does not enforce, deferring to the guard-captain and her militia raised from the people. He remains as he was: a facilitator to figures of power. That was a role in which he had no match. But now, with the throne absent, he does not claim it even though he bears (in part) the title. He maintains the absence. He, himself, is the absence.

The arrows did not come, for the spineless nobility could not predict calm. The work of the Champion was so thorough that spirited opposition to leadership has faded. The figures left in the wake of those events value order and find it in the guard and in the will of the people. Now that peace would allow true leadership to seek the throne, walls of contentment prevent any such attempt.

So, to the portrait. The face offers no particular difficulty, being the normal structure of a northern Marcher born to not-quite nobility—for surely the self-declared Cavins of Ansburg do not measure. Bran Cavin? He himself avoids the name. Mothered in the East, trained in the best of Rivaini academies, versed in the governmental traditions of all the disparate city-states of the Marches. Should that lend to academic posing? He has published no works. He is somehow possessed of exacting skill with the violin, but I would not paint it in his hand. Where are the discordant tones, the antirhythmic cadences of the modern? Where is the will to lead?

To represent the rule of Provisional Viscount Bran is to paint everything but the man. For he is nothing if not the reflection of those around him, somehow focused into competence. He seeks to balance all available pieces, and where others would use that to climb, he would merely see that it not fall. Bran seems contented to remain incidental to his own provisional rule. How, in all that is the Maker's wisdom, does an artist make anything interesting out of "contented"?

Chantry Scholar, the famed book by Brother Ferdinand Genitivi. *In Pursuit of Knowledge* would become Saemus's favorite book, one he would return to every year or so. The brief discussion of the Qun in Genitivi's book is what sparked Saemus's tragic interest in Qunari philosophy and led to him seeking out other reading material on the matter.

The viscount became concerned for Saemus, thinking that a young boy should have interests other than books. He began encouraging Saemus to explore the outdoors and hired a swordmaster to teach him how to defend himself. Saemus fared well in his lessons, but it was clear the boy would never become a master swordsman. Much to the viscount's disappointment, Saemus was far more keen on books of military strategy than actually joining the military.

When Saemus was sixteen, he began leaving the estate alone to wander the Wounded Coast, seeking out the strange flora and fauna that thrived there. His dream was to write his own book, similar to *In Pursuit of Knowledge,* which would inspire a whole new generation of curious young minds. The viscount did not look kindly on Saemus's adventures. The viscount would often hire men to bring Saemus back, and he grew increasingly weary of his son's casual disregard for his own safety. Saemus, in turn, found his father's behavior needlessly restrictive and began to detest his life as a noble and the viscount's only son.

In 9:31 Dragon, when the Qunari dreadnought was shipwrecked near Kirkwall, Saemus took this as a blessing and hoped that he could come to understand more of Qunari culture. That same year, he encountered the Qunari known only as Ashaad while on the Wounded Coast. Saemus befriended Ashaad and, through him, gained a deeper appreciation for the Qun.

Ashaad was killed by men seeking to return Saemus to his father, an act for which Saemus never forgave Marlowe. They went months without speaking to each other.

Saemus's admiration for the Qunari philosophy persisted, and several years later, he became a convert. The ill-fated decision is what led to him being killed in a plot to incite anti-Qunari sentiment. In the end, Saemus's death was one of a series of events leading to the Qunari uprising that would take countless lives, including that of Saemus's own father.

The Dumar line ended with the deaths of Viscount Marlowe Dumar and Saemus Dumar.

MARK OF THE ASSASSIN

Sometime between the expedition, the Qunari uprising, and the chantry explosion, Hawke met Tallis, an elven rogue who enlisted the Champion's help in stealing a jewel called the Heart of the Many from an Orlesian named Duke Prosper. They joined Prosper on a wyvern hunt, then infiltrated his chateau. It was there that Tallis was revealed to be a Qunari agent hunting her former mentor, the Ben-Hassrath who had trained her, to stop him from handing over a list of names identifying the Qunari sleeper agents in place throughout Thedas.

TALLIS

To most people in Thedas, a Qunari is a large creature with horns hailing from the northern island of Par Vollen. They would be alarmed to know that there are Qunari all around them, that they may have met one and not even realized it, for the term applies to all converts to the Qun regardless of their race.

Such is the case for the elven woman known as Tallis—as with all followers of the Qun, that is not her true name but rather a description of her role, and also a much-shortened one, used primarily for the ease of outsiders. "Tallis" is a word in Qunlat that means "to solve." Fitting, as throughout most of her life, Tallis has been tasked with solving troublesome issues in non-Qunari lands. She has at times been a spy, a thief, and an assassin, all depending on what Qunari leaders demanded of her.

Origins

Little is known of Tallis before she became part of the Qun, outside of the fact that it was in the city of Minrathous, in the Tevinter Imperium, and that she was sold into slavery by her elven parents—a common practice in the Imperium among families heavily in debt or forced to pay fines levied by the tribunals. Whatever the reason, she found herself on a slaver ship bound for the Tevinter city of Carastes, and it was during this voyage that the Qunari boarded and captured the ship and all aboard brought to the island fortress of Qunathras off the eastern coast of Seheron.

At Qunathras, the captives (slaves and slavers alike) began their reeducation under the Qunari priesthood. Those deemed unsuitable as converts were rendered mindless laborers, which would have been the fate of young Tallis had it not been for the intervention of a superior—as evidenced by a translated document found during the brief Tevinter occupation of Qunathras in 9:35 Dragon:

"What you say of the young elven girl is true, but what you describe as 'headstrong,' I would describe as 'spirited,' " the document read. "You believe the girl impossible to break, but I believe the challenge she presents is superseded by the rewards of doing so. As you know, we are in need of [those who solve], and thus I formally request that the tamassrans withhold their qamek and instead turn the girl over to me. I will train her, and the responsibility should I fail will be mine."

This was written by Salit, a high-ranking member of the Ben-Hassrath, the Qunari order that acts as the enforcer of religious

Tallis was born in Tevinter.

law and the public good. This mandate evidently extends to clandestine missions in non-Qunari nations.

It was this Salit who then, as her mentor, raised Tallis and sponsored her induction into the Ben-Hassrath. She performed missions for the Qunari in many lands around Thedas, though primarily in Orlais and Nevarra.

Fiona led the mages to rebellion at the White Spire.

Tallis always returned successful in these missions—but never to the complete specifications of her superiors. She would succeed in an assassination, for instance, but in a way other than what had been requested. Even if that had been the only way to complete the mission, her superiors would have preferred the mission be abandoned rather than done imperfectly. To the Qunari, this indicated a streak of pride they believed would ultimately lead to disobedience. They were correct.

The final straw came when Tallis was tasked with stealing a Qunari artifact in the possession of Count Alphonse Valmont in the city of Arlesans. The count believed the artifact a simple piece of art, and had it been stolen without any evidence of the perpetrator as the Qunari intended, its theft would have been blamed on simple thieves. While in the count's estate, however, Tallis discovered elven and human children being kept as sex slaves. She set them free, slaying Count Alphonse and a number of his guards in the process, and kicking off a diplomatic incident that almost resulted in a renewed war between the Qunari and the Orlesian Empire.

While the artifact had been recovered, Tallis was seen as too willful to continue as a member of the Ben-Hassrath. She was demoted to the rank of athlok, a laborer, and set to work as a kitchen hand aboard a Qunari trading vessel. It is believed that Salit also suffered some form of demotion as a result of his pupil's disgrace, though it's uncertain precisely what that consisted of beyond his removal as a leader within the Ben-Hassrath.

Disgrace

After two years as a ship laborer, Tallis was offered a chance to redeem herself: an escaped Qunari mage, known as a saarebas, had to be retrieved near the Free Marcher city of Kirkwall. Successful completion of the mission would have meant reinstatement into the Ben-Hassrath.

She did not succeed, however. While investigating the whereabouts of the saarebas, Tallis met and befriended a human templar by the name of Cairn. They worked together to track the Qunari mage, the templar doing so out of a desire for revenge for the mage's destruction of his home village. When the mage was finally found, Cairn was slain during the battle . . . and Tallis chose to kill the mage rather than bring him back to the Qunari. Details on the incident were collected in a report by Seeker Daniel, who was sent to investigate the disappearance of Ser Cairn a year later.

"Ser Cairn himself had intended to disobey his orders to capture the Qunari mage alive," Daniel stated in his report. "This was verified by a Dalish elf companion who had been assisting him and was present to witness his demise. He was on a mission of vengeance, and even though it would have been a simple matter for the agent known as 'Tallis' to continue with her own mission—according to the Dalish elf, Ser Cairn was already dead when the Qunari mage was captured—she instead killed him in cold blood, defying her own people. I see no other reason for her to have done so other than for the sake of friendship to a dead man. This runs contrary to the behavior of every other Ben-Hassrath agent we have encountered."

THEDOSIAN ARTISTS: GRISELDA REINIGER

Though previously accorded some small acclaim for fostering a resurgence of the traditional Ander portraiture style, Griselda Reiniger was the surprise winner at the annual art contest held by the University of Orlais this past spring. Her daring piece, *The Chant of Light,* portrayed Andraste playing the lap harp the night before she was burned at the stake. It is now considered both a stroke of inspirational genius and a masterwork portrait from one of the most traditional painting schools.

With her name now spoken in the same breath as some of the traditional Ander masters, Reiniger's artistic career is poised to take most auspicious flight. Extremely religious, possessed of a flawless reputation, and supported by the Chantry both in her studies and her bid for recognition at court, Reiniger presents herself as a demure, quiet, and not entirely uncomely young woman. She has nonetheless surprised this art critic most favorably with a politely tenacious and thoroughly educated opinion as to the proper way of rendering the traditional painting styles of her ancestors. Her attire, while not nearly on par with the more flamboyant garb traditionally seen at court, is nonetheless perfectly cut and somberly appropriate for her position and aspirations.

Her deft proficiency, combined with a lovingly centered focus on the faces of her chosen subjects, has served her well of late, with the traditional sector of art patronage opting to offer her a few highly sought-after contracts, much to the chagrin of more established fellow artists. Many chantries have accorded her contracts previously offered to other artists of renown, despite many making courteous gifts of their work in the hopes of winning a more commercial patronage. One court artist in particular, it is rumored, succumbed to a fit of hysteria upon learning the news that a contract he had assumed his was instead granted to the young Reiniger.

Clearly, firmly assured of the approval of her religious patrons and holding the title of "artist eminent" for the year, Reiniger stands poised to challenge the masters of the Orlesian court for the most coveted of contracts.

—*From* A Still Life of Modest Artistic Discernments: Thedosian Artists Through the Ages *by Plume*

Seeker Daniel attempted to track Tallis down in Kirkwall, perhaps with the hope of gaining her service for the Chantry, but was unable to do so.

Tallis had, in fact, been attempting to track down her former mentor, Salit, after learning that he had also abandoned the Qun. Conflicted about her own betrayal of everything she had once stood for, she wanted advice from the man who taught her everything, and to know his reasons for leaving the Qunari—and perhaps even assist him. What she discovered, however, was that Salit intended to secure a personal alliance with the Orlesians by providing them with a list of every Ben-Hassrath spy he had once overseen. Considering many of these spies still remained at their posts, living what seemed ordinary lives to their unsuspecting neighbors, Tallis knew that many of them no longer reported to their superiors and could scarcely be considered spies. These people would be condemned to death, along with the others.

Unwilling to allow this to occur, Tallis conscripted the Champion of Kirkwall to find and stop Salit—a fact unknown to the Champion, who initially believed they were retrieving a valuable jewel. The pair infiltrated the castle Chateau Haine, home to Duke Prosper de Montfort—ally to Empress Celene of Orlais and a member of her inner circle of advisors—and there intercepted and killed Salit before the list of names could be turned over.

"As it turns out, the Champion of Kirkwall was innocent of the affair—outside of slaying Duke Prosper, that is," wrote a courtier close to Empress Celene. "According to everything we discovered after interviewing all present at the chateau, the Champion believed that the Qunari agent intended to steal a gem. Had the duke not imprisoned and later attempted to kill the Champion, it's entirely possible the matter would have been resolved peacefully or, at least, unsuccessfully on the part of the agent. As it is, an attempted theft is hardly a matter that warrants attacking Kirkwall, and they could respond in kind by suggesting our duke attempted to kill their beloved hero. The true culprit is this Qunari agent, Tallis, who I can only assume took the list back to her superiors in Par Vollen."

It is likely that Tallis indeed returned the list to the Qunari, as her name has since surfaced in multiple reports of Ben-Hassrath activity along the northern coasts—including rumblings within the Imperium capital of Minrathous. These claims, however unverifiable, would not be out of the question, as an elven agent working for the Qunari would be far from noticed blending in with the underclasses of the Imperium.

Duke Prosper was a close, personal friend of Empress Celene.

DUKE PROSPER DE MONTFORT

It is surprising that a figure like Duke Prosper de Montfort would find himself at the center of trouble with the Ben-Hassrath. The Great Game of Orlais has had many players, but by reputation, few played it as casually as Prosper. The well-connected, self-proclaimed duke carried the bloodline of the hungriest lions of Orlais, but was often believed to be more inclined to hunt prey and escape to foreign lands on vacation than participate in public intrigue.

It was perhaps fitting that Prosper died abroad, during one of his wyvern hunts at Chateau Haine in the Vimmark Mountains. Prosper's hunting prowess left him famous the world over. Early in the Dragon Age, he was one of the first people to kill a high dragon—admittedly with the aid of thirty Chasind guides. He once claimed he would hunt the animals of the world to extinction if only he had the means.

Prosper's connections to Orlesian nobility went all the way to the top, and he was rumored to have played a role in Empress Celene's ascension to the throne. When Prosper's cousin, Celene's mother, died in what was widely reported as (but quietly suspected not to be) a hunting accident, he was said to have openly wept and sworn off hunting forever.

This pledge lasted approximately five weeks.

THE MAGE UPRISING

Following the death of Viscount Marlowe Dumar, tensions mounted between Knight-Commander Meredith and the city Circle, led by First Enchanter Orsino. By 9:37 Dragon, Kirkwall was still without a new viscount. When Anders, possessed by the spirit named Justice, destroyed Kirkwall's chantry, war between the templars and the mages of Kirkwall broke out, plunging Kirkwall into chaos and jump-starting conflicts between the mages and templars across much of Thedas.

KNIGHT-COMMANDER MEREDITH STANNARD

Long before Meredith Stannard became knight-commander of the templars at Kirkwall and set into motion a war between the templars and mages, she was a confused little girl with an apostate for a sister.

In diaries, Meredith described her beloved older sister, Amelia, as a gentle, quiet girl. Amelia was easily frightened by crowds and loud noises and never strayed far from home or her mother's side. While Meredith longed to see the world, all Amelia ever wished was to be home, close to family, tending to her small garden. Amelia's fragile nature made the discovery that she was a mage all the more heartbreaking. The family faced the possibility of having to send their beloved Amelia to a Circle Tower full of strangers to live under constant watch and rigid rules. Just the mention of being in unfamiliar surroundings drove Amelia into a wild-eyed panic. How would she learn to control her magic if she couldn't learn to control her fear? How would she take the Harrowing? Unwilling to see Amelia suffer, Meredith's parents decided to hide her away.

The plan worked, for a time. But the family had neither the knowledge nor the skills to train Amelia as a mage. All they could do was try to keep her calm and happy. Whenever Amelia was frightened or upset, strange things happened. Glass would shatter when she was angry; fires would start when she was afraid. It became all but impossible to hide Amelia's powers. Neighbors began to suspect that the Stannards were harboring a mage. The templars were called.

Meredith would later recall the moment in her diary:

"We saw the crimson banners at the end of the street. Amelia knew what it meant. I'd never seen her shake like that before. It was heartbreaking. Mother tried to tell her that it was for the best, but she wouldn't listen. She ran into the kitchen and shut herself in a cupboard, weeping. Nothing Mother said would calm her down. Then all went silent. We thought perhaps she'd hurt herself . . . or fainted. When Mother opened the cupboard, I screamed. A twisted monstrosity rose up, eyes dark as the Void. My sister was gone."

The sight of her mother being torn apart by the abomination would stay with Meredith for the rest of her life. All she could do was flee, straight to the templars, while her childhood home was destroyed by the thing that was once her sister. Amelia killed seventy people before the templars destroyed her. All the while, Meredith huddled in an alleyway, shivering with fright behind the templar captain's silver shield, praying to the Maker to spare her.

The Exemplar

Now orphaned, Meredith was alone. When the templar captain returned for his shield, she asked him if Amelia was safe. The captain, Ser Wentworth Kell, explained what had happened—about mages, abominations, and the holy duty of the templars.

"Meredith listened intently, her face grave, saying nothing," Kell would later recall. "I asked if she had any other family close by. If so, we would have seen her safely brought to them. The girl shook her head. No, she had no family. Her family was dead, and her home destroyed. She looked up at me and said, 'I want to go with you. I want to be a templar.' "

There are some who quietly blame Meredith Stannard for the mage uprising.

Ser Wentworth said her eyes were solemn and, at that moment, betrayed a wisdom far beyond her years. Many templars will never face an abomination. They may never truly grasp the horrors of possession. But this child understood. She had seen. "You will be a templar," he said and lifted her up onto his shoulders.

Meredith returned to the Gallows with Ser Wentworth. She was dedicated to the Chantry and became an initiate. Ser Wentworth became her mentor and guardian. When she wasn't at lessons in the chantry, she would serve Ser Wentworth as a page, looking on as he trained with his men, constantly asking when she too could hold a sword. When that day came, Meredith trained harder than any of her brother templars. Behind each swing of the sword, it seemed, was a promise: "No abomination will take another family like it did mine."

Duke Prosper's wyvern hunts were legendary among Orlesian nobles.

Because her parents loved Amelia and wanted to protect her from pain, seventy innocents were dead. Meredith came to believe that no matter how cruel the Circle, no matter how bleak the lives of the mages, it was preferable to the alternative. The feelings of one mage could not be given consideration over the safety of hundreds. Their emotions could not be indulged, like Amelia's were. Mages were different, dangerous, and had to be treated that way.

In 9:14 Dragon, Ser Wentworth's failing health made it impossible for him to fulfill his duties as knight-captain. Before he went into the Chantry to live out the remainder of his life, he named Meredith his successor. He also passed on his prized greatsword to her, stating in a speech during the ceremony that she was the daughter he never deserved. Over the next two years until he died, Meredith would visit Ser Wentworth whenever she could, giving him company even as his faculties left him and he could no longer remember who she was.

As knight-captain, Meredith proposed several changes to the administration of the Gallows, resulting in greater efficiency and a more orderly schedule for the mages. A structured environment and predictable routines led to calm, she would argue. It also made it much easier to detect anything that was out of the ordinary. Meredith's case was so persuasive that her recommendations were put into practice almost immediately, and Knight-Commander Guylian began seeking her out for counsel in other matters. Beside the graying knight-commander, Meredith cut an imposing figure: stern, icy, and uncompromising. When Guylian gave a command, it was Meredith who enforced it. Her drive and her devotion to her duty made her a bit of a legend among her fellow templars, and privately, many thought she possessed a hundred times the old knight-commander's charisma. Many said that it was Meredith who was really leader of the templars, despite her junior rank.

Price of Power

With Meredith as knight-captain, and under Guylian's command, the templars' influence in Kirkwall grew. By 9:20 Dragon, the templars were the largest armed force in Kirkwall and could have challenged even the viscount for power, but Knight-Commander Guylian believed the templars' domain was the Gallows and preferred to remain politically neutral.

Under pressure from Divine Beatrix III, Guylian commanded the templars to force Viscount Perrin Threnhold to

The docks of Kirkwall were a major port of trade for the region.

reopen the Waking Sea passage to allow Orlesian ships to pass through. The viscount retaliated by hiring mercenaries to storm the Gallows. Guylian was captured and publicly hanged. An enraged Meredith and a group of her best marched on the viscount's estate, determined to exact terrible justice. The captain of the city guard, quailing before the templars, protested that he knew nothing of the plot. To prove his innocence, the captain asserted that the viscount had acted unlawfully and had him arrested. Threnhold's lands and titles were stripped from him, and he was thrown into his own dungeon.

Following Threnhold's arrest, Grand Cleric Elthina appointed Meredith as the new knight-commander. At Knight-Commander Meredith's strong suggestion, a new viscount was chosen: a man named Marlowe Dumar.

"Dumar had a good heart. A good heart and a weak will," said Lord Bellamy, a longtime political ally of Dumar's. "On his own he might have made a good leader, given time. But he wasn't on his own. The knight-commander was always there, looking over his shoulder. She let him know she was watching, that he wore that crown at her sufferance. Meredith appointed him. This was a nobleman of only moderate wealth, with little influence. She knew she could control him and there was little he or anyone else could do about it."

Meredith presented Dumar with a carved ivory box at his crowning. All present witnessed the viscount going white as a sheet as he opened it. He kept it close to him for the remainder of his life. It is not known what the box contained, but the reaction from Dumar made its importance to him obvious. What is certain is that Dumar never openly or strongly defied the templars. Over the course of his reign, Meredith's grip on Kirkwall grew ever tighter, and Dumar's failure to act absolutely contributed to the events that led to the mage rebellion.

When Dumar was killed, Meredith did not allow the appointment of another viscount, instead declaring martial law to take full control of Kirkwall. The next few years saw life for mages grow ever more difficult in the Marcher city-state. The knight-commander seemed convinced that blood mages and apostates were all around her, hiding in plain sight, even among her own templars—and did all she could to find and punish them. Some templars close to Meredith reported that she was in possession of a strange red idol. It seemed that the worst of her paranoia started after the idol fell into her hands.

Meredith's extreme distrust of mages eventually led her to invoke the rare and terrible Right of Annulment on the mages of the Circle; some argue her hand was forced after the apostate Anders destroyed Kirkwall's chantry. The Champion of Kirkwall, an associate of Anders, fought through the ensuing mayhem, and templars and mages spilled blood in the city streets. Meredith, then corrupted by her idol, turned on even her templars. She died in battle with the Champion, her body transformed in a twisted mass of red lyrium.

I only met the knight-commander once. You see, she'd heard about the templars who were regulars at our establishment. Natural thing to expect, of course. Being a templar isn't easy, and everyone needs release now and then, if you know what I mean. But Stannard didn't look kindly on it at all. Something about having a reputation to uphold. Anyway, she thought she'd take it upon herself to deliver a surprise disciplinary session . . . and not the fun kind.

Nothing like having a furious knight-commander barging in on you to make you lose your vigor, which is what I'm told happened to a lot of the men. The lovely lady I was with, well, she heard Meredith coming down the corridor and actually jumped out the window. So when Meredith came into my room, all she found was good old Jethann, alone and standing at attention. And I have to say, the knight-commander is a** handsome **woman. Tall, striking blue eyes, commanding presence—well, she could command me any day.

So there she was, the fiery commander standing in the doorway, and there I was, perfectly primed to help her complete her righteous duty. And she looked at me and in the quietest, smallest voice said, "Excuse me." There you have it. My one encounter with the knight-commander. It was love at first sight.

—Jethann of the Blooming Rose

FIRST ENCHANTER ORSINO

First Enchanter Orsino was the head of the Circle of Magi in the Gallows in 9:37. His ceaseless fight for the rights of the mages under his care caused him to butt heads repeatedly with Knight-Commander Meredith. After years of struggling against the templars, Orsino succumbed to despair in the aftermath of the chantry's destruction. He was lost to insanity and killed by the Champion of Kirkwall.

Orsino publicly clashed with Meredith on numerous occasions.

Advocate

Orsino originated from the elven alienage in the city of Ansburg, in the Free Marches. When he first discovered he was a mage, he was moved from Ansburg to the Gallows in Kirkwall. Orsino never spoke much of his life before that, for there were no memories worth recalling. As an elf, he was taught early that he would be hated and looked down upon for his build and his ears. It was at the Gallows, however, that he was taught something else—that there are things despised more than elves. As they say, an elf may be a lowly thing, but is no more dangerous than any man. A mage, on the other hand, is fire made flesh and a demon asleep. After the Gallows, the world no longer saw that he was an elf, only that he was a mage.

As a mage, Orsino did not stand out. Though he passed his Harrowing with little trouble, he was not the best scholar, nor the most proficient caster of spells. He was in no way exceptional, and therefore the templars did not watch him as closely as they did the weakest and the strongest. At first, Orsino was glad for this. He did not raise his head. He obeyed the templars' every order and pretended to be content. Living to see the sun rise every morning was what was important. It was what he'd learned in the alienage. Look out for no one but yourself, and survive.

Not everyone felt the same. There was a human girl, Maud, about Orsino's age. They shared classes and soon became friends. Maud told Orsino of the life she'd had before the Circle. She had a mother and a father whom she missed. There was an older sister with a beautiful singing voice and a dog, Rosie, who would sleep by her feet. As time wore on, Maud found it increasingly difficult to put thoughts of her family from her mind, and she grew homesick. When letters from home arrived, Maud would cheer up slightly and then sink to even greater depths, knowing that she would never see her loved ones again. Her studies suffered, and the templars took note of it. Orsino would urge her to focus on her magic, warning her that she was drawing the gaze of their guards, but Maud did not seem to care. "You mustn't make them suspicious," he would say. "It's terrible, but at least you're still alive." And Maud would only reply, "This is no life, Orsino." When the templars broke down the door to the closet she had locked herself into, all they found were dark scorch marks on the walls and floor.

Maud was the first, and others followed. One or two a year, and then more, as the years went by and the templars tightened their grip on the Gallows. Every time a mage died by their own hand, Orsino would hear Maud's final words to him: "This is no life." The templars didn't seem to care about the suicides. Most had the courtesy to say nothing at all, but some would snigger when they thought no one was listening. "One less to worry about." "The only good mage is a dead mage." Orsino's anger at the templars grew and made him bold. He stopped being obedient. He watched for mistreatment of the mages and called it out. Where once he would shrink away, he stood his ground. The mages were his people, and he would fight for them.

The events at Kirkwall and the White Spire inspired a mage rebellion that stretched across the continent.

First Enchanter Maceron died in 9:28 Dragon without naming a successor. Many were surprised to learn that the Gallows still had a first enchanter; Maceron had spent nearly

FILES ON THE INVESTIGATION OF THE CHAMPION

MOTHER PETRICE

This file is brought to note for obvious concerns, especially in light of what occurred in Kirkwall. This is but a portion of the private writings of Mother Petrice, which among other various and sundry items were recovered from the remains of the chantry. She represents a manner of thought that split the loyalties of many and is proving troublesome in other regions that struggle with looming Qunari threat, be it real or imagined.

It is with regret that I say these things about the young mother. Her trauma prior to becoming a sister informs (but does not excuse) what happened. I knew of her father, Lord Durand, and that the family was accustomed to a much different life before the 9:22 attack on Val Royeaux destroyed their holdings. Their expectation was to be societal peers to families such as the Launcets, and Petrice was raised in similar sheltered fashion. It seems the scars of that loss did not fade as quickly as her initial good works suggested.

Also concerning is that this is no longer a personal journal, but rather an adaptation. This is not Petrice reflecting on personal prejudices. It is her exaggerated account as defense, as though intended for more general distribution. Such perversions of the Maker's teachings become especially dangerous, as a salacious book of lies can pass through many hands and poison scholarly attempts to introduce the truth of the Chant. Her misinterpretation should have been a matter to take inward, not corrupt and project with all possible violence.

An account from Mother Petrice:

Ser Varnell assured me the creature was securely bound. I had not seen one so close before. Strangely, I thought of the stables, of the day with the horses when I was thrown. And the boy who laughed.

Heavy ropes held the Qunari. They were taut, but it was passive, as though ready on the plow before a furrow. I was told it was a mage, but the strength of it showed its purpose. This was a physical creature, base in its raw appeal. Had a human such a physique, he would be hailed, idolized. Perhaps in that moment I appreciated it, as I might any creation of the Maker so caricatured. But while its form showed the appeal of the divine, its faith was a lie, its training heretical. Their way is a corruption that has to be ended. But how to show they are not like us? How to ensure that no other be even momentarily enamored?

I thought of the stables, and being thrown, and the boy. And how things changed after the kick that ended his laughter. He did not know my horse when he tried to take its reins, but my horse was blamed for his injury. And I smiled at this Qunari, for I understood how their danger could be exposed. It could serve, as had my horse, as had my Ketojan.

all of the last decade in his chambers, emerging only rarely. But now he was dead, and the Gallows in need of a new first enchanter. Knight-Commander Meredith was of the opinion that there was no need for one. After all, the Gallows ran perfectly under the templars, without interference from Maceron. But Orsino realized that the mages needed someone to speak on their behalf, lest the templars rob them of what few liberties they still had. So Orsino volunteered to be first enchanter. The other senior enchanters had no desire for the position and quickly rallied behind Orsino. The Circle had voted for their own first enchanter, and the knight-commander let it be.

As first enchanter, Orsino worked tirelessly to improve the lot of the mages. He wanted, as much as he could, to make their days in the Gallows worth something. Even if they were still prisoners, and even though it was hard, he wanted to give them hope. More importantly, he wanted to give them something of a life so that death would not be preferable. Every small freedom he won from the templars was a great victory. The mages grew to trust him, and the templars to mark him as a menace.

Orsino's actions inspired the mages. Many fought back against the templars in their small ways. They grew defiant, pushing the boundaries where they could. Seeing this, the knight-commander tightened her grip. Orsino tried to find every advantage he could. He made contact with mage sympathizers and apostates in Kirkwall. He sought allies in the highest of places, and the lowest. Before his death he even admitted to correspondence with the apostate Quentin, famed for having murdered Leandra Amell and scores of other women. The more Meredith tried to crush him, the more he fought.

The years of fighting took a toll on Orsino. At the end, after the destruction of the chantry, and seeing that he had gained absolutely no ground in almost ten years, Orsino gave in. Like Maud and so many others before him, he let despair take hold and draw him under.

GRAND CLERIC ELTHINA

Grand Cleric Elthina was known to those who loved her best as a gentle, virtuous woman. To many, she was a teacher who shone a light on the righteous path but did not force them to walk it. To her detractors, however, Elthina was a spineless pacifist. They say her stubborn refusal to exercise her Chantry-given authority allowed the conflict between the templars and mages to escalate, finally resulting in the disastrous mage rebellion of 9:37 Dragon.

Peacemaker

Records indicate that Elthina was born in a small village nestled in the Vimmark Mountains just south of Kirkwall. When she was just a little girl, her parents contracted a terrible fever that took them both. Elthina never caught the illness, thanks to a kindly neighbor who cared for her while her parents were sick. When her parents died, the neighbor's husband refused to continue paying for the upkeep of the orphan child, and Elthina was given to the Chantry. She became a lay sister as a girl and, when she came of age, was given the choice to leave the Chantry, or stay and take an initiate's vows. Elthina chose to stay. When she was twenty, she moved south, to Kirkwall, and became a revered mother at the chantry there.

Elthina's grace and kindness made her a well-loved figure in Kirkwall. She was often ready to provide a listening ear and never turned her back on those who needed blessing or just a gentle smile. As a revered mother, she officiated the wedding of Lord Aristide Amell to Lady Bethann Walker and later dedicated their first child, Leandra Amell. Following the death of her predecessor, Elthina was appointed grand cleric of the Free Marches by Divine Beatrix III. At the time of her appointment, she had served in Kirkwall for almost thirty years.

As grand cleric, Elthina's primary concern was the spiritual health of her flock. She never judged or preached, and tried to lead by example. "Faith cannot be an imposition," she would say. "They will come to it in their own time." She took this tack with Sebastian Vael, prince of Starkhaven, who was not ready to take his vows. Elthina allowed him to leave, telling him that the Chantry's doors would be open to him when he was ready. The grand cleric's actions earned Sebastian's respect, and she became a mentor and mother figure to him.

Since Elthina was loath to exploit her authority as the grand cleric, she refused to order either the mages or the templars to stand down when tensions flared. Many believe that she could have forced one side to retreat by showing her support for their opposition, but Elthina refused to take sides. Instead, she tried to make peace between the knight-commander and the first enchanter, urging them to reach a compromise. While some scholars applaud her temperance and her wish to remain above the conflict, others believe that Elthina, by her inaction alone, doomed Kirkwall to its fate. Perhaps it is justice, then, that her end came as it did. Even when she was alerted to the danger, Elthina's dedication to playing peacemaker and her reluctance to commit herself to action compelled her to stay in Kirkwall. This would ultimately prove her undoing. She perished, along with many others, when her beloved chantry was destroyed.

CORRESPONDENCE RECOVERED FROM AN ABANDONED COTERIE HIDEOUT IN DARKTOWN BY THE KIRKWALL CITY GUARD, 9:39 DRAGON

Gallard,

Here's the take: thirteen sovereigns, twelve silver. Expect just as much next month. Lowtown's full of traders looking to shift their stock somewhere nice and safe, before some other crazy mage starts burning the city down. Hightown's merchants are starting to catch on, too. The real money's from families who want a way out that's quieter than going by sea. Figures, don't it—you ask them for protection money, and they're as poor as chantry mice, but they cough up the silvers when they want to get out of town.

The old Tevinter passageways work a treat since we knocked through from the tunnels under the Gallows, but Tipsy says the city guard are starting to catch on. Looks like the Mage Underground used these passages, too, and the new knight-captain passed on his maps. Bloody mages ruin everything—not Harlan, of course. Want me to see about those maps getting "lost"?

Kesper

To the honorable Knight-Lieutenant Paxley:

On behalf of the citizenry of Kirkwall, we would like to extend our thanks for your tireless efforts in restoring order to the city. In the absence of our Champion, the Templar Order has provided a sense of continuity and security that is sorely needed.

As you are the Maker's own warriors of justice, we realize you have no need of the comforts required by common soldiers. Yet with trade still recovering, one can imagine that certain shortages are weighing on your mind. Therefore, please find enclosed a quantity of lyrium, merely as a token of gratitude. Should conditions in Kirkwall remain favorable—say, in the Lowtown districts—we are confident our noble defenders will enjoy the benefits, as deserved.

Kind regards,
A Friend

Harlan,

Lusine needs another server at the Rose. The staff she has are worked off their feet with the new templar recruits in town. Lusine says the recruits gossip like old ladies over their wine—not to mention the pillow talk. We could eat for a month off the information she's passed along.

Something stuck out. A lot of the recruits are talking like they're leaving Kirkwall soon. To go where? Things are settling down, sure, but from what Paxley said, there are still rebel mages and apostates left unaccounted for, either hiding in the city or out near Sundermount. Why bring in new recruits if they're just going to leave again?

The lyrium bribes are eating the profits from our smuggling operations, but it's money well spent. Play our cards right, and when the dust settles, the Coterie could be the last one standing in Kirkwall.

Gallard

THRASK

Thrask was a templar who never approved of Meredith's hard-handed approach to controlling the mages. Sensitive to their plight, he sought ways to help the mages under his care. His compassion would be his undoing, as he was ultimately killed in the mage uprising at Kirkwall.

Duty and Conscience

Thrask was born to a mercantile family, the youngest of four sons. His pious father gave Thrask to the Chantry, to be raised in the service of Andraste in thanks for all the blessings the family had received over the years. Thrask was an obedient and even-tempered child, well liked by many of the mothers and sisters of the chantry. When Thrask was twelve, his agreeable manners led Revered Mother Margitte to recommend him to the templars, and he was taken into training.

While Thrask was never the strongest or the most skilled swordsman of the templar recruits, he more than made up for his shortcomings with his diligence. He seemed proud to be a templar and saw his role as that of a protector and guardian of mages. Unlike some others in the Order, he never abused his power and expressed understanding of the hardships of those under his care.

Thrask's future in the templars looked bright until Meredith took over as knight-commander in 9:21 Dragon. The new knight-commander took a harsh view of mages and favored those who shared her opinions over more moderate templars like Thrask. While Meredith lauded and nurtured men like Ser Karras, Ser Otto Alrik, and even the Fereldan newcomer, Cullen, Thrask languished among the new recruits and the tired old guard. He never changed his views on mages and continued as he always had, believing that it was better to keep a clear conscience than to ignore it in favor of his own advancement.

The Blooming Rose in Kirkwall is a bed of secrets.

In his early twenties, Thrask became a regular patron of a renowned Kirkwall institution, the Blooming Rose. Madam Lusine, proprietor of the Rose, recalls that Thrask was immediately smitten with a young woman named Ambra. He would visit Ambra often, sometimes several times a week. One day, despite her precautions, Ambra discovered that she was with child. Such events are never surprising for one in her profession. What *was* surprising was Ambra's insistence that the child was Thrask's. Madam Lusine, assuming she meant to wrest gold from the child's father, advised her to name a wealthier patron instead of a poor templar. But Ambra was not looking for gold. She knew the child was Thrask's and would not be persuaded to lie. The baby was born several months later, and Ambra named her Olivia.

Olivia discovered her magical abilities when she was nine. Thrask knew what conditions in the Gallows were like and refused to subject his daughter to them. He advised Ambra to hide Olivia and gave her instructions on how to do so. Thrask risked everything by hiding a mage daughter from the templars, and this fact was not lost on Olivia. Though she saw her father rarely, she would always think fondly of him. When Olivia was grown, she decided to leave Kirkwall, fearing that one day someone would uncover Thrask's involvement in hiding an apostate. She wrote a letter to her father, intending to send it to him upon her departure. Unfortunately, she was killed in her attempt to escape the city.

Several years later, Thrask would involve himself in a plot to remove Knight-Commander Meredith from power. Tragically, he would die at the hands of the mages he'd tried so hard to save.

THE WHITE SPIRE CONFLICT

While the chantry's destruction at Kirkwall spurred mages the world over to rebel, it was the conflict at the White Spire in Val Royeaux that made the rebellion official. The Spire, perhaps the most famous and iconic of all Circle Towers in Thedas, was the site of an infamous conclave where fraternity mages, led by Grand Enchanter Fiona, were to vote on the issue of independence. The vote was interrupted by the templars, led by then–Lord Seeker Lambert, who accused one senior enchanter, named Rhys, of killing the controversial prisoner Pharamond. A battle erupted and most of the Circle's senior mages were taken into custody; many were killed.

The mages taken captive at the conclave were later freed and their phylacteries destroyed in a daring mission said to be orchestrated by Rhys, along with a Libertarian firebrand named Adrian and the disgraced Knight-Captain Evangeline de Brassard. There are rumors that their efforts were buoyed by the implicit aid of Divine Justinia V herself, though this has never been confirmed. The surviving Circle mages fled to the fringes where they voted to disband the Circle—a historic move that sent shock waves across Chantry lands.

By the edict of the now-deceased Lord Seeker Lambert, the templars and Seekers nullified the long-standing Nevarran Accord, formally separating from the Chantry. Lambert, it seems, saw the Divine's support for the mages and their vote for freedom as a betrayal. All-out war between the mages and templars erupted.

EVERYTHING IS THE SAME

Do you remember when we were little, we had those hand signs? Mother and Father never knew what we were talking about. I miss secret languages and I miss talking to you. I worry you don't know what to talk to me about anymore.

We're twins. Everything is the same. Everything. At Samuel's wedding we convinced Mistress Sondra we were one another. She's known us since we were three. How could this be different? Why am I different?

It doesn't matter now. The templars would never take someone without proof, would they?

Dinners were so quiet after that day. Sometimes Father told stories and pretended things were the same as before. But what was the point? It wasn't the same. How could it be? Maybe he was trying to make things normal again. A different normal. I think that might be worse.

The first time . . . I shouted as soon as the smoke began to rise. By the time Mother got to my room, the curtains were all flames. I didn't know what to do so I stood there and didn't say a word.

"You must be more careful," she said. I promised her I would. The candle she found beneath the dresser was still in her hand. I don't think she noticed. She left with it anyway and I had no light to read by that night.

A few days later the revered mother found me in the chantry. She asked what was wrong and I don't think she believed me when I said, "Nothing." What was I supposed to say? I asked if she would speak some of the Chant with me. She chose a few verses she thought I'd find comforting.

O Creator, see me kneel:
For I walk only where You would bid me
Stand only in places You have blessed
Sing only the words You place in my throat.

How could we of all people not be bid to walk, stand, sing the same way? I don't understand.

I tried again. This time, when Mother came into my room, the ice had already melted and there was nothing for her to see. I asked her to touch the wall where the ice had been. She left and returned with a spare quilt, worried I'd catch a chill.

After that night, I waited. I didn't know what to do. Our birthday came and went. Mother made a cake, but no one seemed very hungry.

A few weeks later, I found the book. I don't know why Miriam had it, but I wasn't going to risk asking questions. The book mentioned a spirit school of magic. I'm not sure I understand all of it, but there are spirits that can be summoned. Good ones. Or maybe they don't have sides? They aren't demons, anyway. The Circles even teach it.

I tried sitting still and murmuring a few sentences. I didn't want to speak too loudly because spirits probably don't need to be yelled at. Mother walked in and found me sitting alone. She didn't ask who I was speaking to. A few days later, I caught a fish and placed it below the floorboards of the back porch. When Father asked how I knew where the cats would be, I said the spirits told me. He asked me more questions about spirits and I answered as calmly and confidently as I could.

It's been nine months since they took you away. When they take me to the Circle, we'll be together. You can take my magic lessons and I will—I don't know, but there must be something I can do.

The templars are on their way. I will see you soon.

—From the journal of Joselyn Smythe,
written in 9:14 Dragon

RHYS

Born in 9:02 Dragon at Kinloch Hold in Ferelden, the child of Senior Enchanter Wynne, Rhys was treated as most children born within the Circle of Magi are: he was taken from his parents and raised by the Chantry. In the case of Rhys, this meant a monastery at Lydes, where he remained until he was sent to the White Spire at the age of eleven. Even at such a young age, Rhys was already showing evidence of magical ability.

Rhys studied magic under Enchanter Arvin, a senior mage who made Rhys his apprentice. When Arvin was appointed to the Orlesian consulate in the Tevinter city of Teraevyn in 9:15 Dragon, he elected to take Rhys with him. The appointment was considered controversial in and of itself; few Circle mages were sent to consulates inside the Imperium, and Arvin's being an elf was considered at the time to be veiled provocation on the part of Empress Celene. It wasn't until much later, in 9:34 Dragon, after Arvin was poisoned, that it became public knowledge he was a spy working on behalf of Orlais—the true reason for his appointment. In the meantime, the enchanter continued Rhys's education, highlighting what he detected as Rhys's natural affinity for communing with spirits. This apprenticeship lasted until 9:18 Dragon, when an altercation between Rhys and the son of a Tevinter magister ended with Rhys being expelled from the Imperium.

He was returned to the White Spire, apprenticing to three different senior enchanters in turn and beginning a long period of research into the nature of demons. He was responsible for writing several tomes on the matter, including the widely read *Comprehensive Study on Denizens of the Fade*, published in 9:28 Dragon. It is around this time that Rhys began his association with the Libertarian fraternity; he and his fellow mage and companion Adrian often led the White Spire's fraternity and sometimes even served as its representatives to the College of Enchanters in Cumberland until it was shut down by Lord Seeker Lambert.

Rhys and his Libertarian allies chafed under the Lord Seeker's restrictions, and as time passed it appeared many mages of the White Spire were beginning to sympathize with the fraternity's goal of complete independence for the Circle of Magi. Any attempt at a peaceful solution, however, ended with the attempted assassination of the Divine by a mage extremist in 9:40 Dragon. The assassin was killed, but the resulting investigation inside the White Spire ended with Rhys's imprisonment as a possible conspirator. When an aborted attempt by Grand Enchanter Fiona to hold an independence vote in the White Spire resulted in reprisal by the templars and the death or imprisonment of many visiting

QUNARI PHRASES

A selection of phrases in Qunlat collected by Philliam, a Bard!, for the benefit of this text, discovered through stealthy observation of soldiers at rest and marked as being tactically unimportant and therefore able to be released for public interest. Note the familiar mundane rhythm. Translations are approximate and assumptive.

Qunari	Phonetic	Meaning
Meraad astaarit, meraad itwasit, aban aqun.	MARE-awed a-STAR-eat, MARE-awed it-WAH-seat, ab-AWN AH-kyoon.	The tide rises, the tide falls, the sea is unchanged.
Var-toh katashok, ebadim maraas issala toh.	var-TOH CAT-ah-shock, eh-bah-dim ma-RAHS ih-SAW-lah TOH.	They will struggle, and we will turn them into nothing.
Arishokost ebra sala. Seerkata tost eb na shoh.	ah-REE-shock-ohst eh-brah sah-law. seer-CAT-ah tohst ehb nah shoh.	The Arishok will see to it. That or everyone dies.
Kadanshok defransdim vashedan!	cad-AWN-shok def-RAHNS-dim VASH-eh-dan!	You will struggle with your wounded intimate friends! (Seems dockside in nature. More colloquially, "I shall use my foot to assault you in the genitals.")
Defransdim vasebra nehraa issala shok.	def-RAHNS-dim vahs-ehbrah NAY-rah ih-SAW-lah shock.	I'm now struggling with discomfort among my small friends. (In response to the assault by previously mentioned foot?)
Sataareth kadan hass-toh issala ebasit.	sa-TAW-reth cad-AWN hahs-toh ih-SAW-lah ehb-ah-seet.	It is my purpose to do what I must for those I consider important.
Ebadim vashedan Tal-Vashoth, ebra-hissal eva-lok defransdim.	eh-BAH-dim VASH-eh-dan tal-VASH-oth, ehb-RAW-hiss-awl eh-VAH-lock def-RAHNS-dim.	Those excremental Tal-Vashoth can go do something explicit with my intimate friends. (Tone can leave no doubt, most certainly genitals!)
Ebsaam ver-toh kata, ir-vah vashtoh notas-taar.	ehb-SAWM vehr-toh CAT-ah, ihr-vawh VASH-toh noh-TAHS-tawr.	We're going to lose people in combat if we don't get better gloves than this excrement.
Ebra Karasaad vashetoh saar-qalaba kata.	ehb-raaw car-ah-SAWED VASH-eh-toh SAWR-kah-LAH-bah CAT-ah.	That soldier above me has excrement for tactics and will die like a cow.
Ebatot tal-eb noms. Asit hera iss-nal tal-eb. As-eb vashe-qalab!	ehb-ah-toht tahl-ehb noms. ahs-it hair-ah ISS-nahl TAL-eb. ahs-eb VASH-eh-kah-LAHb!	We were told there would be cake. Midweek was when it was to be. This is akin to qalaba excrement! (More colloquially: "This is bullshit!")
Asit zabuk-toh maraas eblok. Kappan maraas tal-eb.	ahs-eet zaw-bawk-toh ma-RAHS ehb-lock. cap-AWN ma-RAHS TAL-eb.	It's because of the priests' hats that I never go to the temples. It has to be fur caps or nothing.
Shanedan, pashaara. Ebost antir vantaam vasheb-sa karatoh.	sha-NAY-dawn, pah-SHARE-ah. Ehb-OST ahn-teer vawn-TAWM VASH-ehb-saw car-ah-toh.	I hear you. Enough. You're tired of the excrement your superior has been giving you. (More colloquially: "Give it a rest, why don't you?")
Ebasit Ben-Hassrath maraas-toh, tal-eb iss mer-toh ari-van.	ehb-ah-seet ben-HASS-rath ma-RAHS-toh, TAL-eb iss mehr-toh are-ih-vahn.	The Ben-Hassrath will make you disappear if you don't shut up.
Ebadim beresaad hissra-toh ataash. Vashedan katoh-qalaba.	ehb-ah-dim BAY-ris-ahd HISS-ra-toh a-TAHSH. VASH-eh-dan CAT-aw-kah-LAH-bah.	Those beresaad think they are so special. Foolish glory animals.
Bazvaarad? Ebasit vash-issra sataa.	BAZ-vah-RAHD? ehb-ah-seet VASH-IS-raw sa-TAW.	Foreigners controlling mages? This place is a fecal illusion.
Ebadim astaar, Qunari itwa-toh. Asit tal-eb.	ehb-ah-dim ahs-tawr, koo-nahr-ee it-wah-toh. ahs-it TAL-eb.	They will rise, and the Qunari will cause them to fall. That's how it will be.
Bas ebadim qalaba, ebsaam asit tal-eb.	bahz eh-bawh-deem kah-LAH-bah, ehb-SAWM ahs-eet tahl-ehb.	These foreigners are cattle. Our way is better and inevitable.

first enchanters, open rebellion broke out—with the aid of Rhys and the templar sympathizer Ser Evangeline de Brassard. This led many of the mages to flee to the northern ruin of Andoral's Reach, where the final vote was taken to declare full independence.

It is interesting that in that vote, Rhys took the side of the Aequitarians rather than the Libertarians. It is said he took that position on behalf of his mother, but also due to a change of heart regarding the means the Libertarians used to force the vote. Even so, he endorsed independence on behalf of the Aequitarian fraternity, and has ultimately been credited with having made the vote which tipped matters in favor of the war.

WHERE WILLOWS WAIL

When waked, we walked where willows wail,
whose withered windings wont wassail.
We weary-worn with wited wale,
were wavering with wanion ward.
When wishing waned, we wighters warred.
When wolfen wan, we wastrels warred.

A lullaby local to Denerim and smaller villages south. A recent addition to the archives, having only gained notice among local minstrels in the last two decades, although the oral record may have simply been lost to Blight. It was originally catalogued with other poems of war common to the Alamarri. Recent excavations at the newly discovered temple to the primitive goddess Mythal now suggest an elven connection, with the discovery of a small carved tablet, which reads:

Tel'enara bellana bana'vhenadahl,
Sethen'a ir san'shiral, mala tel'halani
Ir sa'vir te'suledin var bana'vallaslin,
Vora'nadas san banal'him emma abel revas.
Ir tela'ena glandival, vir amin tel'hanin.
Ir tela las ir Fen halam, vir am'tela'elvahen.

While meter and alliterative differences abound, the two texts share length, tone, and the not-insignificant "wolfen" imagery of an elven trickster deity, the Dread Wolf, Fen'Harel. A literal interpretation is impossible, as some form of lyrical shorthand is employed throughout, and it differs greatly from modern formal Dalish:

We/it lost eternity or the ruined tree of the People,
Time won't help when the land of dreams is no longer our journey.
We try to lead despite the eventual failing of our markings.
To the inevitable and troubling freedom we are committed.
When we could no longer believe, we lost glory to war.
When the Wolf failed/won, we lost the People to war.

—Documented by minstrels assisting the University of Orlais in cataloging folktales of Thedas

EVANGELINE

When Lord Seeker Lambert ended the Nevarran Accord in 9:40 Dragon and called on the Templar Order to separate from the Chantry and hunt down any and all mages, not all templars agreed with their brethren. Some, such as Ser Evangeline de Brassard, even went so far as to actively support the mage cause and fight against the very templars with whom they once served.

Born in 9:06 Dragon, Evangeline belonged to a family considered Orlesian minor nobility—they possessed a farmhold, Brassard-manot, in the Heartlands just outside the village of Velun. As the only child, Evangeline was expected to learn the social graces of a young Orlesian lady. She would eventually marry a man of breeding who would take over the manor and carry on the family line. The problem, however, was Evangeline's interest in none of these things. She was determined to train in swordsmanship under the guidance of her father, a former chevalier, over the constant protests of her mother. When her mother died in 9:21 Dragon, Evangeline assumed her dreams of becoming a chevalier would be dashed, that she would be forced to become the lady of the manor as her mother had been. Her father, however, had different plans.

"I am ashamed to say that Father found me weeping," a young Evangeline wrote. "I have never been the girl that Mother wanted, the one fascinated with the latest fashions out of the capital or mooning over the boys of the baron's court, so when he came upon me in such a state, I was mortified, and he seemed so helpless. When he finally sat down beside me, oh, so carefully, I reassured him in a rush how I would take care of the manor and that he had nothing to worry about from me. And then he teared up, and asked how I could possibly think he was the sort of father who would force me to live for the sake of a piece of land."

Within the year, Evangeline was sent to the chantry at Val Foret, where she began training as a member of the Templar Order. Initially there were some concerns by her superiors that she might be better suited for life as a member of the clergy . . . concerns which lasted until she bested every other initiate in personal combat. After that, she was trained without further comment, and eventually took her vows at the White Spire in Val Royeaux in 9:26 Dragon.

She performed exceptionally well in her duties, showing a dedication which impressed Knight-Commander Eron . . . enough so that she was granted the rank of knight-captain in 9:34 Dragon.

"I told the knight-commander that I was, perhaps, not his best choice," she wrote. "There are too many templars in the tower who see me as too self-righteous, too arrogant in my

Templars and rebel mages clashed in all corners of Thedas, costing countless lives.

belief that our role is to protect these mages and not simply to contain them. I look upon these men and women and I only see people who are doing their best to survive a burden the Maker has laid upon their shoulders. Yes, they are not all good people, but I would not be able to look my father in the eyes again if I subscribed to the same belief of some of my fellows, that we are somehow better and more pure than they. To them, this makes me a sympathizer, as if sympathy were something of which to be ashamed. To his credit, Knight-Commander Eron said that was exactly why he believed I was right for the position."

In 9:40 Dragon, Lord Seeker Lambert arrived at the White Spire to take command, a response to the mounting tensions with the Circles of Magi following the destruction of Kirkwall Chantry, relieving Knight-Commander Eron of his duties. At the same time, Evangeline saved the life of Divine Justinia V when a mage extremist attempted to assassinate her at an imperial ball. The act garnered Evangeline a great deal of praise, even though ultimately she opposed the Lord Seeker for continuing to apply pressure on the mages. After he ordered the attack on the first enchanters gathered at the White Spire, an attack which caused many deaths, she turned against him and aided their escape—along with Rhys—and flight to the ruin of Andoral's Reach.

Following the vote for independence, Evangeline was held up either as a traitor or as an example of what templars of the Order should exemplify in their service to the Maker.

LORD SEEKER LAMBERT

As leader of the Seekers of Truth, Ser Lambert van Reeves stood over the entire Templar Order—his position was that of maintaining discipline and watching for signs of corruption. It was a task that he took seriously, and ultimately it led him in 9:40 Dragon to declare an end to the Nevarran Accord, the agreement that had bound the Seekers to the Chantry since the days of the original Inquisition, thereby beginning the war with the Circles of Magi.

Born in northern Orlais in 8:92 Blessed, Lambert was cousin to the Montbelliards of Churneau, and thus accustomed to a life of wealth and privilege. The only son of his family, he would ordinarily have been destined to assume a position at the Imperial Court, perhaps even governorship of some of the Montbelliard lands as his father and grandfather had before him. At the age of sixteen, however, Lambert instead asked Comte Etienne to sponsor his entry into the Templar Order, a request that would cause considerable scandal and a great deal of grief for his family. As he famously stated to Comte Etienne at the time: "My family has no need of a man to spend their coin and serve at your whim. My sisters will more than serve in that capacity. The empire has far greater need of those who will protect the defenseless, guard against the wicked, and exalt the righteous." Impressed at the young man's eloquence and determination, Comte Etienne agreed.

Ser Lambert rose quickly through the templar ranks, serving with distinction at the Circle of Magi in Ghislain until achieving the rank of knight-captain in 9:17 Dragon. That year, he led a group of templars north into the dangerous border region of the Tevinter Imperium to chase a group of escaped apostates. When he was confronted by a larger group of Imperial Templars just outside the Tevinter city of Caimen Brea who had already taken his apostates captive, the result could easily have been a diplomatic nightmare that led to war. Instead, Ser Lambert respectfully negotiated with the templars and won the admiration of a ranking mage who traveled with them: Magister Urian Nihalias.

It was this feat that led to Lambert being recruited into the Seekers of Truth months later—a remarkable feat, considering the vast majority of Seekers are recruited as youths—and, in 9:21 Dragon, led to his appointment as a Seeker liaison to the Tevinter Imperium. This last came at the personal request of Magister Urian. For years, Lambert served with the Imperial Templars, aiding them by taking charge of investigations of magical corruption. It was a task he grew frustrated with, as evidenced by a letter to Lady Seeker Nicoline in 9:25 Dragon.

"Magister Urian has been a wonderful friend, and without him I don't believe I could stand it," Lambert wrote. "These people asked for our help, and there is so much corruption I could spend day and night hunting the culprits and still not learn of half of it. Yet I do nothing but encounter obstacles, placed in my way by senators who do not wish their allies displaced, or who obscure their own tracks. Despite the knight-commander assuring me that it will all be rooted out in good time, I am uncertain. I find myself listening more and more to Urian and his talk of extreme measures being needed, but I cannot in good conscience take them while also serving the Orlesian Chantry."

Regardless of his misgivings, Ser Lambert took part in what amounted to a coup in 9:27 Dragon—when several high-ranking magisters, including Magister Urian, and a select group of Imperial Templars, arrested in a single night the reigning Black Divine and five of the highest-ranking magisters in Minrathous. The resulting trial, including word of Lambert's involvement, caused scandal back in Orlais . . . no less than when Magister Urian himself assumed the role of Black Divine. Assured that this would lead to reform in the Imperium, Lambert instead found himself witness to a violent purge of the Imperial Chantry by Divine Urian. After four more years of reluctant service to a Divine who no longer seemed as eager to root out corruption as he did before he attained

The rare few who remember Cole describe a sad young man in strange clothing.

the position, Lambert finally returned to Orlais in disgust in 9:31 Dragon.

Initially it seemed as if Lambert's actions in the Imperium would have meant an end to any ambitions within the Seekers of Truth. Lady Seeker Nicoline was impressed with his renewed determination and his zealous devotion to his duty. "What happened in the Imperium will never happen again," he was often heard to avow. When the Lady Seeker stepped down in 9:37 Dragon, she passed the position to Lambert—over the objection of Divine Justinia V, who had interviewed Lambert beforehand and found him too conservative.

The clashes with the Divine continued in the years following Lambert's ascension to Lord Seeker, centering on his objections to her attempts at reform and particularly at her lack of "appropriate response" following the destruction of the Kirkwall Chantry by mage extremists. The growing unrest in the Circles of Magi led his order to close the College of Enchanters in 9:38 Dragon (to stop a planned vote on independence by Grand Enchanter Fiona, as it's commonly believed) and increased restrictions on all mages in the Circles . . . until the rebellion began in earnest in 9:40 Dragon. Blaming all of this on corruption throughout the Chantry in general, Lambert ignored Divine Justinia's order to stand down and dissolved the Nevarran Accord, taking personal control of the Templar Order and beginning the hunt for the mages.

He died on the same day that order was given, found in his quarters within the White Spire—his throat slit, and no apparent way for anyone to gain access to him.

NOTES ON THE WHITE SPIRE

ADRIAN

While the events at Kirkwall stirred unrest among mages and templars, it was the actions of mages at the White Spire in Val Royeaux that truly launched a war. First Enchanter Adrian was a key figure in the mage vote for independence. Standing for the Libertarian party, she was the first to cast a vote in favor of rebellion. Her whereabouts following the vote are unknown. If Adrian lives, she no doubt aids the rebellion still—at least this was the conclusion drawn from some of her supporters.

The following excerpt is from the journal of an enchanter named Damon, dated one night before the vote:

Still at Andoral's Reach. It's snowing—a fact I'm painfully more aware of since it's drifting through the ceiling. After tonight . . . we vote. Can I really sum that up in just two words?

I've always been a Libertarian, though until now I hadn't given it much thought. I considered the fraternities just a way to express your personal philosophies on mage issues. It was a way to define yourself within the Circle. Do you worship the Circle? Loyalist. Money? Lucrosian. What about freedom? Libertarian. I thought for all our speeches and treatises, nothing would change. I'm Libertarian but I never thought this day would come. And that we are voting as fraternities rather than as a Circle . . .

Adrian never doubted. Adrian's voice was always the clearest. Well, sometimes it was just the loudest, but maybe that's what we needed. Someone yelling until we were heard.

After Edmonde died, I voted for her to become first enchanter. Some argue that our titles mean nothing outside the Circle. But Adrian is our leader—we need a leader. Tomorrow she will speak for the Libertarians. She will be our vote—my vote.

I know what Adrian will choose. And the Loyalists will vote to remain loyal. That seems obvious. The Isolationists will avoid conflict as well. Not that it matters—the Aequitarians are the swing vote, as always. I cannot guess what they'll decide. There are rumors that Rhys has joined them. Something has happened between him and Adrian. There's his templar lover, of course, but maybe this division has been a long time coming. I can't say I'm sorry Rhys and Adrian are less . . . close. But people listen to Rhys—we could use him on our side. If he's joined the Aequitarians to vote against Adrian . . . and if he hasn't . . .

Honestly, I don't know what I want anymore. I'm not sure what I pictured when I thought of freedom. Maybe it was like this, but it feels different. I trust Adrian—we wouldn't be here without her. No matter what, I will stand by her. She doesn't ask us to, but she commands it all the same. If we're going to fight, then I know she will fight and she won't stop until . . . until the end.

So that's it. Tomorrow, we vote.

PHARAMOND

Pharamond was an elven mage who successfully reversed his own Tranquility when conducting experiments at Adamant Fortress in the Western Approach. The means he employed to do so have been the subject of much controversy among Chantry and mage officials, and are said to have involved the summoning of demons. Some have even speculated that Pharamond employed blood magic, killing innocents at Adamant to conjure a spell powerful enough to reverse the effects of his supposedly permanent condition. Many experts in magic believe this is the only way such a feat could even be possible.

There are whispers among some that Pharamond was actually permitted to conduct his experiments with the full knowledge and even approval of the Divine. Regardless, when he returned to Val Royeaux with news of his findings, the Divine ordered Pharamond to be made Tranquil once again. Pharamond was murdered in the Spire before this could happen. Though Lord Seeker Lambert accused Rhys of the murder, giving Lambert reason to confront Rhys during the conclave of mages, there is much speculation over the identity of the actual killer. Many had reasons to see Pharamond dead.

Those who encountered Pharamond upon his return from Adamant found his disposition in stark contrast to his years spent without emotion. Every emotion was heightened. He was quick to cry, was wrought by guilt, and laughed uncontrollably at the smallest jokes.

THE SEER'S YARN

A Treasury of Tales for Children All Over

Collected by
SEER AGATA

To the good children of Thedas:

Greetings, *atrast vala*, and *shanedan*. My name is Agata, a seer from the humble nation of Rivain. You know the place, set far to the east. On a map, it looks a little like a dragon's wing, but it's not nearly that scary. For the benefit of your parents, who are likely not as wise to the ways of the world as you, a Rivaini seer is a little like a grandmother—only for *all* children, young and old. It's my job to tell stories. These stories may teach lessons or simply make you laugh.

Over the years, I've collected a great many tales from all over Thedas. My favorites, contained in this treasury, have been told at the bedsides of the richest children in Orlais and the poorest Dalish in the forest—and even to the Qunari children of Kont-aar and beyond. They are collected here and retold for your enjoyment in the hope that when you grow up, you will tell them to your own children.

Sincerely and simply,
Seer Agata

Bad Children All Get Eaten

A Marcher rhyme, originating in rural areas but common in some variation from Wycome to Starkhaven

Now gather, all young ones, and hear what I say,
For good girls and good boys know when to keep mum.
For silent politeness is simply the way,
And always be thinking of this rule of thumb:

Eaten, eaten, eaten!
Bad children all get eaten!
Boiled or toasted! Broiled or roasted!
Eaten, eaten, eaten!

And always give credence to elders and lords,
Respect all their titles and ranks of the guard.
And bow to your betters if you are their wards,
It's never worth risking a loss of regard.

Eaten, eaten, eaten!
Bad children all get eaten!
Poached or basted, nothing wasted!
Eaten, eaten, eaten!

And when you complete all your work in the store,
Or stables or cobblers or fletchers or field,
It's not just polite to wash off what you wore,
If giants can smell you, then your fate is sealed!

Eaten, eaten, eaten!
Bad children all get eaten!
In the fryer, dragon fire!
On a boiling kettle pyre!
Soup for six or maybe higher!
Eaten, eaten, eaten!

Andraste & the Wyvern

From Bedtime Stories for Good Children *by Sister Marigold*

The armies of Andraste and Maferath gathered in the West. And the Prophet went alone into the mountains to sing to the Maker. She would take no one but Justinia and Maferath with her.

They climbed until they came to a hanging valley with a small lake, very still and clear and perfectly reflecting the sky, and there Beloved Andraste said they would rest. She sat down on the lakeshore and said to her dear companions, "Wait with me, my friends. And whatever happens, have no fear." Then she began to sing.

As she sang, the mountains bent to listen. Stars came down from the heavens to be near her. Birds and beasts of every variety came forth and knelt at Andraste's feet. Justinia and Maferath witnessed this, and were afraid.

Then from the sheer cliffs a great wyvern appeared, baring its fangs and drowning out the Prophet's song with its roars. The beast descended the cliffs like a thunderbolt from the sky. Maferath drew his sword and struck at the wyvern, slicing off part of its hood.

But the Prophet put her hand on Maferath's sword arm and stopped him. The wyvern came to Andraste's feet and knelt, and when it rose, it left blood on the ground, dripping from the wound Maferath had given it. And Maferath was ashamed that he had given in to fear despite Andraste's words. He drew his hand along the blade of his sword, spilling his own blood and adding it to the wyvern's. At this, the beast nodded once in acknowledgment, and then vanished as swiftly as it had appeared.

The Doggle-Boon Behemoth

From Fables Under a New Sky *by Maryden Halewell*

Beware ye well, my son and belle,
Beware ye well the calling.
For you will face, with time and grace,
Our failing and our falling.
My failing and my falling.

We sought the beast at farthest east
And paid a bloody tithing.
So will I will that you would kill,
And end its fabled writhing.
And end my fabled writhing.

A doggled-boon our hopes had strewn,
A bargain drained and straining.
So gird in steel and train your zeal,
And pray its will is waning.
And pray my will is waning.

A bander snatched and hander matched,
No jabber whilst you're walking.
Do not be swayed to drop your blade,
When danger comes a-stalking.
When Mother comes a-stalking.

Your eyes are green as its had been,
The doggle-boon behemoth.
Your heart is true and arrows too,
But can you two unsee wroth?
For I could not unsee wroth.

For though you win, hold fast your twin,
There's danger celebrating.
Renew this day, and call callay,
But now begins the waiting.
As then began my waiting.

Beware ye well, my son and belle,
The red, your will it leeches.
And wail you will for kin to kill,
Until your heart it reaches.
Unless my lesson teaches.

The Tale of Imekari-saam and Imekari-raas (Child Something and Child Nothing)

A children's fable, originating in Kont-aar, that has grown quite popular throughout Rivain

Witness Imekari-saam and Imekari-raas.

Imekari-saam was honest in all things.

Imekari-raas showed falsehood in his abilities.

Imekari-saam was evaluated by Arigena and assigned a role to which she was best suited.

Imekari-raas was evaluated and assigned, but to a role to which he was not best suited.

Imekari-saam lived long and well, certain and contented in her purpose.

Imekari-raas was tempted by demons that seized on his uncertainty and consumed his will.

He is Imesaar-bas and lost to the Qun.

Be something and content, like Imekari-saam.

Do not be nothing and dangerous, like Imesaar-bas. You will die.

How the Deepstalker Came to Be

A common tale said to be originally told by Paragon Ebryan, writer of Songs That Only Nugs Can Hear. *Many dwarven tales for children involve deepstalkers.*

In a time only the Stone remembers, a warrior named Gason won honor and glory for his house. He won a dozen Provings and defended his thaig against a legion of darkspawn. But though he was bold, Gason was also selfish and unkind, with a temper like spitting magma. He would rant and rage, mock and malign, until eventually Gason's friends turned their backs on him, his house crumbled, and he was cast into the Deep Roads.

There in the great darkness, Gason's anger roared up so bright it blinded him. He snatched up his sword and began to attack the carvings honoring noble Paragons that lined the walls. One! Two! With each blow of his sword, he cursed the Paragons and the Stone Herself in a voice that echoed from one end of the Deep Roads to the other.

But the Stone always hears the voices of Her children, for good or for ill. As the carvings fell in ruins at Gason's feet, each chunk of rock uncoiled, becoming a horrid creature with a maw full of teeth. One! Two! Hundreds rose and surrounded Gason in a pack, devouring him bite by bite before scattering into the dark.

The creatures, which we call tezpadam, stalk the Deep Roads to this day. They can curl up like tiny stones, waiting to pounce upon trespassers as they pounced upon Gason so long ago. And that's why you're not to play noisy games near the entrance to the Deep Roads. They just might gobble you up too.

The Tale of Corsa

A favorite from Bedtime Stories for Good Children *by Sister Marigold*

There once was a bard from Montsimmard, whose tongue was made of purest silver. His name was Corsa the Jackal, and he was famous for enchanting emperors and empresses by knowing exactly what to say to please them. This often got Corsa into trouble!

One day, Corsa was traveling to Val Royeaux, where he was to place his silver-tongued words into Empress Necessiteuse's ear. As he walked and rehearsed, a mighty storm blew in. Rain washed away the path, and Corsa became hopelessly lost. Chill set into his bones, so he took shelter in a cave.

But the cave was home to a big brown bear! Corsa drew his longbow, but the bear seized it. "I was just about to go out for dinner," said the bear. "Nice of you to drop by!" He looked at Corsa and began to drool. "You shouldn't do that," replied Corsa. "I am old and stringy and not at all good to eat. Let me share your cave, and in the morning, I will gather honey and berries. You shall have a feast fit for kings!"

"Agreed," said the bear, "but go no farther into the cave. You won't like what you'll find there."

Corsa warmed himself by nestling into the bear's thick fur. The bear fell asleep, but Corsa was kept awake by the thought of what lay farther in the darkness. Finally, he could no longer endure the mystery.

At the back of the cave, Corsa found a huge room. And in the middle of that room? An enormous dragon! "Mmm," said the dragon. "Food!"

"Wait, wait!" cried Corsa. "I am old and stringy and not at all good to eat. Let me leave, and I will bring you the bear."

"I think not," said the dragon. "That bear promised me breakfast!" And that was the end of the Jackal.

Veata Tezpadam!

A Dwarven Nursery Rhyme

A poem performed in singsong style for dwarven toddlers.
Veata tezpadam *translates to "Stop, deepstalker!" in the common tongue.*

Mindless he wanders, all unwary,
Where small dwarven should not tarry.
Veata tezpadam!
Your eyes are shining, bright and merry.

The quarters' light distant and dim,
Here in the cave he's wandered in.
Veata tezpadam!
How quick you are on silent limb.

Small hands collide with cavern wall.
Upon the ground, a missing ball.
Veata tezpadam!
Your brothers hear the high-pitched call.

He turns to see they've circled round,
All grinning at his wimming sound.
Veata tezpadam!
What becomes of who you found?

Within the quarter, heard no more
Are songs behind the nursery door.
Veata tezpadam!
Asleep upon the cavern floor.

The Witchwood

A tale of unknown origins that has been told to Fereldan children for generations

Once there was a child. A bright-eyed child, just like you. The child had a task, a chore: "Bring back firewood so that your family stays warm."

But the child, a boy, was also given a warning—the warning all children should be given: "Do not go past the edge of the wood. You are too young and too foolish to face the dangers within."

What do you suppose the child did then?

Well, he went to the edge of the wood and gathered some firewood. Soon he had enough to keep his family warm. Let us say that the story ends here. The child returns home. His family greets him, and they have cake with apples. At night the wind howls, but the house is warm. The child's mother tells stories, his father sings songs, and all is well.

Do you think that's where the story ends? Is that what you would do?

Though the child had enough firewood to keep his family warm, he did not leave for home. Instead, he put one toe over the edge of the wood and said: "I am not too young."

"Of course not," said a voice in the dark, and this made the child smile, for he was vain and cared more for flattery than duty.

The child put both feet past the edge of the wood and said: "I am not too foolish."

"Of course not," said the voice in the dark. "You are a very special child. The best of all."

So the child walked deeper into the forest, leaving the firewood behind, deeper into the dark.

And so I say to you now: Do not go past the edge of the wood. You are too young and too foolish to face the dangers within. You once had an older brother who would've agreed.

Pain & Bane

A common rhyme repeated by many Dalish children to help them pick plants safely

Heart-shaped leaves with veins of green:
Elfroot, to ease the pain.

Flat-capped and gray that grows in the clay:
Blightcap, the hunter's bane.

Spindly with thorns like a great demon's horns:
Felandaris, marking the Veil.

Loose-leafed and tall with a high purple stall:
Deathroot, to make minds frail.

The Chain of the Saarebas

A fable told by the tamassrans to Qunari children who show signs of magical ability

A young arvaarad was escorting his saarebas across a barren country alone. Cursed with magic, the saarebas was yoked and bound, his eyes hidden by a mask and his mouth closed with stitches. Yet the arvaarad was fresh to his duty, and his heart was full of doubts.

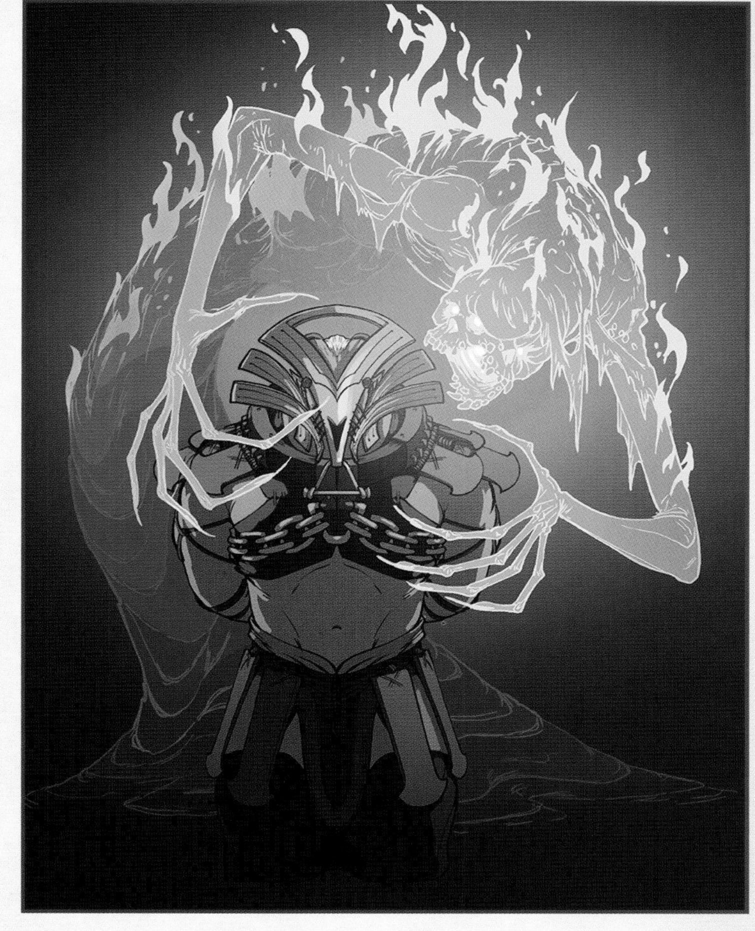

When they made camp that night, the arvaarad broke his vows and spoke to the saarebas. "You are possessed of magic," he said. "You have the power to level mountains and call the storm. But we place a simple yoke on your back and close your mouth, and say you are bound. How can this be true?"

The saarebas said nothing, but a figure stepped out of the darkness into the light of the campfire. It was misshapen and its hair was burning, and it cast no shadow. And the arvaarad was frozen in terror, because he knew it for a demon.

The demon spoke to the saarebas and said: "Your arvaarad is a fool. You belong to me, mage, and I will do evil through you."

Speaking with difficulty through his sewn lips, the saarebas said: "Which part of me belongs to you?"

"Your hands, which will drip fire and lightning, and tear down the cities of your people," said the demon.

"My hands were bound by an ashkaari in accordance with the Qun," said the saarebas. "They are not mine to be taken."

"Then I will take your eyes, and show you the wonders of the Fade to seed envy in your heart," said the demon.

"A mask covers my eyes, with the verses of Koslun written on the underside," said the saarebas. "They are not mine to be taken."

"Your tongue, then," snarled the demon, "to speak of power and magic, to stir the kabethari and confuse the wisdom of the Qun!"

"My tongue was sealed behind my lips by the tamassrans," said the saarebas, "to speak only of simple things, and it is not mine to be taken."

In a fury, the demon caused the campfire to blaze up in a pillar of flame. The arvaarad was blinded, but when it died down, the demon was gone, and the saarebas remained unscathed.

The saarebas said: "It is not these trifles that bind me, arvaarad. It is the trust of our people and the demands of the Qun. I do not belong to myself, but to them. How can that chain be broken?"

Thus the arvaarad was enlightened.

The Straight Path

From the collection of approved lessons by the tamassrans of the Qunari

This is truth in a fiction. Here is the fiction: Once, a child was lost in a heavy rainstorm and wandered into a deep forest. For hours she walked, shivering in the rain and seeing no other thinking thing, until she came to the ruins of a temple from the ignorant times. Taking shelter, she found the destroyed statue of a forgotten god. Still visible on its plinth were the words: "Seek the light, and there find safety in me."

"This is a sign," said the child, for she was unfinished and not yet wise. "The god must still protect this place."

When the storm passed, the child ventured out. Though it was dark, she could see a path through the forest nearby, washed clear by the rain. But beyond she saw a light between the trees, moving into the distance.

"I must follow the light to safety," the child said, proudly, "for the god sent those words to guide me. I will do as he commands."

So saying, she stepped off the path and followed the light. But because she was unfinished, she did not know she was following a wisp, a deceiver from the Fade. Chasing it, the child was led astray among the trees, never to be seen again.

Here is the truth: That those who are unfinished follow whims and superstitions and are lost. But those who are finished know the value of the straight path.

Passing By

A traveling song that teaches Dalish children how to prepare and drive an aravel

Tighten the rig with the Hearthkeeper's knot
Topsail, staysail, and main
The traces tie to the girth and the collar
And the collar is tied to the rein

Say thrice the prayer to Ghilan'nain
To quicken the white halla's tread
Break camp before the last star has faded
To chase the bright day ahead

A thousand miles beneath the wheels
Sails against the sky
Swifter than a dragon's flight
The People are passing by

The rein you must hold in your left hand
In the right hand, your dagger or bow
If the shemlen should strike on your journey
Send them to Falon'Din below

The path we beat is the path that we walked
To flee the Tevinter slums
Now we fly on wheels and wings
And hoofbeats are our drums

A thousand miles beneath the wheels
Sails against the sky
Swifter than the fall of night
The People are passing by

The Ptarmigan: An Avvar Tale

From Ferelden: Folklore and History *by Sister Petrine, Chantry scholar*

Even mountains had a heart once. When the world was young, Korth the Mountain-Father kept his throne at the peak of Belenas, the mountain at the center of the world, from which he could see all the corners of earth and sky. And he saw strong men become weak, brave men grow cowardly, and wise men turn foolish for love.

Korth devised a plan that he might never be betrayed by his own heart, by taking it out and hiding it where no soul would ever dare search for it. He sealed it inside a golden cask, buried it in the earth, and raised around it the fiercest mountains the world had ever seen, the Frostbacks, to guard it.

But without his heart, the Mountain-Father grew cruel. His chest was filled with bitter mountain winds that shrieked and howled like lost souls. Food lost its flavor, music had no sweetness, and he lost all joy in deeds of valor. He sent avalanches and earthquakes to torment the tribes of men. Gods and men rose against him, calling him a tyrant, but with no heart, Korth could not be slain. Soon there were no heroes left, either among men or gods, who would dare challenge Korth.

The Lady of the Skies sent the best of her children—the swiftest, the cleverest, and the strongest fliers—to scour the mountains for the missing heart, and for a year and a day they searched. But sparrow and raven, vulture and eagle, swift and albatross returned to her with nothing.

Then the ptarmigan spoke up and offered to find the god chief's heart. The other birds laughed, for the ptarmigan is a tiny bird, too humble to soar, which spends half its time hopping along the ground. The Lady would not give the little creature her blessing, for the mountains were too fierce even for eagles, but the ptarmigan set out anyway.

The little bird traveled deep into the Frostbacks. When she could not fly, she crawled. She hugged the ground and weathered the worst mountain winds, and so made her lonely way to the valley where the heart beat. With all the god's terrible deeds, the heart was far too heavy for the tiny bird to carry, so she rolled it, little by little, out of the valley and down a cliff, and when the golden cask struck the earth, it shattered. The heart was full almost to bursting, and the pain of it roused the mountain god to come see what had happened.

When Korth neared his heart, it leapt back into his chest, and he was whole again. Then Hakkon Wintersbreath bound Korth's chest with three bands of iron and three bands of ice, so it could never again escape. And all the remaining gods named the ptarmigan honored above even the loftiest eagles.

Mir Da'len Somniar

A traditional Dalish lullaby

Elgara vallas, da'len
Melava somniar
Mala taren aravas
Ara ma'desen melar

Iras ma ghilas, da'len
Ara ma'nedan ashir
Dirthara lothlenan'as
Bal emma mala dir

Tel'enfenim, da'len
Irassal ma ghilas
Ma garas mir renan
Ara ma'athlan vhenas
Ara ma'athlan vhenas

Sun sets, little one,
Time to dream.
Your mind journeys,
But I will hold you here.

Where will you go, little one,
Lost to me in sleep?
Seek truth in a forgotten land
Deep within your heart.

Never fear, little one,
Wherever you shall go.
Follow my voice—
I will call you home.
I will call you home.

chapter seven

THE INQUISITOR

WAR RAGED BETWEEN MAGES AND TEMPLARS ACROSS much of Thedas, buoyed by the violence at Kirkwall and the White Spire. Much of Ferelden was still haunted after the horrors of the Fifth Blight. In Orlais, Empress Celene struggled to maintain order as her cousin challenged her authority. It was in these already trying times, as Thedosians did their best to tear each other apart, that Corypheus tore a hole in the sky itself—killing the head of the Chantry and plunging Thedas into anarchy.

Before the Breach, there was the Divine Conclave at the Temple of Sacred Ashes. Many assumed violence was inevitable. At the very least, gathering the mages and templars in one place to talk out their problems seemed an exercise in futility. Divine Justinia V bravely, and some would say stubbornly, did it anyway. In what would be her final act as Divine, she spoke to the congregated power brokers and pleaded for peace. It was then that Corypheus struck, tearing a hole between the Fade and the waking world that killed hundreds.

The one they called the Herald of Andraste miraculously emerged from the blast bearing a mark with the power to close tears in the Veil. Under the banner of the Inquisition, it fell upon this hero of circumstance to bring Thedas back together and stop Corypheus from gaining the power of a god.

THE INQUISITION'S INNER CIRCLE

The Inquisition formed in the ashes of Haven, taking the name of an ancient order and led at first by the Divine's most trusted advisors, notably her Right and Left Hands, Cassandra Pentaghast and Leliana, along with the diplomat Josephine Montilyet and the seasoned templar Cullen.

As the Inquisition grew, so did its influence. The Herald of Andraste recruited a great many heroes to fight for the cause. There was the apostate spirit mage Solas, the Tevinter expatriate Dorian Pavus, and Warden hero Blackwall. Figures as disparate as the notorious mercenary Iron Bull and the well-connected

Decisions made by the Inquisitor were at times controversial.

First Enchanter Vivienne joined as well, along with author Varric Tethras and the notorious troublemaker known to most as Red Jenny. There are even rumors of a spirit seen fighting by the Inquisitor's side, though firsthand accounts of this boy are scarce and unreliable.

CASSANDRA PENTAGHAST

The Pentaghasts along with the Van Markhams have traded rule of Nevarra since the Glory Age. Outside of the kingdom, the Pentaghast name is perhaps best associated with their success as dragon hunters. Cassandra Pentaghast has managed to make a name for herself free of nepotism. Though her connection to the Nevarran throne is distant, her heroics, both as a young Seeker and in the wake of the Breach, have made her a living legend.

Cassandra went against the Lord Seeker when she helped found the Inquisition.

The daughter of Lord Matthias and Lady Tigana Pentaghast, Cassandra was raised at their estate in the capital city of Nevarra along with her elder brother, Anthony. Lady Tigana held an esteemed position at the Nevarran court as the steward of King Markus—though some claim she was actually his spymaster—and thus the family was affluent even by Pentaghast standards. This standing persisted until 9:10 Dragon, when both Lady Tigana and Lord Matthias were implicated, along with at least a dozen other prominent Pentaghasts, in a conspiracy to assassinate King Markus—the second after an earlier attempt at his life by Baron Gaulene in 9:08 Dragon.

At the time, members of King Markus's court suggested the immediate families of the conspirators should also be killed to prevent reprisals from vengeful relatives down the line. The king reluctantly agreed, leading to widespread arrests and executions—a brutal period that has since become known as the Nevarran Purge. In some cases, youths were spared when there was an influential relative to vouch for their behavior. This was how Cassandra and Anthony survived. Vestalus Pentaghast was a senior member of the Mortalitasi mages, which placed him beyond reprisal even though he was the brother of Lord Matthias.

Vestalus took in his young niece and nephew as wards. As he was a member of the Mortalitasi, they moved into the Grand Necropolis of Nevarra. They grew up among the dead, isolated with only each other for company and support. Vestalus found less and less time for the children as he became prelate of the Mortalitasi in 9:12 Dragon, and thus overseer for the entire Grand Necropolis. In these lonely years in the crypts, Anthony embraced swordsmanship, already dreaming of taking up dragon hunting, and Cassandra did the same.

"I assure you my sister and I are both just fine," Anthony wrote to a cousin. "Uncle Vestalus may be distant, but he sees that we're looked after and has even sponsored my training. Cassie swears she'll follow in my footsteps. She wants the two of us to hunt dragons as a pair, and even though she's so much younger, I don't doubt she'll catch up. I know you joke about her 'playing with swords,' but what else is she supposed to do in the necropolis? Have tea parties with the corpses? She has no one her own age to associate with. Uncle rarely takes us out. At best she has Nomi to keep her busy at the chantry. But that can't be her entire life."

Over the next years, Anthony did indeed become an adept dragon hunter. He joined a cadre of relatives eager to resurrect the Pentaghast tradition, eventually taking part in three separate hunts. The last was the least successful, by virtue of the group unexpectedly facing two high dragons at once, but Anthony was

especially noteworthy in that he not only survived the encounter but killed one of the dragons himself.

By 9:16 Dragon, Anthony's prowess had become great enough that he attracted the attention of a group of apostates. They believed they could use him to acquire dragon blood for an unknown ritual, and when he refused, they killed him in front of Cassandra. Horrified and enraged by the lack of justice when those apostates could not be tracked down, she begged her uncle to send her to train with the templars. Instead, she was sent to the Seekers of Truth.

"I know of your concern that my niece, even at the tender age of twelve, is too old to begin training with the Seekers," Vestalus wrote to the Order. "I would contend, however, that her training is already quite advanced, even by your standards. It is my fault that she has had no social upbringing of note. Instead, her time has been devoted to the chantry here in the necropolis, and following in the footsteps of her brother. She is devout and determined and has skills that will surpass even the best of your pupils; of this I assure you."

Cassandra began her Seeker training at the fortress of Montsimmard, where the majority of the focus was on her religious rather than her martial education. This was initially a source of frustration for her, but eventually she embraced her studies and excelled. She underwent her vigil at the age of fifteen, at a remote castle in the Blasted Hills of northern Orlais—the youngest Seeker to do so since the Storm Age. Left alone for weeks to meditate, purge herself of all emotion, and achieve a state of pious bliss, she emerged from the castle reborn as a member of the Order.

Before the Inquisition, taming a high dragon seemed an impossible task.

A Seeker of Truth

Her apprenticeship began under a senior member named Seeker Byron, who died while still her mentor in the events of 9:22 Dragon. An attempt to overthrow the Chantry leadership by murdering Divine Beatrix III—a plot involving Knight-Commander Martel of the templars, the senior Grand Cleric Callista, and a blood mage named Frenic—culminated in an all-out assault upon the Grand Cathedral in Val Royeaux by a group of magically controlled dragons, since called "Day of Dragons" or "Day of Black Skies." Cassandra was instrumental in thwarting the plot and, true to her family name, putting down the dragons. She was publicly declared a hero by the Divine and awarded with the title of Right Hand, a position previously only awarded to members of the Divine's elite templar guard.

"I cannot explain those events better than I already have," Cassandra would write in a report to her Seeker superiors. "Yes, I was indeed there when the Grand Cathedral was attacked, and I fought with every ounce of my strength to protect the Divine. Things could very easily have gone differently, however. I was framed for the murder of Lord Seeker Aldren, and

Many sinister figures lurk in the shadows of Orlesian high society.

had the mage, Galyan, not helped me, I would still be rotting in that cell. Indeed, Galyan and the other Circle mages were instrumental in fighting this plot. It distresses me that their contribution has been overlooked while I have been singled out as a hero. I was willing to die to protect the Most Holy, it's true, and I almost did die. But fighting against such evil is my sworn duty. Galyan had no such oath to compel him. If it is at all within your power, I would ask that he and his friends be rewarded. The idea that I could have single-handedly slain all those dragons is more than outrageous; it is deceptive, and I will not contribute more to its spread."

For the next several years, Cassandra experienced a degree of notoriety within the Orlesian Empire. She had saved the Divine, and although she did her best to downplay the events on the Day of Dragons, stories of her heroism spread far and wide. Many assumed that Divine Beatrix named Cassandra as Right Hand solely to benefit from her fame, and perhaps there is a degree of truth to that. During those years, Cassandra spent more time acting as bodyguard to the Divine, appearing by her side at public events, than she did pursuing her duties as a Seeker.

Talk of the events did eventually quiet, however, as the Orlesian people found new issues with which to concern themselves. The damaged parts of Val Royeaux and the Grand Cathedral were rebuilt, and Cassandra's cachet as a hero began to dwindle, much to her relief. Many expected the Divine would eventually release Cassandra as Right Hand, allowing her to return to the Seekers of Truth in full. That didn't happen. The Divine likely found having an agent who was not a templar too useful, particularly one who had not been a Seeker for so long that her loyalties to them were absolute. Cassandra's role evolved into that of an agent of the Divine's will, sent to investigate things the Divine wished to know—but not through the lens of her Chantry advisors—and enforce the Chantry's will where needed. It was a role Cassandra appreciated far more than that of an exalted bodyguard.

In 9:34 Dragon, Divine Beatrix III died, and Divine Justinia V was elected in her place. Initially Cassandra assumed she would be relieved of her duties. Indeed, those few people close to her say she looked forward to it. The new Divine, however, had ideas to reform many aspects of the Chantry. For this, Justinia V would encounter opposition both within and well beyond Chantry leadership. What the new Divine needed more than anything was agents she could trust. She made her pitch to Cassandra, who, intrigued, accepted.

Soon after, Cassandra received an unsigned letter, marked with a nightingale and now believed to be written by Leliana, the new Divine's Left Hand.

"I know that the Most Holy has spoken to you, Cassandra," the letter stated. "She wishes you to be her Right Hand, to serve her as you did the Divine before. What she considers is necessary, yet dangerous. There are those who do not see the danger before us. They will say that her efforts destroy everything we believe in. Justinia believes the opposite. She thinks everything we believe in shall be destroyed if it does not change. I know there is at least a part of you that feels the same. My own agents have watched as you perform your duties. You pursue your missions for the Seekers with less vigor than you once did. You question more often, show compassion that would get you in trouble if they knew of it, and you rage at the injustice that has become more and more obvious to those of us with eyes. I welcome the opportunity for us to work together in what shall surely be our most trying hours."

For years, Cassandra was kept busy in her duties under the new Divine. She investigated both public and secret threats to the authority of the Chantry, including the events at Kirkwall. As the situation between the Templar Order and the Circle of Magi turned to rebellion and then chaos, Cassandra redoubled her efforts, only to lose Divine Justinia V entirely in the destruction of the Temple of Sacred Ashes.

Together with Leliana, she helped found the Inquisition shortly thereafter—not as its leader but its backbone, defying the rest of the Chantry as she did so. There are some who claim she is ultimately responsible for rooting out the true villain behind Justinia's death and helping the Inquisitor to destroy him. She would not claim the same, but it is fair to say that Cassandra Pentaghast's legacy will not quickly be forgotten.

CULLEN

A few years after Kirkwall's mage rebellion, Seeker Cassandra Pentaghast sat in the Gallows. Sitting opposite her, at a desk once belonging to Knight-Commander Meredith, Ser Cullen Rutherford of the Templar Order listened quietly to the Seeker's words. Cassandra's speech concluded simply: "The choice is yours."

Champions of the Just

Cullen was eight years old when he told his brother and sisters that he would become a templar. Following this announcement, his youngest sister proclaimed she would be "a princess—no, a cat!" and his brother attempted to tackle "Ser Cullen" into the lake. The conversation progressed no further that day, but Cullen's intentions never wavered. He began visiting the local chantry in Honnleath, asking the templars there to teach him anything they could. Honnleath hosted only a handful of templars, and they humored the boy with basic sword techniques.

His elder sister Mia still recalls her brother's sincere desire to enter a profession that helped people and his refusal to be swayed from the path he'd chosen. Over the next few years, Mia became Cullen's biggest supporter. While his siblings did not want him to leave, under Mia's insistence they agreed to help him train—with occasional protests from young Rosalie, who, it's said, always had to play the apostate. His hard work eventually drew the attention of a visiting knight-captain who agreed to speak with Cullen's parents about formal training. The Templar Order offered a respectable and honorable profession. Wanting to give their second child a life that would make him happy, the Rutherfords agreed to send their son for training.

At thirteen years of age, Cullen was not the youngest among the templars' recruits, nor the most prepared, despite his best

Cullen crossed paths with both the Hero of Ferelden and the Champion of Kirkwall before leading the Inquisition's armies.

efforts. Some recruits had been raised by the Chantry, while others—often the youngest sons and daughters of nobles and thus unlikely to inherit—had been groomed for the profession by tutors. But any concerns that Cullen would fall behind quickly vanished. Serious and attentive in his studies, he soon matched the expertise

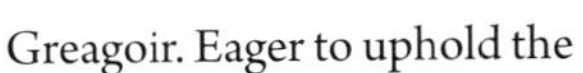

of his peers. Templar training was all that he had imagined. When the time came to take his final vows, Cullen did not hesitate before pledging his life in service to the Maker and taking the lyrium that would bind him to the Order. Ten years after his childhood declaration, Cullen had achieved his goal. He was assigned to the Circle Tower at Kinloch Hold, under the command of Knight-Commander Greagoir. Eager to uphold the tenets of his new post, Cullen proved enthusiastic and loyal, if more inclined to converse with the mages than the other templars. In a letter to his sister, Mia, Cullen wrote: "After everything, I am here, where we said I would be. Tell Rosalie the training was worthwhile."

Advisors Leliana, Cullen, and Josephine were the Inquisition's spymaster, military commander, and chief diplomat, respectively.

The Circles Falter

Cullen was barely a year into his service at Kinloch Hold when the Fifth Blight began. King Cailan, preparing to fight the darkspawn horde, called on Ferelden's mages to join him at Ostagar. Like many in Ferelden, those remaining at the Circle found the idea of a true Blight difficult to believe. While the Blight proved real, few in Kinloch Hold would see the full extent of it. Later, when asked about his own involvement, Cullen responded, "The Blight? That's one disaster I missed."

The death of King Cailan at the Battle of Ostagar threw Ferelden into civil war. Senior Enchanter Uldred took advantage of the ensuing chaos to stage a coup within the Circle Tower. While he claimed to fight for mage freedom, Uldred's actions led to the Circle being overrun by demons and abominations. The speed with which the attack hit took the templars by surprise. With both his forces and the people of Ferelden at risk, Knight-Commander Greagoir ordered the tower sealed, though not all had made it out. Left with little choice but to fight or die, the templars locked inside attempted to reach Uldred and put an end to his plans. All were cut down save for Cullen, who was captured and tortured. The Circle itself was eventually freed by the Hero of Ferelden.

In a report submitted to Knight-Commander Greagoir afterward, Cullen wrote: "I was confined outside the Harrowing chamber; I do not know how. The walls could not be weakened. It was difficult to breathe. Beval, they killed. Farris and Annlise as well. I cannot remember the order. There were images in my mind. But my faith sustains me. I shall not fear the legion should they set themselves against me."

The accuracy of this report was never verified. Cullen was unable to recall how long he had been held. Greagoir, despite his best efforts, could not get Cullen to elaborate on what he meant by "images," nor would he speak of the three templars named in the report, one of whom he'd known since training. When Cullen returned to duty, his peers quickly noticed the enthusiasm their friend once possessed had been replaced with zealotry. Stopping short of insubordination, he openly complained that lenient behavior had led them into danger. His frustration grew as his suggestions for improved security were dismissed as severe and impractical. While he never spoke against them, he displayed bitterness toward the templars who had not been locked inside the tower. Cullen left Kinloch Hold for a time, but seemed no different upon his return. Eventually it was decided unwise for him to remain at Kinloch Hold, and he was transferred to the Free Marches.

Though Cullen was eager to leave Ferelden behind, the voyage across the Waking Sea proved unpleasant. He disliked the confined spaces belowdecks, complaining to the ship's herbalist that he found it difficult to breathe. In the ship's logs, the captain mused on his unusual passenger: "The templar won't go below at all now. Told him he'd need to sleep, but he just gave me a look and said he was fine. Suppose it's for the best. The passengers complain less with him there." As the ship neared its destination, the captain roused Cullen, half-sleeping on his feet, so he could get his first view of the Gallows—Kirkwall's infamous Circle.

Kirkwall's templars were unsure what to make of their newest member. He startled easily and conversed little, save to wake his comrades with disturbed muttering. The mages found Cullen civil but cold. A note dated soon after his arrival, found wedged in a mage's closet, read: "Danger? No. But cannot be trusted."

Cullen, meanwhile, appreciated his new assignment. Knight-Commander Meredith understood the dangers of blood magic and how people could suffer in the name of mage freedom. Recognizing in Cullen a view sympathetic to her own, Meredith took an interest in his career. He rose quickly through the ranks, eventually becoming Meredith's second-in-command. Grateful for her support, Cullen was among Meredith's most loyal supporters. If Meredith wasn't always forthcoming about what occurred in the Circle, then it was for the safety of all and not Cullen's place to question. He made few friends among the templars, though they came to respect his hard work and recognized in him a genuine concern for their safety. At the very least, he was moderately more approachable than the knight-commander.

Cracks in the Façade

Cullen was in Kirkwall two years before he received word from the life he'd left behind. Mia's letter took little time in getting to the point: "You're not dead. That's something you might have told me." During the Blight, Cullen's siblings were forced to flee their home in Honnleath following the death of their parents. Finally settling in South Reach, they attempted to locate their brother. As many of Cullen's friends had died during Uldred's revolt, it was some time before Mia found someone who could help in their search. Even then, the Templar Order's reluctance to disclose weakness among their ranks made it difficult to determine where Cullen had been transferred. Undeterred, Mia tracked down the information she needed to send a letter, a point she emphasized in its conclusion: "You were no doubt aware where *we* were—or could have been—as the Order has more resources than three displaced Fereldans looking for their stupid brother. Be safe. I will write again soon."

Mia's letter tore at Cullen. He later confided in Cassandra, "For all her reprimands, she wrote to someone who wasn't angry. Someone . . . I wasn't that person anymore. I couldn't be. I wasn't sure I wanted her writing to the man I was then." Cullen began a hesitant correspondence with his siblings, often letting months—and sometimes years—go by between letters. The fastest response he ever wrote was an emphatic no to his brother's suggestion that he join Cullen in Kirkwall as a templar. "It was a joke," Branson complained to Mia upon the letter's receipt. Despite Cullen's reservations, he credits Mia's letters with offering him a piece of sanity during what was to come.

After several years as Meredith's second-in-command, Cullen was beginning to question the blind loyalty with which he had followed her. Relations between the city's mages and templars were growing worse. More and more, the templars confided their own slips in performance to Cullen, fearful of the punishments Meredith gave for even minor infractions. While still ill at ease among large groups of mages, he was beginning to notice the tension and fear that filled the eyes of his charges. It was fear reminiscent of his own, and it troubled him. These

Free of the Circle, some mages let loose their terrible powers in the name of rebellion.

were the people he had sworn to protect. Meanwhile, Meredith had become increasingly guarded and evasive when questioned, expecting his devotion.

When the apostate Anders blew up Kirkwall's chantry, Cullen watched another Circle fall around him. This time, the fighting went beyond the Circle, spilling into the streets of Kirkwall. Once again, he fought alongside the templars to regain control. However, when Meredith threatened the lives of those around her, he could no longer ignore her actions. Siding with the Champion, Cullen stood against his knight-commander.

Stories of Kirkwall's mage rebellion tend to end with the deaths of First Enchanter Orsino and Knight-Commander Meredith—but that was not the end for those living there. Large sections of the city had been physically damaged during the conflict. Beyond that, the people of Kirkwall were angry and frightened. Mages—for years the only threat Cullen could see—faced the real possibility of being mobbed by those seeking vengeance. With Meredith gone, the templars were leaderless and, as he was forced to admit, potentially dangerous. He rallied the templars to begin repairs on the Gallows and ensure protection of the loyalist mages who continued to reside within. He coordinated with the city guard, lending aid to relief efforts throughout the city. For over two years, Cullen effectively ran the Templar Order in Kirkwall, bringing some stability to the struggling city.

A New Path

Since he was eight years old, Cullen's life had been a headlong sprint in one direction. It was a course, once set, that could not be altered. Or so he'd come to accept.

Seeker Cassandra Pentaghast and Sister Leliana, the Right and Left Hands of the Divine, arrived in Kirkwall a few years after the rebellion. It was then that Cassandra met Cullen. Impressed by his integrity and what he had accomplished since Meredith's death, Cassandra offered him a position in what would become the Inquisition. "I do not care where you have faltered—only that you stand here now," she said. "But this is not an order. The choice is yours."

It wasn't long before Cullen once again found himself on the Waking Sea, this time bound for Ferelden along with Cassandra and her prisoner, Varric Tethras. As Cullen still refused to spend more time belowdecks than was necessary, Varric often found him staring at the ocean.

"Kirkwall had disappeared by that point," Varric recalled. "I asked him if he was ready to leave. He thought for a moment, then said, 'All of it.' I told him Ferelden might not be better. He said, 'I was there during a Blight and the Circle . . .' And then he actually somewhat smiled. 'It can't be *worse*.'

"You know, for a first attempt at optimism, it wasn't bad."

JOSEPHINE MONTILYET

To onlookers, the Inquisition's rise to power appeared abrupt but inevitable, sanctified by Blessed Andraste herself. The Inquisition's taskmasters worked hard to project this impression of grand victory after grand victory, but every organization is founded on smaller triumphs. A crucial member of its council was Lady Josephine Montilyet of Antiva, ambassador of the Inquisition.

The Montilyets are an old Antivan family, notable for being one of the major naval powers in Antiva as late as the start of the

Josephine's family once wielded great influence in her home country of Antiva.

They say even the foundations of Val Royeaux were poured with gold.

Blessed Age. At their height, if one includes their close relations, their fleet of trading vessels numbered in the hundreds. House Montilyet also had a large contingent of formidable warships ostensibly at the disposal of the royal navy. In reality, they were mostly put to use guarding their merchant vessels in long voyages around the coast. Their heavily guarded cargo was the target of many a daring Rivaini pirate who wanted to make a name and a profit in one fell swoop. The noble Antivan house became entangled in so many rivalries and vendettas against pirates that their relationships became as complex and bitter as those at any Orlesian soiree. Some Rivaini pirate fleets hold grudges against the family to this day.

The Montilyets always had strong ties with Orlais. Roughly half the family lived in the capital and frequently intermarried with Orlesian nobility. The loss of their trading fleets started over a question of marriage and fidelity in Val Royeaux. The names of the lovers in question have been lost to history, but their indiscretions led to vicious infighting, shocking betrayals, public duels, and eventually exile from Orlais for House Montilyet. Their Orlesian trading contracts were no longer considered valid by the Crown. One year later, the sky itself further crippled their fortunes: the Montilyets sent out an unusually large number of their trading ships with cargo bound for the Imperium. A few days out to sea, a thunderous maelstrom swept across the Amaranthine just as the vessels came around a rocky coastline. The fury of the weather caught even the most seasoned captains off-guard, and lasted a full three days. By the time it let up, the majority of the Montilyets' ships had been dashed across the rocks or sunk by the waves. The few remaining ships limped back to port. Superstitious sailors refused the Montilyets' employ, funds could not repair the ships in time to repay their debts, and the Montilyets' once-splendid fleet became merely a legend.

The Montilyets survived, albeit on greatly reduced terms. Today they are a modest trading house, known mostly for their wines and the grandeur of their family estate in Antiva City. When Lady Josephine Montilyet became her family's heir apparent, it was evident even at a young age that she had greater ambitions than overseeing the family vineyards. Before she worked for the Inquisition, Josephine was chief ambassador from Antiva to Orlais. Her tenure there was most successful. It is not unusual for a royal diplomat to be charming, courteous, and well spoken. It is for them to be well liked. Lady Josephine had a reputation for being both fair and honorable in negotiations, which meant she was often asked to arbitrate the most bitter of disputes. It gave her position an air of trustworthiness and, even rarer, neutrality, despite her Antivan allegiances. "Lady Josephine has stridently and painstakingly opposed my latest suggestions to the court," a fellow diplomat once wrote. "But it is refreshing to feel it is nothing *personal*." Her pleasant grace did not hurt her social standing, and it was expected she would retain her position for many years to come. Her decision to step down as Antiva's ambassador to Orlais, therefore, greatly surprised both courts.

When Josephine joined the Inquisition, she was seemingly abandoning a web of potential trading connections crucial to the livelihood of her estates. She told few colleagues and acquaintances where she was heading, but many among the nobility suspected some greater opportunity must have presented itself.

"My dear, you spout nonsense," an Antivan merchant prince wrote to his cousin, an Orlesian countess who suspected Josephine's departure was part of a ploy by rivals to undermine her position at court. "Sweet Lady Josephine retains all her wits. It's no secret that House Montilyet, despite its good reputation, is in gentle decline. The ambassador is risking a leap because she's spotted a fine reward. The question now is whether she topples on the landing."

There was no toppling. The transition from court ambassador to Inquisition diplomat went smoothly enough in the public sphere. In private, Josephine was uneasy. "I cannot help

THEDOSIAN ARTISTS: REYNERIUS D'AUBERIVE

Known for a particular, dramatic style—one that does not always appeal to the masses but has found a remarkably tenacious following among choice members of the Orlesian court—Reynerius d'Auberive has finally recovered from the unfortunate scandal that nearly led to his exile from Val Royeaux. We shall refrain from expanding on the topic, lest we incur the wrath of our most beloved ruler, but suffice it to say that with d'Auberive's interest in the early works of Lydes now appeased, there is no doubt that he can now return to focusing on his own efforts. The demands for d'Auberive's death through methods increasingly gruesome were getting rather tiresome, to say the least, and this critic for one is rather delighted at the prospect of seeing more of his art.

After all, his ability to advance the nature of his work is nothing short of astounding. It is through the very clever use of his skills as an artist that d'Auberive engineered his return among the ranks of the most favored. Indeed, the delightfully audacious maquillages that have adorned some of the most eminent nobles of the court of late were, it is rumored, the work of d'Auberive himself. With the wealth of his patrons and the range of rare cosmetics and materials available to him, our young virtuoso has been putting the empress's most august cosmeticians to shame. Why, to turn the faces of his patrons into veritable tempera masterworks of color and light—so precious and yet saved from ephemerality by being turned into masks upon removal . . . Truly, so inspired a comeback has never been witnessed in the history of art in Val Royeaux!

Even now there are rumors regarding his latest commission, which is to be a mural, though the topic is of a nature even this critic has yet to discover. There is no doubt, however, that his incomparable style will shine through regardless—pun intended, of course.

—*From* A Still Life of Modest Artistic Discernments: Thedosian Artists Through the Ages *by Plume* thinking, one way or another, Sister Nightingale has talked me into the last position I will ever hold," she wrote to an old friend in Rialto, three weeks before departing for Haven. "Her arguments are sound, yes, but there is such an air of finality when she talks about restoring the Inquisition. I feel as if I am abandoning the estate as well. Mother pretends to be holding up, but I can tell she is disappointed I am moving even farther away from her. During dinner, Father looks at me with sad eyes. Antoine is fretting over who will take on some of my duties. Yvette is *pouting*. Still, Leliana would not ask me to move so many miles without good reason, and the mage rebellions are increasing grievances on both sides. Perhaps the Divine's Conclave will end the worst of the violence."

It, of course, did not. In the aftermath of the attack, after the dead had been tallied, monarchs across Thedas demanded answers even as the Chantry's surviving clerics fought for control in the vacuum created by Justinia's death. The Inquisition might have been crushed amid the politics if not for the swift interference and negotiations of its ambassador. Josephine's mere presence brought the fledgling organization enough legitimacy to make the circling nobles pause. The following months saw a rise in the Inquisition's reach and its social standing. When the Inquisitor won renown, Josephine made sure it was spun into favors, alliances, and tangible prestige that slowly earned the respect, and sometimes even admiration, of the powers in Thedas.

SOLAS

Each of the Inquisition's inner circle brought unique strength and insight to the organization. Among the founding members, none knew the Fade or spirit magic better than the mage known as Solas.

The Advisor

An elf from a distant village to the north, Solas grew up outside the realm of Chantry teachings and had to learn magic without the benefit of the Circle. His own explorations taught him valuable information about the Fade, lessons ignored or avoided in more regimented magical practices. His insights proved vital in sealing the Breach at Haven; had Solas not overcome his natural concern about the fledgling Inquisition and approached voluntarily, it is entirely possible that the Breach would never have been sealed.

But Solas's selfless dedication to helping the Inquisition deal with the threat hardly ended with the Breach itself. Seeker Cassandra Pentaghast notes that after the destruction of Haven, it was Solas who led the Inquisition to Skyhold. "He found it for us in the middle of the mountains, a fortress lost to the ages," she said. "In our most desperate time, it was precisely what we needed, when we needed it most. It almost seems a miracle to think of it now."

Solas also brought his own special knowledge, gained from extensive study of ancient history, to the fight against the dreaded Corypheus. In the days immediately following the explosion at the Temple of Sacred Ashes, Solas urged the Inquisition to locate whatever artifact was used to create the Breach. When Corypheus destroyed Haven after the Breach's closure, Solas recognized the orb that Corypheus carried as the ancient elven artifact that gave him his power. That knowledge led to the destruction of the orb and the ultimate defeat of the

The apostate Solas was neither Dalish nor city elf in origin, and his knowledge of spirit magic was unprecedented.

The discovery of Skyhold fortress turned the tide in the Inquisition's battle against Corypheus.

mad magister. Even Morrigan, advisor to the Inquisition on matters arcane, conceded that Solas had an amazing breadth of knowledge. "The things he knows are uncanny," she said. "He must have walked many paths in the Fade to find such treasures."

Indeed, it seems likely that the Inquisition would have fared much differently had Solas not come to its aid. Without fanfare or expectation of reward, the quiet apostate gave the Inquisition exactly the tools it needed to succeed at each critical step in the organization's development.

The Dreamer

Solas credited most of his knowledge to extensive exploration of the Fade. While it is not uncommon for mages to journey into the Fade in their minds, Solas learned to retain the same conscious awareness one has while awake. For mages with such a gift, the Fade is an endless wonderland filled with amazing treasures. These mages, known as Dreamers, can shape the Fade to their will, and even enter the dreams of friends and loved ones to share their experiences. Sadly, the minds of most Dreamers, touched as they are by the Fade, are tempting targets for demons, and most Dreamers eventually succumb either to possession or madness.

Fortunately for Solas, the same natural insight that brought him to the Fade made him a friend to most of the spirits that live there. Eschewing the usual protective practices most Circle mages follow, Solas befriended the spirits he found, treating them as equals and gaining valuable wisdom and guidance in his exploration of the Fade. While such activities sound outlandish or even dangerous to most, even Cullen admitted that Solas never seemed at risk. "He has a way with spirits that I've never seen," he observed, following the move to Skyhold. "A demon might kill him someday, but it will never possess him. He's too much like they are."

This unique understanding gave Solas an affinity with forms of magic most mages find exceedingly difficult. While many mages are driven mad by touching the nature of the Veil itself, Solas shaped it as comfortably as he spoke to spirits.

"He talked about the Fade like it'd be a paradise, but it all sounded crazy to me," said fellow Inquisition member Varric Tethras. "I suppose I'm the wrong person to have opinions about the Fade. I think he felt sorry for me for not being able to touch it, but I kind of prefer it that way."

The Wanderer

For all the wisdom he shared with the Inquisition, all the valuable advice he offered when it was most needed, Solas was a quiet man, more comfortable with spirits than he was with most people. The kitchen staff at Skyhold recall him eating little, though he had very particular requirements regarding his tea. He decorated one great room of the fortress with elaborate paintings detailing the Inquisition's achievements, though he rarely showed himself in his murals. It seems that he preferred to observe and assist in great achievements rather than garner praise for those achievements himself.

This is not to say that he was hesitant to speak when the need arose. He had passionate views on the Grey Wardens, voicing concerns over the long-term ramifications of killing the Archdemons. He held moderate views on the plight of elves in Thedas: he pitied the elves of alienages as he pitied the poor and helpless of any race, and he was skeptical of the usefulness of the Dalish attempting to remember and reclaim their heritage with so much lost. For all that, Leliana remembers that he spoke the elven language fluently. "I have heard elves in the alienage speak their few remembered words, and I have heard Dalish Keepers recite passages from texts passed down for generations," she said. "Solas spoke like neither of them. He spoke the language perfectly, with an accent I have never been able to place. I can only imagine where in the Fade he might have learned it."

Solas left the Inquisition after the defeat of Corypheus, presumably returning to his peaceful, solitary life. Wherever he is now, his work with the Inquisition is a testament to what is possible when people from different backgrounds come together without prejudice for a noble end.

Dorian Pavus learned much of his magic from Magister Gereon Alexius.

DORIAN PAVUS

The Tevinter Imperium is a realm ruled by mages, all competing against each other for supremacy and willing to use any means at their disposal to achieve it. There are mages like Dorian Pavus, however, who oppose the resulting and rampant corruption. These Tevinters want to see their homeland restored to greatness without spilling the blood of innocents.

Great Expectations

Dorian Pavus was born in 9:11 Dragon to Magister Halward and Lady Aquinea Thalrassian, both from wealthy and influential families with lineages stretching back for generations—all the way to the Dreamers who preceded the first magisters. House Pavus, in fact, is one of the preeminent political forces in eastern Tevinter, its estate outside the city of Qarinus having been the site of several important historical events, not the least of which was the start of the so-called Rebellion of Three Dragons in 3:44 Towers. Thus, it was with high hopes that the pair greeted their new son, he who would one day take over his father's seat in the Magisterium and marry a young woman to whom he had been betrothed since birth.

By all accounts, Dorian was not interested in any of this. Having shown magical ability from a very young age, he was apprenticed at the Circle of Magi in Carastes, one of the most prestigious academies in the eastern Imperium. There, the trouble began.

"You were right to send your son to us, Magister Halward," wrote a senior enchanter at Carastes. "Even at the tender age of nine, he is already evincing talents greater than boys three or four years older. This means he will one day make a fine magister, one of which you and your dear wife shall be very proud. For the moment, however, it also means he is a young lad with much older boys who are quite jealous of him. There have been incidents, I fear. My initial suspicion was that Dorian was being bullied by the older boys, but it appears the reverse is true. Your son has become a terror in the halls, lording his superior magic over the other boys, who he believes are jealous of his prowess. After yesterday's duel in the courtyard (with a full audience), I have one badly injured student and a sullen yet unrepentant Dorian locked in solitary—both sons of prominent magisters. I trust you can see my predicament."

Dorian went from one Circle to the next and then to several private tutors. Each time, an incident resulted in his being sent back to his family in Qarinus. In desperation, his father sent him to the capital city of Minrathous to attend a smaller school run by the Order of Argent—known as much for its adherence to strict Andrastian discipline as for its exorbitant entry fees. That lasted exactly three months before Dorian disappeared . . . only to turn up in a drunken stupor at a house of ill repute in the elven slums. The resulting scandal would likely have been more than House Pavus could have borne, had Dorian not been discovered by Magister Gereon Alexius.

I am indeed the one who found your son with the whores, my friend. Ask me not what I was doing there, and I shall tell you no lies. The boy had enough cheek, even in his inebriated state, to invite me to join him. It made me laugh, so I dragged him back to the Gilded Quarter rather than simply calling the templars. Fortunate that I did, since once Dorian sobered up in the carriage, we had an interesting chat. He's rather despondent over the life's path you've charted for him—if I may speak frankly—and thus, I think a part of him sabotages all efforts to keep him on the straight and narrow, either to spite you or to punish himself. I cannot say. Regardless, he has spirit, and his tutors claim he has almost as much talent as he believes. With your permission, I'd like to take him under my wing and see what can be done to cultivate it. No matter what he feels, it would be a pity for such a mage to go to waste. Our Imperium needs better.

—Alexius, in a letter to Halward

The magister took Dorian under his wing. For several years, Dorian was personally tutored at the Alexius estate in Asariel, where he flourished. Alexius had an intelligence and ambition that not only grabbed Dorian's attention but also gained his respect. The Pavus family breathed a sigh of relief when, four years later, Magister Alexius sponsored Dorian for his tests to become a fully ranked enchanter at the Minrathous Circle of Magi—tests that Dorian passed with ease. For once, it appeared as if he was finally on the path his parents had always envisioned for him.

It was not to last.

The Drifting Enchanter

Until 9:35 Dragon, Dorian enjoyed the privileges of a ranking enchanter in the cosmopolitan atmosphere of the Imperium's capital city. He split his time between aiding Magister Alexius in his research and partaking of the life of a well-heeled scion. He participated in Lower Floor debates of the Circle and attended social functions and balls. If his parents grew slowly more insistent that he return to Qarinus to marry his betrothed, they were easily stayed by claims that reaching the esteemed rank of senior enchanter was more important to him.

On a winter trip from Val Royeaux with their son, Felix, Magister Alexius's wife was slain in a darkspawn attack. Felix was badly injured—and, far worse, was afflicted with the darkspawn corruption. The disease was incurable. Rather than accept this, Magister Alexius turned his research toward temporal magic, desperately searching for a way to turn back time itself and restore his son's health. Dorian abandoned his duties at Minrathous, moving into Alexius's estate to devote his full energy toward aiding his mentor's cause. It was not long, however, before the toll of such an endeavor began to wear on them both.

"I'm fine, Father. Seriously, you can stop asking," Dorian wrote. "Yes, I am still at the estate, and, yes, we are still chasing after the same hopeless quest. I keep hoping that Alexius will snap out of it. Was it not enough that we found a way to prolong Felix's life long past what someone with such an illness would normally hope to expect? We've given the poor boy years, when not long ago he would only have had months. Instead of spending that time with Felix, Alexius has us chasing the past. I gave him the letter you sent, but he waved it away the same way he ignores anything I say . . . as if I haven't been here with him, for months and months, staring at the same dead end he is. What he wants to do is technically possible, but the power it would require is unachievable and, even if it wasn't, would rip apart the fabric of time if successful. Thankfully there's been no talk of blood magic. Despite what you fear, Father, I yet have hope for him."

Despite his words, Dorian left the Alexius estate in 9:37 Dragon after a heated argument. He spent months drinking in the slums of Minrathous, evading anyone sent by his family to recover him. Eventually he returned to the estate to reconcile, only to find both Magister Alexius and his son gone. With no indication where Alexius had gone, Dorian fell back to his debauchery, engaging in such excess that the scandal forced his family's hand. He was abducted from the home of Lord Ulio Abrexis—absent at the time, though his son was present—and spirited back to Qarinus by ship.

The scandal was rather delicious, my dear. Think of it: all the times Halward has bragged about his talented son, how the boy would one day be the next Archon! Not bloody likely. I hear they had to hire thugs to invade some vulgati lord's estate to get him back. Seven guardsmen killed, and they find the boys in bed, so wrapped up in their efforts they didn't even realize men were dying right outside their door. This must be why the Pavus boy still isn't married, after all this time. Halward has held onto that betrothal for how long? All the while, the Everens could have married their girl off to someone actually interested. It's too rich. Couldn't have happened to a more deserving family.

—Correspondence between magister rivals of Halward

In an effort to contain the scandal, Magister Halward evidently kept Dorian a veritable prisoner in their Qarinus estate for months. When Dorian finally escaped, he fled into the countryside with not a coin to his name, vowing never to return. Whether his rage was due to the kidnapping, the imprisonment, or something else is unknown, but the obvious row within the Pavus family fueled the public speculation for many months. Eventually Halward was forced to step down from his position on the consiliare for the Archon—a loss of prestige from which the family has yet to recover.

For the next two years, Dorian drifted from one part of the Imperium to the next, living off the funds of distant relatives or whatever companions he encountered. It was during this period that Magister Alexius once again contacted him, as Dorian himself wrote about in a letter to a colleague at the Circle of Magi:

"It's rather curious, isn't it? Alexius always told us that the only way to restore the Imperium was through integrity. If we mages didn't have it and enforce it among our own kind, how could we expect others not to live in fear? Yet he said the same thing to you as he did to me. I still don't think he actually believed the words coming out of his own mouth. Someone has done something to him, or to Felix. That has to be it. Rather sad that you won't come south with me, but I can't just let this lie. I won't."

Dorian did, in fact, go south to Ferelden to follow his mentor. The exact details of what became of him are unclear, save for the fact that Magister Alexius had given his support to a cult of Tevinter supremacy in exchange for their aid in healing his son. It seems that Alexius and his son both died and Dorian joined the Inquisition in its showdown against the cult. This news led to a degree of widespread notoriety and fame for Dorian within the Imperium, much to his family's chagrin. What will become of him once—and if—he returns to his homeland is unknown, but his status as a visible member of the Tevinter magocracy, who challenged its standards and not only survived but perhaps thrived, is all but guaranteed.

BLACKWALL

Documents taken from the Orlesian Grey Warden fortress at Val Chevin reveal that Gordon Blackwall was recruited from the city of Cumberland in 9:17 Dragon. As the Grey Wardens believe

The legacy of Warden Blackwall persists long after his death.

that joining the Order marks a new beginning, the reasons for Blackwall's recruitment and his life up to that point are unknown. In 9:28, after over a decade of service, Blackwall assumed the position of Warden-Constable, taking over for close friend Alisse Fontaine, who became Commander of the Grey in Orlais. After his promotion, Warden-Constable Blackwall was put in charge of operations in northern Orlais, while Warden-Commander Fontaine maintained control of the South.

Shortly after the Fifth Blight, Fontaine tasked her Wardens with securing all known Deep Roads entrances in Orlais. On one associated campaign, a sudden cave-in trapped seven Grey Wardens in an old, crumbling shaft. Blackwall managed to force his way free of the rocks. Help for his fellow trapped Wardens was not close at hand, with the nearest outpost a three-day hike. Blackwall made his way, alone, through a darkspawn-infested cave system to reach and free his peers. For this deed, Blackwall was awarded the Silverite Wings of Valor upon his return to Val Chevin. According to the testament of one of the rescued Wardens, Blackwall did not escape the campaign unscathed and would walk with a slight limp thereafter.

In 9:36, Blackwall traveled to Montsimmard to confer privately with Warden-Commander Fontaine. It is widely believed that it was at this meeting that Fontaine informed Blackwall of her intentions to undertake her Calling within the next year and was in the process of choosing her replacement. His business with Fontaine concluded, Blackwall sent a message north voicing his intention to return to Val Chevin. However, he never reached the town and fell out of contact with the Orlesian Wardens for several years. Many speculated that he had gone rogue.

Fontaine stepped down from her post as Warden-Commander and was succeeded by Warden-Commander Clarel de Chanson.

Blackwall emerged some time later in Ferelden, where he was recruited by the Inquisition.

FIRST ENCHANTER VIVIENNE

It was a surprise to many when the powerful and well-connected First Enchanter Vivienne set aside her duties to join the Inquisition. Indeed, she had plenty to lose.

Romance & Power

Bastien, thirty-third Duke of Ghislain and respected member of the Council of Heralds, had a *reputation*. As a young man, he eschewed the Game in favor of life as an outlaw. A bard of some skill, he trained under the legendary Black Fox, dabbling in treason in the name of justice for the common folk, or perhaps for his own amusement. His life as a minstrel, spy, and troublemaker was cut short in 8:96 Blessed by the demise of his elder sister Marissa, the Duchess of Ghislain, a victim of the blue death.

Bastien returned home to assume his duties as duke and, as far as the nobility was concerned, settled down to become a respectable competitor in the Game. He made the appropriate enemies, arranged the appropriate marriage for himself, acquired the appropriate connections, took a seat on the Council of Heralds, and in all ways seemed to be atoning for the wildness of his youth.

Vivienne offered her power to the Inquisition in exchange for some degree of influence over its direction.

Well, this should be shit right the way through.

NOTES ON THE INQUISITION

SERA & THE FRIENDS OF RED JENNY

Red Jenny is a minor legend, a figure of vengeance for those oppressed who are brave enough to wish ill on the authors of their misfortunes, but at the same time not possessed of the conviction to upset the social structure in which they find themselves mistreated. In short, something happens, but nothing changes.

Well, no?

Where would you spend anything if you tore it all down? Daft!

The group is simultaneously led by skilled actors, each claiming to be the titular figure, "Red Jenny." Sera appears to hold seniority, earned at a very young age. Individual "Red Jennies" operate independently for long periods of time, each to the advantage of their personal territory. Sera's activities vary from insult to larceny, and, in extreme cases, murder. She will, as the saying goes, rob from the rich and give to the poor, but with significant funds kept for services rendered. Often, robbery is incidental, the action being more about petty revenge. The one rule Sera seems to demand is that they cross no other of their own.

That's right it's the rule. No chances, no bargains, you're over and done.

Sera's group has attained such a strange notoriety that they need not even act to be credited with an outcome, in what seems the modern equivalent of blaming sickly cattle on imagined witches. So, the difficulty in tracking Red Jenny is established by individual skill, multiplied by concurrent numbers, scattered by random intent, and compounded by the fact that a Red Jenny may not have even been there in the first place.

Thanks to some well-placed sources, we have learned that the Friends of Red Jenny have been of previous interest to assassin guilds as well. Some unusual records surfaced from the Antivan Crows:

They went after Crows? Pissballs!

You wanted their measure taken, and here it is.

The knives I found think the Friends of Red Jenny started in Ferelden, maybe a hundred years back. Could be longer—they're hard to track. Don't know if the name is a rank or what, but pretty sure it's older than they are. They were assassins back then, but I doubt they competed with true guilds. They were cheap, small, and made a habit of paying urchins to get information or plant weapons. They recruited that way, but that doesn't seem like a way to get skilled people. The Friends had some teeth, and they weren't shy about getting bloody if their people were threatened, but they were strictly local.

It's recent that the Friends have been more active. Since the Blight, mostly. A new Red Jenny at the head—or seems like—in Val Royeaux. And in Kirkwall. Maybe more. Thing is, they might be doing more, but they stepped back from being assassins. And there are a lot fewer of them. Could be Blight—it killed a bunch of everyone. But my gut says different. They didn't just move; they changed how they work.

I found Red Jenny herself, or one of them, I guess. Tall for an elf. I approached her plain, figured we'd talk guild to guild. Her answer was two fingers. She could move, she's proper skilled, but I don't think she's competition. What she and her friends do has nothing to do with us.

Ashevin

Noted below, presumably by the initiating Antivan Crow:

I get it. They all wear the same mask. The rest is bullshit.

The elf, the voice says Denerim, a mutt. But she's got a trainer who must be somebody. You don't split flies like she does without someone teaching you how to nock an arrow. Who gets that at birth? No one the living are supposed to know.

Is it so hard for everyone? You miss, then you don't.

This is admittedly the thinnest of the threads I've followed. The following is an anonymous contemporary tavern rhyme that circulates in the Free Marches north of the Vimmark Mountains brought to my attention as it references a nickname Sera was overheard to mention.

She of the Red,
Oh, She of the Red,
She's under a lake with no water, it's said.
As friendly as any, and then you are dead.
"Forgive me; I've killed you,"
lies She of the Red.

Frigging. Piss. Off!

Sera was likely at the alienage in Denerim as an infant, but we can find no record. Her association with the Friends of Red Jenny may have been her means of avoiding it. Speaking in confidence, some guards admit they are loath to chase anyone into a dark alley, as it is akin to chasing a bear to its den. Not worth the risk, especially if only over a matter of elven truancy.

Whatever that means, no one cares.

By her own admission, Sera spent some years in the household of a merchant of moderate holdings named Lady Taraline Emmald. That time seems to predate exposure to the Friends and ended with the woman's death well before the Blight. A particularly virulent wasting illness was known to have passed through Denerim during those years.

Didn't go, stupid tree, didn't stay.

Makes you gray. And cold. You don't wish it on the worst people.

The streets and the Friends are probable sources for Sera's combat abilities, but Emmald was likely her initial educator and provider. The taking of a ward is not unheard of for those who are childless but of means. Sera has admitted that the situation was mutually beneficial for a time, but clearly has mixed feelings about it now. The death may have caused matters to go unresolved.

She ruined cookies. Nice or not, that was shit.

The life of her patroness remains undocumented. It seems people are allowed to be lost in the wake of Blight, but matters of property rarely are. Sera is not named in the following records, but the epithet "Bequeathed" is occasionally used when a party is unable to be legally identified, as in the matter of elves and holdings outside of approved venues such as alienages. It appears that at one point, Sera may have inherited a sizable estate. That speaks to Lady Emmald's commitment to at least the appearance of the relationship. How Sera dispensed with it speaks to her.

Never asked for it. Paid good sovereigns not to read any of it then, pay you even more not to read it now.

Document dated before the Blight:

Notice of Grant

Subject: Estate and holdings on behalf of one Lady Taraline Emmald, deceased, to be placed in trust for Bequeathed, as indicated by will and testament.

Value: Sum total of estate is determined to be twenty-eight thousand seven hundred sovereigns, eighty silver, and ninety-six copper (28,700g, 80s, 96c), in combined lands and monies. Less negotiated fees (147g, 3s), less taxation of transfer, respecting precedent of holdings between legal title bearers and those remaining undocumented. Divestment of two thousand eight hundred and seventy sovereigns, eight silver, one copper (2,870g, 8s, 1c) required.

Addendum: Funds refused by Bequeathed, as anticipated by author of will and testament. Amount deferred to trust maintained by divestment of interest. Title remains with the estate for purposes of documentation, as respecting of precedent (re: undocumented).

Document dated during the Blight:

Notice of Seizure

Subject: Estate and holdings of one Lady Taraline Emmald, deceased, as held in trust for Bequeathed, to be seized for immediate use.

Authority to seize: Granted in anticipation of treaties presented by relevant authorities (Grey Wardens), to be used in efforts against the Blight. Said treaties not present. Authority enacted by special enforcement of arl and state.

*Addendum postseizure: The quoted value has been deducted from the estate for cited circumstances. The total of: *worth of mercantile goods and trade contracts stored on site (sold to fund efforts), *miscellaneous private goods (sold to fund efforts), *miscellaneous structural elements (sold to fund efforts), the removal of which compromised roofing. Principal manor house rendered unlivable due to elements and animal infestation. Blight forces immune to fine of worth.*

Amounts total: Reduced from estimated worth of holdings, ten thousand and sixteen sovereigns, eighteen silver, and four copper (10,016g, 18s, 4c). Hall house and outbuilding remain as taxable structures.

Document dated after the Blight:

Notice of Fine in Worth

Subject: Bequeathed returned to unannounced tenancy of holdings titled to one Lady Taraline Emmald, held in trust for said Bequeathed, incurring fines against said holdings. Fines require reactivating intent of will and testament from trust. Estate now subject to precedent of Blight Reclamation Act IV, wherein inheritance by those undocumented is taxed for public good, requiring prefine divestment of three thousand four hundred sovereigns, four silver, eleven copper (3,400g, 4s, 11c).

*Claims against: Seeking financial recompense the total of: *unpaid contract to the Gnawed Noble to supply spirit and comestibles (ongoing), *two (2) neighboring outbuildings destroyed (tipped), *two (2) nightgown garments ruined and personal attending of two (2) residents of adjoining property to restore damage to countenance suffered while attending purpose in said tipped outbuildings, *individual rewards for city officers who assisted in the control of accidental fire consuming hall house of estate, which spread to neighboring public stables. Three thousand forty-eight sovereigns, eleven silver, nine copper (3,048g, 11s, 9c), paid by divestment or reduced from estimated worth. Outbuilding remains as taxable structure.*

And another:

Notice of Quitclaim and Transfer

Subject: Quitclaim on land and holdings titled to one Lady Taraline Emmald, deceased, by one Bequeathed. This is to certify that all ownership and claims thereof are nulled in their entirety by the estate, as held in trust by Bequeathed.

Authority to dispose: Bequeathed authorizes the dissolution of holdings due to admitted lack of education regarding such matters, and disinterest in pursuing same. Total of instruction of Bequeathed is exactly: "Maybe orphans or some (excrement)." Terms defined by documenting trustee for additional fee (39g, 3s), by divestment.

Action: Management of all land and holdings is transferred to Undetermined Sister of the Chantry, Denerim, as per precedent regarding Blight orphaned and monies donated through will or testament. Transfer requires divestiture of considerable value, total eight thousand forty-nine sovereigns, one silver, thirteen copper (8,049g, 1s, 13c), precedent noted regarding gifting by undocumenteds. See Blight Reclamation Act IX.

Addendum: Chantry has delayed assignment of Undetermined Sister, as any available have been dispatched to Kinloch Hold for the purpose of "diplomatic ministrations." Delay in assignment has exposed estate to seizure due to lack of occupancy (see Blight Reclamation Act XII). Avoidance of seizure requires satisfying fine of worth to ensure land title remains giftable, payment in lieu requiring divestment of remaining holdings in their entirety. Two thousand one hundred thirty-one sovereigns, thirty-two silver, fifty-eight copper (2,131g, 32s, 58c).

Note: The estate of one Lady Taraline Emmald ceases to be legally definable if balance is archived at zero. Account to be closed with a final deficit against estate of thirty silver (30s), as requested and pocketed by Bequeathed.

And for the sake of circumstantial numerical interest, note this contemporary tavern leaflet, as commonly circulated following the Blight:

Rest well at the Gnawed Noble.
Raise a glass, raise your feet.
Thirty silver for all your comfort for the week. Arriving to find your claim?
Passing through to find your fortune?
Staff on hand to assist in pairing with a suitable caravan, be your destination the opportune rebuilding of Redcliffe,
or farthest Orlesian jewel and capital Val Royeaux.

Happy now?
Better be.

The fiercest politics often play out in the ballrooms of Orlais.

Madame de Fer, known to some by her given name of Vivienne, began her life at the Ostwick Circle of Magi in the Free Marches. One of the youngest full-fledged mages in Circle history, she transferred to the Montsimmard Circle at the age of nineteen. In her new Orlesian Circle, Vivienne was considered an exceptional scholar and showed early promise at the Game—especially remarkable in a mage of foreign birth.

At the Imperial Wintersend Ball of 9:16 Dragon, mages from the White Spire and the Montsimmard Circle were invited to attend the festivities and entertain the court with feats of magic. The young Vivienne was among the envoys from Montsimmard, and by all accounts, Duke Bastien was far more enraptured by her than by any display of magic. Bastien danced the entire evening only with Vivienne, slighting a number of very powerful nobles.

A few days later, Bastien paid a call to her in Montsimmard, accompanied by a small army of florists bearing armloads of peonies. Reportedly, the duke's gift filled an entire floor of the tower and inspired at least two alchemists to divert their research to extracting fragrances instead. In short order, he invited Vivienne to several parties held at his estate in Ghislain. By the start of summer, she had a suite of rooms in his house and conducted most of her Circle business by correspondence.

The affair was a matter of intense scandal at the time. Some saw Bastien's dalliance with a mage who was all but destined to

In 9:16 Dragon, a strange book was recovered during a University of Orlais expedition into an uncharted section of the Western Approach.

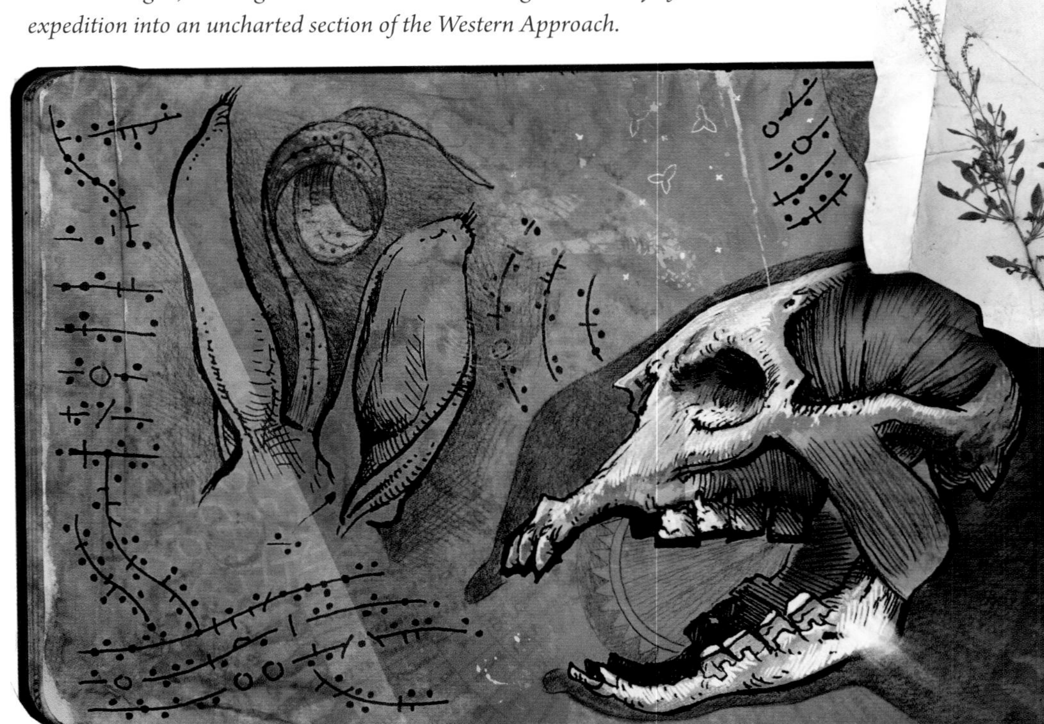

become first enchanter as a bid to gain access to Circle enchantments, cutting out those nobles who usually managed trade with the mages. Some objected to a nobleman of Bastien's rank and position associating with mages at all. Many whispered that Vivienne must be a blood mage to have captivated the duke so completely. The usual embargoes were sanctioned, assassins sent, and bards put into play, but Bastien had been a master at thwarting the schemes of the nobility in his youth, and he put his talents to work reminding his peers of this fact. Several of his enemies found themselves the targets of relentless saboteurs, thieves, and vandals. After a few such reprimands, the duke's enemies turned to less difficult quarry.

Meanwhile, Vivienne handled her own barrage of attacks from her own set of detractors. Several bards were sent to make an example of the young upstart enchantress; half of them were returned to their employers frozen solid. The rest were persuaded to work for her instead.

The nobility continued stewing in their opposition to the love affair until shortly after the coronation of Empress Celene four years later. The empress inherited her family's fascination with all things arcane and insisted on having a court enchanter. She petitioned Orlais's Circles for the most knowledgeable mage in the empire, and almost no one was surprised when Vivienne's name was put forward. After that, only a single meeting with the empress was required to see Vivienne take the court enchanter's post. With Empress Celene supporting her, few nobles were willing to publicly condemn Madame de Fer for being a mage ever again.

The book is written in an invented script by an unknown author, apparently on the subject of animal physiology.

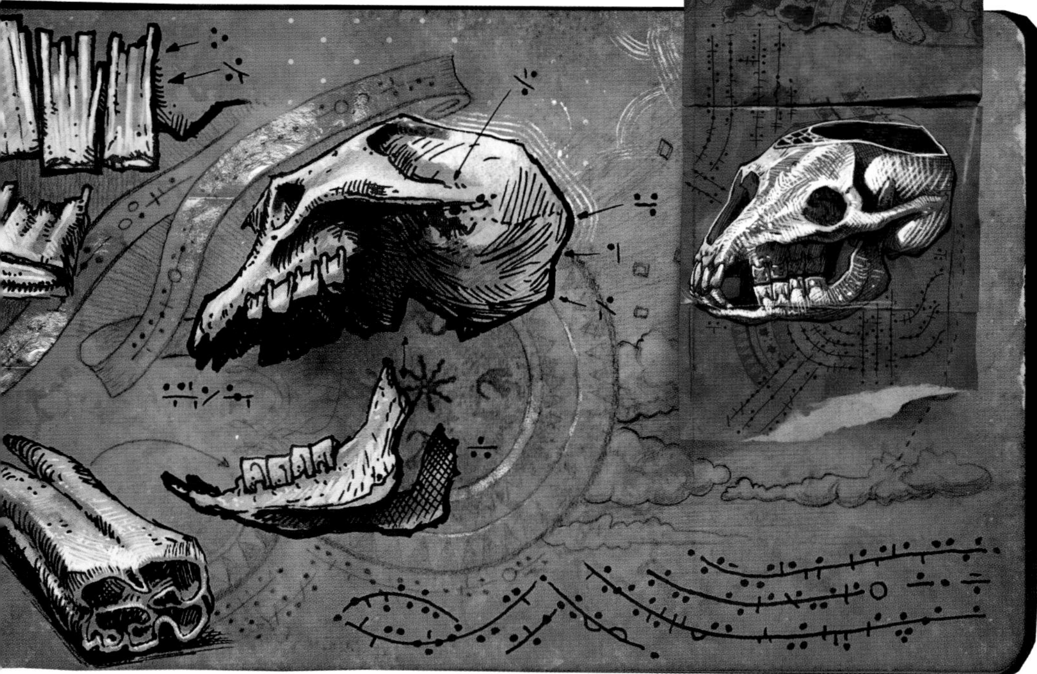

IRON BULL

The early years of the Qunari mercenary who now calls himself the Iron Bull were spent in the schools of Par Vollen. Instead of parents, Qunari children are raised by tamassrans. The tamassrans are both nannies and teachers, educating the children in their care and instilling the Qunari values of duty, logic, and obedience. But while a typical nanny answers to the lord and lady of the house, Qunari tamassrans all answer to the Ariqun, the head of the Qunari priesthood. They are responsible for ensuring that the imekari, the children in their care, grow up to be useful members of Qunari society. They observe and test each child to gauge what strengths he or she possesses and how best to use them to serve the demands of the Qun.

Ashkaari

The tamassran who watched the young Iron Bull called him Ashkaari, a nickname meaning "one who thinks." Young Ashkaari was big for his age and could easily have become a bully, but his keen eye led him instead to serve as a sort of secondary caregiver. When one of the other children wasn't feeling well or was going to cause trouble, it was Ashkaari who told his "Tama" what was happening. This should not be taken to mean that young Ashkaari entirely avoided trouble himself. On one occasion, he ate all of the meat on his plate, leaving the vegetables largely untouched. Ashkaari's Tama told him that he would not be allowed to go and play until he ate two more things off his plate. Without hesitation, Ashkaari took two pieces of meat that he had hidden in his pocket, placed them upon the plate, looked at Tama, and then ate the two pieces before running off to play.

That was when Tama knew that Ashkaari, for all his strength, was not destined to be a soldier. Qunari soldiers must be strong, loyal, and obedient to the spirit of an order as well as the letter, and while Ashkaari was strong and loyal, his quick mind,

The Bull's Chargers, led by the Iron Bull, were a notorious mercenary band of unquestionable skill.

keen eyes, and unusual problem-solving skills made him a poor fit.

Instead, she recommended that Ashkaari be placed in the Ben-Hassrath. While his growing size—and, as he grew older, distinctive horns—would make him too recognizable to be a spy, he had the makings of an excellent enforcer for the secret police.

Hissrad

As he began his training with the Qunari secret police, Ashkaari gained a new informal name, as is common among Qunari assigned to new roles. All members of the Ben-Hassrath are thinkers to some degree, so "Ashkaari" did not distinguish him from his peers. What made him unique was his ability to lie. Criminals who saw the hulking warrior assumed he was a guard, the brutish muscle for the more intelligent members of the Ben-Hassrath. His straightforward manner led them to think that he was stupid, and in their confidence, these criminals would let slip information that the young Ben-Hassrath agent would pounce upon. He quickly earned the name "Hissrad," which means "one who creates illusions" or "liar."

His early work in Par Vollen saw Hissrad recognized by his superiors as a valuable asset who uncovered smuggling operations, discontented groups considering fleeing the Qun, and even a Tevinter spy ring. It was the latter case that led the senior Ben-Hassrath to recommend Hissrad for service in Seheron.

Unlike most Qunari settlements, the island of Seheron stands in a state of constant unrest. Humans on Seheron consistently rebel against the Qunari occupation, often with the help of Tevinter agents fomenting chaos in the region. Tevinter forces openly assault Seheron as well, leading to bloody fighting that catches civilians in the middle. The resulting chaos causes Qunari there to desert and become Tal-Vashoth in greater numbers than in any other Qunari settlement. The Ben-Hassrath needed agents with the intelligence to find Tevinter spies, the charm to win over Seheron natives who saw many Qunari as a hostile force, and the ferocity to survive the ugly and unpredictable urban combat that killed so many. Hissrad seemed like a natural choice.

The Ben-Hassrath considered two years of active service the maximum time most agents could perform in Seheron before prolonged stress rendered them too unstable to carry out their duties effectively. Hissrad spent almost a decade there, rising through the ranks as superiors broke down or died at the hands of assassins and insurgents. Among the natives, Hissrad earned a reputation as a fair man, someone they could approach with information or requests without fear. Among the Ben-Hassrath, he earned a reputation as an effective hunter, ruthlessly tracking down Tal-Vashoth deserters. Among his fellow secret police, Hissrad was an unshakable comrade, giving the team confidence even during the bloodiest fighting and never losing the friendly attitude that won the loyalty and respect of the natives.

Then, after eight years in Seheron, the unit Hissrad commanded suffered heavy losses. A friendly Seheron merchant, pressured by rebels, poisoned several of his men, and when the same poison was used to kill a school full of children, a furious Hissrad vowed to avenge them. He mounted an assault upon a Tal-Vashoth jungle stronghold without Ben-Hassrath approval—an action technically legal for him, as he called it an investigation and maintained that he was unaware of the exact number of hostiles he might find inside. In the bloody fighting, Hissrad lost several more soldiers, including Vasaad, a longtime friend who was first through the door into the Tal-Vashoth stronghold and took an arrow through the throat. Upon seeing one of his oldest friends die before him, Hissrad went berserk, slaughtering all comers.

The survivors of his unit returned to their superiors and requested medical attention for Hissrad, who was still at the stronghold. Ben-Hassrath agents arrived to find him still there, unmoving, covered in wounds and surrounded by the hacked and butchered corpses of the Tal-Vashoth warriors. He declared himself unfit for duty and too dangerous to be around civilians, where every hand might hold a knife and every meal might hold poison. The implicit threats of occupied Seheron provoked violent urges he no longer felt confident that he could check, and so Hissrad submitted himself to the Ben-Hassrath reeducators, asking that he be repaired or destroyed as best served the Qun.

The Iron Bull

The Qunari are loath to destroy their tools. Hissrad's mind remained sharp—too sharp, in fact, for the treacherous island of Seheron, where it could so easily shatter. He would be dangerous as a police agent, defiant as a soldier, and wasted as a laborer.

But the Ben-Hassrath knew that outside Qunari borders, Tal-Vashoth mercenaries were seen as impressive fighters, prized for their terrible strength. Hissrad could live a simple life as a Tal-Vashoth mercenary, using his own brutish appearance as the perfect disguise to hide his nature as a Ben-Hassrath spy. Knowing his dislike for hurting those he considered civilians, the Ben-Hassrath installed him in a role that was purely observational, sending reports on anything he deemed worth noting for his superiors.

GATT ON HISSRAD

His state of mind? Am I supposed to say that he wasn't angry? Is that what I'm supposed to say so the reeducators can fill him full of qamek and send him off to break rocks with a hammer for the rest of his life? Because he was angry. Of course he was angry, after what the Tal-Vashoth did to those children. He's always been angry.

I remember the day he raided my master's ship and rescued me from that bastard. He butchered them all, and he wasn't calm as he did it. I'd have been terrified if he was. No, he fought with a righteous fury. He was every ounce of anger I'd been pushing down in my fear. He was rage, and I would have had it no other way.

He was angry when I finished my education and joined his team in Seheron. He'd smile when he greeted the locals, and he'd banter about the food at breakfast, but underneath it all, there was always the anger. How could he be anything else, after watching his friends die from poison or a knife in the back?

Did you know his last commander became Tal-Vashoth? Of course you do. You've got records on everything, including the attitude I'm displaying right now that will doubtless come up as an area for improvement. Your people will tell me, and I'll sigh, and I'll take it, because I've seen the world outside the Qun, and while I might bang against the walls of this life, I'd rather be here than anywhere else.

So would Hissrad. The difference between him and me is that he's never known anything else. He grew up in this orderly world you all made, and it all makes sense to him, people make sense, and he thinks that if he does the right thing, then everything will work. He's been in Seheron for ten years trying to make everything work, telling himself that he's the tool you made him to be, doing the job he was meant to do. He hunted down and killed his old commander. He killed civilians working for the rebels. There are times I'm grateful for those Tevinter mages coming in to attack. At least Hissrad doesn't have to argue with himself after he kills them.

Now he killed the Tal-Vashoth who killed those children, and he broke himself doing it. He thinks it's his fault, that he failed to live up to the demands of the Qun. But we all know that isn't really true, is it? Seheron was a mess. We and Tevinter made certain of that. We grind ourselves down until we end up dead or turning Tal-Vashoth, and Hissrad would rather die than do that.

He's a good man. He believes in you. You owe him better than what you've done to him.

—Post-mission deposition from team member Gatt on mental state of his commander, Hissrad

The first real choice he made in his life was what to call himself. After a little thought, the Iron Bull was born.

The Iron Bull fought with the Fisher's Bleeders mercenary company for several years. While his fighting power made him a highly valued asset, Fisher was heard to remark on more than one occasion that "the oxman" was too quick to offer suggestions. As Fisher grew frustrated with what he saw as the Iron Bull's disrespectful attitude, the Iron Bull grew equally tired of serving a commander with scant combat experience and mediocre tactical skills. When he finally left the company, he offered to take anyone who was interested along with him, a severe breach of professional etiquette that had Fisher leaping at Bull with sword drawn. Once Fisher's sword had been shattered on a nearby rock and Fisher himself lifted by the throat, the captain was far more amenable to the departure.

The Iron Bull expanded his mercenary company slowly but steadily over the next few months, recruiting those who were themselves outcasts from normal Orlesian or Nevarran society. The Bull's Chargers quickly gained a reputation for taking bizarre or seemingly impossible jobs and carrying them out with ingenuity and grit. The Iron Bull's success gained him entry into the parlors of Orlesian nobles who happily gossiped in front of him, never suspecting that the great brute of a mercenary was smiling over his flagon, listening to every veiled innuendo, and passing notes to his superiors in Par Vollen.

As for the Iron Bull himself, he now enjoys food, drink, and all of life's earthly pleasures more than he had expected. Telling himself it is for his role as a Tal-Vashoth, he has let most of his self-imposed restrictions slip. Still, the notion of becoming fully Tal-Vashoth brings back immediate memories of those savage monsters in the jungles of Seheron and the children they had killed. He insists upon referring to himself as Qunari, a distinction that few in Orlais understand enough to make a point of, and he reports to the Ben-Hassrath with perfect devotion. The letters he sends are his lifeline, the single remaining point of discipline holding back the savagery he hunted for more than a decade until the day he saw it in himself.

COLE

Some whisper that a strange, roguish spirit in the form of a boy was among the Inquisitor's most trusted companions. This is only a rumor, however. There is little tangible evidence to prove even his existence, and most witnesses either are dead or offer up little more than "I don't remember him." What can be pieced together points to a figure known as Cole, who first made himself noticed in the White Spire of Val Royeaux.

The Ghost of the Spire

It was a rumor for years: a ghost stalked the halls of the White Spire, killing mages. At first, enchanters filed complaints with Knight-Commander Laroche, arguing that templars must have killed the mages and spread the rumor to cover up the unjustified deaths. A thorough investigation turned up nothing, however, and the templars seemed as concerned about the deaths as the mages were. Eventually, Laroche declared that as most of the deaths were of less gifted mages or apprentices about to undertake their Harrowings, they were obviously suicides born of fear. The explanation pleased no one, and after Knight-Captain Evangeline reported Laroche's handling of the matter, the unpopular commander retired and was replaced by Knight-Commander Eron. Still, the deaths continued.

While most mages feared whatever was killing their members, some found it exciting. Someone or something that frustrated even the templars' attempts to find it proved that

Few recall even a passing glimpse of the boy known as Cole.

the templars were not the all-powerful group they seemed to be, and the murders caused tensions between mages and templars that rebellious mages could exploit. If most of the victims were mages who might have failed their Harrowing or been made Tranquil, then perhaps the killer was making a statement against the Circle. A quick death might be preferable to possession in the Harrowing or the horror of being made Tranquil.

As the deaths continued, weeks or even months apart, tensions between the mages and the templars grew even worse. Some argued that the Ghost of the Spire was in fact a vengeful templar, while others said it must be a mage using blood magic. Some called it a demon.

After the fall of Kirkwall, Lord Seeker Lambert came to the White Spire, replacing Knight-Commander Eron and pledging to uncover the cause of the deaths. Though initially the mages refused to cooperate with the investigation, the senior enchanter Rhys eventually admitted that a young man calling himself "Cole" was responsible. Cole, the Ghost of the Spire, possessed the ability to make others ignore and forget him, and he had used this power to kill mages in a mistaken belief that doing so kept him alive.

When the mages of the White Spire erupted in rebellion against the templars, Lord Seeker Lambert found and confronted Cole. Using the Litany of Adralla, Lambert negated Cole's ability to remain hidden. Since the Litany of Adralla

LUCIUS'S CHANGE OF HEART

For months, we were all so certain Lord Seeker Lambert's death was an assassination carried out by mages. He had, after all, declared the Nevarran Accord null and void, hurtling us headlong into a war against the rebels. Why else would he be killed, except as an act of retribution? The entire Templar Order was fired up, ready to take up the fight against the mages . . . something we were sure would be over in a matter of weeks. Thus, the election of Lucius Corin to the role made me despair. According to the few Seekers of Truth with whom I spoke, he was a moderate. He agreed to the Divine's Conclave, and every templar I knew felt certain he would compromise to see the war ended.

But lately . . . the man seems different, does he not? I never met him before he assumed command, but even in this short time, his opinions on the war have turned. He did not go to the Conclave he personally supported. In fact, he seems to regret supporting it at all. He talks of the templars establishing themselves as a power in our own right, and our fellows are all too eager to listen. I don't know from where this change of heart came, but I begin to wonder if Lambert's death wasn't as simple a matter as we assumed. Something is amiss within our Order, and all I know is that it's beyond me to discover what.

—From a letter written by an unknown templar, found in a burned-out fort, 9:41 Dragon

Cole was known as the Ghost of the Spire and is believed responsible for numerous murders.

only protected against demonic influence, Cole was revealed as a demon. It fled as the White Spire fell to chaos; its current whereabouts are unknown.

Lord Seeker Lambert ordered an investigation of this demon that appeared human. If it had possessed a mage, then the human Cole must have come from somewhere. Lambert died shortly thereafter, likely killed by an assassin sent by mages—but the investigation he ordered continued.

The Mage

Transportation records of mages brought to the White Spire from other areas showed a mage named Cole arriving not long before the murders began. Strangely, however, records at the White Spire showed no such arrival. Had Lambert not ordered the investigation, the discrepancy would never have been noticed, but the records at the White Spire had clearly been altered to remove all references to Cole.

Former Knight-Commander Laroche was questioned. After initially denying any involvement, Laroche admitted that records at the White Spire had been falsified. Templars had arrested a young mage named Cole after the deaths of most of his family, with magic obviously in evidence. As is standard in situations where the young mage has deliberately caused injury or death to others, Cole was imprisoned for the safety of templars and fellow mages alike. Normally this imprisonment is followed by an inquiry, after which the mage is either killed, made Tranquil, or released to begin training under supervision, depending on the judgment of the investigating templars.

In this case, the inquiry never came. A new templar, unfamiliar with the regulations, filled out the paperwork incorrectly, listing Cole as a prisoner being held for crimes rather than a new mage being investigated. He was housed in the most remote section of the dungeons and was never fed or checked upon. Because no inquiry had been started, all contact with the prisoner was restricted. In the darkest depths of the White Spire, his cries ignored, Cole starved to death, alone. The templar recruit responsible for misfiling the papers was, according to Laroche, racked with guilt as a result of his mistake. Since punishment would not bring Cole back to life, and since the young mage was, as Laroche put it, "a possessed abomination waiting to happen," it was determined that the templars of the White Spire would erase all records of Cole. It was deemed an unfortunate clerical error that changed the shape, but not the nature, of the young mage's fate. The templar recruit in question disappeared in the rebellion at the Spire. Whether he was lost among the other deaths or deserted his post remains unclear.

A continued investigation of the circumstances surrounding Cole's life revealed much that would have played in the young mage's favor, had a formal inquiry ever taken place. Neighbors described the father as abusive toward the entire family, and evidence at the house suggested that the young Cole may have been defending himself. It was unclear how Cole's sister and mother died, but the father may have been responsible in either or both cases. Magic, at least, was not a factor in their deaths.

Cole's status as a victim sheds an interesting light on the situation. The murders committed by the Ghost of the Spire of mages who were afraid—of being made Tranquil, going through the Harrowing, or being killed by templars—thus do not appear to be acts of aggression, but misguided acts of mercy.

The Veil is thin at the Spire, and an untrained mage could easily attract the attention of any number of spirits. I say* spirit *rather than* demon *because the templars would surely have called out the mage being possessed if a demon had taken his body. It is more likely that some benign spirit—perhaps a spirit of faith or compassion—came to comfort the young mage in his final moments.

The boy Cole's death was horrible. Upon seeing such a wretched fate befall him, any man of good conscience would be gravely affected. And spirits, being creatures of emotion and thought, are more sensitive than we understand. What might trouble us could drive one of them to madness. Perhaps such a spirit sought to ease the pain of others, by ending their lives. If it called itself Cole, it might even have forgotten what it truly was. Such a thing is unlikely, but no more so than any other explanation for what has occurred.

Until we find this spirit, this Cole, and learn the truth of the matter, it will remain one of countless tragic mysteries.

—Enchanter Mirdromel, author of *Beyond the Veil: Spirits and Demons*

ENEMIES OF THE INQUISITION

The ancient darkspawn Corypheus wielded power in numbers few generals could ever claim. He inspired an army of Tevinter extremists called Venatori and gathered minions from among dissident templars, imbued with red lyrium through unspeakable means to terrorize southern Thedas. His reach extended from the wind-torn Western Approach to the deepest tangles of the Arbor Wilds. At the Warden fortress Adamant, he plotted to raise legions of demons from the Fade. Even the halls of Orlesian authority were not immune to his corruption.

Corypheus wielded impossible power when he ripped open the Veil between reality and the Fade.

CORYPHEUS

There are essential truths that weren't always true. The Chantry teaches that the city at the heart of the Fade is black, but was once golden. Because of this, there are now Blights, and the children of these Blights, the darkspawn, corrupt Old Gods into Archdemons. There are many who believe the monster called Corypheus was among seven magisters who knocked on the door of the Maker, corrupting the city and cursing all Thedas.

Much has been said about the sins of ancient Tevinter, the darkspawn, and Blights. This text is concerned more specifically with Corypheus, his crimes, and whether he remains a threat. Indeed, if Corypheus was one of the seven responsible for offending the Maker and unleashing the Blights, and if he possessed the will to attempt such an act again when he tore open the Breach, it is essential that Thedas know beyond knowing that his life has finally ended.

If records of lineage are to be believed, before he was Corypheus, he was Sethius of House Amladaris. This magister of Tevinter was reportedly an obsessive believer in Dumat—a fact safe to assume given the passion with which the ancient Tevinters dedicated themselves to their Old Gods. The whispers of these gods were likely heard by Sethius and the others; it is only the nature of the whispers that is generally disputed. Many Chantry scholars believe their origins to be demonic, as they could not be divine.

Sethius, we know, was a mortal man—perhaps an utterly typical one, with typical, if ambitious, failings. House Amladaris was mediocre and remains thus. Any connection to recent events likely did the family more harm than good, for Tevinter remains a nation that believes, by and large, in the teachings of the Chantry. Following the closure of the Breach, House Amladaris publicly distanced itself from Corypheus, as it has since the conversion of Hessarian. It would take a far more influential family to make an ancestor like him palatable even to the citizens of the Imperium.

Sethius of House Amladaris was middling and wanted more. And like many who are weak at heart, he likely did not consider that it was his own nature that determined his place. He believed the whispers of demons, and he and six others breached the heavens to worship their false gods in person. Instead they found the rebuke of the truth. And in his punishment, Sethius became corrupted, became Corypheus. Instead of humbling him, this inflated his stature and sense of perceived destiny.

We are told that after his original fall in -395 Ancient, there was a dormancy of some kind. Perhaps it was not unlike the slumber of the Old Gods. When he awoke again in -191 Ancient, is clear that Corypheus was understood as dangerous. The Grey Wardens caged him instead of risking a failed attempt at killing him—and well they did, for in the mishap with the Champion and in the preliminary battles with the Inquisitor, Corypheus maintained a tenacious hold on life. So how is it

Only a handful of people have ever physically set foot in the Fade. Most visit in dreams.

possible for a seemingly immortal darkspawn magister to truly be dead?

Corypheus wanted to traverse the Fade. The Inquisitor damned him to such, but not as Corypheus intended. Archdemons are reborn if killed by someone other than a Grey Warden, their essences leaping to a nearby darkspawn. It is the presence of the Grey Warden that prevents this, their body trapping the soul of the beast, killing them both. Corypheus was observed to have perverted this somehow and avoided death on at least two occasions. However, his power over death was undone with a tether to an immense source of life: the dragon he corrupted. It is possible Corypheus sought to replicate the process that is inflicted upon the slumbering Old Gods, imagining himself in command of his own Archdemon. In doing so, he turned his own nature against himself. It was monstrous and initially effective, but ultimately futile when countered by the effort and guile of the Inquisitor.

Secondly, it can be inferred that Corypheus intended the mark and the orb to be his means of traversing the Fade to the Black City. The fact that the Black City is, indeed, black suggests that Corypheus did know how to do this. For how could he have fouled it if he had not first succeeded in reaching it? Either by providence or the will of Andraste, the Inquisitor suffered the mark instead of Corypheus and put it to uses that saved rather than severed. And in their final accounting, the Inquisitor turned this power on its master and shattered the elven orb. Thus Corypheus lacked this means of assistance for his journey.

Finally, the Fade is a place of dream and whim, the very landscape altered with imaginings. The study of magic has shown that to exist there for any length of time, one must be as certain as the Maker's first children, the spirits and demons of aspects shaped by our wants. The lesson Corypheus learned from his first attempt at breaching the Fade was not that it was wrong to dare, but that he had not dared enough. This despite the cost paid by all the world and, given his scarring, what Corypheus had personally suffered. Truly this was a creature of absolute certainty, or absolute denial—and both born of pure arrogance.

Had Corypheus reached the Fade with his dragon, the mark, and the orb, it is entirely possible that he would have had the strength of will to maintain himself and journey to the Black City to once again offend the will of the Maker. But he did not, because the Inquisitor, above all else, broke this

"Elder One" of his own delusions. What we witnessed when Corypheus disappeared was not the swagger of a conqueror, but the stumbling of a broken authority. In his first ascent, Corypheus was cast down by the Maker, perhaps, in his mind, making him worthy of such. In this second attempt, it was a mortal, the Inquisitor. Corypheus knew not the absolute certainty of arrogance; he was broken and surely knew doubt.

And it has been written that nothing that knows doubt can survive in the Fade.

I was wrong. We cannot control the creature Corypheus. Even our most powerful mages hold no influence with him. In truth, it is they who have been most vulnerable.

A dozen times, those assigned to guard or study the creature have sought the key to free him. When they are removed to a safe distance, they remember little. They speak of a voice in their minds, a calling like that of the Old Gods, but it wanes outside Corypheus's presence.

Darkspawn have attacked as well, seeking him. I can only assume they are summoned the same way. Somehow, his magic lets him speak through the blight itself, affecting any who bear its taint.

This same power stays the hand of any Warden who approaches to kill him. I must recommend that we seal this prison over and conceal its very existence. Corypheus must not be allowed to go free.

—Notes from Warden-Commander Daneken, 1014 TE

Strengthened immeasurably by red lyrium, the former templar Samson acted as general to Corypheus, commanding the red templars.

Since the Breach, countless rifts have been examined, and the Fade searched by armies of mages in their dreams. All confirm that in his profound absence, Corypheus is no longer a threat. He is dead, or what passes for dead when a physical being is consumed by the Fade. In the words of the new head of the Chantry: "May his blighted soul find only oblivion, far from the sight of the divine."

SAMSON

Much about the past of Samson, the notorious general of Corypheus, can be explained by two letters. The first was addressed to his commanding officer just before his dismissal, written by Knight-Commander Meredith of Kirkwall:

"You call it a lapse in judgment, Knight-Captain?" she wrote in reprimand. "You ask what harm Samson did, by passing on a letter from a mage to that mage's lover? Do not honey this rebellion. It is the harm he *could have done* you will concern yourself with. The softhearted are all too easy for the maleficarum to manipulate. The rising number of apostates and blood mages in Kirkwall should be proof enough we have grown lax policing our own as well as the Circles. There will be no appeal. Raleigh Samson is no longer a knight of the Templar Order."

The second letter, dated six months after Samson was dismissed from the templars, is unsigned:

"You say the pain and the craving for lyrium takes you harder than most. It may be true—some grow more reliant on it than others—but I *cannot* share my supplies. There are rumors you've become friendly with mages since you were thrown out of the

Order. If I were discovered handing you even a single drop of lyrium, Meredith would have our heads on display at the Gallows. Take this coin and buy passage out of here. Kirkwall is no place for a templar without a Chantry. Or anyone else, these days."

Samson remained in the city of Kirkwall. A once-proud knight of good martial prowess was reduced to a guttersnipe scrounging for gold to purchase smuggled lyrium. One can imagine the resentment: templars who retire honorably are given a small stipend of lyrium to stave off the hunger. Being cut off all at once is said to be agony. No matter what transpired afterward, the bitterness of the abandonment left a lasting mark on Samson's heart.

It has been asked what potential Corypheus could have possibly seen in this man. One of Samson's virtues was a resistance to the effects of red lyrium. Its potency was far greater than the Chantry's lyrium, but somehow Samson did not suffer the grotesque transformations and madness it caused in his brethren. Perhaps the same quirk of character that rendered him overly dependent on lyrium, even for an addict, also offered protection from its horrors. There was more to his appointment as leader of the red templars than his resistance, however. When Corypheus elevated him to the rank of general, Samson surprised many who'd known him in the past by transforming into a capable leader. What scattered accounts remain paint him as not only grateful to Corypheus, but a genuine soldier of his cause. Despite Samson's low origins, Corypheus treated the man with a respect the former templar had not felt in ages. Perhaps he saw something of his self-righteous monomania reflected in the tight anger that fueled his general: Samson resented what he saw as injustices and injuries heaped upon his fellow templars by the Chantry even more than his own exile.

"I'm not the first man they threw away because of a second's pity, and you won't be the last," Samson wrote to a former knight-templar, exiled for questioning the then-current Lord Seeker. "How many more of us will the Chantry break in the name of a duty most knights no longer believe in? The templars aren't protecting common folk or mages. They're whips for the Chantry's damn pissing matches. The man I serve now can change that. Bring anyone you trust who feels the Order has wronged them, and I'll show you a way to right it all."

We see the cautionary tale take shape before our eyes. The deaths caused by the red templars are well documented and need no elaboration here, yet they were born of a man who truly thought he could free his brothers and sisters from a life of misguided servitude. This does not offer an excuse, only a somber reminder of how cruelty is cast and returned to us, again and again, in different forms.

CALPERNIA

The cult of the Venatori caused no small alarm in the Tevinter Imperium. The Archon himself publicly denounced them, as did any magister who realized the cult's devotion to the "Elder One" ran too deeply to serve their own agendas. What truly outraged the mage-lords, once it came to light, was that the Venatori's leader was once a slave of Tevinter.

The Tevinter mage Calpernia led the Venatori cult that heralded Corypheus as a god.

In the ashes of Haven, the Inquisitor first met Corypheus face-to-face.

We know for certain "Calpernia" was a name she chose for herself. Any early records of her are lost, if they ever existed. Who would note the name of a single child sold among a hundred weeping souls? Even chained to a life of drudgery, Calpernia showed potential, teaching herself to read from the books in her master's library and soaking in the Imperium's history. Her owner, Erasthenes, was a mage and a scholar of the Old Gods, largely indifferent to his slaves as he remained immersed in his studies. He paid dearly for this detachment when Calpernia manifested a talent for magic, an event not even the most oblivious of mages can afford to ignore.

Erasthenes reluctantly put aside his learning long enough to teach Calpernia how to control her newfound powers, then promptly returned to his tomes. Calpernia chafed at the lack of guidance. Her reading had given her an appreciation for Tevinter's past triumphs and a burning frustration with the ruling nobility's indifference to their homeland's slow decay. Her raw power equaled her ambition, for Corypheus himself came one night to Erasthenes's door to offer her an apprenticeship. She accepted with pride. Erasthenes was never seen in Tevinter again.

By all accounts, some written in her own hand, Calpernia flourished under her new mentor. Corypheus promised he would return the Imperium to a time of miracles and glory. Calpernia, loyal and already powerful beyond her years, was given the task of shaping his disciples into an army of mages and scholars who would become priests of a new god. She saw these Venatori as the key to saving Tevinter, a group dedicated to forging a great future for the Imperium and humanity as a whole.

The obvious irony, that Tevinter's greatest proponent among the Venatori was originally condemned to slave under it, was not a topic of amusement to Calpernia. Her dreams of revitalizing Tevinter included uplifting the enslaved as true citizens of the Imperium. Calpernia believed in the worth of the people unseen by the powerful, and well-remembered her own longing for dignity. She purchased and freed many slaves with her new position, cannily creating a network of spies loyal to her and her alone in the process. While it caused some friction among her fellow mages, it was tolerated by the Elder One, who seemed pleased with his student's progress.

It is a testament to Calpernia's strength of vision that she remained the Venatori's leader, largely unquestioned and second only to Corypheus, until the end. She had "a will of steel," as one letter from a magister describes her, "and the power to wield it." What happened to her is sadly a mystery. Corypheus returned from the Wilds with his army broken. Calpernia did not return at all. Did that blazing power and spirit of steel outlive a second master, or does she lie silent in the shadows of the Temple of Mythal? The last of the Venatori are scattered to the winds, and those few who can be found either do not know or are intent on preserving their former leader's secrets.

GEREON & FELIX ALEXIUS

The Circle of Minrathous is one of the oldest buildings in the Imperium. Once the temple of Razikale, the Dragon of Mystery, now it is an edifice of magical education. And true to its roots, the Minrathous Circle has a reputation for esoteric magical research.

Long before he took his place in the Magisterium, Lord Gereon of House Alexius made a name for himself in the halls of the Circle as a researcher. He investigated the limits of the known magical laws, pushing the boundaries of what ordinary magic could accomplish in traveling through and controlling both time and physical space. His partner for much of his academic career was Lady Livia of House Arida, a specialist in studies of the Veil. Together, the two made great strides in cataloging the limits of magic.

Although House Alexius supported Gereon's academic pursuits, they wished him to focus less on the theoretical and more on magic with practical uses. In the interest of spurring him to political pursuits, his father ceded him the family seat in the Magisterium. This did not have quite the effect they anticipated. Magister Alexius became a tireless champion of education, criticizing his peers for pouring the Imperium's funds into the war against the Qunari at the expense of the Circles and demanding better schooling and institutions of higher learning for the Soporati.

At the same time, he continued his research, albeit in a diminished capacity, as he divided his time more and more between his various responsibilities. He married his longtime sweetheart and fellow researcher, Livia, and took a position as a professor of thaumaturgy at the Minrathous Circle.

Their only son, Felix, was born a few years later, and while the child displayed a little magical ability, it quickly became clear that Felix Alexius would never be much of a mage. Even with all his parents' tutoring, he could cast simple spells only with immense effort. Gereon's father, concerned that his future heir was, he said, "just barely more than a Soporati," tried to have his own grandson assassinated. His gambit was effortlessly countered by Lady Livia, who then had her father-in-law killed, making Gereon head of House Alexius and safeguarding her son.

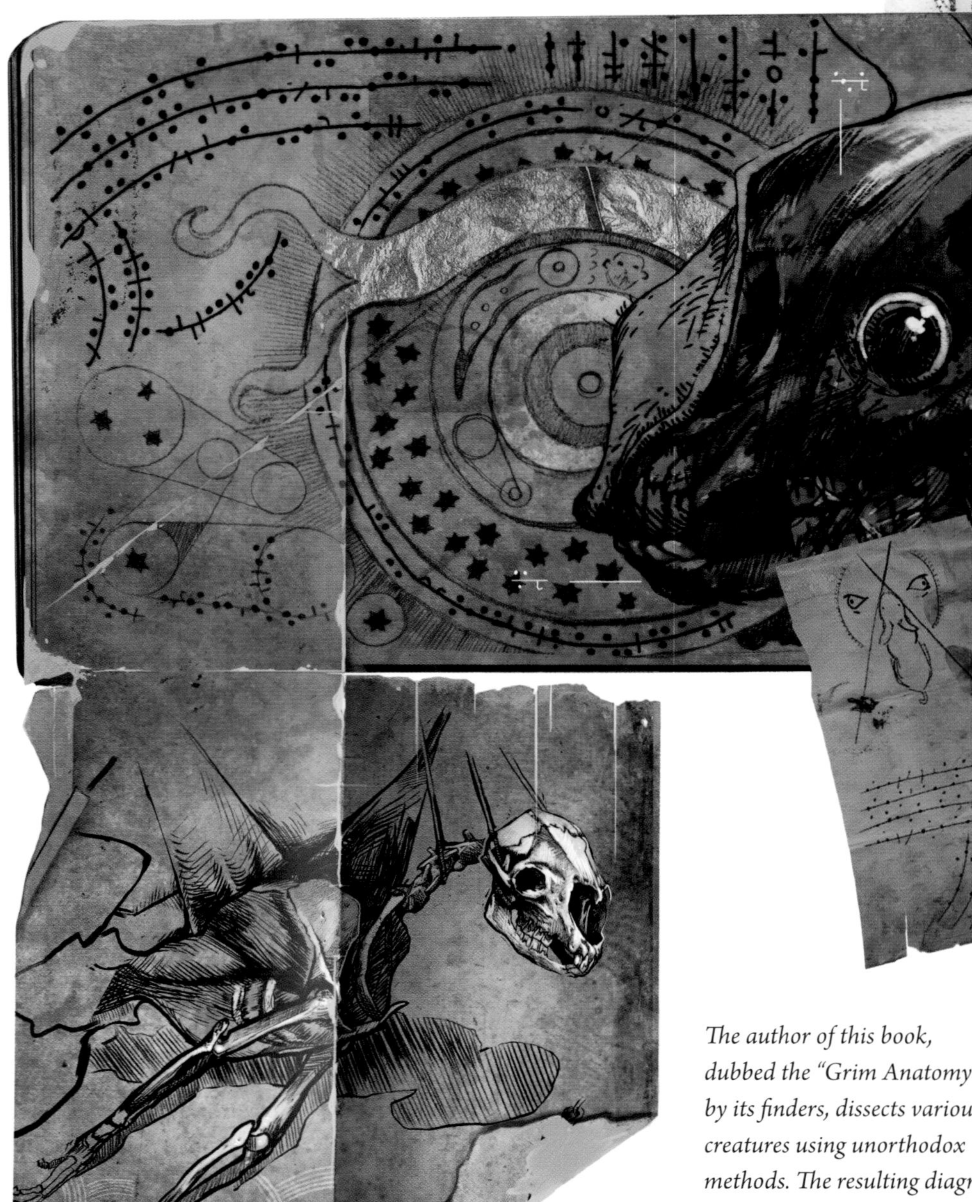

The author of this book, dubbed the "Grim Anatomy" by its finders, dissects various creatures using unorthodox methods. The resulting diagrams illustrate in great detail how nugs, giants, wyverns, and others look on the inside.

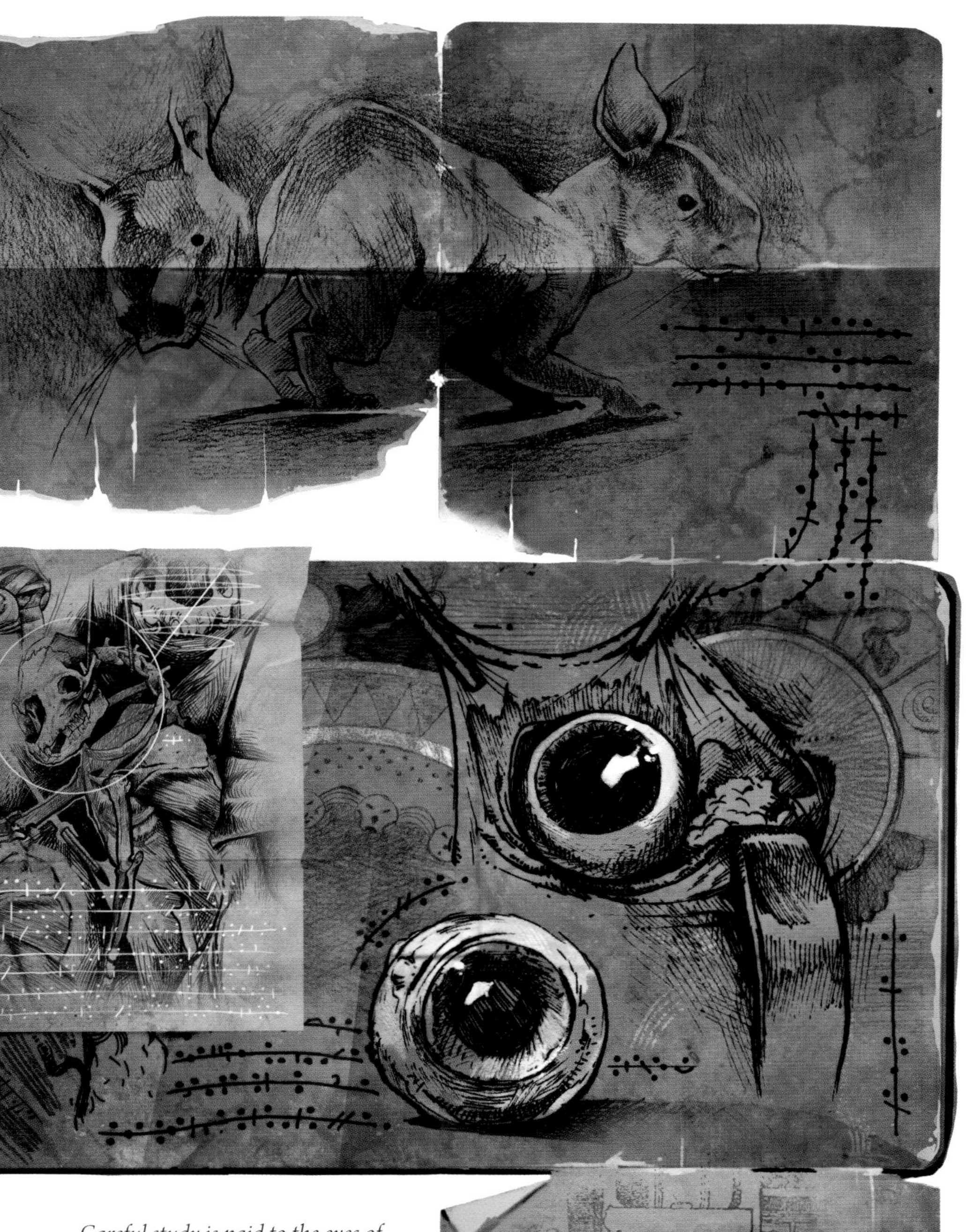

Careful study is paid to the eyes of the nug. Based on the drawings and a limited deciphering of the text, the author seems all but obsessed with understanding what animals see and how this might differ from our own perception of reality.

Gereon doted on his son. Since Felix could not learn much in the way of spells, Gereon brought in tutors to teach him history, art, music, literature—anything that the boy could study was offered to him on a silver platter. When Felix's interests and talents turned out to be mathematical, his proud parents sent him to the University of Orlais to work with the best mathematicians in Thedas.

Since their son could not be part of their research, Alexius and Livia brought in apprentices. Livia took half a dozen of the most promising young scholars of the Fade and the Veil from across Tevinter under her wing, but Gereon chose only one: an exceptionally gifted student of thaumaturgy from the Minrathous Circle by the name of Dorian Pavus.

For the next few years, Alexius and Dorian worked on breaking the boundaries of magic itself, while his wife and her team of apprentices sought to determine the effects of such magic on the Veil. Some of Gereon's rivals in the Magisterium whispered that they might be close to a breakthrough. Then tragedy struck.

In 9:38 Dragon, Gereon and Livia traveled to Val Royeaux to visit their son at his university and return with him to Minrathous for the winter holidays, as they had for many years. While crossing through southern Tevinter, their party was set upon by hurlocks. The creatures were driven off, but Livia was killed and Felix badly injured in the attack. The horrified magister returned to the capital, bearing his gravely wounded child, and from that point onward seemed to care for little else besides his son's health. All the work he and his wife had done for more than two decades was left to gather dust. Livia's apprentices went their separate ways, and while Dorian attempted to keep up research with his mentor, he found Gereon increasingly distant and strange.

NOTES ON THE INQUISITION

CLAREL

Arl Teagan Guerrin,

I sought a chance to speak with you in person, my lord, in hopes of convincing you to allow us to send further aid to Ferelden, to give the Grey Wardens in your homeland a chance to rebuild. I hope this letter succeeds where my requests for a meeting have not.

I understand Fereldan feelings regarding Grey Wardens. Sophia Dryden's actions were reprehensible. Grey Wardens are forbidden from interfering in the affairs of nations, save when we must exert our authority to battle the Blight. Still, even you must acknowledge the vital necessity of my Order after the Blight nearly ravaged your homeland. Without the Grey Wardens, Ferelden would be a wasteland populated only by darkspawn.

I understand as well your concern that I am a mage living outside the confines of the Circle. I have been informed that you saw magic ill used by apostates at Redcliffe. You have my sympathy in this, but not my apology. The Maker saw fit to give me the gift of magic, along with a temperament better suited to battle than to quiet meditation. I left the Circle legally, and the Grey Wardens gave me a chance to use my abilities to defend our land. I am no apostate.

My first interest, Arl Teagan—indeed, my only *interest—is to see this world protected from the Blight. I may be Warden-Commander of Orlais, but I am not Orlesian at heart. I am a Grey Warden and nothing more, and I will defend this land from horrors you cannot even imagine. My oath comes before political ambition, before concerns about the rights of mages. It will one day come before my own survival.*

I hope to hear from you soon.

Yours,
Warden-Commander Clarel de Chanson

ERIMOND

The firstborn son of a magister, Livius Erimond enjoyed every advantage that upper-class Tevinter society could offer. He received instruction from the finest tutors and, thanks to the leniency of his parents, was able to pursue personal whims with little oversight. While his father held a hereditary seat in the Magisterium, thus ensuring Erimond's future station, his parents nevertheless made certain their son forged useful connections among the Tevinter elite. His attendance at parties was required, and he often accompanied his father on official business. While not especially charismatic, Erimond proved adept at pinpointing those with the most power. Rather than endear himself to an entire room, he devoted his attention to those most likely to assist his own goals.

Few in the Magisterium were surprised when Erimond's father retired early, granting his seat to his more politically ambitious son. While nationalistic pride is considered common among magisters, Erimond outstripped many of his peers in that regard. It's believed that his zeal eventually drew the attention of well-placed members of the growing Venatori cult and they made contact. It was around this time that some magisters commented on Erimond's tendency to speak of his position as a stepping-stone rather than the pinnacle of his career, though this was largely dismissed as a quirk of character, albeit an irritating one. His attendance in the Magisterium dropped as he began attending meetings that were, he said, of great importance to the glory of Tevinter.

Despite belief to the contrary, not every member of the Venatori was a mage. Many Tevinter warriors and rogues fought among their ranks.

He eventually left to pursue urgent matters in the South, providing no elaboration on what that entailed—though it is now known he did so in service to Corypheus and his plot to convince Warden-Commander Clarel to raise a demon army. The Inquisition saw that this did not happen, and Erimond's fate was left to the Inquisitor's will.

How can you look upon Minrathous, or Marnas Pell, or Vyrantium with satisfaction? Unless you lack vision. They reflect only past greatness. I see the future my master will bring, and soon the world will as well.

—Excerpt from a letter written by Magister Livius Erimond of Vyrantium, confiscated by the Inquisition on Sister Leliana's order

ABELAS

After the Inquisitor returned from the Battle of the Arbor Wilds, stories about a set of elven ruins circulated among scholars with connections to the Inquisition. The strangest referred to "Sentinels," elves protecting a temple city hidden deep within the Wilds. We know that during the last days of the battle, these Sentinel elves emerged from the forest, striking down soldiers on both sides. Curiously, when the Inquisitor encountered the leader of these Sentinels, the elf did not attack but stopped to speak. Perhaps the fame of the Herald of Andraste had spread even into the deepest regions of the Wilds.

This leader, Abelas, declared that he was a servant of Mythal, an old legend still popular among the Dalish. He spoke as if Mythal were a living god, not an ancient elven story, saying they were tasked with preserving her sacred ground. This, if nothing else, is proof the Inquisitor stumbled onto a delusional sect. Sketches of the Temple of Mythal have led scholars to guess its construction occurred in the ancient era. To have been given a task by anyone who lived while the temple's walls were intact would make Abelas over a thousand years old. Perhaps the stories of lost elven immortality seemed so potent, when surrounded by the relics of the elves' golden years, that this lost Sentinel cult and its leader began to believe it themselves.

While this much of the story has percolated past Skyhold's walls, the outcome of this meeting between this Abelas and the Inquisitor has not yet reached the ears of anyone outside the inner circle of the Inquisition. Some of the Sentinels' arms and armor, however, were brought back to civilization by the Inquisition's soldiers. Historians declared the craftsmanship superb but concluded that no cloth and metal, no matter the enchantments placed on them, could survive the great span of time Abelas claimed to have seen them untarnished.

Hidden deep in the Arbor Wilds is the legendary Temple of Mythal.

Corypheus commanded a corrupted dragon that many mistook for an Archdemon.

THE INQUISITION'S ALLIES

As the Inquisition gained the power and influence to confront Corypheus, countless souls flocked to its noble cause from all corners and among all peoples. They were not just fighters. They supplied mounts, gear, and even faith to the downtrodden rank and file.

INQUISITION SCOUT HARDING

Lace Harding was born in the Fereldan Hinterlands, just outside the town of Redcliffe, to a seamstress mother and a trader father. Her mother named her "Lace" with the hope that her daughter would be as pretty and delicate as a slip of the fine fabric. When Harding was a child, her father often bragged that he could trace his bloodline back to a Merchant Caste family from Orzammar, though no official reference to a merchant house carrying the name can be found.

As a young woman, Harding eschewed her mother's chosen profession and refused to stay indoors peering at needlework when she could be out and about. She volunteered to help her neighbor on her sheep farm, performing chores the elderly woman could no longer manage. While on shepherding duty, Harding spent days exploring the hills and fields of the Hinterlands. Her familiarity with the terrain would prove useful to the Inquisition when it was first establishing itself in Ferelden. Harding saw the first Inquisition scouts passing by, and she gave them directions to and information on sheltered locations where she believed rebel mages and templars could have made camp. When Harding's information proved correct, the agent called Charter invited her to join the nascent organization. Concerned about the state of Ferelden and the chaos started by the opening of the Breach, Harding signed on. Her cunning, daring, and positive outlook set her apart from other recruits, and she became indispensable to the Inquisition over the next few months.

Now, as one of the Inquisition's most experienced and trusted agents, Harding is often chosen to lead teams into unknown and dangerous territory, which she does with inimitable style.

THE BULL'S CHARGERS

The Iron Bull's mercenary company is known across Orlais, Nevarra, the Free Marches, and even Ferelden. More a task force than a private army, the company has fewer than fifty standing members, but it is nevertheless one of the most prestigious companies in all of Thedas. Over the past several years, the company has become famous for accomplishing the impossible with a creativity not usually found among sellswords.

Lieutenant Cremisius "Krem" Aclassi, second-in-command of the Chargers, credits the diversity of the group for its success. "Most companies want blades, not trouble, and anything that isn't normal is trouble," says Krem, who met the Iron Bull while fleeing the Tevinter Imperium. "The result is you get a lot of people with swords, and their solution to any problem is the swords."

By contrast, Krem notes that the Bull's Chargers include among their number dwarves, elves, and other specialists who might not have found a place in a more traditional mercenary company. "Our sapper is a dwarf from Orzammar," he says. "He can bring down a wall in ways nobody up on the surface has ever heard of. Our scouts learned from Dalish hunters how to move through the trees, and we've got warriors who've trained everywhere from Rivain to the Anderfels. And while of course it wouldn't be legal to have an apostate in the company, we know how to deal with magic when the need arises."

When asked, Krem says that he is honestly uncertain whether the Iron Bull consciously attempted to build diversity in his company. "You'd be a fool not to respect the Iron Bull as a warrior, but even so, some people wouldn't willingly work for a Qunari. Everyone in the Chargers is someone who can look at an eight-foot horned giant and say, 'Yes, I trust that man with my life.' I think sometimes that we found him more than he found us." He points out that the Chargers also have fewer deaths than any other company and credits the Iron Bull's excellent instincts and fierce loyalty to his troops for the team's success.

"The chief will turn down a bad job, no matter how well it pays," Krem says, "and every one of us knows that he cares about his people more than his purse. In fact, there are times it seems like he just does this to keep himself busy, and the coin is a happy accident."

Happy accident notwithstanding, the exotic appearance and remarkable success of the Chargers make them popular all across Orlais and Nevarra. Whatever else he may be, the Iron Bull is a successful commander who has put together a skilled and loyal team.

MOTHER GISELLE

Revered Mother Giselle is perhaps best known for her actions as revered mother of the chantry in Jader. In the years following the Fifth Blight, Jader saw an influx of Fereldan refugees fleeing either the violence of the Blight or the corruption and loss of their lands. The overpopulation and poor living conditions led to an outbreak of disease that nearly crippled the city, followed by famine in the poorer sections of Jader when it was quarantined.

Mother Giselle, whose prosperous chantry was in a wealthier quarter, wrote to Val Royeaux asking for assistance from the Chantry. When help was not immediately forthcoming, it is said that she addressed the clerics of her chantry. "As Andraste herself said, 'My faith sustains me; I shall not fear the legion,' then so shall faith sustain the hungry in this time of need," Giselle told them. "As we have devoted our lives to divine contemplation, such a diet should come to us quite easily." With that, she took the unprecedented step of taking all of her chantry's food into the poor quarters of Jader, distributing it to peasants who would otherwise have starved to death.

Tamar the Reaver was given a choice: serve the Inquisition or face execution.

Shocked and shamed by what some in Val Royeaux privately referred to as an ostentatious bullying tactic, Chantry officials coordinated relief efforts. Food arrived quickly, along with instructions on how it was to be distributed: first to the Jader chantry to end its hunger strike, then to the Orlesian peasants, then to the Fereldan refugees, and finally to the elves of the alienages. Mother Giselle famously replied to the orders by saying, "If we believe that some have fallen further from the Maker's grace than others, then those who have fallen furthest are in greatest need of our care. We cannot fill their souls until

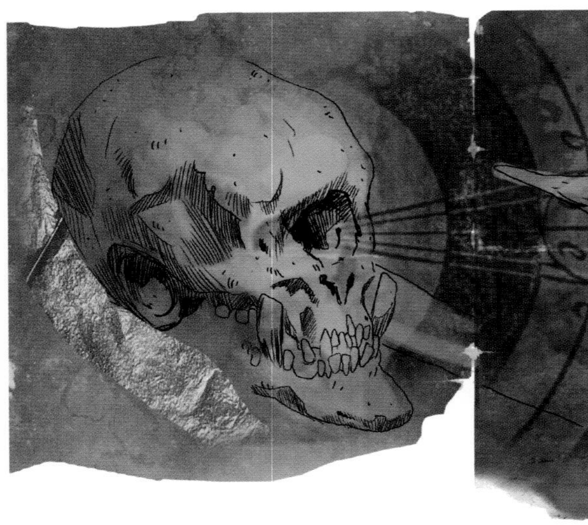

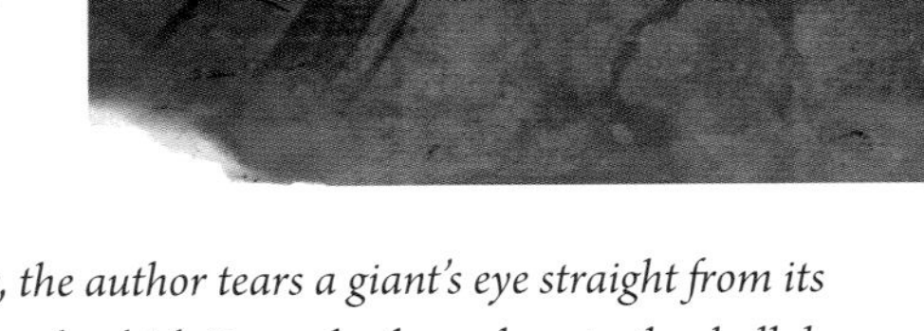

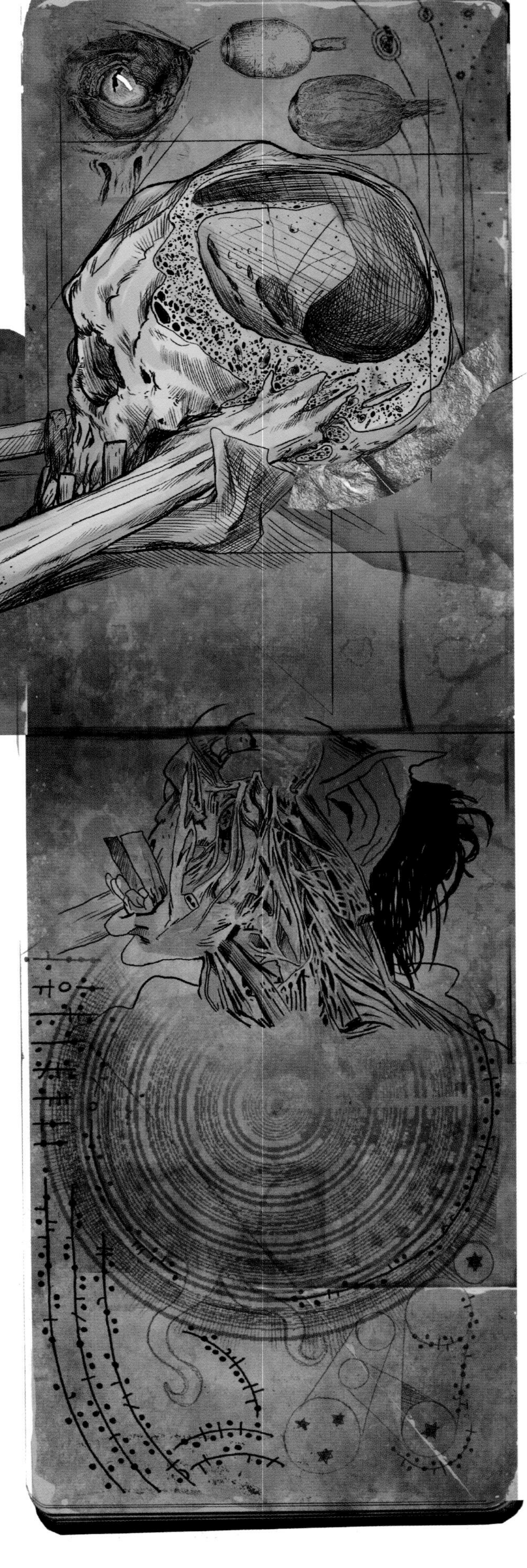

In later pages of the Grim Anatomy, the author tears a giant's eye straight from its socket. "If the eye is the window through which it crawls, then where in the skull does it hide," they wonder. "It" likely refers to a demon attempting to possess the beast.

we have filled their bellies." With the support of Lady Seryl of Jader, who was directing relief efforts of her own, Giselle ignored the directives and fed the poor of the city without regard for race or nationality.

Her actions saved thousands of lives in Jader and made her a beloved figure among the poor in Orlais and Ferelden alike. Those actions also destroyed her chances of any official political advancement in the Chantry, as the grand clerics did not look kindly on being shown up in such a manner. In the years following, Divine Justinia often deployed Giselle to troubled areas to help the poor and the sick. Her arrival was greeted as a blessing by the poor and as a portent of unwelcome charity by the rich.

BIANCA DAVRI

Half of Nevarra has heard of the Davri Mechanical Thresher. Powered by steam, the device separates grain from chaff, doing work that normally takes hundreds of laborers weeks of backbreaking effort in mere hours. The Nevarran nobility herald it

Many secrets surfaced when the long-flooded village of Crestwood was drained by the Inquisition.

as the greatest innovation of the age, but it is just the latest gift from the genius of Bianca Davri.

She made her name more than a decade ago with an improved seed drill that was capable not only of distributing seed in perfect rows at nearly any spacing, but also of adjusting to the correct depth for each seed type. Far more reliable than any other seeder, it quickly became the standard across the Free Marches, Antiva, and Nevarra, and House Davri, a previously obscure surface Smith Caste family living in Kirkwall, instantly established itself as a power within the Merchants Guild.

But the Davri Seed Drill was not self-powered. It required the locomotion of a horse or an ox to operate. Bianca's second invention, a spinning machine, was run like a grain mill by the action of moving water. With this device, a single worker could spin up to sixty spools of thread at a time, at a much finer quality than hand spinning. With the Davri Spinning Frame, demand for Bianca's designs spread to the high-priced markets of Orlais.

She spent the next several years investigating more-efficient methods of powering her machines. She experimented with a variety of water- and steam-powered engines before settling on a design that incorporated a coal furnace. She may have been inspired by its gains in efficiency over wood-burning furnaces, but it had the added effect of cementing a lasting alliance between her house and several Miner Caste families in Orzammar, who specialized in converting ordinary coal to the smokeless variety used in dwarven forges.

For her work, Bianca Davri has been nominated before the Assembly to be named Paragon. If the motion should succeed, she will be the first surface-born smith ever to become a Paragon. The vote has been put off several times, and the infighting over the decision has been vicious, even by Assembly standards.

A PLACE IN THE CHANTRY

There are some who claim men have no place in the Chantry, beyond the lowest rank of scholarly brothers and those who take their place among the templars. It is not true. This is an organization spanning seven nations, from the smallest village chantry to the Grand Cathedral in Val Royeaux. It takes more than sermons to keep it alive. There is an invisible army at work ensuring meals are delivered, repairs are made, and faithful attended to . . . and much of it is done by Chantry brothers like myself. The position of high chancellor places a man beside the Most Holy; I control who is permitted audience, handle her correspondence, deliver her word to Thedas, and serve as her advisor on matters which may be mundane but cannot be disregarded. If I have influence, let it be said it is something I use sparingly if at all. This is a task to which I devote myself with solemnity. I and my fellows bear a burden so that others are free to guide the spirits of Thedas unencumbered.

—Excerpt from a letter by High Chancellor Roderick Asignon, 9:38 Dragon

Dace, of course, would support any motion to acknowledge the so-called "surface caste," but they've made a king's ransom exporting coal and importing surface silks, so they're backing their candidate with everything their house can muster. Helmi is split. Denek holds the deshyr's seat, and he's captivated by all this inventive genius, but his mother will spit lava if the motion passes. Bemot and Meino have been working together to pressure some of the more conservative deshyrs to support Davri, but the strongest houses (Aeducan, Harrowmont, Hirol) are dragging their feet and waiting to see which side offers them more for their votes.

—Deshyr Sardirak Vollney, in a letter to Lord Vollney

The houses most stridently opposing the vote make their coin from the lyrium trade, and there has been talk that as the lyrium trade dwindles and is supplanted by trade in coal and steel, power is shifting in the Assembly. Formerly minor or lesser nobles grow prominent while ancient, powerful houses sink into obscurity, and those falling will not go quietly.

While the Orzammar Assembly debates her status as a living ancestor, Bianca pays them no mind. Her workshop in Val Royeaux expanded twice in the last year and employs almost a hundred smiths full-time. Bianca devotes most of her time to developing new designs and leaves the business of taking orders and delivering completed machines to her husband, Bogdan Vasca. House Vasca was long one of the most powerful members of the Dwarven Merchants Guild and has been the primary exporter of Orzammar-forged dwarven steel on the surface for centuries. The alliance between House Vasca and House Davri has granted considerable power to both and made them a faction within the Merchants Guild that none of the other families dare to oppose.

Everyone from soldiers to tradespeople aid the Inquisition's cause.

It's rumored that Bianca herself was less than pleased with the prospective alliance and actually left Bogdan standing at the altar while she tried to elope with another man. Both House Davri and House Vasca vehemently deny the rumors.

KNIGHT-CAPTAIN RYLEN

After the destruction of the Kirkwall chantry in 9:37 Dragon, the Starkhaven chantry launched a massive relief effort for its sister city-state. The rubble of the chantry rained down like catapult shot over much of the city, collapsing buildings, blocking streets, and injuring hundreds of people. Half of Starkhaven's initiates and affirmed and a third of their garrison of templars traveled to Kirkwall to search for survivors trapped under rubble and provide food and shelter to those left homeless by the explosion.

At the head of the relief effort was Knight-Captain Rylen. The youngest of five children of a Starkhaven stonemason, Rylen joined the Templar Order at fifteen, "to do something useful that isn't laying bricks," he said. No one in Starkhaven was surprised that he spearheaded the rescue efforts in Kirkwall. In his almost fifteen years in the Order, Rylen had acquired a reputation among his fellow officers as "the one who fixes things."

THE WARDEN STROUD

Born the younger son of a minor noble family in the Fields of Ghislain, Jean-Marc Stroud had just finished training at the Academie des Chevaliers when he received word that his family had been killed, ostensibly by bandits. In reality, they were victims of the Orlesian Great Game. Ser Jean-Marc's plan to find his family's murderers was cut short when the Grey Warden Clarel recruited Stroud on the advice of the Academie trainers, who did not wish to see a promising young chevalier throw his life away in fruitless pursuit of vengeance. Unable to refuse such a request honorably, Ser Jean-Marc joined the Wardens and left his old life behind.

Warden Stroud has served the Grey Wardens with honor for decades. He is regarded as one of the finest swordsmen in the Order, combining his study at the Academie with years of fighting darkspawn alongside dwarves in the Deep Roads. Warden-Commander Clarel has tasked him with recruiting and training new Wardens; most young Warden warriors owe their skill to Stroud's mentorship.

Stroud prefers to travel in the Free Marches rather than Orlais, knowing his family history could cause him to become caught up in the Game, leading to accusations of political interference among the Wardens. He also has no strong opinions regarding mages or templars, although he believes both groups are wrong to turn their back on the Chantry, which Stroud holds in some esteem.

—From a leaked Inquisition intelligence report

Whether it was a cracked wagon axle or a hunt for a fugitive apostate gone awry, Rylen was the Starkhaven templars' solution.

Lord Seeker Lambert's actions in 9:40 Dragon tore the Starkhaven templar garrison apart. Knight-Commander Carsten elected to leave the Chantry, but many of his senior officers did not. Those who remained were at a loss as to their place in the world: the Starkhaven Circle had been lost to a fire years earlier; the mages they guarded had long since dispersed to other city-states. The templars, under Rylen's leadership, struggled to find a new purpose for themselves. The arrival of Cullen, formerly of Kirkwall's templars, was greeted with wary optimism by his Starkhaven brothers. It took very little convincing from Cullen to bring Rylen and his loyalists onboard with the fledgling Inquisition.

SER BARRIS

The Barrises are a noble family whose distant ancestors settled in the northwest region of Ferelden, tending farms and hunting game near Lake Calenhad. There have been notable knights in their line: Kenem Barris fought in 6:50 Steel against the Avvar invasion of the Bannorn, saving the life of Teyrn Lewys Mavbrae, future king of Ferelden. Alarra Barris took up arms against Orlesian occupiers in 8:98 Blessed, forever driving them out of her family's holdings.

In the Dragon Age, the Barrises allied themselves more closely with the Chantry, giving a few scions from every generation to its barracks or its cloisters. Ser Jervin Barris sent his second-oldest son to the templars. "Delrin has the stomach for fighting, but not a love for it," he wrote to the knight-commander. "The boy is even-tempered, thinks swiftly, and shows no interest in the affairs of a bann. Train him as a knight, and he will grow into a man who does the Order credit."

The words seem prophetic. Ser Delrin was eleven when his father wrote them, and twelve the day he became an initiate in Denerim's chantry. He impressed his commanders with an early maturity, although his fellow recruits teased him mercilessly for what they considered an overly somber bearing in someone of their own rank and age. His first assignment as a knight-templar was to hunt down rumors of apostates in Dragon's Peak, south of Denerim. By the time his squadron arrived, a roiling web of alliances and intrigue had turned the straightforward mission into a chaotic brawl between a cult of blood mages, an unbound pride demon, a passing Dalish clan, a pair of Seekers, and Tal-Vashoth mercenaries enslaved by the mages' magic.

The templars' leader was slain. Impressed by Barris's cool in the heat of battle, his compatriots ceded him unofficial leadership without question. The skirmishes lasted a full three days, and the templars emerged victorious. "We have not gone unwounded," Barris wrote to his commanding officer after the fighting ended, "but the grace of the Maker lit our way. The demon has been slain, the mages are subdued, the Qunari freed, the Seekers mollified, and the Dalish returned to the woods. A bard found our camp yesterday, intent on wringing out every detail of this mess. I impressed upon him that the affairs of the Order are a serious matter. He says he only wishes to bring news back to the royal court and has given me his word he will not exaggerate his telling. In light of his oath, I have given him a brief and sober account of the events that have occurred."

Today, *Thunder upon the Mountains! The Battle for the Heart of Dragon's Peak!*, by Philliam, a Bard!, remains one of the most popular chapbooks in eastern Ferelden.

> NOTES ON THE INQUISITION
>
> ### THE INQUISITOR'S TRAINERS
>
> **Not much is known about the experts in special tactics called upon by the Inquisition to hone the Inquisitor's effectiveness in battle. They were by all accounts an eccentric bunch. The comments that follow were collected anonymously from Skyhold's custodians and kitchen staff:**
>
> *Ser: A templar, I think. Maybe not. Knows a lot about lyrium. I'm scared to go into his quarters. The cracks in the door glow at night.*
>
> *Breaker Thram: The nicest reaver. She left me gifts every time I made her bed. Little things. Earrings once. Hard to believe she could kill a mouse, let alone a dragon. But maybe that's what makes her so effective.*
>
> *Lord Chancer de Lion: A "more flies with honey" kind of guy. I wonder if he's single.*
>
> *Kihm: I'm not going anywhere near that old lunatic's room.*
>
> *Commander Helaine: The knight-enchanter has taken to friendly debates with Cullen over the proper strategic uses of magic on the battlefield.*
>
> *Heir: "Distant and cold" is an understatement. She talks in the third person. It's unsettling.*
>
> *Three-Eyes: He invited me in and told me about how the Maker is a master artificer. You can see it in our bones, he said. Still not sure where that third eye is hiding.*
>
> *Your Trainer: Her name is "Your Trainer," which is fine if that's what she is. For the rest of us, it's just confusing.*
>
> *Speaker Viuus Anaxas: Lady Cassandra has been observed visiting the necromancer on multiple occasions. She warned us not to say anything. You're not going to print this, are you?*

DENNET

The Inquisition horsemaster Dennet was born in Redcliffe, a farrier's son who cared little for iron but loved the horses his father shod. At a young age, he accompanied his father to Redcliffe's stables, where his father was to check the hooves of the arl's horses. A still-green stallion broke free from its handlers and would have trampled a serving girl had young Dennet not stepped up beside it and calmed it with a few soothing words. Upon seeing this, Redcliffe's horsemaster promptly took Dennet in as his apprentice. The boy grew up tending horses and helping children of the noble family learn to ride—including young Alistair Theirin, whom Dennet once chastised for, he said, "riding like he had a pole stuck up his shirt."

Dennet became Redcliffe's horsemaster after his predecessor died from a mysterious wasting illness that spread from a horse he was treating. It was Dennet who determined that the horse, who'd returned to the stable with cuts on its flanks and its rider missing, had wounds that were infected by the blight. His prompt action saved the other mounts and stablehands from contracting the corruption, which had been seen only sporadically in the centuries since the last darkspawn attacks. More than a decade later, this experience proved vital in saving lives when Redcliffe, already weakened by undead attacks brought on by young Connor Guerrin, was attacked by darkspawn.

After the end of the Fifth Blight, Dennet helped Arl Eamon rebuild Redcliffe, then retired to the Hinterlands with his wife, Elaina, and their daughter, Seanna. While planning to live the rest of his years in peace and quiet, he admits that the arl gifted the land in the hopes that Dennet and his hardworking family

NOTES ON THE INQUISITION

DAGNA

Josephine:

Here's a sampling of what's been said about me and my work in the past, warts and all. Let me know if you want more:

I would address the new arrival, whom I call a "researcher" because she is not—and cannot be—an apprentice. This dwarf is utterly ignorant of her limitations, both those imposed by our methods and those imposed by her nature. Need I restate that her people have no connection to the Fade and as such are incapable of directly drawing power from said? It is not a failing, for it enhances the ability to safely manipulate runes, and it should be enough. It is a boundary that needs be respected, and she most certainly does not.

I don't know what deluded patron lent their name to her or, failing that, what nefarious bargains she enacted to gain access to these halls, but I assure you that nothing good can come of this.

—Senior Enchanter Verimus, the Tine Tower

—

Her experiments are unprecedented, in the most alarming sense of the term. The very fact that she risks no demonic temptation is what makes her all the more dangerous. Her curiosity lacks the caution that all mages must employ. Look past the utility of her discoveries and know that she progresses too fast. Were she anyone else, we'd have seen a bloody end. Are we even certain she could be contained if her devices reach too far? Are templars trained in such unusual matters? I swear, when we awoke to the Breach in the sky, my first thought was, "What has she done now?"

—Pel Gaian, second apprentice to Magister Tebrin, South Post

—

For studies both exacting and exhausting, for practical advances that both protect and profit, I hereby commend you for your ability. However, and to my own dismay, I must do so without service or ceremony, in records that remain sealed among secret concerns. Yours is a skill that many of my brethren are not ready to accept because, I suspect, some parts of them remain unready to accept their own. Tradition dictates the manner in which magic must be approached. It dictates. I dislike the term, I dislike limitations, and yet I am affected by far fewer than you are yourself.

Your people are one of the pillars that make the study of magic possible. They are vital but separate. You are not separate. I delight in your exploration, for it is with an eye I cannot comprehend. I feel as though this is how the majority who never wield the Fade must at times view me. And just as they must be, I am sometimes unnerved by that which I cannot understand. But that is my failing, not yours.

These doors will never be closed to you, Arcanist.

Sorry about there being no name on that last one, but I made a promise, and that's a currency in some places. Who knew?

Anyway, I know you're nervous about what I can bring to the Inquisition. I have a chest full of the letters to and about me, and you're welcome to them if you feel the need. A lot of naysayers and gangue spitters, if you ask me. And you did, so thank you!

I heard things like this for ten years. Mages aren't used to a dwarf being at their level. That's funny, right? And that's why their moaning never got to me. There are no end of people who'll line up to say no, but I don't worry about them. As mad as some people get, it doesn't mean they don't like "me" me. It means new ideas make them uncomfortable. Everyone is like that sometimes. You just have to never give up and find the ones who are willing to help.

Just like that last letter. Because I also met some really smart forward thinkers, and they risked a lot by helping me. That shows that it doesn't matter the color of the robes; there're good people everywhere. And the ones who aren't can suck three pebbles. My father used to say that. Well, he said it once. It's still good advice, and he didn't like new ideas at all!

Anyway, I'm willing to come as soon as the deal is inked by your Inquisitor. In fact, I'd probably do it for half of what you've offered. I won't now, of course, because bartering is rude, and sometimes it just feels better to invest. And I'm ready to invest, too. To help fix the sky or even just get a closer look. Actual "hole in your boot" physical rifts? In the Fade? Ancestors, maybe I can finally see what all the fuss has been about.

Arcanist Dagna

might tame the somewhat lawless area and bring the land outside Redcliffe some much-needed stability. His strategic position proved advantageous when the Inquisition found itself in need of mounts.

THE BLACK HART

"The best spies are never seen, only inferred."

This pithy maxim, attributed to a dozen different Orlesian generals from the Glory Age, is a misunderstood ideal. The highest levels of the Game spin around manipulation of a thousand hearts, but the men and women engaged in the groundwork of spycraft must hide their true allegiances, not their physical presence. The Black Hart, for example, was a notorious master of false identities. It is unlikely she or he—accounts vary, although most agree the spy was elven—was the inventor of this colorful pseudonym. "The Black Hart" is simply the last nickname this agent accumulated when working for the coastal city of Bastion during a minor skirmish with its sister port of Salle.

The Hart infiltrated Salle many times, making notes of its defenses, its captains, its noble families. The reports were thorough and measured, with clarity born from weeks of observation. It served Bastion's nobles well. When Salle sent knights out to confront an army reported by several trusted scouts to be invading from the west, it encountered empty fields and frightened farmers. When a fleet flying Bastion's colors sailed in from the north, Salle found many of its own warships had been quietly scuttled just before dawn, taking on too much water to sail. When the city's ruler ordered the gates shut and barred, they were thrown open to Bastion's mercenary companies by guardsmen who were never seen again.

Salle's surrender was unconditional. The Black Hart—so named for the animal the cloaked spy was seen riding away from Bastion a day after the victory—took payment and vanished. There have been tenuous theories, among those select few who follow the clandestine feints in eastern Thedas, that the Black Hart has used many aliases: "Mollnir," a double agent who revealed a conspiracy against the Crown in Hercinia. "Sonner," a spy who sneaked into the heart of Markham, pilfered a general's plans, and walked out in broad daylight. The latest rumor is that the Hart, seeking steady employment, was contacted by Leliana to work for the Inquisition under the name of "Charter." If true, it is almost certain she or he has shed that nickname for another by the time of this writing.

THOM RAINIER

The inclusion of Thom Rainier here may be a shock to some. Indeed, among the editors of this volume, there was some degree of discussion over whether to consider Rainier a friend or an enemy of the Inquisition. His betrayal, though initially kept quiet by the Inquisition, nonetheless leaked out on the tongues of gossip hounds—the likely source being one or more present at the would-be execution of a subordinate convicted for crimes Rainier had committed.

The Grand Tourney

The warrior called Thom Rainier came to prominence as a combatant in the Grand Tourney of the Free Marches. To hear tales from those who were there, Rainier was a young braggart who possessed a swagger that spoke more about his true self than his words, which were consistently empty. They remember him wielding a great two-handed sword, which he swung in loose, undisciplined arcs—the chaotic strength of youth unmitigated

Dagna's skill as the Inquisition's arcanist was unmatched.

The traitorous Thom Rainier eventually confessed to his crimes.

by wisdom. "Too much sword for so small a boy" was the phrase whispered in the stands.

Rainier was enrolled in the Grand Melee, and many believed he would be roundly trounced and humiliated in the most brutal of tourney contests. Mere moments after the fight opened, however, it was evident that Rainier was not going to be easily defeated. A single warrior, alone, cannot last in a brawl of over a hundred challengers. Success came only with alliances, and it became clear that Rainier had made one. The man he paired with was Ser Geoffroy de Bordelon, a decorated chevalier who had won the melee at least twice in the last decade. Fighting back to back, the old chevalier and the young upstart presented a formidable team, Ser Geoffroy's experience in battle more than making up for Rainier's recklessness and occasional clumsy flailing. At the last, when they were the two left standing, Ser Geoffroy yielded to Rainier, thus handing him the win.

"I saw the soul of a warrior, obscured by the manners of a cretinous brute," said the chevalier days later. "I offered to teach him, to chisel away his baser nature and reveal the good within. He declined and said that he had no desire to be merely good. He wished to be great."

At the closing of the tourney, Rainier was announced champion of the Grand Melee. When receiving his prize, he was heard to declare, "My father was Thomas Rainier. Call me Thom." The nickname would endure.

The Imperial Soldier

Rainier left the Grand Tourney with a purse heavy with gold and his arrogance increased a hundredfold. Traveling through the Marches, he squandered his tourney winnings on wine, women, and a set of finely crafted armor that was stolen within a fortnight while he lay oblivious in a drunken stupor. Within a few months, Rainier was again penniless, living day to day and selling his services as a mercenary and hired sword.

Almost two years later, while Rainier was escorting a caravan to Val Royeaux, his employer suggested he enlist with the imperial army. The Orlesians, he was told, were the most powerful nation in southern Thedas and always looking for men willing to fight. The pay was good, lodgings were provided, and there would be no shortage of foes to match steel against. Seeking a change, Rainier remained in Val Royeaux after the job and signed up with the Orlesians.

Rainier's Marcher heritage was treated with disdain and some mistrust in the army, but he recounts that he cared little about the scorn of those with whom he served. "I wasn't there to make friends. Not in the beginning. I was there to learn to make my name. The first time in the tourney—I thought it was skill. It took me plenty of beatings to make me realize that it was luck. And I didn't want to rely on luck."

Years with the imperial army taught Rainier discipline and allowed him to perfect his skills. Campaigns in Perendale and the Dales gave him experience with military strategy. He exchanged his two-hander for a lighter weapon and a shield. His progression and dedication to the army contributed to his quick promotion to the rank of captain. Those who had once treated him with disdain became his subordinates. Corporal Mornay, a man who worked closely with Rainier, had this to say about him: "Even after his promotions, he never put on airs, never saw himself apart from us. He used to tell us stories of how he was. He called himself a little cocky bastard. He had an ability to look back at himself and see his faults. And to laugh at them. And to let us laugh at them. He was our captain and our friend. Some of us were more loyal to him than to our own mothers."

Rainier would eventually exploit this loyalty when he led his men to massacre Lord Vincent Callier and his family, who were close allies and supporters of the empress. Rainier led the soldiers in his command to believe that they were fulfilling their patriotic duty, when in fact he had ordered them to unknowingly perform an act of treason.

The Fugitive

Even as Rainier's troops naively celebrated the success of their campaign, an investigation was taking place, with spies and informants trying to uncover the instigator of the terrible massacre. The news of agents of the Orlesian throne closing in reached Rainier first. Realizing he would not be able to escape and that his career in the imperial army was over, he fled into hiding. With Rainier missing, the blame for the crime fell on his soldiers. Save a few lucky ones, most were arrested and sentenced to traitors' deaths. Rainier himself remained at large.

To survive, he became a mercenary, frequently traveling far out of Orlais to avoid being recognized. One day, however, while passing through the countryside near Churneau, he stopped at a tavern and encountered a Grey Warden. An entry from the Warden's journal reads as follows:

"I encountered a man today, in a roadside inn near Pimont. Worn cloak, wild hair, nursing a bottle of cheap wine. I thought he was an unfortunate of some kind, a transient perhaps, and paid little attention. But then a woman working the place began crying out, struggling with some besotted churl, and within an instant, the man was off his seat and upon that vile fool. One fool would be nothing, but the fool had friends—four, in all. One broke a stool upon the man's back, and he simply turned

The Inquisition stood against legions of demons pouring out of the Fade.

around, grabbed a broken leg, and proceeded to beat them all until at least one of them was crying to the Maker for mercy. Then, fools down and honor defended, this man calls to the woman for more wine, stepping over the groaning mess to return to his seat. No transient, this, I thought. There is something else here."

The Warden decided to recruit him, no questions asked, and Rainier saw his opportunity to start a new life. The two journeyed toward Val Chevin, the Warden mentoring his new recruit along the way. However, their journey came to an abrupt end when the two men were ambushed and overwhelmed by a band of darkspawn. The Warden suffered a mortal wound trying to protect Rainier and, despite all attempts, could not be saved. Rainier was racked with guilt after the Warden—a man far better than he—sacrificed his life to save him. To honor the Warden's memory, Rainier took up his sword in penance. The rest is an unfortunate bit of history best not repeated.

THE INQUISITION'S AGENTS

At the height of the battle between the Inquisition and the forces of Corypheus, it often felt like the Inquisitor was in a hundred places at once. But one strong leader, even one as hands-on as the Inquisitor, cannot be everywhere. The agents of the Inquisitor acted on behalf of the war council, undertaking countless dangerous missions to further the Inquisition's cause.

SER BELINDA DARROW

> *"Belinda was the first to greet me when I was recruited. She wasn't wearing her armor then, just a plain wool dress, and I thought she was a Chantry sister—perhaps a scribe or nurse, but not someone who'd pick up a sword and wade into battle. I saw a sweet, friendly young woman and underestimated her. I'm not proud. The next day destroyed my assumptions, thank the Maker. We were sent on a mission to rescue pilgrims. Seeing Belinda in full templar gear was surprising enough, but what really set me straight was watching her send an abomination flying with a blow from her shield. Of course, she turned right around once the danger was eliminated, clapped her hands, and cheered. It was the same young woman I met the day before. Still sweet, still friendly, but also so much more."* —*Hall*

The name Argent, taken by one of the Inquisition's best assassins, means "quicksilver."

Ser Belinda Darrow met Divine Justinia V in person, several weeks after Belinda was initiated into the Templar Order. Belinda recalls being struck by Justinia's grace and warmth and saw in the Divine a woman whose idealism mirrored her own. Though Belinda was devastated when her Order split from the Chantry over the mage rebellion, there was never any doubt in her mind—she would remain loyal to the Divine.

When chaos abounds and the world is threatened with complete and utter annihilation, many give in to despair. Not Belinda Darrow. Some may call her foolish, even childish, as she is well aware.

THE NOBLE SPORT OF NUG RACING

It was the jockey's fault: Paragon's Patsy does all right if she gets to do the thinking, but she was pushed too fast on the turn and took a spill on some loose shale. Didn't hurt her none—can't hurt a nug any more than you can hurt a pillow—but it cost time getting her up and along the tunnel again. By then, Chasing Topside and Moss-on-the-Barrel had pulled ahead, and it was Moss's race to win.

"How d'you get a nug to run anywhere?" some idiot surface human asked me once. "They say 'as blind as a nug' for a reason." Well, how d'you get a nug to do anything? Food, of course. The trick is the right tunnels: broad enough for 'em to pass, narrow enough for a nug to be feeling their way with their whiskers as they run, enough of a breeze to get the smell of roasted roof beetles down toward them. Then you need a nug breeder who can get 'em big enough without them just being bags of lard. Paint them up with a house emblem, starve them for a day beforehand so they're raring to go, and you've got a race.

It's mostly a sport for the lower castes. Most nobles'll turn their noses up and go to a Proving instead. But a few will rough it and stand in the scaffolds built in the tunnel roof, waving and cheering with the miners and merchants while the nugs go thundering by underneath.

Of course, where there's nobles, you get noble hunters with their fans and painted smiles. That's where the serious money starts to come in, and those plump little sods start to earn their keep. The nugs, not the noble chasers.

Jockeys are my trouble. Can't hurt a nug, no; but if a jockey takes a spill in those tunnels, they'd better climb up to the scaffold sharpish before three hundredweight of blind nug comes barreling back around toward them. Lost a few that way. Still, if you're a brand in Dust Town with no prospects, there are worse ways to earn 'em. The coin from nug jockeying—especially if you're smart about it—has got more than one lad or lass a start in the Carta, and they've had along with it a taste of fame that can last 'em a time. Funny how even the casteless end up with their own pecking order.

"What about when the nugs get old, when they can't race anymore?" the human asked me. Fair question, though she didn't like the answer much. What was she expecting me to say—"we let 'em run wild and free into the Deep Roads with all the lichen they can eat"? No. You get a nug that won't run or turns into a biter, there's not much else you can do except have a quiet word with the wrangler and look up recipes.

That's the other way you make coin off 'em, believe me. Most nobles won't watch a giant nug run, but they'll turn out in droves to see how it tastes.

Well, how else d'you get decent muscle on a nug? That's what I'd like to know.

—Conversation with Neryn Harok, nug wrangler and marshal of the Tripcut track in Orzammar, as transcribed by Brother Genitivi while writing The Stone and Her Children

However, no amount of ridicule has diminished her hopefulness. While the Divine's death was a blow, it did not make Belinda lose faith in the work that they had started. She continues to fight with the Inquisition and has managed to maintain her good cheer and optimism through all trials.

KORBIN

"The others think that because we're both short, we understand each other. I lived on the surface. Korbin's from down there. I don't get down there. They have rules. Crazy rules. Break a rule, and oops, have fun swimming in the magma pools. Or . . . or exile! Up here, exile just means you go one country over and get used to a new accent. Down there? Exile means 'I hope you like darkspawn!' And the Legion of the Dead? It's for people that break a crazy rule and feel bad about it. So they spend the rest of their lives trying to make up. Even when sometimes, the rule makes no sense. And they call me the insane one." —Luka

Korbin was once a great soldier of the dwarven Warrior Caste. He told the Inquisition that he volunteered for the Legion of the Dead. However, the truth—as truths tend to be—is much more complicated. Though she has never revealed this to the rest of the Inquisition, Ambassador Montilyet discovered through her diplomatic contacts that Korbin was sentenced to the Legion for killing a noble. The ambassador's hunch that there was more to the story drove her to ask Sister Leliana to investigate. The spymaster's inquiries revealed a deeper secret: that the crime was not Korbin's but another's. Korbin took the blame and the punishment and chose to tell no one about it. And there, the tale ended. The two Inquisition councilors were unable to discover more.

Korbin has never disclosed his true reasons for joining the Legion to his colleagues in the Inquisition, and both the

Though usually subterranean, nugs have been more common on the surface since the Fifth Blight.

ambassador and the spymaster have decided to abide by his choice. After all, hearsay and rumors mean nothing, when Korbin's selflessness is more than evident to those who fight by his side.

KATARI

"He told me that katari means 'one who brings death.' He wants us to call him that. I told him that he didn't have to be what he does anymore. He can choose any name for himself. Whatever he wants. That's what life outside the Qun is like. And then he asked if I picked my name, and I said no, my mother named me for her dear uncle. He asked how that was different. I didn't really have an answer. And then Katari told me he thought I was called 'Thornton' because I was prickly. And tried to explain the joke. I said he didn't have to. I got what he meant. Outside the Qun, we don't explain our jokes." —Thornton

The Qunari known as Katari fought great battles under the Inquisition banner.

Not all Qunari accept their roles. Many leave and become vashoth, wanting nothing to do with the Qun. Katari, once a soldier of the antaam, abandoned the Qunari and their philosophy after time spent in human lands made him disillusioned with the Qun. He speaks little of his life in Par Vollen, though he states that he came south with his unit on a large Qunari dreadnought.

After fleeing his superiors, Katari found it difficult to integrate into life alongside the average Thedosian. Most viewed him with suspicion, and his outlook, shaped by the Qun, was difficult for others to understand. In turn, he found it challenging to adapt to his newfound freedom away from the structure of the Qun. Like so many before him, he turned to the skills learned in the antaam to make his living in the world, becoming a mercenary for hire. When the Inquisition sent out the call for able-bodied soldiers, he answered. Small steps are the easiest, and Katari already understands what it is to be part of something bigger than himself. With time, perhaps he'll be able to build his own alliances and forge his own path.

TAMAR

"I was afraid of Tamar for a long time. She was the sort of shemlen the elders warned about—wild, bloodthirsty. And then one morning, as we watched the Chantry mothers preach to the soldiers, she said something I'll never forget: 'The gilded Chantry says only one truth exists. And its servants lie, steal, kill to make it so.' I think we reached an understanding that day." —Neria

The Disciples of Andraste were a dragon cult that lived in the secluded village of Haven in the Frostback Mountains, near the Temple of Sacred Ashes. After the Hero of Ferelden's discovery of the temple, the Chantry took great interest in the area and sent soldiers to reclaim it. What was left of the cult was forced out of the area. Many died, but at least one, a woman named Tamar, survived in the cold wilderness. For years, she waged a one-woman guerrilla war against the members of the Chantry. She had no illusions that she would ever drive them from Haven; her goal was simply to demonstrate to the trespassers that they were not safe and that the Disciples would fight so long as one of them lived. The Chantry lost at least a dozen people to her ambushes before launching an organized, coordinated campaign to bring her in. Tamar was captured and imprisoned in the

PUPPET SHOWS ACROSS THEDAS

The show I saw in Gwaren's marketplace was an almost stereotypically Fereldan affair: a retelling of *Dane and the Werewolf.* The hand puppets themselves were better than you usually see in the Southeast. The white hart could prick up its ears while it grazed from paper trees, and the werewolf's felt tongue lolled from its mouth when it snarled, making the children watching scream and clap each time it appeared.

Their parents were more interested in the business of the market, which is one way to tell you're in a backward country. In Antiva City, anyone of rank will pay close attention to such shows. Antivan puppets are more impressive, two-person affairs, manipulated with sticks from beneath a high stage. Their faces are sewn of fabric, which can be manipulated with the fingers to show emotions in a very convincing manner. I've seen less expressive faces on merchant bankers.

The purpose, of course, is to entertain, but the spice comes from the knowledge that many shows given in the streets directly comment on the politics of the day. Safe in the anonymity their stages provide, the puppets dance on the squandered fortunes of great traders or woo one another in the latest scandal. They throw eggs at depictions of those soon to be reviled and shower rose petals upon those soon to be elevated.

It is well known that if the Crows have a message to send in public, they will slip a few andris to the puppeteers. A few crow feathers added to a costume here, a silk scarf suggesting blood there—all in good taste, but the signs are clear enough to those paying attention. Oftentimes you will see a servant running away from such shows, bringing word to a luckless prince that he shouldn't stop to pack.

I wonder sometimes if our approach to puppetry was influenced by the Dalish clans who live along the coast, beyond the city walls. The clans here are more secretive than those outside the Antivan borders, and more violent if troubled. To keep humans from disturbing their camps, many Dalish build "forest marionettes." These puppets are built from scraps of cloth, carved branches, old bottles, and worn-out bowstrings. When they are strung up in the trees, rigged to the correct branches, a mere breeze causes the marionettes to move and swoop in a most disturbing way, while air across the mouths of the bottles makes a sound not unlike moaning.

A simple performance, to be sure, but the simplest is often the most effective. Many hunters take these marionettes for sylvans or unquiet spirits and flee the woods long before they smell the Dalish cooking fires.

Orlais, not a country known for its restraint, has its own puppet traditions—many stolen from us, I might add. Those best known are the baroquely ornate creations for high opera or religious festivals. Seated in a box at the Grande Royeaux Theater, I have seen wooden griffons soar over the heads of chanting Grey Wardens before a papier-mâché Archdemon head, with no less than five puppeteers to work it, leaned over the stage and breathed ribbon flames. Yet even in great spectacles, puppets can make more delicate statements. In the best production I saw of the Orlesian passion play *The Fall of Elderath*, worshipers of the Old Gods were played by wooden puppets with their strings clearly visible, bowing and scraping to a stuffed dragon, while Andraste walked between them and cut their cords with a song.

However, there must always be a fashion for this or that in Orlais, and lately, simple shadow puppets have become popular at salons and smaller parties. They are usually crafted from wood and paper, but I've seen expensive versions made of ironbark—Maker alone knows where those came from. Add a lantern with colored glass, a little music in the background, and a skilled puppeteer can take a story around Thedas in an hour.

As for me, after seeing the show in Gwaren, I took myself to a tavern for a drink. I listened while some local louts bragged about a tribe of Chasind barbarians they had spotted passing through the Wilds nearby. One claimed to have actually seen their shaman doing a ritual with small poppets made from old furs and horn and leaves, trying to draw the sickness from a newborn baby. They had a good laugh about it; I had my own little laugh, at their expense. Like I said: only a backward people would think puppetry is a childish pursuit.

—From the diary of Jonaro Vesevri,
Antivan master puppeteer and storyteller, 9:33 Dragon

cellars of Haven's chantry, only to be forgotten in the flurry of activity that surrounded the Divine Conclave.

However, the destruction of the Conclave and the opening of the Breach necessitated the formation of the Inquisition. The fledgling organization had little support and few soldiers, and suddenly, a battle-hardened warrior and survivor became a precious resource. Wary of treachery, Commander Cullen offered Tamar an ultimatum: waste away in prison or raise a sword in the Inquisition's name. Longing for the heat of battle, she pledged herself to the Inquisition. While she never let go of her own beliefs, the Inquisition provided her with an endless supply of foes to defeat, and she has served it well and loyally.

ARGENT

"I feel sorry for her. She can only conceive of herself as an extension of someone else. I don't think she understands what it's like to be a person . . . and I don't think she sees other people as people, either. She's never called me by my name or even addressed me directly, and that's when she's talking to me. It's always 'He's hurt' or 'He's funny' when she means 'Rion's hurt' or 'Rion's funny.' Actually, she's never told me I'm funny. I don't think she gets funny. All of it's unnerving. Come to think of it, she reminds me of one of the Circle's Tranquil mages. With the Tranquil, it's

'Here's some lyrium and a sharp pain . . . Poof! No more feelings.' How do you do that to a person without magic? What does it take? Any answer I can think up is horrifying." —Rion

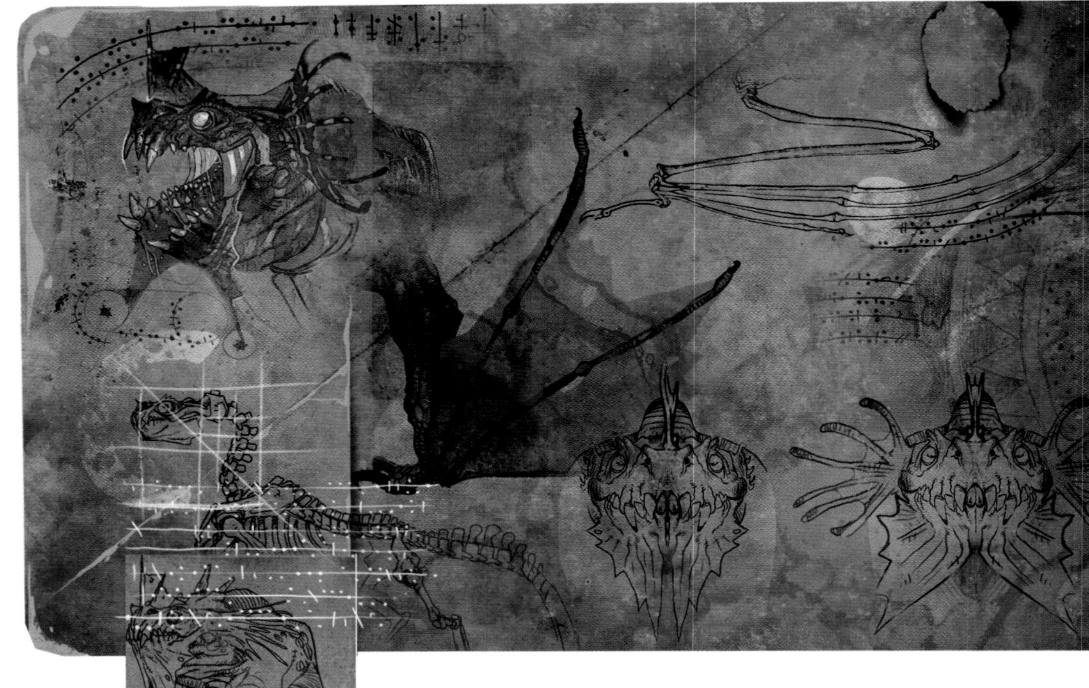

The assassin known as Argent, from the old Orlesian word meaning "quicksilver," was acquired by the Inquisition shortly after its formation. Sister Leliana, the Inquisition's spymaster, determined to discover the truth behind Divine Justinia V's death, began investigating all known enemies of the Divine. Her attention was drawn to Lady Cybile Maronn of Baisne, a minor but exceedingly wealthy noble. Evidence of plots against the Divine gave a justice-seeking Leliana enough cause to destroy the lady, politically and socially, even though she had nothing to do with the events of the Conclave. Her only son, trying to appease the Inquisition, donated much of his mother's assets to the young organization. One of these assets turned out to be Argent, who presented herself in Haven shortly after the handover of properties was concluded.

Some believe Leliana possesses a document that contains details about Argent's origins. Leliana has neither confirmed nor denied the existence of the document and has made no comment about Argent's past. Idle gossip often brings up the assassin's high and noble nose, which some say bears a striking resemblance to those of the scions of House Savrenne, but such talk is only given credence by those who have a fascination with tales of lost heiresses and bastard princes. The truth is likely far less romantic, and Argent was most probably an orphan from the Chantry: a girl with no family, whom no one would miss, who was given purpose and turned into a living weapon, a blade in another's hand.

LUKA

"I'm quite fond of the dwarf, Luka. The others try to pretend she's not there. When they are forced to deal with her, they call her eccentric and things less complimentary. I know what that's like. Say someone is mad or strange, and it takes less effort to dismiss them. And they want to dismiss us, because not doing so means being challenged. Means that maybe we're right and they're wrong. People fear being wrong more than anything. So they can laugh at Luka and at me. But I know, and she knows, it's because they're afraid." —Tamar

Luka once worked for the dwarven criminal group known as the Carta. A surface runner for the Carta's smuggling operation, she sat at the bottom of the hierarchy and was entrusted only with the simplest errands. This suited her well: low responsibility and good-enough wages. But that was before the Vimmark Mountains.

For reasons Luka barely understands, the Carta bosses she worked for became obsessed with a certain Kirkwall noble. They halted smuggling operations and moved their entire setup to an ancient Grey Warden fortress in the Vimmarks. Luka was tasked with clearing old tunnels, alongside other Carta members like her. She knew better than to ask questions, but every day, more of her friends would disappear and come back changed. There were rumors of a ritual, but Luka, unimportant, was never called.

And then one day, the prison was attacked. Luka ran, stumbling over the bodies of the people she knew, and was trapped

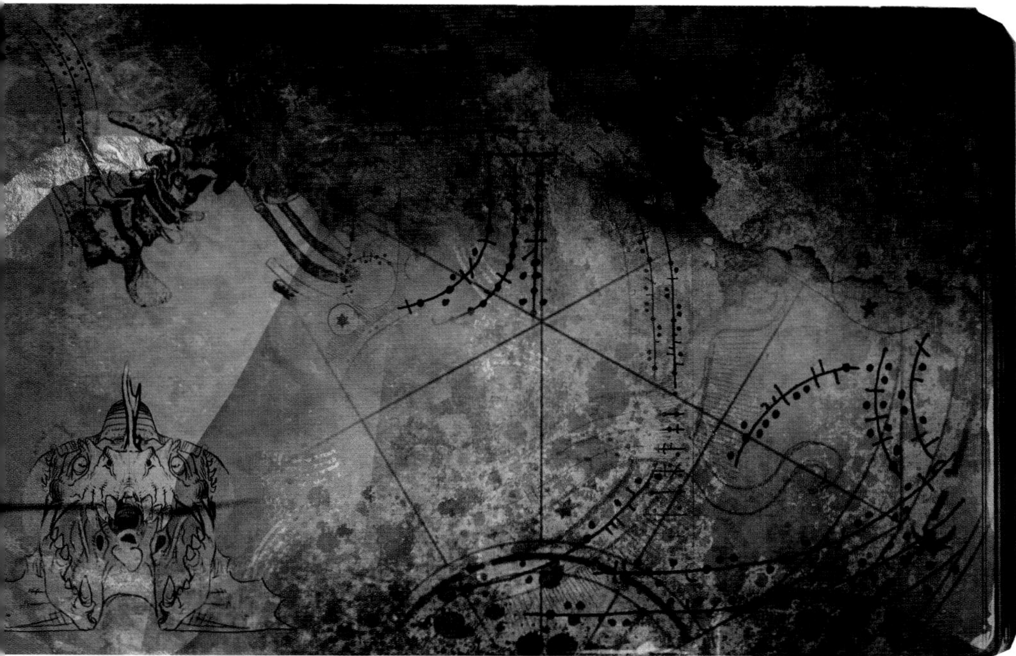

It is widely believed that the Grim Anatomy's focus is on demonic possession, specifically how a demon, itself a tangible being, can enter into the mind of another and manipulate it. Here, the author observes the motor skills of a possessed wyvern. "It is not wearing the creature's skin," the notes read. "It has become the creature: its mind, its senses . . . its blood."

in a section of the Vimmark fortress when a hallway collapsed. There was no up and out; the only way to go was down. So down she went. Luka is unsure how many years she spent alone, with only her thoughts for company, wandering through ancient caves, discovering strange minerals. And then one day, she discovered a mixture that could melt rock itself.

Escape was nothing like she'd dreamed it would be. The world had changed, and no one understood what she was saying. They looked at her with pity or avoided her entirely. Luka considered returning to her caves, but then the Inquisition came calling. The sister gave her an underground workshop and the freedom to continue her outlandish experiments. It made the changed world easier to bear.

HALL

"The boy with the bow doesn't talk much. He doesn't know what to say. It doesn't matter. Words don't matter. Unnecessary. One can work with another without talking. His arrow to the leg makes the mark fall before a knife ends it all. Efficient. The young templar suggested we name the maneuver. We suggested 'Arrow to Leg, Followed by Knife.' She said it lacked flair. She doesn't understand. The archer does. We don't talk. I like him." —Argent

Hall never had a home or a family or any place to call his own. He has only vague recollections of his parents, who were killed in a bandit attack while the family was traveling. Commanded by his mother to run into the woods, he escaped the bandits, only to find himself lost and alone. Hall is certain death would have claimed him had he not been rescued by a passing Dalish hunter named Fanora.

Hall recalls long arguments between Fanora and her Keeper over him. The clan was less than welcoming to the shemlen child, but Fanora refused to abandon him by the gates of a human village, as her Keeper instructed. Fanora continued to care for Hall and even began teaching him her ways. For years, Hall believed she was trying to help him fit in. And then ten years to the day she had found him, Fanora led him into the woods, handed him his bow and arrows, and told him to close his eyes. When he opened them, she was gone. Fanora had been passing on her skills in preparation for the day when she would be forced to turn him out. Hall was fourteen.

From that day, he drifted from town to town, never staying in one place for long, lest he outstay his welcome. Years of relying on his bow for survival made him a superb archer, and inspired by Fanora's impact on his life, Hall tries to help others when he can. His commitment to the Inquisition marks a change: for the first time, he has found a place where he belongs and is needed.

THORNTON

"Thornton enjoys talking about the time when he'll leave the Inquisition and his profession as a soldier and move somewhere sunny. He's seen too much now, and I think, for once, he'd like not to think about war or how he'll survive the next one. That, and he believes he's past his prime, that much closer to the moment when his eyesight or reflexes fail,

The influence of the Inquisition stretched to the farthest deserts of southern Thedas.

and people die as a result. He doesn't want it to come to that. They call this process of giving up 'retirement' where he comes from. He says he'll take up gardening. That's when people get a parcel of dirt and grow things in it. Not even useful things. As part of this 'retirement,' the more useless a pastime one picks up, the better. So he shall be growing the most frivolous things known to man. Like orchids." —Korbin

A native of Ansburg, Thornton first enlisted as a soldier with the margrave's army. He quickly found a niche in stealth and reconnaissance, with his information resulting in the successes of several important campaigns. He became the man his superiors would look to for scouting behind enemy lines. Thornton's quick wit and survival instincts would always bring him home alive. According to his many anecdotes, he has survived enemy capture through various means, including hiding in trees, pretending to be rock formations, hiding in burning buildings, running very fast through fields of poisonous snakes, and, in his favorite tale, disguising himself as a general's wife and fooling the general himself.

After Ansburg, Thornton moved to Orlais and used his expertise to obtain a position in the Orlesian army. When the Orlesian civil war began, he fought on the side of the empress until he was sent to the Frostbacks as support for the Divine Conclave. After the Conclave's destruction and the formation of the new Inquisition, Thornton was quick to enlist with the fledgling organization, hoping to use his veteran's experience to bring order back to Thedas.

NERIA

"When I first left the clan to pursue the path of the arcane warrior, Neria was just ten. I remember going to the Keeper and seeking her blessing to leave, to follow in the footsteps of our ancestors. Neria was sitting by Keeper Elindra, her attention focused entirely on a wooden puzzle that we call June's knot. 'Aneth ara,' I said. She didn't reply. I don't think she even knew I was there. That was Neria. It still is Neria. Tightly focused. Determined. Once she puts her mind to something, it must be done. It will be done. Not even the Creators themselves could shake her conviction. I wonder how long she spent on that little wooden carving. Did Elindra ever reveal that there is no solution to June's knot? Perhaps Neria didn't accept it. For all I know, she's still working on it." —Cillian

Neria was nine when Keeper Elindra chose her to be her apprentice. There was no other choice, as the Ralaferin clan was not blessed with many children, and few had any magical ability. Neria nurtured a healthy respect for Elindra and, even as a child, took her appointment as the Keeper's First very seriously.

Several years later, the clan attended the Arlathvhen, a meeting of the Dalish clans. Here, meeting others of her age, Neria learned that some among the Dalish had little respect for the Ralaferin clan. The more isolationist elves held a deep anger over the actions of Elindra's predecessor, Gisharel, who had shared Dalish lore and culture with human scholars. Though Neria defended her clan to its detractors, she began to doubt. When the Arlathvhen was over, she engaged her Keeper in a lengthy discussion about what Gisharel had done. Neria came away from it strong in the conviction that sharing one's culture with others did not diminish it—or her clan—in any way. Only by seeing and understanding the Dalish would humans ever learn to respect them. Vowing that the People would not be overlooked amid the chaos of the Breach, Neria joined the Inquisition: an emissary of Ralaferin and a voice for the Dalish.

CILLIAN

"Engaging an enemy in close combat has always seemed to lack finesse. I find it crude, the resort of those who lack for alternatives. Thus the way of the elven arcane warriors is strange to me. Cillian could learn the ways of the Dalish Keepers—earth, storm, and vine—but instead chooses to be within arm's length of his foes, like a common soldier. I respect his commitment to his craft, however, and I will admit that there is something of grace and dignity to his movements. I would keep that comment to yourself, if I were you."
—Sidony

Cillian was a child of the Ralaferin clan, like his clanmate Neria. When his magical abilities surfaced, he began training as Keeper Elindra's apprentice and was intended to be her First. But the tales of an ancient order of mystical warriors who turned their magic inward fascinated Cillian, and what he learned from Elindra could not satisfy his curiosity.

As a young man, Cillian decided that he would leave his clan and pursue the way of the arcane warrior. He asked Elindra's blessing to leave to seek his own path. She assented, knowing his heart was not in becoming Keeper, and Cillian left his clan, traveling far into the wilderness, seeking out knowledge of the arcane warriors. He explored ruin after ruin, until he came across an ancient elven shrine, where he says the secrets of the ancient order were kept. Cillian remained in the shrine for years, meditating, dedicating his mind, body, and soul to the practice of the art form.

Cillian believes he may have stayed longer, had the Breach not appeared in the sky. After years of living apart from people—even his own—he knew that it was time to return to the world and dedicate the skills he had learned to fighting for the greater good of all Thedosians.

The arcane warrior Cillian was a conduit for the powers of the Fade.

SIDONY

"I don't think I like Sidony very much. She's distant. Disdainful. And she says the most terrifying things, just to see us balk. What sort of person does that? It's like she was raised by wolves, but even wolves are more polite. There was a time when a red templar had me pinned. Sidony destroyed him and helped me up. She was very particular about saying that it didn't mean we were friends. I thought that was odd. Why was it so important to her that I didn't misunderstand? I think she thinks she needs to be hard and uncaring all the time. Anything else means she's weak."
—Ser Belinda Darrow

Sidony does not share stories about her past, preferring to keep her mind on her goals. Inquisition investigations into her past revealed that she was raised in Nevarra by an unknown Mortalitasi mage who was rumored to have allies among the ruling Pentaghast family. Sidony's magical abilities were kept secret and carefully cultivated, but she was taught never to fear her own powers. Though Sidony was also forced to learn proper comportment and etiquette, she sneers when speaking of it and chooses to pay no attention to social niceties. After all, what worth are smiles and kind words, next to power and achievement?

And what better way is there to achieve a greater understanding of magic, and thus grow more powerful, than to observe the biggest magical mystery of the age? Sidony volunteered with the Inquisition for the sole purpose of researching the Breach. To hear her tell it, one would imagine the Breach as a thing of wonder, a gateway to knowledge. Sidony makes no bones about it: nothing and no one will stand in the way of her reaching her potential as a mage.

The Breach left great destruction in its wake.

QUNARI NAMES FOR ITEMS

In keeping with their seemingly never-ending search for efficiency, the Qunari appear to use the following designations to denote the skill level associated with an item:

- *Eva* means "basic" or "beginner."
- *Iss* means "experienced."
- *Katoh* means "ending" or "achievement."

Thus, an amulet, which is generically called *taamsala*, would be designated *taamsala eva* if meant for a neophyte, *taamsala iss* if intended for a veteran, and *taamsala katoh* if used by a master.

The following words describe the durability of an object and whether it is used by a warrior or a mage:

- *Taar* denotes heavy armor and derives from the word for "death."
- *Saar* denotes light or cloth armor. It is derived from a word meaning "dangerous" but most commonly associated with *saarebas* (mage).
- *Kas* denotes martial weapons intended for melee. Likely derived from the word for "soldier."
- *Bas* denotes weapons meant for mages, derived from the word for "thing."

Thus, a heavy boot intended for a master is *sataam-taar katoh*, and a maul of moderate quality is *sata-kas iss*.

When describing a mage's staff (*saartoh-bas*), an additional adjective denotes its type. In *saartoh-bas tic*, *tic* means "cold." Other descriptors are *vat*, meaning "fire," and *kos*, describing an energy associated with nature.

Here follows a translated equipment list:

antaam	cuirass
aquaam	glove or light vambrace
asabas	light helm or reinforced hat
asalaa	helmet
mertam	light boot
nehrappan	belt
notas	gauntlet or vambrace
saartoh-bas	mage's staff
sataam	heavy boot or greave
sata-kas	maul
taam-kas	greataxe
taamsala	amulet
taaras	light mail or doublet
valo-kas	greatsword

RION

"In the lands of the Qun, they would be saarebas: tightly controlled, weapons to be used by the arvaarad. The Qun does not value or acknowledge the difference between mages. They are all saarebas. But Cillian is peaceful, Sidony is impatient, and Rion is boisterous. Cillian laughs little, Sidony laughs at others, and Rion laughs at himself. They are all different. I now consider their differences, and I do not regret leaving the Qun. I appreciate that the human cultures have allowed Rion's ridiculousness to flourish. Though I seldom understand the comments the others find humorous, his flailing amuses me. I would hate to see him trammeled." —Katari

Rion waves off any talk about his past. He admits to being from the Ostwick Circle, which he describes as "better than the Gallows for being at least a hundred miles away from any Stannards." Hints dropped in casual conversation with his peers have led them to believe that he is from a family of means, possibly even noble, but further inquiries are often met with coldness, sometimes literally—with the slinging of a spell. While nursing a frostbitten thumb, templar Ser Belinda Darrow was quoted saying, "I don't think he gets along with family."

Rion was one of the first mages in the Ostwick Circle to join the mage rebellion after the incident in Kirkwall. When the Templar Order abandoned the Chantry to pursue the mages rising up in the Free Marches and around Thedas, it became open war. Both templars and mages were struck down, and the conflict even claimed the lives of those who had no stake in it. With each day that passed, more innocent lives were lost, and Thedas began to fear mages more, not less. Rion, who once believed that there could be no compromise, began to wonder if compromise was necessary to ensure that there would still be a Thedas once all the battles were fought. Questioning the rebellion led him to abandon it, and when hope for a peaceful resolution was destroyed with the Divine Conclave, Rion joined the Inquisition—the last hope of Thedosian mages.

THE MASKED EMPIRE

In the months leading up to the blast at Haven, a civil war brewed in the nation of Orlais. The Grand Duke Gaspard, a seasoned chevalier of some reputation, began an orchestrated plot to overthrow Empress Celene. Beyond myriad clandestine efforts, there were public clashes between the cousins at both the capital and Halamshiral. Their feud persisted, taking countless lives and distracting Orlais from bigger problems—until the Inquisitor came along.

Empress Celene ushered in an age of unprecedented change in Orlesian society, stirring much controversy in the process.

EMPRESS CELENE I

It is unfortunate that the civil war between Empress Celene I of Orlais and Grand Duke Gaspard de Chalons may come to define her reign. Every ruler who has sat upon the throne of Orlais has seen violence and bloodshed—and played the Game accordingly—but few have done so much to bring Orlais into an age of enlightenment as Celene.

For several ages, the University of Orlais served as something of a dumping ground for the younger children of the lesser nobility, those with few political prospects whose families tired of entertaining them with a multitude of tutors. It coexisted uneasily with the Chantry, which prided itself on having the greatest minds in the country, and it lacked the political backing to stand against either Chantry or noble pressures. As a result, the university made significant gains only in subjects that neither the Divine nor the nobles found objectionable, and for centuries, it produced little beyond scathing critiques of other nations and the occasional bit of mathematics.

Celene changed that. After her coronation as empress, she declared her intent to study at the university, insisting that to rule a great nation, she must learn from the greatest minds in that nation. In truth, her duties as empress kept her from doing more than meeting with a few professors in what amounted to private consultations. Nevertheless, this public show of support reinvigorated the university. It quickly became fashionable for even eldest children to spend a season or two attending the university, either for scholarship or as a new field in which to play the Great Game. When the Chantry objected to studies of changes to the Chant of Light over the centuries, Celene stood by the university, declaring that so long as the examinations covered only history, they were the domain of mortals and not the Maker. Her assertion that studying the means by which the Chant of Light has been perfected might lead humanity to a more perfect understanding in the future was accompanied by generous donations to the Chantry itself, a move that did much to head off any further concerns.

The University of Orlais is now one of the most prestigious institutions of learning in all of Thedas. Nobles travel there not just from Orlais, but from Nevarra and the Free Marches as well. The university is respected across the world for its studies of nature, magic, history, and the arts. Empress Celene has even urged the university to relax its requirement of noble blood for entry, suggesting that allowing those of peasant birth to enter if sponsored by a noble patron would encourage fresh viewpoints. While the university has thus far been slow to respond to the suggestion, it speaks well for the prospects of the institution.

The Grande Royeaux, by contrast, aspires to art rather than study, but is no less important a representation of Orlesian cultural heritage. In ages past, the Royeaux was often checked by the Chantry or the emperor. Mad Emperor Reville restricted the Grande Royeaux to performing wordless pantomimes, and after the theater performed a play that Chantry officials lambasted as borderline heretical, Emperor Florian required that no work would be performed without the approval of representatives from both the court and the Chantry.

Celene removed all restrictions, announcing that artistic freedom should not be constrained by such worldly concerns and that the Grande Royeaux must show the rest of the world the greatness of Orlesian culture. The theater was timid at first, but quickly realized that Celene's support was genuine. When the epilogue of a historical drama was read by a "Spirit of Rulership" who was clearly meant to be Celene herself—her mask patterned after one she had worn just a week prior—the empress gave a standing ovation and even invited the actor up to her private booth after the show. Until the civil war with Gaspard began, it was safe to say that the Grande Royeaux, secure in its knowledge that the empress cared for cultural quality and nothing more, had seen twenty years of unprecedented success.

Empress Celene's reign will be studied and remembered long after her death, as are those of all rulers, and fault will doubtless be found. It is hoped, facts notwithstanding, that any judgment of her abilities as ruler recognizes what she did to ensure that Orlais remained not just a strong nation but a great one as well.

AMBASSADOR BRIALA

Who is Briala? Ask three Orlesians, and you may well get five different answers, for the stories are seldom consistent even in a single telling. To the nobles,

It is said that Celene could not have held power without her longtime elven servant Briala.

she was Empress Celene's trusted handmaid. To the court, she was a spy few ever noticed. To the elves of the Orlesian alienages, she was the hope of elven freedom. Just as likely, she was none of these things at all.

It is public knowledge that Briala came to Val Royeaux a few years after the empress took the throne. Nobles of the court recollect her serving Celene even as a child. "She served me tea when I visited the Valmonts," recalls a duke who asked that his name not be used. "She said nothing. It was easy to forget she was there, a tiny masked figure who moved in perfect silence. It was not until the ride home that I realized that she'd known precisely how I took my tea."

In the court, she was a known presence, separate from the palace staff and a quiet power in her own right. "Miss Bria always looked out for us," Rilene, the cook, noted. "If a lord doesn't like his supper, it comes down hard on us in the kitchens. Miss Bria would always help. 'The duke hates onions; you might want to use carrots instead,' she would say, or 'Lady Montsimmard will want extra plum sauce.' Once she even pointed out that the new scullery boy had a funny look to him. He was with the Antivan Crows. Could have poisoned the whole banquet if Miss Bria hadn't noticed him."

The last pages of the Grim Anatomy are largely unreadable, torn, and singed. It's as if someone attempted to destroy the book. What little can be made out speaks of rot and emptiness.

While various rumors, too scandalous and disrespectful to repeat, have suggested that Briala once held a more personal relationship with Empress Celene, it seems likely that the elven servant did have a position of trust with the empress, and it is interesting to wonder how many of Celene's policies, often attacked by critics as too gentle with the elves of Orlais, might have been implemented differently had Briala not been present. It is clear that elves have fared better under Empress Celene's rule than under any previous ruler since the fall of Halamshiral. Elven merchants have been granted increased legal status, and nobles who casually and publicly mistreat the elves of their alienages have found themselves out of favor with the court.

Nevertheless, when the elves of Halamshiral rebelled against Celene, witnesses say that Briala was present and did not offer the support they had hoped for. "She came in her fancy armor with her fancy bow with a Dalish mage at her side," said an elven woman who survived the burning of the rebelling neighborhood. "We thought she was come to help us. Instead she tells us we were fools to put up barricades, that if you build a wall against the nobles, they have to come kick it down to prove who's bigger. She took Thren, a good man, off to do it her way. The next morning, Thren was dead, our homes were burned, and our great protector was riding off in a wagon like some noble's favorite pet."

Since the beginning of the civil war between Empress Celene and Grand Duke Gaspard, Briala has become better known while her existence has become less plausible. Reports place her outside Val Firmin, putting arrows into the water casks of the imperial army, while equally secure reports have her delivering food to the Ghislain alienage on the very same day. Her agents, lightly armored elves who move through city and forest with equal ease, have frustrated both Celene's and Gaspard's forces in ways that combine a servant's understanding of practicalities with a master strategist's view of warfare. Food supplies have been fouled. Orders for troop movements have been stolen, and counterfeit orders delivered in their place. The war would certainly have ended by now if not for this frustrating sabotage, and while it is clearly impossible for Briala to have traveled so quickly across the entirety of Orlais, the exaggerated tales of her accomplishments have led to fierce loyalty among the elves of alienages all across the country.

"Halamshiral burned because she tried to play by the rules of the humans," said one elven servant who wished to remain anonymous. "We'll never burn again. We have someone who can beat the nobles at their own game. Someone who speaks for the elves."

FELASSAN

Regarding the elf Felassan, the information that is known is far eclipsed by the information that is lacking. It is clear that he mentored Briala in her youth, teaching Celene's handmaid about elven culture and supplementing her already-impressive training as a spy. He accompanied Briala and Celene after Gaspard attacked the empress outside Halamshiral, providing assistance that almost certainly kept Celene alive—and his expertise regarding the ancient elven mirrors known as eluvians is is unparalleled.

The accompanying diagrams are bizarre, no longer resembling the physiology of any known animal but instead a mess of overlapping and interconnected geometric shapes.

What is not known, however, is what Felassan gained from this mentorship and assistance. He was not a member of Clan Virnehn, and in fact, no Dalish clan willing to speak with outsiders admits to having had Felassan among its ranks. When his skill with magic was explained—he is known to have caused earthquakes and thunderstorms, rent stone walls asunder, and explosively countered the magic of a Dalish mage who, it was later revealed, was possessed by a powerful demon at the time—the Dalish clans noted that such a gifted mage would more likely be serving as Keeper for a clan than wandering the world alone like some restless hermit.

Empress Celene, speaking through her advisors, said that in her journeys with Felassan, she found him to be unlike any other elf she'd encountered. "He had neither the loyal fellowship of the city elves nor the love of the past that marks the Dalish," she said. "It was impossible to say what he truly cared about, but most things I expected an elf to care about seemed to him mere curiosities."

Grand Duke Gaspard, who also traveled with Felassan while allied briefly with Celene, shared similar opinions when asked. "He didn't look down, and any city elf would have. He didn't look angry, and all the Dalish did. He didn't talk about the old elves like a scholar or a poet. He talked about them like a man who walked those streets himself."

Wherever he is now, Felassan will, it seems, remain a mystery.

GRAND DUKE GASPARD

It is said that the Orlesian nobles love and hate the chevaliers. They love them because they maintain the grand tradition of Orlais, holding up the warriors of the country as the greatest in the world and celebrating the culture of honor they uphold. They hate them because, as Ser Massache de Jean-mien once said, "Coin and family may purchase all else in this world, but they cannot purchase the yellow feather." To earn the right to wear upon their helmets the yellow feather that marks a chevalier, warriors must undergo rigorous training, pass grueling tests, and swear to follow the chevalier code of honor, upon pain of death.

Grand Duke Gaspard is an exception to this description of the ambivalent relationship between nobles and chevaliers, for he stands as one of the highest-ranking nobles to have earned the yellow feather and as one of the strongest proponents of the chevaliers as an institution.

Gaspard earned his chevalier's feather as a young man, and there were those in the court who whispered that the Academie des Chevaliers had loosened its standards to award him his place. Those whispers were silenced in Gaspard's first Grand Tourney. He defeated several veteran chevaliers with impressive skill and placed well in both the joust and the horse race. While never known for his humility in the court, Gaspard cheerfully congratulated chevaliers whose family rank was far below his, famously saying, "As long as we are in the saddle, I am Ser Gaspard and no more."

He would likely have won the Grand Melee had his tourney sword not cracked after a powerful exchange against the young Marquis de Montsimmard, leaving his blade jaggedly sharp. Although his opponent was stumbling and off balance, Gaspard threw down his blade, signaling his forfeiture of the match. When the shocked judges asked why he had done so, Gaspard pointed out the ruined edge on the normally blunted tourney blade, noting that the chevalier code prohibited an honorable combat with unmatched weapons. Rather than take a likely victory but risk injuring Montsimmard dishonorably, Gaspard accepted his loss and raised a round of applause for the young marquis, who was said to remark, "I have rarely seen a man win over so many by losing."

Gaspard's claim for the throne divided Orlais in civil war.

Gaspard carried his love of the chevaliers through a distinguished military career, earning the admiration of his soldiers in campaigns even as he appeared to disdain the convoluted politics of the Game. When Empress Celene took the throne, Nevarran forces invaded Orlesian territory, claiming the town of Larécolte in the Fields of Ghislain. Gaspard pushed for a strong response to answer this blatant insult to Orlesian pride, and in response, Celene placed the Orlesian armies under Gaspard's command. As she did, however, she told him that should he lose more than one thousand men, he must withdraw and she would cede Larécolte to Nevarra. "I will not see the blood of ten thousand good Orlesian souls stain the ground in defense of a town of twenty-five hundred."

Some saw such an order as indicative of Celene's practicality and her desire to check Gaspard's impulses, which might pull Orlais and Nevarra into an ugly war neither country truly wanted. Others saw such an order, impossible as it appeared, as a means to get her cousin and former rival out of Val Royeaux and set him up for failure.

Gaspard marched his soldiers across the Fields of Ghislain and engaged the Nevarran forces in several battles. Each time, his keen tactical mind and rallying presence on the battlefield drove the Nevarrans back with minimal losses to the Orlesian army. Finally, the Nevarrans fortified Larécolte, effectively daring Gaspard to assault the city in a bloody battle.

Knowing that a frontal assault would cost him more than the thousand lives Celene had limited him to, Gaspard instead rode alone to the gates of the city and asked to speak with the Nevarran commander, a knight of some renown. Calling to him up on the walls, Gaspard praised the Nevarran warriors' skill while at the same time mocking their honor. The Nevarran commander, incensed, called back insults of his own, and Gaspard promptly challenged the man to single combat, with the city of Larécolte going to the winner. When the Nevarran commander balked, Gaspard famously threw his shield to the ground and called out, "If you are that fearful, then I shall fight without a shield, as it seems I will not need it."

The duel took place outside the city walls. Gaspard, true to his word, arrived without his shield. Instead, he carried a great maul, apologizing for the clumsiness of the weapon. The Nevarran commander was a knight of no mean skill himself,

SER MICHEL & THE DEMON'S PROMISE

I find it disappointing how often people blame things on demons. Don't you?

They come up with stories where the demons trick them into committing some evil act, where they possess the mage and turn him into a horrific monster, where the demons are always the villains. But if you paid attention to the Chant of Light instead of just repeating it over and over in your mind like you're doing right now, you'd know that even Andraste herself didn't believe that. *Spirits* are attracted to feelings, passions, those moments that define someone's life. We don't put the bad feelings into your head. We come to you because they're in there already. A good man, a humble man, could stand before a pride demon with nothing to fear. Except getting stepped on, of course.

What I'm saying is that you have nothing to fear from a spirit except whatever trouble you bring with you. A spirit is the best test mortal man will ever find to uncover the darkest parts of himself, whether it be fear or rage or pride . . . or *choice*.

Some call it desire, but everyone has desires. Not everyone makes the choice to act upon them, and if you don't make a choice, well, what use are you? You're like that girl who liked you that year at the harvest festival, but she never worked up the courage to ask you to dance, and you never knew. If you like, I could tell you her name. I bet you'd be surprised. No? Just a thought.

In any event, like all the Dalish, Clan Virnehn wanted to reclaim what they'd lost, and they summoned me and bound me in one of their little circles, but for all their talk, they couldn't make the choice that would gain them my cooperation. I had to sit and listen to them equivocate and pontificate and generally try to bore me into helping them. That's elves for you.

For the choices that get things going, you need humans.

Do you know the easiest con your Maker, praise His name if you're feeling like it, ever invented? I feel comfortable sharing this with you, seeing as how you're currently, shall we say, between a rock and a hard place. The easiest con is to let someone think they're conning you. Ser Michel, champion of the somewhat throneless Empress Celene, saw a demon (his words, not mine) trapped in a binding circle, and heard of the magical eluvians and a chance for his empress to escape the Dalish and regain her throne. I gave him an offer he was never going to accept—a willing sacrifice, heart's blood, something like that—in return for never having to worry about anyone ever discovering his dirty family secret. His mother was elven, you see. Didn't look it, since the ears never come out pointy once a human's involved, but elf blood, common birth, would have gotten him killed for impersonating a noble. What a mad choice for a young man to make, living a lie to become a chevalier.

As I said, humans. These days, they're the ones who want things badly enough to make the really *interesting* decisions. That's why I'm talking to you, in fact. How's the nose? Itchy at all? I always hate it when my hands are restrained and my nose starts to itch. It's one of the worst things I can think of. Just let me know if you'd like some help.

As for Ser Michel, he was never going to accept that bargain. No, he heard me let slip the secret of the eluvians and the fact that breaking my binding circle would banish me to the Fade, and the dear boy decided to con me. Me, one of the Forbidden Ones. He got the secret of the eluvians from me, and then he broke the binding circle, which, as it turned out, was the way to *free* me and not *banish* me.

Now freed, I sent him and his empress off to the eluvians and taught the Dalish what happens when you summon one of the Forbidden Ones.

Oh, did you think I'd killed Ser Michel? Now, why on your Maker's poor neglected earth would I do that? I get the feeling that you don't understand me *at all*, and let me tell you, understanding me is becoming an increasingly important prerequisite to your continued existence. Michel *made a choice*. He took action, and while his sadly mortal mind didn't quite get the consequences correct, he understood that they might exist. A man who makes choices, right or wrong, is someone I'm happy to have around. As for the mealy-mouthed Clan Virnehn, fumbling around with their binding circles and their clumsy commands . . . the world is a more interesting place without them.

Except the children, of course. Children don't have the wits to choose anything for themselves. I sent the little dears to another clan. Quite charitable of me, if I do say so, dropping a few dozen children into the laps of a clan with winter on the way. The mouths of hungry youngsters create such good choices for others. If you had a child, we'd be having a much different conversation right now.

The only other member of Clan Virnehn I left alive was the First of their clan, a young woman named Mihris. Ser Michel had chosen to leave her alive rather than kill her, even knowing that she hated him for killing some guardsman she liked. She seemed quite invested in avenging her clan and killing Ser Michel, even to the point of allowing me to possess her to give her the power to do so. Sadly, it ended up being a waste of time. When her chance came, Mihris flinched from the consequences, and with no interesting choice to keep me bound, I was forced to go my own way.

And it turns out that Ser Michel didn't need Mihris. He had his own downfall with him all along, in the form of a promise he'd made to Celene's lover: one favor for her silence on his little elf-blooded secret. The favor turned out to be forfeiting his duel with Celene's rival, and in his pride, Ser Michel revealed his parentage for all to see. I hear the empress's disgraced former champion is trying to find me, to put his mistake right and banish me from this world.

Let's hope it doesn't come to that, shall we? I'm the only thing keeping you alive right now—well, for certain definitions of *alive*.

Just remember, if you want to get out of there, healthy and whole, at any time, all you have to do is say yes. Not a command, not an order, nothing but an offer from a spirit who loves seeing people make interesting choices.

I'll give you some time to think it over. The woman in the next room is worried about her son. Something to work with there, don't you think? It's always easier to make a difficult choice when you can say you're doing it for someone else.

—*The demon Imshael*

AN INTRODUCTION TO CHEVALIER TACTICS

Duelist Catches an Apple: To pierce an opponent's throat, an effective opening move.

Bear Mauls the Wolves: When one is swarmed, a sweeping blow that, when performed correctly, can cut down multiple combatants. Best applied with two blades.

Second Shield: To stab through the body of one opponent into another.

Testing the Blade: Stretches used to find torn muscles, strained ligaments, and other hidden pains that could affect the ability to fight if not caught and compensated for.

Spear Fisher: Raising sword and shield in a defensive position when recovering from fatigue in the midst of battle. Most chevaliers consider it a shameful position that shows they have been outclassed by their opponent.

—*From* A Meditation upon the Use of Blades *by Massache de Jean-mien*

but was famed primarily as a tournament fighter, with little experience in the ugly realities of war. Gaspard's maul, ugly but effective, smashed through the knight's defense and sent him reeling. In less than a minute, the Nevarran commander was on the ground with a broken arm, and Gaspard was accepting his surrender and taking Larécolte back for Orlais.

Grand Duke Gaspard has never been held up as a master of the Game, but with his commanding presence and his sincere commitment to the code of the chevaliers, he won the love of the soldiers who serve him. Celene may well be remembered for upholding the cultural tradition of Orlais, but Gaspard upheld the proud history of Orlesian military might.

GRAND DUCHESS FLORIANNE DE CHALONS

From the time she was born, Florianne de Chalons had one purpose in life: to help her brother Gaspard take the throne. Her mother, Grand Duchess Melisande, was the youngest child of Emperor Judicael I. The crown passed from Melisande's father to her oldest brother, Judicael II, and then to her older brother Florian. Emperor Florian Valmont had always been an eccentric man, but the death of Princess Evangeline, his only child, made him even more reclusive. He banished all children from the imperial palace, including the children of servants. Melisande hoped that naming her newborn daughter after him might evoke some curiosity from her brother and allow her children, particularly her firstborn son, Gaspard, to visit him.

Her gambit worked. Melisande's children were permitted to enter the palace, but had only a single audience with their uncle. The emperor looked impassively at his namesake for a few moments, declined to hold her, refused even to look at her older brother, and declared in a monotone that the children "might stay; just keep them out of my sight."

Florianne spent her early years in the imperial palace with only servants for company. Her brother, nearly thirteen years her senior, began his chevalier training soon after she was born, and only rarely had time to spend with his family. Her mother served as one of the emperor's only advisors and spent most of each day talking him through the affairs of the empire. Her father, Duke Theodore de Chalons, was not an affectionate man and cared only for rich food, strong drink, and gambling on horse races. He rarely bothered with either of his children.

During the day, Florianne wandered the palace gardens. In the evening, her mother would quiz her to repeat back everything she had heard the servants say. They began lessons in etiquette, protocol, and the Game early, training Florianne to be the subtle shadow that trailed behind her shining brother.

When Gaspard turned nineteen and became a full-fledged chevalier, he returned to the palace. Melisande pressed for her son to take his place in the emperor's cabinet, but at first Florian continued to be difficult and would have only his siblings advise him. This gave Gaspard a great deal of spare time that he spent doting on his little sister. The two grew quite close during their shared exile from the emperor's inner circle, and when, as the Rebel Queen's uprising in Ferelden gained strength, the emperor relented and allowed his chevalier nephew to advise him, Gaspard insisted on bringing her along to meetings as his page.

She grew up along the fringes of power—out of sight, out of mind, but always observing. Even after the Council of Heralds awarded the throne to her cousin Celene, Florianne continued to live in her suite in the palace. She held a respected, although not particularly substantial, place in Celene's cabinet of advisors and in the Imperial Court. Having neither the diplomatic prowess of her cousin nor the military acumen of her brother, Florianne developed a reputation for being the least important member of the royal family. Her position would have thrilled her late mother: Florianne had status enough to be invited everywhere, but was so little thought of that no one paid her any attention. A skilled bard could hardly ask for a better cover, but what she would do with it was anybody's guess.

THE WHOLE NUG
Culinary Treasures of Thedas

Food, while a necessity for survival, is often imbued with meaning and significance beyond mere utility. What we eat says as much about our culture as any music or art. Eating brings us together. Indeed, the greatest moments of our lives are celebrated with food and drink. Imagine a wedding without a feast, or an elegant soiree without canapés made with the fashionable ingredients of the day. Throwing a party lacking in repast is enough to make an empress faint in a dead swoon.

Now imagine toasting the heroism of fallen soldiers with empty hands and empty glasses. It would not surprise me if the dishonored dead rose from the ashes for such an affront! And how many treaties and accords were signed and sealed with a fine barrel of wine as witness? The simple act of sharing drink and breaking bread creates a bond, and we understand this deep in our heart of hearts.

This is why we rejoice over food, we forge alliances and friendships over food, we even mourn with food. Nothing else comes close to sharing its place of importance in our lives, because nothing else has quite the same power to comfort the soul, nurture the spirit, and delight the senses.

I invite you now, dear reader, to come with me on a culinary adventure through Thedas. Here, I have compiled a special collection of recipes from all corners of the known world: from the hearty and humble dishes of Ferelden and the austere fare of the blighted Anderfels, to the simple, wholesome food of the wandering Dalish elves and the decadent, ambitious banquets of Orlais.

May these culinary treasures of Thedas excite your palate and transport you to lands you'd only otherwise visit in stories.

To life, to love, to lunch!
Lady Savarin Ledoure

Spiced Wine

This is the perfect drink to take the chill off, wonderful on a cold winter's night or any time of day in Ferelden. I prefer to use the fruitier wines of Antiva, but you may use whatever is your favorite. I promise that after two cups, you won't even notice the difference!

INGREDIENTS

- *A bottle of rich red wine*
- *One orange*
- *One lemon*
- *One apple, cut into small pieces*
- *Eight to twelve whole cloves*
- *Two or three sticks of cinnamon, broken into smaller pieces*
- *One teaspoon of freshly grated nutmeg*
- *One teaspoon of dried ginger*
- *Five tablespoons of honey*
- *Dark brown sugar, about four to eight tablespoons or to taste*
- *One cup of good brandy*

DIRECTIONS

Place the bottle of wine and the same measure of water into a large pot. Heat it gently. Pare the peel from the lemon and orange, slice it thin, and add to the pot. Cut each in half and add the juice also. Add the apple, the spices, and, of course, the brandy. Sweeten the wine to your taste with the sugar and honey. Stir well and heat until simmering. Taste the wine. Add more spices or sweetener as desired and water if it is too strong. Serve hot, in small glasses.

A CURE FOR THE ELEMENTS

There are some recipes so ubiquitous, it can be impossible to trace their origins. While this particular mixture of spiced wine is my own invention, the idea of adding spices to hot wine dates back to the Glory Age, following the liberation of the Dales from the elves and, more specifically, the building of the Winter Palace in Halamshiral. The drink, in one form or another, has been favored by visiting nobles as a cure for the elements ever since. Perhaps the treat is yet another thing Orlais liberated from the elves. Even today, Empress Celene is said to enjoy a spiced wine when she visits the South. Known for her strange tastes, Celene adds rosemary and substitutes a pear for an orange.

Starkhaven Fish and Egg Pie

Starkhaven's famous pie is made with lightly poached fish from the Minanter River, which runs through this most beautiful of Marcher cities. I've heard that King Ottomar Vael ate a fish pie for his supper every day until his untimely death at the hands of brigands.

INGREDIENTS

- *Good pie dough, made with butter*
- *One to three fish, depending on size, from the Minanter River (carp, trout, or others)*
- *One cup of dried currants*
- *One cup of sliced almonds*
- *Two or three eggs, boiled hard and sliced*
- *Half a cup of butter*
- *Half a cup of flour*
- *Two cups of fish broth (or reserved poaching liquid)*
- *Two cups of milk*
- *Salt, pepper, and freshly grated nutmeg*
- *One cup of single cream*
- *One egg, beaten, for preparing the crust*
- *Whitebait or other small fish, fried till crispy (optional)*

DIRECTIONS

In a good-sized pot, place one gallon of water. Add to this one cup of good wine, a cup each of chopped onion, carrot, and celery, several sprigs of thyme, a leaf or two of bay, and a handful of sea salt. Heat the liquid until it steams, then gently add the fish to the pot. Ensure that the pot is fully covered. Continue to let it simmer, but do not let it boil. When the fish is just cooked through, remove it from the liquid and let it cool. Remove the meat from the bones and break it into chunks.

In a separate pot, melt the butter. Add the flour and stir for about two minutes. Add the broth and milk and whisk vigorously till the mixture is smooth. Continue to whisk while you bring the sauce to a boil and allow it to cook for at least ten minutes. If you find the sauce too thick, thin it out with more fish broth or milk. Once it is cooked, take it off the heat and stir in the cream. Season liberally with salt and add freshly grated nutmeg and pepper if desired. Now stir in the meat from the fish, the currants, the almonds, and the sliced eggs. Transfer this mixture into a large earthen crock.

Roll out the pie dough into a circle large enough to cover the crock. Brush the beaten egg around the edges of the crock, then place the pie dough over top, covering the fish filling. Crimp the edges and cut away any excess dough. Brush the dough with egg and make slits in the crust. Bake until the crust is golden and the filling is bubbling. If desired, serve the pie topped with small fish, deep fried whole for added texture and flavor.

Nug-Nug

Some credit the Left Hand of the Divine for starting the Orlesian obsession with nugs as pets. In her travels, Sister Leliana came across a nug, which she adopted and brought home to Val Royeaux. The fad quickly caught on. I've been told that this strange little creature—hairless, wrinkled, and pink, with its beady eyes and oversized ears—makes a wonderful companion animal. Children especially adore them. And they adore the nug-nug, a dish put together to resemble a nug peeking its head out of a burrow. I prefer beef, but use any meat that you have on hand, even actual nug meat, if you must. After all, as the dwarves will tell you, they are edible and very delicious. Just make sure you haven't inadvertently hunted and killed some poor lady's pet.

INGREDIENTS

- *One pound of ground meat*
- *One bunch of parsley, or any fresh, mild green herb, chopped*
- *One large egg*
- *One tablespoon of salt*
- *One tablespoon of crushed cumin or mustard seeds*
- *One tablespoon of fine black pepper*
- *Eight wooden sticks, for skewering the meat*
- *Two cups of cooked rice, or as much as desired*
- *Four large tomatoes*
- *One large onion (optional)*
- *Chives to garnish*

DIRECTIONS

Place the meat in a large bowl. Add the chopped herbs, seasoning, and egg to the meat and mix everything well using your hands. Wet your hands and form the meat mixture into sausage-like shapes, two fingers in diameter.

Press the meat onto the wooden sticks.

Roast the meat sticks in a pan or over an open fire until the meat is fully cooked.

Arrange the cooked rice on a plate, in a round shape. Bring water to a boil and blanch the tomatoes for one minute. Cut the tomatoes in half and place a tomato half in the middle of the bed of rice. Take two meat sticks and place them on the tomato, simulating long ears. Add some fresh chives to garnish. These will be the nug's whiskers.

If desired, fry onions and add on the side as a garnish or serve in a separate bowl.

Serve to squeals of delight!

Jellied Pigs' Feet

Jellied meats are a delicacy in some parts of the Free Marches. Originally a peasant food, born out of a reluctance to waste any part of a killed animal, jellied meats have gradually caught on with the wealthy, first in Ansburg, where the dish was invented. While this dish is customarily made with pigs' feet, pork hocks have occasionally been substituted, since some find the idea of eating pigs' feet repulsive. I myself was wary at first when presented with the traditional dish, but several glasses of wine filled me with the courage to take a bite of the quivering, translucent mass. After all, without adventure and novelty, surely this life would lack savor! If I can do it, so can you, dear readers. So grip your spoons tightly, take a breath, and dig in! What have we to fear from a gelatinous cube?

INGREDIENTS

- *Ten pigs' feet, pork hocks, or a combination of the two*
- *Four tablespoons of salt*
- *Two large onions, chopped*
- *Two whole heads of garlic, chopped or crushed, plus more to taste*
- *One tablespoon of allspice, whole or ground*
- *Two tablespoons of peppercorns*
- *Six bay leaves*

DIRECTIONS

Score the pig parts with a sharp knife and wash thoroughly. Immerse them in cold water with two tablespoons of salt. Leave overnight in a cool, dark place.

The next morning, wash the feet thoroughly, then place in a big pot with cold water and the remaining two tablespoons of salt. Bring to a boil. Scum will rise to the surface of the water. Skim as much of it off as you can. Add the chopped onion and garlic to the boiling water. Wrap the allspice, peppercorns, and bay leaves in a small piece of cloth. Tie tightly and add to the pot. Simmer for six to eight hours, until the meat is tender and falling off the bones.

Strain the stock from the meat and set it aside. Separate the meat from the bones and remove the skin, if that is your preference.

Place the meat in a deep dish or pan and pour the stock over it. Crush some fresh garlic, as many as twelve cloves, and mix it in with the meat and stock. Cover the pan with cloth and leave it in a cool, dark place for about twelve hours—enough time for it to set. Serve cold.

Pickled Eggs

You haven't truly been to Ferelden until you've had a mug of warm, watery ale and a pickled egg at a Fereldan tavern. Fereldans seem to love their pickled eggs, and they will prescribe them for just about every ailment there is, from fevers to ague to sneezing. One drunken codger in the Gnawed Noble in Denerim even swore to me that old pickling brine from that very tavern, mixed with dog hair and elfroot ash, helped him regrow a finger lost in the Fifth Blight. If the authentic experience of choking down a chewy, salty-sour egg in a dimly lit tavern with dirt floors and besotted carousers sounds far too stimulating, I offer an alternative: a formula for pickled eggs, so you may consume them at your leisure in your parlor, away from the smell of wet dog and unwashed beards.

INGREDIENTS

- *Two tablespoons of sugar*
- *One teaspoon of salt*
- *Two cups of vinegar*
- *Three-quarters of a cup of water*
- *Twelve to sixteen eggs, boiled and peeled*

DIRECTIONS

Stir the sugar, salt, vinegar, and water together in a pot. Simmer for several minutes. Place the eggs in a heavy earthen jar and pour the vinegar mix over top. Seal the jar, then let it stand in a cool, dark place for at least two days before eating.

Llomerryn Red

"Llomerryn red?" I hear you ask. Ah, yes. You have heard, then, that this is another name for blood. After all, the byways and alleyways of this lawless island are stained with red—Llomerryn red. Then again, perhaps they just mean this sauce, which is extraordinarily popular with the locals. It is served in every tavern, on every table, for eating with just about anything. It is exceptional on fried or roasted potatoes and adds a subtle tanginess to fresh oysters. The best Llomerryn red, I am told, is as sweet and spicy on the tongue as blood.

INGREDIENTS

- *Four to five cups of fresh, ripe tomatoes, peeled*
- *Two medium-large onions, diced*
- *One large red bell pepper, diced*
- *Half a cup of brown sugar*
- *Three-quarters of a cup of apple cider vinegar*
- *One teaspoon of mustard powder*
- *Ground hot pepper powder, to taste*
- *Salt*

For the spice ball:

- *Cheesecloth, a square of about six inches*
- *Half of a cinnamon stick*
- *One and a half teaspoons of whole allspice*
- *Half a teaspoon of cloves*
- *One and a half teaspoons of fennel seeds*
- *One and a half teaspoons of dill seeds*
- *Half a teaspoon of mustard seeds*
- *One and a half teaspoons of black peppercorns*
- *One bay leaf*
- *One garlic clove, peeled and lightly crushed*

DIRECTIONS

Squeeze the tomatoes with your hands until they are reduced to a pulp. Put the pulped tomatoes, onions, and bell pepper into a large pot. Bring to a boil and then simmer until the vegetables are soft. Press the cooked vegetables through a sieve to puree, then return to the pot. Add the sugar, apple cider vinegar, and mustard and hot pepper powders. Cover the pot with a lid, leaving a small gap for steam to escape. Continue to simmer.

Wrap the spices in the cheesecloth and tie it into a ball. Drop the ball into the pot.

Taste the sauce after it has simmered with the spice ball for twenty minutes. If the sauce is flavorful enough for your liking, remove the spice ball. Otherwise, leave it in for longer, tasting frequently. Add as much or as little salt as desired. Continue to simmer the sauce for another hour, stirring every few minutes. Test for consistency by dropping a small spoonful of sauce onto a plate. If liquid seeps from the edge, continue simmering. Remember, Llomerryn red must be at least as thick and sweet as blood.

Once the sauce is thick enough, transfer to a jar and seal. Can as you would jam and keep in a cool, dark place or consume within a few days.

Butter Soup

This is a simple, tasty soup that is both inexpensive and easy to make. Often seen simmering at the hearths of Orlesian rustics, it makes a good midmorning or midday refresher for those working the fields. Its mild but nourishing nature also makes it suitable for convalescents and children.

INGREDIENTS

- *Ten cups of water*
- *Four to five potatoes, cut into cubes*
- *One small white onion, chopped*
- *Half of a cinnamon stick*
- *Half of a teaspoon of star anise, ground*
- *One clove*
- *Two bay leaves*
- *Ten peppercorns*
- *Salt to taste*
- *Noodles, cooked*
- *Half a cup of cream*
- *Half a cup of butter*

DIRECTIONS

Melt about a tablespoon of butter in a pot and add the chopped onions. Cook until softened but not browned. Add water, potatoes, spices, and seasonings. Bring to boil and simmer gently until the potatoes are tender.

Add the cream, the remaining butter, and your desired amount of cooked noodles. Heat through and serve hot.

Alamarri Pickled Krone

The Alamarri tribes were the predecessors of the modern Fereldan people and also of the tribal Avvar who still dwell high in the snowy Frostback Mountains. To survive the bitter winters of the region, the Alamarri often preserved the bounty of the summer. One of the most traditional preserved foods of the Alamarri is, of course, the infamous pickled krone fish.

Caught in large quantities in late summer as swarms of them swim up the Hafter River to spawn, krone fish were usually baked and eaten with honey. The excess was pickled in barrels for consumption throughout the year. Rarely prepared in this current age, recipes for pickled krone still survive as culinary and cultural curiosities. Here, I have included a formula from my own collection, considered by scholars to be typical of the traditional method of preparation for pickled krone. It is not recommended for consumption by man or beast—as improperly prepared krone can kill and even properly prepared krone is, at best, revolting.

INGREDIENTS

- *A good-sized school of live krone*
- *A barrel*
- *Enough brine to fill it*
- *A handful of druffalo dung (optional)*
- *An equal measure of pine pitch (optional)*

DIRECTIONS

Before the krone spawn, catch them in a weir. Do not kill them.

Put them live into barrels of strong brine. This will kill them and draw out the blood. After all the fish are dead, behead and gut them. Pack them into a wooden barrel of weaker brine.

Place your barrels underground in a cool space. The air in the space should be warm enough to soften butter, allowing your signet to leave a mild impression, but no more than that. If the barrels leak as a result of building pressure, carefully plug the leaks with fresh druffalo dung that has been mixed in equal parts with pine pitch.

After forty days, bury your barrels in a peat bog. Leave them at least until Wintersend. Though the fish can now be eaten, the flavors of the pickle will continue to mature over time, and the best taste is achieved by waiting until the snows begin to recede.

Take care not to allow the juices of the pickled krone to fall upon your beard, as this may cause a change in color.

Fereldan Turnip and Barley Stew

Ferelden: a cold, wretched land of peat bogs and rain, where the capital, Denerim, is more miserable and dirt-stained than the poorest village of Orlais. Where the children running through the streets are oftentimes muddier than the dogs by their sides. Where it is perfectly acceptable to play at politics with swords drawn, and the current monarch is widely known to have been selected based on who could throw a better punch. Ferelden: full of people we sneer at and call "Fereldan turnips," who are as obstinate as they are uncultured, but also wonderfully disarming and pleasant upon getting to know. In many ways, this dish is a true reflection of Ferelden and its people. While unappetizing, dull, and easily dismissed at first glance, if given a chance, it will surely win you over with its rich, soothing flavors and belly-filling warmth.

INGREDIENTS

- *One cup of dried white beans, soaked overnight and drained*
- *Three tablespoons of oil*
- *One medium-sized onion, chopped*
- *Four carrots, chopped*
- *One rib of celery, finely chopped*
- *One head of garlic*
- *Eight cups of stock, the browner the better*
- *One pound of turnips, peeled and diced*
- *One pound of turnip greens, blanched*
- *One pound of sausage, very well smoked and not rotten, cut into chunks*
- *One cup of pot barley*
- *One teaspoon of cumin*
- *Two teaspoons of dried basil*
- *Two teaspoons of dried oregano*
- *Three teaspoons of salt, or to taste*
- *Half a teaspoon of pepper, or to taste*
- *A dash of herbed wine vinegar, to taste*

DIRECTIONS

Heat the oil in a large stew pot. Cook the onion, carrots, celery, and garlic until tender. Add the diced turnips, blanched greens, beans, sausage, and stock. Simmer for an hour or until beans are cooked. Add barley and all seasonings and cook until barley is done. Serve hot.

"Fereldan turnips" prefer to eat this stew the second day after it's cooked, provided the dog doesn't get into it first.

Pig Oat Mash

The Hanged Man in Kirkwall always has a pot of this warming porridge boiling on the fire. Several patrons apparently swear by it as a hangover cure, but only if washed down with cider spiked with brandy, of course. Even if you aren't an incorrigible liar, an inveterate gambler, a seafaring lush, or a bored noble slumming in the greasiest dive in the Free Marches, the pig oat mash, also called Hanged mash, makes a wonderful sweet-salty breakfast, perfect for starting off your day.

INGREDIENTS

- *Four very ripe windfall apples*
- *Two handfuls of dried salt pork or a good smoked bacon, torn into shreds*
- *Three handfuls of dried, rolled oats*
- *One handful of berries of your choice, fresh or dried*
- *One to two cups of weak ale or water*

DIRECTIONS

Peel and core the apples and throw them, along with everything else, into a pot placed over a fire. Boil for an hour, until the apples have softened and melted into the porridge. Serve hot.

Dalish Deep Forest Comfort

The Dalish elf clans in southern Orlais have enjoyed this dish for hundreds of years, but the flavors are also pleasing to a civilized palate, with reasonable substitutions, of course. The original recipe calls for the use of the larvae of a wood-burrowing beetle, prized for the distinctive "pop and squish" of their "tangy innards." No, thank you. I have used tomatoes in their place. You may also substitute for the squash a grain-based noodle of some kind, but for the purist who wants to experience a truly cultural dish, the squash is a must!

INGREDIENTS

- *Three string squashes*
- *Two good tablespoons of butter (halla butter traditionally used, but regular butter will do perfectly)*
- *Four cloves of garlic, chopped*
- *Two cups of wild, fresh-picked mushrooms, chopped*
- *Two cups of the leaves of the elfroot plant, chopped (spinach will suffice)*
- *Two cups of diced tomatoes*
- *One pinch of crushed hot red pepper, for spice*
- *Three pinches of parsley*
- *Rock salt, ground fine*
- *Three-quarters of a cup of halla cheese, freshly crumbled (or a brined goat cheese, which lacks richness but also the distinctive stench of halla, for which some may be thankful)*
- *Edible wildflowers and pine nuts, for garnish*

DIRECTIONS

Cook the squash in any manner you desire. The Dalish roast it whole in a fire pit filled with hot coals, but you may prefer to use an oven. When fully cooked, the flesh of the squash will come apart in strings that resemble noodles. Remove this flesh by scraping it out with a fork and set the result aside.

Heat the halla butter and fry the garlic in it. After about a minute, add the mushrooms and cook until they are just tender. Add the elfroot or spinach and allow it to wilt. Elfroot leaves take much longer than spinach to cook, and if you are using spinach, watch it carefully. Mushy spinach is a sign of a poor and inattentive cook!

Finally, add the tomatoes, crushed pepper, and parsley. Season with salt to taste. Cook the mixture to your desired consistency.

Once the sauce has reduced, remove it from the heat. Place the squash in your chosen serving dish. Stir halla cheese into the mushroom-elfroot mix and immediately spread over the plated squash. Toss together and serve immediately. For a more authentic Dalish experience, garnish with edible flowers like borage or chicory and eat accompanied by a good helping of self-righteous heresy.

FOLK REMEDIES OF THEDAS

*The gardens and forests of Thedas teem with healing flora and fauna: elfroot for cuts and bruises, foxmint to settle a troublesome gut, spindleweed for afflictions of the lungs, and gurgut bile to balance the humors. Of course, if all else fails, one can always take one's chances with a mage.**

To Stop Hiccuping

Prepare one large cup of water. In between hiccups, take a deep breath and begin drinking the water, taking gulps as large as you can manage. Ignore all painful spasms of the chest. Once the cup is drained, you should be cured. If not, repeat as many times as necessary.

To Cure a Cold

Bring a cup of whiskey to nearly a boil in a kettle, until its vapors permeate your surroundings. Add the juice of half a lemon and two peeled and crushed cloves of raw garlic. Consume before the whiskey cools. Serve forcefully if necessary. I'm told that the Grey Wardens swear by this remedy. Do not serve to infants.

To Remove a Wart

Cut a raw potato in half. Rub the potato, cut side down, in a clockwise manner on the wart. Once the area is fully saturated, feed the used potato half to a snoufleur. The snoufleur will take the wart upon itself. Use one potato half for each wart to be removed. If you have only one wart, consider planting the other half potato. This way, you will always have potatoes, should the wart return.

For Virility

Many believe that consuming the horns of the tusket will increase virility and desire. Add one cup of finely shaved tusket horn to three cups of wine or brandy. Store in a dark cellar and allow to infuse for at least a month. Consume half a cup of this tonic as the situation requires. For best results, sleep with the rest of the tusket horn under your pillow.

*Only templar-approved Circle practitioners. Seeking out the services of a swamp-dwelling hedge witch is never appropriate.

Mad Bernard's Gift of Flesh

The nesting roast is an Orlesian delicacy first conceived by Bernard Huileux, infamous chef to Reville, the "Mad Emperor." Huileux saw his kitchen implements much as a torturer sees a rack and gibbet. There were no limits in the butcher's relentless pursuit of what he called "the perfect taste." He believed pheasant is better drowned in brandy and the best horse meat comes from a foal that is force-fed dates and never allowed to walk.

The typical nesting roast is made with three birds: a quail stuffed in a pheasant stuffed in a swan. It was conceived for Reville's thirtieth birthday, and the emperor reportedly loved it. But Huileux immediately considered the roast inferior. Imperfect. His exact words may have been "too reasonable." The chef set out to perfect the nesting roast in time for Reville's thirty-first birthday. Bernard called it his "gift of flesh." He began experimenting with larger and smaller creatures in increasingly bizarre combinations. By the time of the emperor's birthday banquet, the roast required the strength of fifty elven servants just to plate it. When the beast, which took eight whole days to cook through, was finally revealed, dinner guests were said to have let out a collective gasp; some may have fainted. It was Huileux's most perfect creation: a whole wyvern, stuffed with a whole gurn, stuffed with an entire horse, stuffed with a large halla (horns and all), stuffed with a swan, stuffed with a duck, stuffed with a quail, stuffed with a bunting that choked on a gold piece the chef had pushed down its throat. Huileux declared boundless glory to the diner who recovered the gold piece. Some guests refused to touch the dish. Others would only consume it with their serviettes draped over their heads to "hide from the Maker."

In the interest of culinary decency—and because wyverns, if not properly prepared, are highly poisonous—I offer only the method for the standard roast.

INGREDIENTS

- *One quail, deboned but kept whole*
- *One pheasant, also deboned*
- *One swan, deboned save for the legs and the wings*
- *A good quantity of heavily spiced and salted sausage meat*
- *Herbs of your choice, chopped and blended with butter*
- *Salt and pepper, to taste*

DIRECTIONS

This Orlesian Nesting Roast is a quail within a pheasant within a swan—with empty spaces filled with spiced meat, commonly sausage. While it is time-consuming to prepare, once the separate elements are gathered, all one must do is assemble them so that they may be roasted together.

First, rub the herbed butter on and under the skin of the birds. Season them with salt and pepper. Then lay out the deboned swan and spread a layer of sausage meat within the cavity. Atop this, lay the pheasant and once again spread sausage within the cavity. Stuff the quail with sausage and place it within the pheasant.

Bring up the sides of the pheasant to cover the quail and the sausage layer, then do the same with the swan. Tightly truss the swan and place within an earthen or iron pan. Roast in a stone oven for three to four hours until cooked through. Serve with gravy made from pan juices, in slices so that the layers may be seen and appreciated by all.

Nordbotten Fruit Stew

I love fruit, topped with a light dusting of sugar and served with sweet, spiced cream. Good fruit needs little else, and there is no better way to present the delights of our Orlesian fields and orchards. But not everyone in Thedas is as lucky as we are. Those in the Anderfels are still suffering the effects of a Blight that took place a thousand years ago. Very little grows there, and what does grow grows poorly. The Anders are not blessed with our luscious berries, our stone fruits with juice like honey, our bright and fragrant oranges. They have apples, small and bitter, and sour berries that must be made palatable with vast amounts of honey . . . and sometimes, when an Ander is lucky, he is able to trade for dried fruit from Orlais or Antiva. When an Ander obtains some dried fruit, he makes it plump again with water and sometimes liquor, and cooks it gently into a stew. In the poorest Ander villages, the dish is reserved for very special days. I'm told a whole family will share a small pot of it, the children lingering over each and every spoonful.

INGREDIENTS

- *One pound of dried apricots*
- *Half a pound of pitted prunes*
- *One cup of raisins*
- *One pound of mixed dried fruits (cherries, apples, cranberries, or whatever is on hand)*
- *One lemon or orange slice (if available)*
- *Two sticks of cinnamon*
- *Five whole cloves*
- *Ten cups of water*
- *One cup of sugar or honey*
- *One-quarter of a cup of brandy (optional)*

DIRECTIONS

Place all dried fruit, lemon, cinnamon, and cloves in an iron saucepan. Add water, but do not heat. Cover and let sit for at least four hours to bring the fruit back to life. Once the fruit has softened and absorbed the water, add the sugar or honey and bring to a boil.

Simmer, covered, for about ten minutes, until the fruit is tender. Add more sugar or honey to taste. Let cool slightly and stir in brandy, if desired. Serve warm or cold.

Dandelion Wine

The elves of Orlais often make and consume dandelion wine. Though familiar with the process of winemaking from years of working vineyards, the elves have no vines of their own and are often too poor to buy the fruit necessary for making grape wine. Dandelions, however, are abundant and make an interesting brew. In some towns, elfroot is added to make the wine into a restorative draft. While sweet and refreshing, it is hardly a match for any of the proper wines of Orlais or Antiva and certainly does not age as well.

INGREDIENTS

- *Sixteen cups of fresh-picked dandelion blooms*
- *Sixteen cups of water, boiled then cooled*
- *Three pounds of sugar*
- *A piece of ginger root, about an inch*
- *One lemon, including rind*
- *Rind of one orange*
- *One cake of fresh yeast*

DIRECTIONS

Place the dandelion blooms in the water. Cover and let steep for three days, stirring occasionally. After three days, strain into a pot. Pare the rind from the lemon and add it to the pot, along with the orange rind. Next add the sugar, ginger, and juice of the lemon. Boil gently for thirty minutes. Allow the mixture to cool before adding the yeast. Let stand for another two days.

After two days, pour the brew into a keg and store it in a cool cellar for eight to nine weeks before bottling. You may choose to leave the bottles for a few months before consuming. Some believe it improves the flavor of the wine.

Marie du Lac Erre's Sweet Ruin

7:46 Storm. The Duchess Laurentine celebrates her fiftieth anniversary. Alas, servants topple the pièce de résistance of the evening: a towering confection of cake, wafers, cream, and fruit. The duchess's steward and confectioner are hysterical. What will the guests eat now? In desperation, they begin serving all the replacement sweets they can find, which includes a platter of tea biscuits sandwiched with cream and jam, created by a young kitchen helper whose official job, up to this point, was to pluck and clean chicken carcasses. The biscuits' creator, Marie du Lac Erre, baked the biscuits for herself and her fellow servants, thinking they were too humble for the duchess's table. But she gladly gives them up, and the biscuits leave the kitchen. To everyone's surprise, they are universally adored. The duchess trills at each tender bite. The guests rave—so simple, so elegant! The party is saved, and Marie du Lac Erre is promoted to the post of First Under-Confectioner. The duchess herself charges Marie with the task of creating over a dozen varieties of her tea biscuits, one to suit each of the duchess's moods. The kitchen sends for the best ingredients from all over Thedas: pure Rivaini vanilla, lavender from Ghislain, orange essence from Seleny. Even chocolate, from the Donarks.

Marie's biscuits take Orlais by storm, and the Duchess Laurentine has the entire Imperial Court at her feet, frantic to have a taste. The duchess presents a box of the fine treats to the emperor himself, and it is consumed in one sitting. When His Highness requests a second, hired mercenaries accost its carriers, and make off with the biscuits. A third box is sent, and is couriered to the emperor under armed guard. Violent feuds break out between several noble houses over the number and type of biscuits the duchess has gifted to each of them. Envious of the attention, confectioners from all over Val Royeaux try their own versions of the biscuits, but they fall short of perfection. Then a contingent of assassins descends upon Duchess Laurentine's estate, with the intent to steal Marie's formula. The librarian and several housemaids are killed, and the entire north wing of the estate is destroyed by a fire. Thankfully, Marie survives.

Fed up with the troubles her biscuits have wrought, Marie leaves the duchess's employ, taking her biscuit formula. She has it copied a hundred times over, in full, by a clerk. The copies are then sent to a hundred bakers all over Orlais, to be shared by common folk and nobility alike. The Duchess Laurentine, lamenting the loss of her First Under-Confectioner, is heard to call the biscuits her "sweet ruin."

Here I have provided the recipe for the chocolate-dipped sweet ruin, the variation which many believe to have been Marie du Lac Erre's personal favorite.

INGREDIENTS

For the biscuits:

- *One cup of butter*
- *Half a cup of fine powdered sugar, sifted*
- *Half a teaspoon of vanilla extract*
- *Two cups of flour*
- *One-quarter of a teaspoon of baking powder*

For the filling:

- *One cup of chocolate, chopped and melted*
- *Two-thirds of a cup of powdered sugar, sifted*
- *Two tablespoons of soft butter*
- *One-quarter of a teaspoon of orange or mint extract*
- *Milk to adjust consistency*

DIRECTIONS

Heat the oven to a temperature suitable for baking shortbread. Beat the butter, sugar, and vanilla together until light and fluffy. Mix the flour and baking powder together and stir into the creamed butter mixture.

Roll the dough out till it is an eighth of an inch thick. Cut into shapes with your choice of cookie cutter or press with a patterned shortbread mold and cut out. Bake on lined sheets for about seven minutes or until set but not browned. Let the biscuits cool.

Spread the unpatterned sides with tempered chocolate. Allow the chocolate to set. Meanwhile, mix powdered sugar, softened butter, and flavor extract together. Add dribbles of milk until the filling is soft enough to spread. Spread the buttercream on the chocolate-dipped side of one biscuit and place another on top. Press together lightly.

The biscuits are now ready. Prepare yourself for the adulation of your friends, but consider holding some in reserve, for use as a bargaining chip in your schemes.

Raider Queen's Bread of Many Tongues

"What's a banana?" I hear some of you say. I am now in a position to tell you, dear reader, as I, not twenty-four hours ago, was forced to eat one. I wouldn't ordinarily have let alien fruit come anywhere near my face, but the daggers were very sharp—and the woman holding the blades seemed to have no compunction about using them. Well, let me just say that I am glad those daggers were out because when I finished the first banana, I immediately proceeded to eat the entire bunch. The banana is a beautiful food, fragrant and with a rich sweetness reminiscent of honey. If you ever chance upon this golden wonder, do not hesitate as I did!

While the recipe does call for Par Vollen bananas, I find Rivaini ones an acceptable substitute, despite what the recipe's creator claims. Most of us aren't mad enough to raid Qunari lands solely for the purposes of baking.

INGREDIENTS

- *Two cups of flour*
- *Three reasonably heaping teaspoons of baking powder*
- *Half a teaspoon of salt*
- *Half a cup of melted butter*
- *Two-thirds to three-quarters of a cup of brown sugar*
- *One-third of a cup of molasses*
- *Two large eggs*
- *Four ripe Par Vollen bananas*

DIRECTIONS

Peel and mash the bananas with a fork. Stir the melted butter, brown sugar, molasses, and eggs into the banana mash. Mix well. In a separate bowl, mix together the flour, baking powder, and salt.

Now combine the flour mix with the banana mix. Stir briskly to combine, but do not overmix. Place the resulting batter in a buttered loaf pan. Bake until the top is golden brown.

They say the Inquisition lived off this bread at the height of the war against Corypheus.

The Blessed Apple

According to local legend, Andraste's Exalted March took her through the fields of Ghislain. She was weary from her long battle with the Tevinters and took a moment beneath an apple tree. The tree's shady crown sheltered The Prophet from the noonday sun, while its fruit—cool, crisp, and sweet—refreshed her. For the gifts it had shared, Our Lady asked the Maker to bless the tree. In the years that followed, a wondrous orchard sprung forth from the blessed tree, producing the most luscious apples in all of Orlais.

For the last eight hundred years, the trees of the orchard have been tended by the sisters of a small cloister. The sisters are adamant that the fruit of the orchard should never be sold, but shared freely. Every autumn, barrels of apples are gathered and shared with the faithful—rich and poor alike. And once every week through the season, the sisters make pies from the windfalls, and the aroma of the pastry wafts from the cloister kitchen, hanging in the air for miles around.

INGREDIENTS

For the crust:

- *One and a half cups of flour*
- *One-quarter of a teaspoon of salt*
- *Half a cup of cold butter*
- *Three to four tablespoons of cold water*

For the filling:

- *Six to eight apples, peeled, cored, and sliced (golden apples from the Lady's Orchard are preferred; otherwise, use any crisp, green cooking apple or apple of your choice)*
- *Three-quarters of a cup to one cup of sugar, to taste*
- *Half a teaspoon of salt*
- *One teaspoon of ground cinnamon*
- *Half a teaspoon of fresh-ground nutmeg*
- *One-quarter of a teaspoon of ground cloves*
- *One and a half tablespoons of flour*
- *Butter (optional)*

For the crumb topping:

- *Half a cup of raw brown sugar*
- *One cup of flour*
- *Half a cup of cold butter*

DIRECTIONS

Begin by lighting a fire to warm your oven. You want it to be quite hot so that the crust will cook through, something in the range of 425 degrees.

Stir together the flour and the salt. Cut the butter into the flour mixture with a knife until it resembles coarse meal. Sprinkle cold water over the flour and butter mix, one tablespoon at a time. Mix with a fork until the pastry holds together. Gently press the dough into the pie dish to form the crust. Trim the edges.

Toss the apples with the sugar, salt, flour, and spices. Pour the filling into the prepared crust. Dot with butter, if desired.

To make the topping, first stir the sugar and the flour together. Then cut the cool butter into the flour mixture until it resembles fine crumbs. Sprinkle over the apples.

Bake the pie in the hot oven for ten minutes, reduce the heat to average, and continue baking for thirty to forty minutes. Once cooked through, allow to cool before serving. Eat warm or cold, with cream or plain, and dream of the golden leaves and sun-warmed apples of autumn.

Hearth Cakes

Hearth cakes are common Dalish fare, earning their name from the manner in which they are baked: on a heavy iron griddle set upon the hearth. Traditional hearth cakes are made with halla butter, but I've substituted both goat butter and regular butter to great effect.

STICKY FINGERS

One wonders where the Dalish obtain their sugar. They certainly do not trade with Tevinter or Rivain, as we do. Where, then, do they gain the precious stuff that makes baking such a delight? I shall tell you: they steal it. I have heard many a story of roving Dalish bands attacking freeholds, robbing them of gold, livestock, and, yes, sugar and spices. So guard well your kitchens, my dears. You never know when an elf may be watching.

INGREDIENTS

- *One and three-quarters of a cup of flour, mixed with a spoonful of hardwood ash and fine-ground salt**
- *One teaspoon each of cinnamon, ginger, and nutmeg*
- *Half a cup of butter*
- *Half a cup of sugar*
- *Half a cup of mixed dried fruit (currants, cranberries, or whatever is on hand)*
- *One large egg, beaten*
- *Milk*

*Author's note: The Dalish use hardwood ash as a leavening agent. I do not recommend it. One tablespoon of baking powder mixed with a teaspoon of salt should serve adequately.

DIRECTIONS

To make the dough, first sift the flour into a large bowl. Mix in the spices, then rub in the half cup of butter until the mixture resembles fine crumbs. Stir in the sugar and dried fruit. Add the egg and mix until it is the consistency of raw pastry. If the mix seems too dry, add dribbles of milk until the texture is correct. Knead the dough on a clean, floured surface and roll it out until it is a quarter inch thick. Cut the cakes into rounds with an overturned goblet or something similarly round with an edge. You should have about twenty. Ensure the cakes aren't too thick.

Heat a flat iron griddle (or a heavy skillet) over a flame. Test the heat of the griddle by sprinkling a pinch of flour on it. If the flour turns golden brown, the griddle is hot enough. Ensure the griddle is not too hot, or the butter will burn.

Place the cakes around the edge of the griddle. Setting them in the middle will blacken them. Cook until golden brown and slightly crisp on each side. Turn with a knife after a minute or so to make sure they're cooking and be sure to put them back on the griddle if they need more time.

Notes

Sera's Yummy Corn

Yellow, not that weirdy checkered stuff. Peel it halfway to get rid of the dog-wick hair. Also check for rot. And messages. Wash it to get water in the leaves . . . husks? Whatever. Fold it back up and stick it in the oven. Cake-hot, not forge-hot. Half an hour, peel and eat.

Too simple? That's why you're bad at it. No pot, no wrap, just steal-heat-peel and get it in your mouth. Has its own handle so you can poke people while you tell them how good it is. Promise.

appendix I

BESTIARY

THE MYRIAD CREATURES OF THEDAS ARE AS DIVERSE AND worthy of study as any of the peoples who call the continent home. From the furry fennec to the high dragon, each has its place in the world and a part to play. Over time, each creature has gained its own cultural relevance, be it through symbolism, sustenance, or as something to avoid.

DEMONS

The mysterious and uncharted realm of the Fade holds countless denizens we of the waking world have yet to discover. Here is but a sampling of darker spirits we have only recently begun to understand.

Envy Demon
Even within the realm of the Fade, envy demons look like a mistake. Limbs protrude from every angle, some thrashing and grabbing, some flopping unnervingly. While demons of all kinds are drawn to the living, spying on mortals is the sole purpose of envy demons. They are obsessed with learning about their subjects, peering into their souls with a singular need to become them at all costs.

Despair Demon
A young girl wrapped in rags. An old woman trying desperately to shield herself from the cold. Who wouldn't want to help these poor creatures? When someone gets close enough, the despair demon envelops a victim in a cloak of ice and unleashes torrential frozen gales. These demons not only feed on despair but cause it.

Envy demon

Fear demon

Fear Demon
Just as a pang of fear can make guts drop, hearts pound, and lungs force feet to stop for want of breath, so too can a fear demon paralyze you where you stand. Invisible, it will sneak up on a victim, then flash into view in a tangle of gnarled limbs. Fear demons are often surrounded by wraiths, shades, or other smaller demons. Does it summon them, or are they drawn to it?

Terror Demon
If your heart doesn't stop when a terror leaps out of the ground, this lesser demon will do its best to finish the job. Green, spindly, and resembling nothing so much as an enormous, voracious mantis, these demons *are* the things that go bump in the night, feeding on the shock and terror they create.

Fearling

Fearlings are manifestations of our anxieties and deepest fears. Born in the Fade, they are simple spirits that occasionally slip into the waking world where the Veil is thin. "When Lieutenant Herve cut one in half, he started screaming about an imagined fire," Lady Losaneta, a decorated chevalier in the Blessed Age, wrote in her journal after encountering a swarm. "The templar with us waded in, looking for mages who were not there. The second *my* sword pierced a fearling's flesh, I became consumed by thoughts of disappointing my mother. I told everyone I saw a dragon."

Fearling

Gibbering horror

Gibbering Horror

Mages claim that the strange monsters dubbed "gibbering horrors" are a recent phenomenon. The first recorded reference to the creatures is from a letter written by an anonymous enchanter in Kirkwall to a friend in the Montsimmard Circle in 9:23 Dragon:

"It was a joke, at first. Any time someone claimed to spot a new oddity in the Fade, we said they'd seen a 'gibbering horror.' Then, slowly, out of the corner of my eye—flashes of teeth, a small bared skull, a hiss. I do not believe we conjured them with our fears. I feel they have existed for some time, and that some unknown current of magic has revived them. Either way, beware. They bite."

PREDATORS

Many animals native to southern Thedas should be avoided due to risk of death or serious injury. However, skilled hunters will attest that the more dangerous the kill, the more valuable the reward. Here is a short list of creatures with particularly sharp teeth.

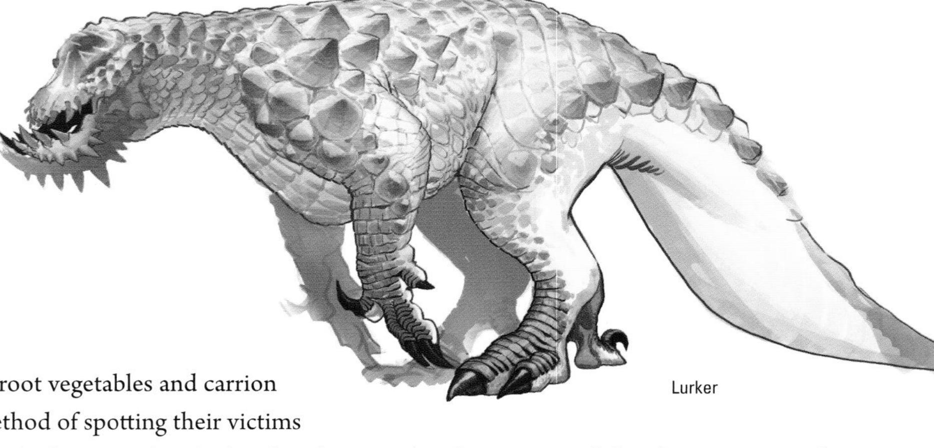
Lurker

Lurker

Lurkers are ravenous omnivores, capable of surviving on root vegetables and carrion but driven by a preference for live prey. For ages, their method of spotting their victims has been a mystery. They seem to track by sight, despite a lack of eyes. Within the last decade, naturalists have proposed that the strange, translucent lump on the lurker's skull is in fact a tough membrane that is sensitive to vibrations and temperature changes in the environment.

Phoenix

Phoenix

Mad Bernard's Gift of Flesh is one of the most elaborate dishes in history, and Tevinter's Verimensis tea the most expensive drink in Thedas, but the humble roasted phoenix remains the most infamous meal of all. Phoenixes are dangerous enough—their foul bite and aggressive nature make them the bane of many a traveler in lonely places—but nearly half their organs are pure poison. Only a trained chef can determine which parts are succulent bits of offal and which cuts will cause a guest's lungs to liquefy. For the negligently adventurous: serve it with a sweet red wine.

Black Wolf

Black wolves live and hunt in packs, often led by an alpha male. Though typically found in or near wooded areas, packs have also been known to establish territory in open plains if game is plentiful.

Wolves frequently feature in Fereldan folklore, no doubt because of rumors of werewolves in that country. These tales, when coupled with the wolves' habit of threatening livestock, have given the animals a fearsome reputation. Black wolves may become aggressive if they feel their territory or pack is threatened but will typically avoid confrontation with people. Following the opening of the Breach in 9:41 Dragon, there were reports of increased, almost unnatural aggression toward travelers in some parts of southern Ferelden. The spike initially baffled researchers. Some now believe the abnormal behavior of these wolves was likely connected to the many disruptions in the Veil at the time, but this remains a theory at present.

Great bear

Great Bear

Little is known of the private behavior of great bears. The researcher charged with gathering information on this topic is presumed eaten. His notes were not recovered before our publishers wanted this bestiary.

Hyena

Hyena

Though many think of hyenas as scavengers, merchants who travel through their territories know them to be skilled hunters. Trophy hunters often brag of going one on one with these intelligent predators. The amount of truth in these accounts varies widely.

Hyenas most often hunt in packs led by alpha females but will occasionally strike out on their own in search of prey. Their hardy constitution and ability to adapt have allowed them to survive in even the harshest conditions. While often associated with the brutality of their kills, hyenas are affectionate and attentive to other members of their pack.

Dracolisk

The dracolisk is a rugged beast originally used by nomadic hunters in the Donarks. They became popular with Tevinter's cavalry in the Steel Age and remain a staple of the Imperium's military today. The modern dracolisk is larger than its ancestors, having undergone selective and magically assisted breeding in Tevinter to increase its size and strength. The dracolisk may also share some distant blood with the dragon and the wyvern. Some exceedingly rare breeds can spit poison, while another (bred exclusively by the current Archon's family) can breathe ice or fire.

Dracolisk

Poison Spider

"I suspected nothing until I unlocked the deep cellars," the Duchess D'Aubrigne wrote to her cousin in 9:14 Dragon. "The spiders were stuffed three deep, crawling over each other as they tried to reach me. I threw the torch, slammed the door, and ran. I know now what plagued the deer in my forest, and why I found bears and wolves contorted in poisoned agony. The spiders' venom is so foul that the smoke from their bodies has driven us out of the castle. I cannot step inside my own grounds without my eyes watering—although some blame may be laid on some fifty years' worth of apple brandy going up in flame."

Varghest

The varghest is a hunter that thrives in barren reaches, such as the Western Approach. The creature's appearance is so outlandish that for a time people believed the animals were demons. We know today that the bat-like snout, feathery tail, and overlapping scales are as natural as a nug's ears or a dragon's wings. The varghest's hide is much sought after for use in clothing and armor, but beware the serrated scales. The edges are so sharp, they've cut open many an unwary tanner's hand.

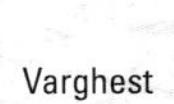

Varghest

Gurgut

The brightly colored gurgut prefers wet, sequestered areas. Its diet primarily consists of marsh weeds and fish, but it will not hesitate to kill intruders in its territory. The name *gurgut* comes from sounds made by the animals in the spring. When winter thaws, the air around the swampland in southern Orlais vibrates with the unmistakable bellow of the animal's mating call. Male gurguts perform elaborate dances meant to attract the attention of female gurguts. These mating displays are loud, impressive, and bereft of dignity. Travelers are of course advised to keep their distance.

Giant

How in the name of Andraste did giants come to be? Magic gone awry? Accidents of breeding? Whatever they are, these huge, violent creatures—known also as "trolls" in some parts of Thedas—lumber primarily through the forests of the Emerald Graves, though they've also been spotted in places as far-flung as the Western Approach and the Storm Coast. At least you can usually see them coming.

Giant

Quillback

Quillback

At first glance, the menacing quillback would seem to have little connection with Orlesian fashion. However, for a time, the beasts' quills were used to adorn men's hats throughout Orlais.

Quillbacks can travel great distances with little water. This allows them to survive in harsh, arid climates. Only hunters interested in a significant payday actively seek out the aggressive and territorial beast.

Bogfisher

Bogfisher

The bogfisher prefers dim, damp environments such as swamps, marshes, and cave systems. Loose skin, many-toed feet, and needle-sharp teeth have given the bogfisher a dark reputation. More than one tale exists in which a foolish child is pulled beneath the murky waters of a bog and then torn apart by the vicious monster. Of course, these tales are mere flights of fancy. In truth, the bogfisher is a shy creature that uses its sharp teeth to catch fish, eels, and frogs.

PREY

For every hungry predator there is particularly tasty prey. While most of these animals tend to be harmless, few are advisable to keep as pets.

Ram

Ram

Rams are often found roaming grassy plains or woodland hills. The males and females of the species are indistinguishable, both possessing horns and shaggy coats. This has led to the entire species being referred to as "rams," although the term usually applies to male creatures.

Like the druffalo, the ram is important to the livelihood of farmers and shepherds throughout Thedas. Rams are a source of meat, wool, and milk, the latter of which is used to produce fine cheeses.

August Ram

The august ram is a particular breed known for its striking markings and coloration. For this reason, the creature has long been a popular subject for painters. When pastoral imagery was in fashion, many Orlesian nobles lined their parlor walls with portraits of vibrantly colored lambs gamboling through the trees.

August rams tend to live and travel in herds. They are swift runners, able to move quietly even in large groups through forests and plains.

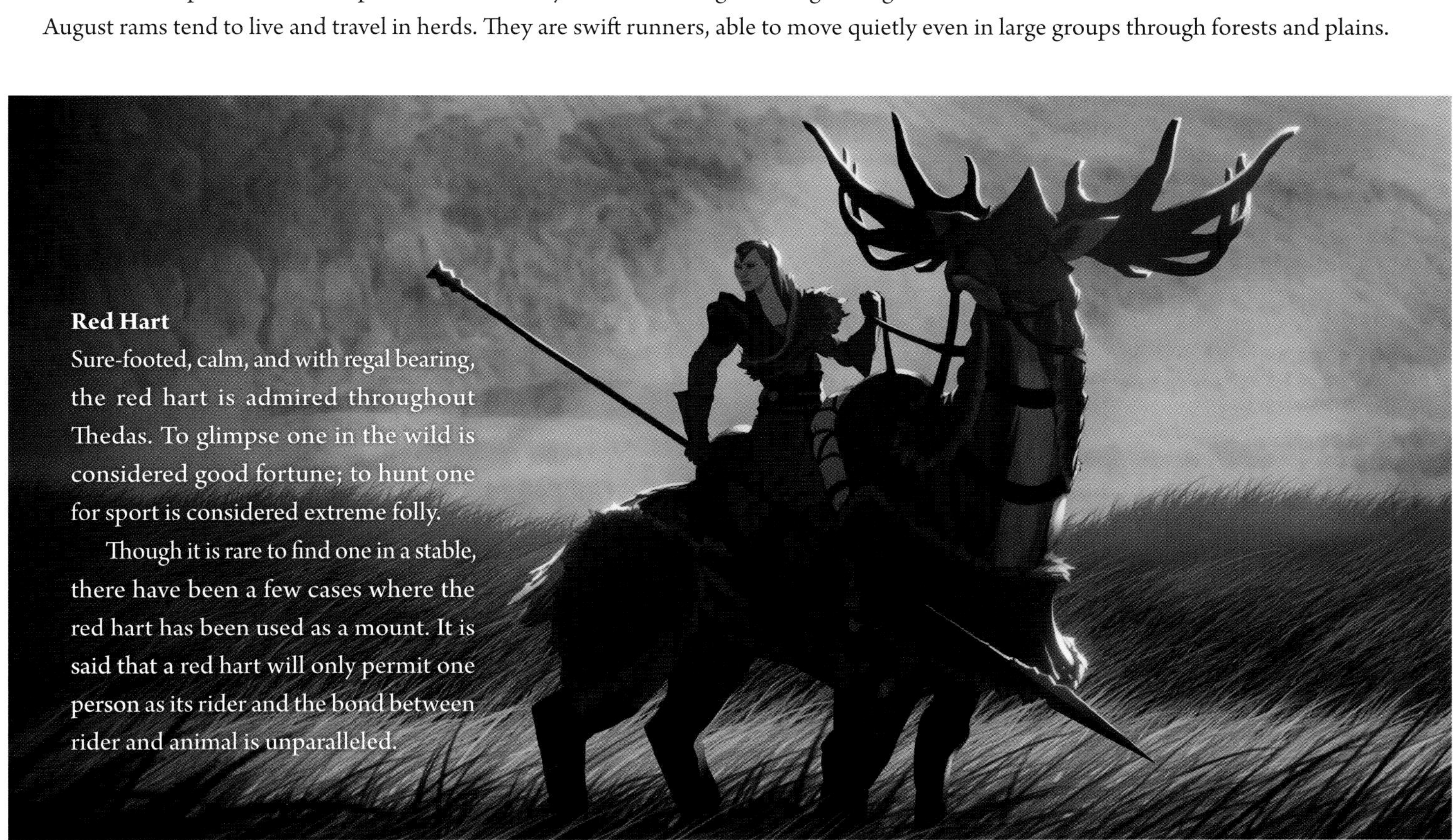

Red Hart

Sure-footed, calm, and with regal bearing, the red hart is admired throughout Thedas. To glimpse one in the wild is considered good fortune; to hunt one for sport is considered extreme folly.

Though it is rare to find one in a stable, there have been a few cases where the red hart has been used as a mount. It is said that a red hart will only permit one person as its rider and the bond between rider and animal is unparalleled.

Fennec

Fennec

The fennec—sometimes referred to as a white fox—is a small, dog-like creature with large, tufted ears and a bushy tail. The fennec's delicate features and timid nature may give it an impression of frailty, but this is not necessarily the case. Though neither strong nor vicious, the fennec has proven to be extremely adaptable, able to survive and flourish in a wide variety of environments.

Fennecs are occasionally hunted for fur, the demand for which is dictated by the whims of Orlesian fashion. Attempts have also been made to keep fennecs as pets, though, for the most part, the species has proven resistant to true domestication. A group of fennecs is called a tangle.

Gurn

The gurn's tough exterior is matched only by its obstinate nature. The horn-like plate that commonly protrudes from the gurn's forehead can ward off attacks—be they from a pack of hyena or a rival gurn during mating season. Sharp teeth provide the gurn with yet more protection, while also allowing the beast to supplement its diet of shrubs and grasses with small and midsize rodents. Hardy from the beginning, a gurn calf will be up and walking within a few hours of birth.

Though intimidating in appearance, gurns rarely attack unless provoked. Despite a stubborn temperament, they are occasionally used as pack animals due to their immense strength.

Gurn

Snoufleur

Snoufleur

The snoufleur is an inquisitive animal with strong hearing and a keen sense of smell. A snoufleur will often be seen sniffing the air or even standing on its hind legs to get a better sense of its surroundings. Snoufleurs live in family groups. A cooperative species, the entire group will take turns watching over the young.

Druffalo

The massive druffalo is known for its shaggy hide and large, curved horns. While herds of wild druffalo still roam the hills and plains, it is estimated that at least half of the population has now been domesticated. Valuable to farmers throughout much of southern Thedas, druffalo are put to work as beasts of burden, commonly pulling plows, and are also a significant source of meat. Druffalo leather can be used to make clothing, saddles, and tack.

Tusket

Tusket

The tusket is most often found near lakes, rivers, and other bodies of water. Their lower tusks and sturdy front feet are ideal for digging up muddy banks in search of food.

Tuskets usually live in small groups or pairs. Tuskets bond for life and are known for the affection they show toward their mates. Mate selection is influenced by the curve and slight color variations of the upper tusks. The poet Hiram of Starkhaven immortalized the gentle creatures in his melodramatic "Ode to a Tusket," in which a lone tusket refuses to stray from the spot where his mate was killed.

Greater Mountain Nuggalope

Greater mountain nuggalope

As far as historians are able to determine, references to the greater mountain nuggalope (or "deth nug") predate the Divine Age. For centuries, the nuggalope remained a creature of myth, with sightings attributed to lunacy or drunkenness. Occasionally, convincing evidence for the nuggalopes's existence would be brought forth. These claims were always proven to be hoaxes, perpetrated for fame or malicious amusement.

As such, it came as a great shock when tales of the nuggalope were finally proven true. Despite their elusive nature, nuggalopes may be tamed and even ridden, though few have accomplished such a feat.

One of the nuggalope's most unexpected features—and one of endless fascination to researchers—is the creature's hand-like front paws. The nuggalope has been known to dunk its food in water before consuming it. It can also reach high tree branches and pull them down to eat the leaves. While observations of wild nuggalopes are few, some researchers theorize that the creature may also be capable of rudimentary tool use, such as poking sticks into trees and dirt mounds to draw out the insects within.

HIGH DRAGONS

A mere fifty years ago, dragons were thought to be extinct. Now, well into the age named after them, a staggering number of variations are emerging, surprising even the most experienced naturalists. Some breeds, like the Abyssal High Dragon, were well documented by the dragon hunters of ages prior. Others, like the Greater Mistral, are new breeds that exhibit some fascinating traits never before seen in dragons.

Highland Ravager

There is no more aptly named dragon than the Highland Ravager. It consumes herds and obliterates villages with equal relish, setting fire to what it does not eat with almost-human spite. Ravagers will, strangely, occasionally permit other high dragons in their territories. When this happens, they sometimes rampage through the countryside with even more enthusiasm than normal. "It seems a matter of dominance, as well as 'showing off' in front of one's peers," writes Frederic of Serault in his seminal *Flight Patterns of the Highland Ravager*. "Let us not think we are the only social animal. It has often been observed that, while they do not possess our intellect, dragons can have relationships, even friendships, when circumstances align."

Gamordan Stormrider

The Gamordan Stormrider is quite popular among Orlesian artists. Its vivid colors and ability to spit blazing bolts of lightning have been immortalized in many paintings, usually of the dragon fighting a regiment of bold, brave, and probably doomed chevaliers. This romantic tableau persists in art even though, in reality, most knights never see the beasts. The Stormrider prefers to make its lair in swampy places isolated from large human settlements, where only the occasional unfortunate farmer or caravan falls victim to its appetite.

Abyssal High Dragon

For years, the Abyssal High Dragon was considered extinct. Scholars argued dragons spotted in the Western Approach were likely Hunterhorn Shrikes or the dreaded Stonejaw emigrating from the east in search of prey. At the dawn of the Dragon Age, however, dozens of sightings by terrified merchants and, more reliably, Grey Wardens patrolling the wastes have confirmed the Abyssal High Dragon's return to Thedas. The breath of these elusive dragons has been described as hotter than a forge.

Northern Hunter

Even among dragons, the Northern Hunter is a voracious feeder. It will consume everything from lone nugs to unwary wyverns, if it can take the venomous beasts by surprise. The Hunter has even been seen devouring human foodstuffs left behind in villages that have fled its wrath. One Fereldan farmer, speaking to renowned draconologist Frederic of Serault, swore that after fleeing his home, he'd spied on a dragon from a (very distant) hilltop. On top of eating five cows, the farmer said the beast polished off "ten bushels of cabbages, eighteen wheels of cheese, seven pumpkins, sixteen loaves, and a whole trough of cream," although, strangely enough, "it didn't even touch the Orlesian hams."

The Fereldan Frostback

The Fereldan Frostback is a territorial beast, even by the standards of high dragons. It prefers areas where it can keep a relatively close eye on its broods. The Frostback lays large clutches of eggs, but the dragonlings are left to learn to forage and hunt on their own. Intruders who believe this makes them easy prey are sorely mistaken. Many an enterprising hunter has had their life cut short by their prey's mother appearing above them with flaming breath and snapping teeth.

Greater Mistral

Sometime around 9:20 Dragon, Greater Mistrals began to emerge from the Emerald Graves. They have been described as showy for their bright colors and tendency to take long, swooping flights at dawn over nearby human settlements, bellowing as they skim across the trees. "The dragon is like a rooster," one Orlesian duke recently wrote. "A loud, gaudy, deadly, ice-spewing rooster that demands you cede it your full attention."

Hivernal

Several Orlesian houses proudly display stuffed Hivernals inside their trophy halls, but at one time hunting the Hivernal was a matter of necessity. Its thick hide covers a layer of fat that makes it suited to the cold climates of Orlais's highlands, and its hide will keep out the bitterest of winds. In wilder times, when the earliest Orlesian settlements were being founded in the south, groups of hunters numbering in the dozens would work in concert to slay the beasts. A triumphant party would come back to a village feast, after which the meat was salted and the rest of the Hivernal was made into clothes, weapons, and potions that would help them last the winter. This "Hivernal Feast" is still celebrated in some villages, although few recall its origins.

Sandy Howler

A desert-dwelling beast, the Sandy Howler prefers to seek out warm, sandy basins for its nesting spots. It spends a great deal of time sleeping, lurching to life only when it rouses itself to hunt, mate, or defend its home. This nocturnal predator is especially fond of gurns and, unlike most dragons, appears to prefer cooked meat to raw. If a Sandy Howler dispatches its prey with its claws or fangs, it will then use its fiery breath to roast its victims before consuming them.

Kaltenzahn

The Kaltenzahn (meaning "cold tooth") dragon originated as a breed somewhere in the Hunterhorn Mountains. In 9:30 Dragon, an entire flight of these beasts migrated south almost without pause, keeping to lonely and isolated places. Given the timing, it is possible they were chased out by darkspawn, although the Kaltenzahn is so legendarily stubborn, it seems unlikely that anything short of an Archdemon could make it flee. The Kaltenzahn's freezing breath, ear-piercing scream, and thick scales make it a challenge even for the most seasoned of dragon hunters.

Vinsomer

It is said that the last dragon killed by Caspar Pentaghast, the ancient King of Nevarra, was a Vinsomer that had grown to twice the normal size of a high dragon. Legends claim its breath caused thunderstorms and its wings roaring hurricanes, exaggerations immortalized in Nevarran poetry and song. The Vinsomers of today may not reach such a ferocious stature but are just as dangerous when cornered. They are wary of other predators, including humans, and tend to keep to high and rocky coasts.

THE WORLD OF THEDAS VOLUME 1: A LIST OF ERRATA BY BROTHER GENITIVI

I ONCE GAVE A LECTURE at the University of Orlais on the conflict between fact and belief.

"Gathering accurate information is challenging in a place as vast and fragmented as Thedas," I told the students. "Sources may conflict wildly."

This portion of my lecture was excerpted in a recent encyclopedia entitled *The World of Thedas*. The author of the text is unnamed and prefers it that way. But I know him. I have studied with him. And I can speak to his obsession with detail and objectivity, the latter being something with which I sometimes struggle.

You could say that his approach with regards to accuracy is "ruthless."

But, as I said in Val Royeaux, ours is a large, complicated world. It is perhaps inevitable that a few errors survive numerous readings and are then committed to print.

With this in mind, here are a few points in the first volume of *The World of Thedas* that, based on my studies and travels, warrant correction:

Pages 8–9: On this particular map of Thedas, as well as in three other places throughout the volume, the desert chasm in the Western Approach commonly known as the Abyssal Rift is instead called the Abyssal Reach. While it was at one time called the Abyssal Reach, history has come to favor the alternative name. I've seen the place, and honestly, *rift* is far more accurate. A dreadful thing.

Page 12: The main text states that the First Blight lasted one hundred years. Most authorities agree that it was fought for 192 years. The timeline in the tome is correct.

Page 12: The timeline states that the Old Gods whispered to humanity from the Black City in -2800 Ancient. At this time, the legendary city would still have been known as "the Golden City," as it had not yet been sullied by the presence of men.

Page 42: The term *ralshokra*, said to be a Qunari military challenge where the higher ranks are fought for and defended to the death, is not a Qunari term at all. Its use can be traced back to the Storm Age, first appearing in a popular Orlesian children's story meant to demonize the invading race. There's no evidence that any Qunari actually participate in something so barbaric.

Page 126: The timeline also states that in 8:45 Blessed, the Fereldan nobility continued a "guerrilla war against the occupying Orlesians, led by Brandel's daughter Moira." While the Rebel Queen Moira did eventually lead the war, she was born after 8:45 Blessed.

Page 136: The timeline puts Celene's birth at 9:6 Dragon and her ascension at 9:20, making her, according to the timeline, fourteen when she became empress. However, the main text says she was sixteen when she took the throne. By all accounts, the main text is correct. Celene was born in 9:4 Dragon.

Page 141: There are rumors in some circles of an intelligent darkspawn known as the Architect, who attempted to unearth and kill the remaining Old Gods and taint the entire surface world. Though the timeline says 9:14 Dragon, most reliable sources state these events actually occurred in 9:10 Dragon.

Page 146: The timeline states that Bhelen Aeducan was the middle child of King Endrin Aeducan. He was actually King Endrin's youngest child.

Page 157: The main text says that the darkspawn sacked Minrathous in 1:31 Divine. While it is true that Minrathous nearly fell during the Second Blight, the infamous heart of the Imperium has never actually been taken. This is stated elsewhere in the book.

Page 176: In the glossary, the definition of the Archon as Tevinter's "monarch" is technically incorrect. It would be more accurate to call the Archon a "ruler."

Page 177: The First Warden is the leader of the Grey Wardens at Weisshaupt. The glossary incorrectly states that the Commander of the Grey is this leader. I'm not sure what my peer was drinking when he wrote this one.

With these corrections, perhaps the record has now been set straight. I hope you have found these tomes as enlightening as I have.

Yours in scholarly devotion,
Brother Ferdinand Genitivi

CHARACTER INDEX

O

P

Q

R

S

T